Democracy and Disagreement

Democracy and Disagreement

Amy Gutmann
Dennis Thompson

The Belknap Press of
Harvard University Press
Cambridge, Massachusetts
London, England

Copyright © 1996 by the President and Fellows
of Harvard College
All rights reserved
Printed in the United States of America
Third printing, 2000

Library of Congress Cataloging-in-Publication Data

Gutmann, Amy.
  Democracy and disagreement / Amy Gutmann, Dennis Thompson.
      p.   cm.
Includes bibliographical references and index.
ISBN 0-674-19765-8 (cloth)
ISBN 0-674-19766-6 (pbk)
1. Democracy.   2. Representative government and representation.
3. Compromise (Ethics)   I. Thompson, Dennis F. (Dennis Frank),
1940–   . II. Title.
JC423.G925   1996
321.8—dc20   96-13732

Contents

Acknowledgments

This book grew out of our experience in teaching courses on political ethics, jointly and separately, at two universities during the past decade. Our students would probably not recognize the product, which took on a life of its own well beyond what we taught in our courses. But we learned much from our students. The discussions we had with them gave us some reason to believe that men and women of very different backgrounds and quite divergent moral views can argue with mutual respect about controversial issues of public policy. The discussions we had with each other forced us to look hard for ways to maintain mutual respect in the face of vigorous disagreement. The hard-won agreement between its authors that this book expresses is not a modus vivendi: both of us contributed equally to every chapter, and both of us are equally committed to all the arguments and conclusions of the book. But the agreement, like the product of democratic deliberation, should no doubt be considered provisional.

We have presented some of the arguments of this book previously in a different form. Chapter 1 is a substantially revised version of our "Moral Disagreement in a Democracy," which appeared in *Social Philosophy and Policy*, 12 (Winter 1995): 87–110. Copyright © 1995 by Cambridge University Press. Portions of Chapter 2 are drawn from our "Moral Conflict and Political Consensus," *Ethics*, 100 (October 1990): 64–88.

We are grateful to our many friends and colleagues who gave generously of their time in deliberating with us about the ideas and arguments in this book. Frederick Schauer, Cass Sunstein, and Alan Wertheimer provided invaluable comments on the entire manuscript. We also received helpful suggestions on drafts of individual chapters from Arthur Applbaum,

Charles Beitz, Sissela Bok, Ezekiel Emanuel, David Estlund, Peter Euben, Robert Fullinwider, Fred Greenstein, Jane Mansbridge, Peter de Marneffe, Henry Richardson, Mark Sagoff, Debra Satz, Thomas Scanlon, and Kenneth Winston. The notes are more complete and accurate as a result of the astute research conducted by Stuart White, who also gave us helpful comments on every chapter. Additional research assistance was ably provided by Ted Aaberg, Carole Gunning, and Simone Sandy. Helen Hawkins, Valerie Kanka, and Jean McVeigh skillfully managed the complex logistics of researching, writing, and revising a manuscript by two authors working in two different locations. Our greatest debts are to Michael Doyle and Carol Thompson, whose support—personal and intellectual— sustained us through the writing of this book.

Democracy and Disagreement

Introduction

OF THE CHALLENGES that American democracy faces today, none is more formidable than the problem of moral disagreement. Neither the theory nor the practice of democratic politics has so far found an adequate way to cope with conflicts about fundamental values. We address the challenge of moral disagreement here by developing a conception of democracy that secures a central place for moral discussion in political life.

Along with a growing number of other political theorists, we call this conception deliberative democracy. The core idea is simple: when citizens or their representatives disagree morally, they should continue to reason together to reach mutually acceptable decisions. But the meaning and implications of the idea are complex. Although the idea has a long history, it is still in search of a theory. We do not claim that this book provides a comprehensive theory of deliberative democracy, but we do hope that it contributes toward its future development by showing the kind of deliberation that is possible and desirable in the face of moral disagreement in democracies.

Some scholars have criticized liberal political theory for neglecting moral deliberation. Others have analyzed the philosophical foundations of deliberative democracy, and still others have begun to explore institutional reforms that would promote deliberation. Yet nearly all of them stop at the point where deliberation itself begins. None has systematically examined the substance of deliberation—the theoretical principles that should guide moral argument and their implications for actual moral disagreements about public policy. That is our subject, and it takes us into the everyday forums of democratic politics, where moral argument regularly appears but where theoretical analysis too rarely goes.

Deliberative democracy involves reasoning about politics, and nothing has been more controversial in political philosophy than the nature of reason in politics. We do not believe that these controversies have to be settled before deliberative principles can guide the practice of democracy. Since on occasion citizens and their representatives already engage in the kind of reasoning that those principles recommend, deliberative democracy simply asks that they do so more consistently and comprehensively. The best way to prove the value of this kind of reasoning is to show its role in arguments about specific principles and policies, and its contribution to actual political debates. That is also ultimately the best justification for our conception of deliberative democracy itself. But to forestall possible misunderstandings of our conception of deliberative democracy, we offer some preliminary remarks about the scope and method of this book.

The aim of the moral reasoning that our deliberative democracy prescribes falls between impartiality, which requires something like altruism, and prudence, which demands no more than enlightened self-interest. Its first principle is reciprocity, the subject of Chapter 2, but no less essential are the other principles developed in later chapters. When citizens reason reciprocally, they seek fair terms of social cooperation for their own sake; they try to find mutually acceptable ways of resolving moral disagreements.

The precise content of reciprocity is difficult to determine in theory, but its general countenance is familiar enough in practice. It can be seen in the difference between acting in one's self-interest (say, taking advantage of a legal loophole or a lucky break) and acting fairly (following rules in the spirit that one expects others to adopt). In many of the controversies discussed later in the book, the possibility of any morally acceptable resolution depends on citizens' reasoning beyond their narrow self-interest and considering what can be justified to people who reasonably disagree with them. Even though the quality of deliberation and the conditions under which it is conducted are far from ideal in the controversies we consider, the fact that in each case some citizens and some officials make arguments consistent with reciprocity suggests that a deliberative perspective is not utopian.

To clarify what reciprocity might demand under non-ideal conditions, we develop a distinction between deliberative and nondeliberative disagreement. Citizens who reason reciprocally can recognize that a position is worthy of moral respect even when they think it morally wrong. They can believe that a moderate pro-life position on abortion, for example, is morally respectable even though they think it morally mistaken. (The abortion example—to which we often return in the book—is meant to be illustrative. For readers who deny that there is any room for deliberative disagreement on abortion, other political controversies can make the same point.) The presence of deliberative disagreement has important implications for how citizens treat one another and for what policies they should adopt. When a disagreement is not deliberative (for example, about a policy to legalize discrimination against blacks and women), citizens do not have any obligations of mutual respect toward their opponents. In deliberative disagreement (for example, about legalizing abortion), citizens should try to accommodate the moral convictions of their opponents to the greatest extent possible, without compromising their own moral convictions. We call this kind of accommodation an economy of moral disagreement, and believe that, though neglected in theory and practice, it is essential to a morally robust democratic life.

Although both of us have devoted some of our professional life to urging these ideas on public officials and our fellow citizens in forums of practical politics, this book is primarily the product of scholarly rather than political deliberation. Insofar as it reaches beyond the academic community, it is addressed to citizens and officials in their more reflective frame of mind. Given its academic origins, some readers may be inclined to complain that only professors could be so unrealistic as to believe that moral reasoning can help solve political problems. But such a complaint would misrepresent our aims.

To begin with, we do not think that academic discussion (whether in scholarly journals or college classrooms) is a model for moral deliberation in politics. Academic discussion need not aim at justifying a practical decision, as deliberation must. Partly for this reason, academic discussion is likely to be insensitive to the contexts of ordinary politics: the pressures of power, the problems of inequality, the demands of diversity, the exigencies of persuasion. Some critics of deliberative democracy show a similar insensitivity when they judge actual political deliberations by the standards of ideal philosophical reflection. Actual deliberation is inevitably defective, but so is philosophical reflection practiced in politics. The appropriate comparison is between the ideals of democratic deliberation and philosophical reflection, or between the application of each in the non-ideal circumstances of politics.

We do not assume that politics should be a realm where the logical syllogism rules. Nor do we expect even the more appropriate standard of mutual respect always to prevail in politics. A deliberative perspective sometimes justifies bargaining, negotiation, force, and even violence. It is partly because moral argument has so much unrealized potential in democratic politics that we believe it deserves more attention. Because its place in politics is so precarious, the need to find it a more secure home and to nourish its development is all the more pressing. Yet because it is also already part of our common experience, we have reason to hope that it can survive and even prosper if philosophers along with citizens and public officials better appreciate its value in politics.

Some readers may still wonder why deliberation should have such a prominent place in democracy. Surely, they may say, citizens should care more about the justice of public policies than the process by which they are adopted, at least so long as the process is basically fair and at least minimally democratic. One of our main aims in this book is to cast doubt on the dichotomy between policies and process that this concern assumes. Having good reason as individuals to believe that a policy is just does not mean that collectively as citizens we have sufficient justification to legislate on the basis of those reasons. The moral authority of collective judgments about policy depends in part on the moral quality of the process by which citizens collectively reach those judgments. Deliberation is the most appropriate way for citizens collectively to resolve their moral disagreements not only about policies but also about the process by which policies should be adopted. Deliberation is not only a means to an end, but also a means for deciding what means are morally required to pursue our common ends.

Despite the revival of academic interest in deliberative democracy, the kind of moral reasoning that it prescribes is not the dominant method in any of the relevant disciplines in universities today. The tendency in moral and political philosophy has been to carry on its inquiries at either the micro or the macro level of politics, ignoring the vast territory in between. Most studies of morality assess the interrelations of individual actions, analytically isolated from any social context, while most theories of justice prescribe the basic structures of an ideal society, morally removed from prescriptions for any non-ideal society.

Much of the best work in philosophy seeks secure foundations for moral principles—at the level of the most fundamental and general philosophical justification. The aim is more often to find out, for example, whether the basic premises of utilitarianism or contractarianism are correct than to

determine whether a government is justified in legalizing abortion or prohibiting preferential hiring. Perfectly proper as the aim of a foundational
philosophical inquiry, it takes us in the wrong direction for understanding
the nature and value of political deliberation. In politics the need is to find
some basis on which to justify collective decisions here and now in the
absence of foundational knowledge of the sort that would (presumably)
tell us whether the fundamental premises of utilitarianism or contractarianism are correct. While philosophers dispute about theoretical foundations, citizens must decide moral issues.

Nevertheless, philosophy is neither helpless nor useless in the face of
foundational disagreement. Some contemporary moral and political philosophers employ a form of moral reasoning that is well suited to deliberative democracy. Leading theories of justice and constitutional democracy provide invaluable guidance for understanding the conditions and
content of deliberation. Important philosophical work on problems of public policy—such as abortion, affirmative action, and health care, among
other issues—also furthers public understanding of particular moral disagreements in politics. We draw on much of this important work, and
indeed could not develop a theory of deliberative democracy without it.

The approach we use in this book also owes much to the method that
some philosophers adopt to develop their own foundational principles.[1]
This method posits a process in which deliberators move back and forth
between general principles and considered judgments about particular circumstances, successively modifying each in light of an appraisal of the
other. In our use of the method, the principles operate in the middle range
of abstraction, between foundational principles and institutional rules;
and the judgments apply as much to particular decisions and policies as
to basic structures of society. Furthermore, in our use the method does not
presuppose any strong assumptions about the philosophical status of
moral judgment or knowledge. We treat the method as an informal reconstruction of a form of moral reasoning familiar in everyday life, a
pattern of argument that many people use when they try to justify to others
in moral terms the positions they take and the decisions they make.

The principles of deliberative democracy that we develop here are variations on familiar themes in political theory and practice. They reflect the
subjects of actual political debate in our time. We try to clarify the themes
and bring them together into a coherent whole, which we call the constitution of deliberative democracy. Although we believe that the principles
are relevant for societies other than our own, we develop them in the

context of American society. As political theorists we begin from where we are, with ideas and concepts in our traditions, broadly understood to include all the cultural resources available for our critical and creative use. As citizens we also begin with these same cultural resources. We can deliberate in politics about only what we can understand, or what we can come to understand through political action with our fellow citizens.

Deliberative principles depend on context in a more specific sense. They are developed and defended through reflection on actual cases. This is one reason why cases—accounts of actual episodes in democratic politics—play a much larger role in this book than in most works of political theory.[2] Another reason is that an adequate conception of deliberative democracy must attend to actual arguments that citizens and officials use or could use in political discussion.

Because context is important, we rely largely on cases drawn from domestic politics in the United States in recent years. Since most readers are likely to be familiar with the social conditions and historical background in which the events take place, we can avoid extensive discussions of the circumstances of the cases and concentrate more on the competing values at stake. The contexts are not primarily the occasions of constitutional cases or national crises. Instead, we feature a number of less renowned episodes, which have taken place in state and local as well as national politics. Part of the reason for using such cases is to emphasize that important moral deliberation goes on at all levels of politics. Deliberation should be part of the fabric of political life throughout government and in public life generally. (Debates in government are prominent here only because they are more often on the record.)

Although the examples we use are specific, their implications are general. We do not claim that the cases prove any sweeping empirical propositions about deliberation. But we expect that readers will recognize features in the examples that are common to many other circumstances. The cases have two main functions in the book. First, they illustrate problems and principles: they help clarify what is at issue in formulating principles of deliberation and what the implications are. Second and more important, they serve as a concrete expression of considered judgments, provisionally fixed points in deliberation, to which we can appeal in justifying or criticizing principles. They are in this sense a critical element in the method we use in this book as well as in the method of deliberation itself.

Neither our discussion of the cases nor our analysis of moral arguments purports to prove empirically that deliberation produces the morally best decisions and policies. We suggest some reasons to believe that deliberation has good consequences for a democracy, and some reasons to value deliberation in the face of uncertainty about its consequences. But we do not undertake any systematic comparison of deliberative and nondeliberative processes or institutions. We focus on what we believe must be prior to any empirical investigation of this kind: the clarification of the character of deliberation itself, the conditions and content that are necessary to determine to what extent adequate deliberation is taking place in democratic politics. For similar reasons, an extensive discussion of the institutions for promoting deliberation is premature. At several points we mention some institutional changes that could facilitate deliberation, and in our conclusion we identify some general implications for institutional reform. But again we believe that the task of institutional design is likely to be misguided without a better understanding of the conditions and content of deliberative democracy we begin to develop here.

Chapter 1, "The Persistence of Moral Disagreement," prepares the ground for this understanding by examining the most important challenge to any moral conception of democracy. We argue that conventional conceptions of democracy do not meet the challenge of moral disagreement as well as does deliberative democracy. They fail to make enough room for moral deliberation in the normal processes of democratic politics.

The three subsequent chapters present principles that express the conditions of deliberation. The principles refer to the reasons that should inform political debate in a deliberative democracy—the kinds of reasons that should be given, the forum in which they should be given, and the agents to whom and by whom they should be given. In each chapter we aim not only to clarify a deliberative principle but also to subject it to various moral challenges, which come either from values based on rival principles or from values intrinsic to the principle itself. In each instance we try to find ways to acknowledge the truth in the competing values while maintaining the core of the basic principle.

In Chapter 2, "The Sense of Reciprocity," we argue that the principle of reciprocity is a more appropriate basis for democratic politics than an approach based on impartiality or one based on prudence, which favors a strategy of bargaining among political interests. We show how reciprocity can accept bargaining under certain conditions while escaping the moral problems that bargaining creates when taken as a comprehensive method for democratic politics.

Chapter 3, "The Value of Publicity," argues that the reasons that citizens and officials give should be public, partly to ensure that they are reciprocal but also to realize the independent moral value of openness in government. We then show how the value of publicity can be reconciled with the values of secrecy and confidentiality, which democracy also demands on occasion.

In Chapter 4, "The Scope of Accountability," we explain how a principle of accountability can be compatible with the process of democratic representation. That principle seems to imply that everyone should give an account to everyone else, but in a representative democracy some people give reasons while others look on. To satisfy the demands of democratic accountability, representatives need to consider the claims not only of their electoral constituents but also of what we call their moral constituents, who include citizens of other countries and members of future generations.

The principles of reciprocity, publicity, and accountability give citizens and officials some guidance in making political decisions, but they also leave a lot of moral disagreement unresolved. The question therefore arises whether some other approach might resolve more disagreement. The most influential theory that claims to be able to do so is utilitarianism, and in Chapter 5, "The Promise of Utilitarianism," we assess its claim to be a comprehensive guide to dealing with moral disagreements.

In Chapter 6, "The Constitution of Deliberative Democracy," we show how a deliberative perspective, without claiming to be comprehensive, can provide better guidance in dealing with the substance of moral disagreement in politics. The "constitution" of deliberative democracy refers not only to the conditions discussed in the previous chapters but also to three substantive principles that govern the content of deliberation: basic liberty, basic opportunity, and fair opportunity. Each of the three subsequent chapters discusses one of these principles.

Chapter 7, "The Latitude of Liberty," analyzes the principle of basic liberty. In the spirit of the approach we took in the chapters on the conditions of deliberation, we defend and revise the principle in response to challenges posed by competing values. In this case one challenge comes from moralists, who would legislate on the basis of social morality in the absence of individual harm, and the other from paternalists, who would legislate on the basis of individual welfare in the absence of individual consent. We show how basic liberty can be preserved while acknowledging some value in the claims of both the moralists and the paternalists.

In Chapter 8, "The Obligations of Welfare," we explore the implications of the principle of basic opportunity, which governs the distribution of goods that enable people to live a decent life and enjoy access to other opportunities. We consider two challenges to guaranteeing either a job or a basic income to all individuals. One challenge asks why society should support people who are unwilling to work, while the other asks why children should be made to suffer for the sins of their parents.

In Chapter 9, "The Ambiguity of Fair Opportunity," we turn to the principle that governs the distribution of goods on the basis of qualifications. We examine two competing interpretations of fair opportunity as applied to skilled jobs—a liberal one that implies a policy of fair competition, and an egalitarian one that calls for a policy of preferential hiring.

The concluding chapter shows how the principles of deliberative democracy interact with one another, and how they can help sustain a conception of democracy with a capacity for moral improvement. Deliberation is an ongoing process, producing results that in a deep sense are always provisional.

In this book, as in deliberative democracy, we neither begin nor end with comprehensive moral agreement. While the locus and content of particular disagreements shift over time, moral disagreement is a permanent condition of democratic politics. We believe that a deliberative perspective can help resolve some moral disagreements in democratic politics, but we suspect that its greater contribution can be to help citizens treat one another with mutual respect as they deal with the disagreements that invariably remain.

–1–

The Persistence of
Moral Disagreement

Reporter: *How fair do you believe it is then that women who can afford to get an abortion can go ahead and have one, and women who cannot afford to, are precluded from this?*

The President: *Well, as you know there are many things in life that are not fair, that wealthy people can afford and poor people can't. But I don't believe the Federal Government should take action to try to make these opportunities exactly equal, particularly when there is a moral factor involved.*[1]

·   ·   ·

[*To end discrimination, AT&T must achieve*] *full utilization of minorities and women at all levels of management and nonmanagement and by job classification at a pace beyond that which would occur normally.*

One thing that really bothers me is moving up in the company . . . I am white, male, twenty-five . . . I have a lot of drive and want to get ahead. I have just been notified there is some kind of freeze, which will last 3 or 4 months. In that time, if I am passed over, the company will go to the street. This is not fair. I work for the company but my chances are less than someone on the street.[2]

·   ·   ·

[*Should society*] *spend money on doing eight heart transplants at 1½ million dollars? Or . . . give more . . . poor people . . . prenatal care [at] about 2,000 dollars a case. [That's] about 700 deliveries for eight heart transplants . . . When I have limited resources, it's women and children first. The* Titanic *concept of medicine.*

Dianna Brown . . . is the first person to die under Arizona's newest death penalty law . . . She had committed . . . no crime. Dianna Brown's only offense was to be poor and sick. Under Arizona's law, that's now punishable by death.[3]

Is IT FAIR that government refuses to fund abortion? Does affirmative action violate the rights of white males? Is it wrong to deny scarce life-saving medical treatment to poor people? Abortion, affirmative action, and health care are only a few of the many moral issues that citizens and their representatives continually confront in public life. The moral claims with which we begin this chapter are also only fragments of larger moral arguments that citizens and their representatives make about public policies.

The sound of moral argument in American democracy may be familiar, but the very familiarity has bred neglect, if not contempt. In the practice of our democratic politics, communicating by sound bite, competing by character assassination, and resolving political conflicts through self-seeking bargaining too often substitute for deliberation on the merits of controversial issues. In the standard theories of democracy—proceduralism and constitutionalism—deliberation likewise receives little attention. These theories are surprisingly silent about the need for ongoing discussion of moral disagreement in everyday political life. As a result, we suffer from a deliberative deficit not only in our democratic politics but also in our democratic theory. We are unlikely to lower the deficit in our politics if we do not also reduce it in our theory.

The conception of deliberative democracy that we defend here seeks to diminish that deficit in theory and in politics.[4] The conception consists of three principles—reciprocity, publicity, and accountability—that regulate the process of politics, and three others—basic liberty, basic opportunity, and fair opportunity—that govern the content of policies. It would promote extensive moral argument about the merits of public policies in public forums, with the aim of reaching provisional moral agreement and maintaining mutual respect among citizens. In its most general form, the demand for deliberation has been a familiar theme in the American constitutional tradition. It is integral to the ideal of republican government as the Founders understood it. James Madison judged the design of political institutions in part by how well they furthered deliberation.[5]

Deliberation should not be confined to constitutional conventions, Supreme Court opinions, or their theoretical analogues. It should extend throughout the political process—to what we call the land of middle democracy. The forums of deliberation in middle democracy embrace virtually any setting in which citizens come together on a regular basis to reach collective decisions about public issues—governmental as well as nongovernmental institutions. They include not only legislative sessions, court proceedings, and administrative hearings at all levels of government but also meetings of grass roots organizations, professional associations, shareholders meetings, and citizens' committees in hospitals and other similar institutions.[6]

In defending this conception of deliberative democracy, we look at moral arguments already present in our political life, criticizing and extending them in light of other principles also present in our political culture.[7] The characteristics of moral arguments we find in actual political debate provide the basis for developing the normative principles with which we assess the ongoing debates. These features of moral disagreement themselves point toward a deliberative way of dealing with the disagreement.

What counts as a moral argument in deliberative democracy? The most rudimentary criterion—sometimes called generality—is one that deliberative democracy shares with most moral and political theories. The criterion of generality is so widely accepted that it is often identified with the moral point of view.[8] Moral arguments apply to everyone who is similarly situated in the morally relevant respects. The poor woman who seeks an abortion, the white male employee who fails to receive his promotion, the mother who needs prenatal care do not assert merely that they, or even only their friends, family, and associates, should receive the benefit; they maintain that all citizens similarly situated should receive it. Their claims, if fully developed, would impute rights and wrongs, or ascribe virtue and vice, to anyone who is similar in the respects that the argument assumes to be morally significant.

As these examples suggest, generality is not a purely formal standard. It always raises a substantive question: What are the morally relevant respects in which people are similarly situated? Does the same argument against preferential treatment for white males, for example, apply equally to preferential treatment of black Americans and white women? Generality forces us to take up substantive arguments (such as those discussed in Chapter 9) which consider whether the differences between whites and blacks, and men and women, in this country are morally relevant in a way that would support a policy of preferential hiring.

In politics, however, substantive moral argument calls for more than merely satisfying the criterion of generality. Political decisions are collectively binding, and they should therefore be justifiable, as far as possible, to everyone bound by them. Three characteristics of moral arguments are especially important in politics. The first corresponds to our principle of reciprocity, a form of mutuality in the face of disagreement (which we develop in Chapter 2). Citizens try to offer reasons that other similarly motivated citizens can accept even though they recognize that they share only some of one another's values. When our deliberations about moral disagreements in politics are guided by reciprocity, citizens recognize and respect one another as moral agents, not merely as abstract objects of others' moral reasoning.

Reciprocity asks us to appeal to reasons that are shared or could come to be shared by our fellow citizens. The reporter and the president both invoke a familiar and widely accepted principle of fairness. The AT&T employee says simply: "This is not fair," and we know at once what he means, whether or not we agree that he has been treated unfairly. The defender of Dianna Brown assumes that we accept the idea that people should not suffer as a result of diseases that are not their fault. Reaching for reciprocity in these ways is of course not always successful. But it is a feature of moral reasoning that is especially important in politics. It enables us, for example, mutually to respect one another as moral agents who share the goal of reaching deliberative agreement even when we disagree with one another's conclusions.

Reciprocity also applies to the empirical claims that often accompany moral arguments. Moral arguments take place in context, and they therefore depend at least implicitly on matters of fact, estimates of risk, suppositions about feasibility, and beliefs about human nature and social processes. Sometimes these assumptions are plausible but controversial: hiring and promoting simply on the basis of qualification will not end racial discrimination soon enough. Sometimes they are widely accepted but questionable: Arizona cannot afford both prenatal care and organ transplants because voters will not approve higher taxes. Sometimes the assumptions are obviously true: only women bear children. If technological advances and cultural changes were somehow to eliminate all the social and psychological effects of this biological fact, our moral attitudes and public policies might be different. But that possibility, even if realized in some other place or some other time, should not affect the moral argument for us now.

The president, the AT&T employee, and Dianna Brown would not be moved if they learned that their moral argument would not be understood, let alone accepted, if they tried to make it in some remote village in Asia or among the Ik in Uganda.[9] Even those who rely on what they regard as universal moral principles do not presume that their practical conclusions are independent of reliable facts and plausible assumptions about particular societies. The arguments begin from where we are, and appeal to those with whom we now live. This is why moral relativism is seldom as important an issue in practical as it is in theoretical ethics.[10]

Reciprocity asks that our empirical claims in political argument be consistent with reliable methods of inquiry, as these methods are available to us here and now, not for all times and all places. Neither relativity nor uncertainty is grounds for abandoning the most reliable methods of inquiry at our collective disposal. By using the most reliable methods of inquiry, we demonstrate our mutual commitment to reach deliberative agreement in the empirical realms that are relevant to moral argument.

Once the fragments of moral argument with which this chapter began are put into context, they reveal two other characteristics of moral disagreement in politics. They take us beyond the nature of reasoning to the forums and the agents of the disagreement. Moral conflicts in politics typically take place in public forums or are intended for dissemination in public forums. The reporter and the president, the AT&T executive and the employee, the defender and the critic of Arizona's health care program speak not only to each other but also in effect to all citizens. The principle of publicity, whose implications we explore in Chapter 3, captures this feature of moral disagreement in politics.

The third feature of this disagreement concerns the agents by whom and to whom the moral reasons are publicly offered. The agents are typically citizens and public officials who are accountable to one another for their political actions. One common way in which public officials offer an account of their actions is by responding to challenges from reporters such as Judy Woodruff, who put President Carter on the spot about subsidizing abortions for poor women. Accountability is ultimately to citizens, who not only vote for or against the president but also speak their minds between elections, often through organized groups and intermediary institutions. Accountability through moral disagreement in public forums extends not only to prominent elected officials such as the president but also to far less conspicuous officials, professionals, corporate executives, union leaders, employers and employees, and ordinary citizens when they act in a public capacity. The principle of accountability, the subject of Chapter 4, captures this characteristic of moral disagreement in politics.

These three features of moral disagreement, then, point to the need and at the same time provide the support for the three principles that refer to the process of deliberative democracy. Taken together the principles constitute a process that seeks deliberative agreement—on policies that can be provisionally justified to the citizens who are bound by them. Accountable agents reach out publicly to find reasons that others who are motivated to find deliberative agreement can also accept. When citizens and accountable officials disagree, and also recognize that they are seeking deliberative agreement, they remain willing to argue with one another with the aim of achieving provisionally justifiable policies that they all can mutually recognize as such.

Even when citizens find some provisionally justifiable principles, their disagreement over public policy may persist. In politics, disagreements often run deep. If they did not, there would be no need for argument. But if they ran too deep, there would be no point in argument. Deliberative disagreements lie in the depths between simple misunderstanding and immutable irreconcilability. The president and the reporter may disagree about what fairness requires, and even about in what way abortion should be a "moral factor" in this dispute. The AT&T executive and the employee disagree about what justice in employment means, as well as about who should suffer its costs. The doctor who puts mothers and children first and Dianna Brown's advocate, although both motivated to justify their position to the people bound by it, appear to favor different priorities: saving more and younger lives versus saving lives immediately in peril. They also may have different views about the obligation of society and the government to save lives of any kind.

Some theorists would abstract from these moral disagreements and imagine a nearly ideal society in which some could be more readily resolved and many would not arise at all. In some familiar theories of justice, moral claims are constructed as hypothetical agreements among individuals who are not accountable to anyone and who are assumed to be living in a just society.[11] In such a society no one would need to argue for or against preferential hiring as a means of overcoming racial or gender discrimination because no such discrimination would exist in that society. Deliberative democracy, in contrast, admits reasons and principles that are suitable for actual societies, which all still suffer from discrimination and other kinds of injustice. Actual deliberation has an important advantage over hypothetical agreement: it encourages citizens to face up to their actual problems by listening to one another's moral claims rather than concluding (on the basis of only a thought experiment) that their fellow citizens *would* agree with them on all matters of justice if they were all living in an ideal society.

Deliberative democracy does not assume that the results of all actual deliberations are just. In fact, most of the time democracies fall far short of meeting the conditions that deliberative democracy prescribes. But we can say that the more nearly the conditions are satisfied, the more nearly justifiable are the results likely to be.[12] Even if, as one critic suggests, "all of the inequalities of society in general" were "replicated in the content of deliberation,"[13] it would not discredit deliberation. The process of deliberation as we understand it here is self-constraining; its own defining principles provide a basis for criticizing the unjust inequalities that affect the process. Deliberative democracy certainly does not accept as equally valid whatever reasons and principles citizens and public officials put forward in defense of their own interests.

Neither should we make deliberation the sovereign guide to resolving moral disagreements in politics, as some "discourse theorists" seem to suggest. Jürgen Habermas writes that "all contents, no matter how fundamental the action norm involved may be, must be made to depend on real discourses (or advocatory discourses conducted as substitutes for them)."[14] Habermas seems to imply that a provisionally justifiable resolution of moral conflicts in politics depends solely on satisfying the conditions of deliberation. Principles such as basic liberty and opportunity therefore are valued only for their contribution to deliberation, not as constraints on what counts as a morally legitimate resolution of disagreement. If leaving "all concrete moral and ethical judgments to participants themselves"[15] means that principles such as liberty and opportunity should never constrain these judgments, then discourse theory does not adequately protect basic rights.[16]

Habermas and other discourse theorists try to avoid this implication by, in effect, building guarantees of basic liberty and opportunity into the ideal conditions of deliberation. They do so by qualifying what counts as a moral ideal of deliberation. The participants in practical deliberations must regard one another as "competent subjects"[17] and "moral and political equals."[18] Their deliberations not only must be free but also must be reasoned.[19] Deliberative outcomes, then, would have to respect basic liberty and opportunity as an ongoing condition of their own legitimacy.

This understanding still does not capture the value of basic rights. Citizens value basic liberty and opportunity, and their mutual recognition by fellow citizens, for reasons other than the role of these values in democratic deliberation. As we shall suggest, even in deliberative democracy, deliberation does not have priority over liberty and opportunity. The condition of honoring basic liberty and opportunity should still be "reflexively" subject to deliberative understanding, as discourse theorists correctly insist.[20] But so should deliberation itself.

We do not assume that deliberative democracy can guarantee social justice either in theory or in practice. Our argument is rather that in the absence of robust deliberation in democracy, citizens cannot even provisionally justify many controversial procedures and constitutional rights to one another. Insofar as deliberation is missing in political life, citizens also lack a mutually justifiable way of living with their ongoing moral disagreements. When citizens deliberate in democratic politics, they express and respect their status as political equals even as they continue to disagree about important matters of public policy.

Before exploring how deliberative democracy deals with disagreement, we need first to examine the sources of that disagreement. Then we can better see why procedural and constitutional democracy can be only partial solutions to the problem of moral conflict, and how deliberative democracy provides a more nearly complete solution.

Sources of Moral Disagreement

Why do we morally disagree with one another about public policy? The temptation is to answer this question by turning moral disagreements into a simpler and seemingly more fundamental kind of conflict. This temptation is especially great in politics. Moral conflict in politics seems slightly mysterious, dangerously subjective, at once naive and complex. In a kind of reverse transmutation, some theorists attempt to reduce moral claims to self-interest. Others, most famously David Hume, suggest more broadly that there would be no moral conflict if social resources were less scarce or human nature more generous. Hume's suggestion illuminates two important sources of moral disagreement, but it neglects two other sources: incompatible values and incomplete understanding. When we take into account all four sources of moral disagreement, we are in a better position to see why deliberation is indispensable for dealing with our ongoing moral disagreements in politics.

THE LURE OF SELF-INTEREST

Some people claim that moral disagreements simply reflect the conflicting self-interests of individuals. This familiar view has been around for a long time—finding its most systematic political statement in the theory of

Thomas Hobbes. On this view, moral disagreements cannot properly be understood on their own terms. Moral terms are "inconstant names," referring to "things which please and displease us," and which vary depending on what individuals take to be in their interest.[21]

Certainly in many political disputes today we are inclined to believe that economic self-interest influences the moral positions that people take. As the joint pursuit of economic self-interest suggests, the "self" in the "self-interest" view of politics also applies to groups whose members are united by pursuit of their partial but similarly self-interested aims. To see the limits of this general view, consider the debate over taxing Social Security benefits. This dispute is often seen as a clash of self-interests. Some senior citizens object to having their taxes raised, while other citizens want to have their taxes lowered, or more tax revenues spent on them. So too is much of the high-minded rhetoric of the politicians who represent these citizens regarded as a cover for their self-interest.

Yet this interpretation is a misleading or at least an incomplete account. Even if self-interest influences the positions that these citizens take in this dispute, it does not completely determine them. Some citizens who would suffer from the tax increase favor it, and some who stand to benefit from it oppose it. Are these citizens deluded about their interest? It seems more likely that their moral understandings are part of what constitutes their interests. Some citizens are willing to sacrifice some personal economic advantage for what they take to be their moral interest in helping others less economically fortunate than themselves.

It is of course possible to define self-interest so expansively that it subsumes all the interests that citizens might have in fulfilling legitimate expectations, upholding rights, rewarding desert, and seeking fair treatment for themselves and people they care about. But such an expansive concept is also misleading. It elides the distinction between interests exclusively in oneself and interests in other people and impersonal values. To criticize someone for being self-interested makes sense only if self-interest is understood as having interest solely in oneself, or at least failing to demonstrate sufficient regard for the interests of others. If all human action is assumed to be a reflection of self-interest, the charge of self-interest loses its critical content, and the claim that moral disagreements can be reduced to conflicting self-interests becomes a truism.

The more limited reduction—all political action by public officials is narrowly self-interested—is not a truism. (Nor is it obviously true.) The reduction is common in political science, where it is often assumed that self-interest for public officials consists in gaining office or remaining in office, most commonly by satisfying the preferences of their most powerful constituents. Whatever the truth of this reduction, it takes the sting out of the criticism of any particular political actor for acting in a self-interested way. In any case, it does not succeed in reducing moral disagreement in politics more generally to self-interest since moral disagreement among public officials may reflect the disagreement among citizens, and that disagreement, as we have just noted, cannot meaningfully be reduced to self-interest.

Even if we stick to the narrow sense of self-interest as an interest exclusively *in* one's self, reducing moral disagreement entirely to self-interest is misleading in another way. Citizens who take positions based on narrow self-interest may still be able to justify their positions by appealing to moral principles. Advocates of increasing taxes on the benefits of senior citizens with total incomes above a certain level argue that government should not in effect provide a tax shelter at public expense for affluent citizens, and that revenue could be better and more fairly used for the less well-off, including other senior citizens. Opponents argue that senior citizens have planned their retirement expecting that their Social Security benefits would not be taxed; it is unfair to change the rules at this point, especially for people who are far from wealthy and are in no position to find new ways of replacing the lost income. If we attend solely to narrow self-interest, we understand only one aspect of the dispute—the motives of citizens—and fail to appreciate another—the justifications for their actions.

Even if economic interests (including both motives and justifications) correlated perfectly with political positions, the issue still would not be reducible to self-interest. All citizens, regardless of what they stand to gain or lose by this policy, could still make a genuine moral claim on behalf of either side of this issue. It would still be possible to stand outside the arena of self-interested combat and judge the merits of the conflicting claims. It is what citizens expect public officials to do at least some of the time, and it is what citizens themselves do more often than the self-interest perspective allows.[22]

If the lens of self-interest tends to distort disputes about tax policy, then it is all the more likely to misrepresent disputes over policies that are less directly linked to economic interests—such as abortion, pornography, and capital punishment. These political issues involve conflicting moral perspectives more than competing self-interests. We may disagree about precisely what is at stake in the debate over whether and when abortion should be legal. Yet even Hobbes, who thought his own birth traumatic, would not have supposed that the abortion controversy is best understood as a battle between the self-interests of women and fetuses.

Citizens and officials sometimes—even often—act on self-interest, but there is no warrant for assuming, as a theoretical postulate, that they always, or even generally, act on this basis. Self-interested behavior is not in any nonvacuous sense presumptively rational. We should not regard the assumption of self-interest as the default position of deliberative democracy. As Brian Barry has argued:

> The equation of rationality with the efficient pursuit of self-interest is . . . pure assertion. It can therefore fitly be opposed by a counter-assertion, namely, that it is equally rational to care about what can be defended impartially . . . The virtually unanimous concurrence of the human race in caring about the defensibility of actions in a way that does not simply appeal to power is a highly relevant supporting consideration . . . Until somebody produces more than an argument by definitional fiat for the equation of rationality and self-interest we can safely continue to deny it.[23]

THE HUMAN CONDITION

Some people assume that if unjustified economic, racial, and gender inequalities could be eliminated, moral disagreement in politics would also disappear, or at least would cease to be so contentious. But moral disagreement appears to be more pervasive and more diverse than this assumption admits. That the deepest source of our moral disagreement in politics may reside in the human condition itself is the more disturbing possibility.

Hume's account of the sources of moral conflict (or, as it has come to be known, the circumstances of justice)[24] begins to explain why we should not expect moral conflict to disappear even in a more egalitarian society. But we can go further than Hume in demonstrating the irreducibly moral character of conflicts over public policy. Hume argues that only in conditions of moderate scarcity do moral conflicts arise that call for a just resolution.[25] Were there such abundance that all of us had enough to satisfy not only our wants but also our wildest imagination, justice would become an "idle ceremony."[26] Moral conflicts demanding just solutions would simply not arise. Hume suggests that *extreme* scarcity would also eliminate moral conflict. The reason presumably is that conflicts over goods in such desperate circumstances can be resolved only by force—

some version of the survival of the fittest. Both abundance and extreme scarcity thus render disputes over justice beside the point. In abundance, people flourish without demanding any goods from others; in extreme scarcity, people fight simply to survive. This is why Hume thinks that it is only under external conditions of moderate scarcity, the most common condition of human society, that moral conflicts generally arise.

Moral disagreements are also internally rooted, Hume argues, in a characteristic of human nature: our limited generosity. Even if social resources remained limited, there would be no problem of moral conflict if human beings were generous without limit—if the human mind were "so enlarged, and so replete with friendship and generosity, that every man has the utmost tenderness for every man, and feels no more concern for his own interest than that of his fellows."[27] But, unfortunately, the human mind is not so enlarged or so replete. As with scarcity, so with generosity: it is in the middle of the range where problems of moral disagreement arise. If we were completely selfish, disagreement would not be moral. If we were completely generous, it would not be necessary.

Hume is surely right that moral conflict is rooted not primarily in certain kinds of societies but in more fundamental and more nearly universal features of societies. Hume must also be correct in claiming that among those features are scarcity of resources and the limited generosity of human nature. But Hume's account does not go far enough. There are at least two other sources of moral conflict that he ignores: incompatible values and incomplete understanding. These make the problem of moral disagreement both more complex and more challenging than he implies. Moral conflict is more deeply rooted in the human condition than the Humean circumstances of justice would have us believe.

Under conditions of extreme scarcity, moral conflicts still arise, and considerations of justice are still relevant. Consider the familiar hypothetical case of the lifeboat full of shipwreck survivors with too little food and water for all to live long enough to be rescued.[28] The survivors are certainly in a situation of extreme scarcity. No principle for distributing provisions can save everyone. Yet moral conflicts about how to determine who survives are likely to arise, and some decisions that resolve those conflicts may carry moral weight. Even if the extremity of the circumstances might *excuse* someone who did not comply with fair principles for survival (such as drawing straws) fairly set, he would still be rightly accused of acting wrongly.

The circumstances of the lifeboat example are not as hypothetical as they may seem.[29] But we do not have to turn to real lifeboats or mountaintop plane crashes to find significant analogues. Americans now live in a society in which many citizens need an organ transplant, and relatively few suitable organs are available. The scarcity is as extreme as the lifeboat example: many people cannot enjoy a normal life, and many cannot live at all, without access to organ transplants. The distribution of extremely scarce organs is a matter of justice and a source of ongoing moral conflict. Similar questions routinely arise regarding other scarce life-saving medical technology. Moral conflict does not end when scarcity becomes extreme.

Neither does it end when generosity disappears. Even if most people were complete egoists, pursuing only the narrowest notion of self-interest, there would remain ample scope for moral conflict. A society where people utterly lacked generosity and fellow feeling would be a strange society indeed. But even here not all disagreement would necessarily take the form of conflicting claims of self-interest. Suppose that many of the egoists "work hard to create valuable objects from the moderate store of raw materials that nature provides." Genuine moral conflicts may break out among these ruffians, each of whom argues for his or her fair share. Even if they argue from self-interested motives, their arguments nonetheless can have genuine moral content.[30]

The problem of moral disagreement arises not only at the grim extremes of Hume's circumstances—extreme scarcity and complete egoism—but also at the felicitous extremes, in conditions of material abundance and unlimited generosity. It might seem safe to pass over this question since no such societies have existed or are likely to exist in the foreseeable future. Nevertheless, by raising this admittedly hypothetical question, we point to another source of moral conflict that is highly relevant to contemporary politics: the incompatibility of values. Many citizens and politicians follow Hume in viewing moral disagreement as a conflict between people who pursue different ends: propertied versus propertyless, rich versus poor, the self-interested versus the moderately public-spirited. The implication of this view is that moral conflicts could be eliminated were people better motivated or social resources less limited. This suggestion seriously understates the difficulty, and distorts the nature, of moral conflict in modern politics. The problem of moral conflict originates not only between *persons* but also between the moral *values* themselves.

Totally benevolent individuals trying to decide on the morally best standards for governing a society of abundance would not be able to reconcile some moral conflicts beyond a deliberative doubt. They would still confront, for example, the problem of abortion. Certainly, devoting more social resources to eliminating poverty would help alleviate unwanted pregnancies, and more generosity and good will on both sides would reduce the tensions and violence that exacerbate the problem. But short of imagining a radically different world in which adults have no emotional attachment to the children they conceive, and children thrive without parental care or education, citizens would continue to face a fundamental conflict between the life of the fetus and the liberty of women. Nor is abortion a unique case. Similar moral conflicts among valued ends characterize significant aspects of the controversies over legalizing pornography, capital punishment, surrogate parenting, and many other contemporary issues on which moral opinion divides.

These moral conflicts can be understood and experienced by *one* person appreciating the competing claims of more than one fundamental value, and therefore struggling internally to resolve the conflict. Rather than eliminating the internal struggle, benevolence may simply intensify it. If some moral conflicts can be recognized by a single person of good will and with adequate resources, then they are not likely to be resolved only through changes in the non-moral circumstances of social and political life. The sources of moral disagreement lie partly within morality itself.[31]

But why should incompatible values produce moral conflict in politics? Finding the right resolution becomes more difficult when moral values conflict, and a conflict among values readily turns into a conflict among persons, as citizens come to different conclusions about the same decisions and policies. Still, why should these political differences be regarded as *moral* conflicts?

It is not clear that they should, so long as the problem is only one of incompatible values. When values are incompatible, there are better and worse choices among them, and better and worse reasons for the choices. There may be a correct resolution of even the most difficult moral dilemmas; there may be a lesser evil. Some citizens may not discover it, but that alone does not warrant elevating their failure into a genuine moral conflict. If we assume that citizens carefully and impartially think through the conflicting values at stake in the issue of abortion, for example, then we might think that each should arrive at the same *correct* conclusion concerning what the law or public policy should be. The conflict of values that is internal to the dilemma—the life of the fetus against the liberty of a woman—should certainly be considered seriously by each person, but this internal conflict alone would not itself create moral conflict in politics.

It would not create a conflict in which each side should—for moral reasons—be taken seriously by the other. Incompatible ends alone do not create moral conflict between people over justice.

But incompatible ends do produce moral conflict in politics if we recognize yet another circumstance: incomplete understanding. We do not know whether, if we enjoyed perfect understanding, we would discover uniquely correct resolutions to problems of incompatible values, such as those that divide us in the abortion debate. But we should be able to recognize that all of us lack that kind of understanding at present. Even if everyone were completely benevolent, some would reasonably give different weight to the many complex factors, moral and empirical, that affect the choice of public policies. Recognizing this human limitation does not imply moral skepticism. It is fully compatible with the belief that there are moral truths, although it does not presuppose this belief.[32] It simply expresses a recognition that at any particular moment in history we cannot collectively resolve some moral dilemmas on their own terms. Some dilemmas may have a uniquely correct solution, and some may not. But at any historical moment our imperfect understanding, manifested in the fundamental disagreements among the most thoughtful and good-willed citizens, prevents us from definitively distinguishing those that do from those that do not. We live in a state of moral conflict over many issues about which we do not (yet) know the right answer.

So to Hume's two circumstances of moral conflict, scarcity and limited generosity, we add incompatible values and incomplete understanding. All four sources are pervasive, and each is often sufficient, none always necessary, to create an irreducibly moral conflict in politics. It is hardly surprising that the moral disagreement in political life is so incessant.

If moral disagreement is so pervasive, how can we ever hope to resolve it? Some basis for hope is to be found in the nature of moral claims themselves. Just as the problem of disagreement lies partly within morality itself, so does the basis for its resolution. The distinctive characteristics of moral argument in politics—most notably reciprocity—support the possibility of resolution. If citizens publicly appeal to reasons that are shared, or could be shared, by their fellow citizens, and if they take into account these same kinds of reasons presented by similarly motivated citizens, then they are already engaged in a process that by its nature aims at a justifiable resolution of disagreement.

We should not expect finally to resolve all or even most moral conflicts. If incompatible values and incomplete understanding are as endemic to human politics as scarcity and limited generosity, then the problem of moral disagreement is a condition with which we must learn to live, not merely an obstacle to be overcome on the way to a just society. We reach some resolutions, but they are partial and tentative. The resolutions do not stand outside the process of moral argument, prior to it or protected from its provocations. We do not begin with a common morality, a substantial set of the principles or values that we assume we share, and then apply it to decisions and policies. Nor, for that matter, do we end with such a morality. Rather, the principles and values with which we live are provisional, formed and continually revised in the process of making and responding to moral claims in public life.

Democratic Responses

There are better and worse ways of living with moral disagreement, and among the better is political democracy. Democracy seems a natural and reasonable way since it is a conception of government that accords equal respect to the moral claims of each citizen, and is therefore morally justifiable from the perspective of each citizen. If we have to disagree morally about public policy, it is better to do so in a democracy that as far as possible respects the moral status of each of us.[33]

But what conception of democracy is most defensible? We should not expect to find a complete resolution of conflicts about these conceptions any more than we can find a complete resolution of more particular conflicts about policies. Nevertheless, we should be able to determine how well different conceptions of democracy deal with the general problem of moral disagreement. We can ask how well each provides a perspective that can be accepted by people who are mutually motivated to find fair terms of social cooperation among political equals.

Both procedural and constitutional democrats go some distance toward providing such a perspective. Both are committed to the basic democratic value of political equality, and therefore in principle are also committed to finding terms of cooperation that each citizen can accept. But they disagree about what those terms should be, and their disagreement can be provisionally resolved only by supplementing their conceptions with that of deliberative democracy.

Procedural democrats call attention to the importance of establishing a fair or legitimate process for making decisions about controversial moral issues. They defend majority rule as the default procedure because, other things being equal, it realizes popular rule. Proceduralists also defend those individual rights that are necessary to create a fair democratic process. Constitutional democrats add another set of rights to those that have priority over the democratic process, rights whose primary purpose is to produce justified outcomes. Procedural and constitutional democrats therefore disagree about what rights have priority over the democratic process, even though they both agree that some rights should have that priority.

Breaking the deadlock between proceduralists and constitutionalists about which rights have priority is part of the promise of deliberative democracy.[34] Procedural and constitutional democrats agree that their disagreement turns on the question whether democratic procedures have priority over just outcomes or just outcomes have priority over democratic procedures. Deliberative democracy rejects this dichotomy. It sees deliberation as an outcome-oriented process; citizens deliberate with the aim of justifying their collective decisions to one another as best they can. As we shall show, neither the principles that define the process of deliberation nor the principles that constitute its content have priority in deliberative democracy. Both interact dynamically in ways that overcome the dichotomy between procedure and outcome.

PROCEDURAL DEMOCRACY

Procedural democrats defend popular rule as the fairest way of resolving moral conflicts.[35] They maintain that the only alternative, rule by only some part of the citizenry, violates the democratic value of respecting citizens as political equals. If political equals disagree on moral matters, then the greater rather than the lesser number should rule. The alternative imposes the claims of the minority on the majority, and this seems to assume that some citizens' moral convictions count for more than those of others. The most straightforward form of popular rule is majoritarianism: members of a sovereign society agree to be governed by the will of a majority or their accountable representatives. The decision of a majority at any particular time is provisional, since it may always be revised by subsequent majorities. Also, some provisions are usually built into proceduralism to protect permanent minorities; most proceduralists would, for example, allow special protections for "discrete and insular minorities."[36] But what the majority decides resolves the moral conflict as a matter of policy at that time and for all citizens.

Procedural democrats do not claim that majority rule always resolves the substance of a moral conflict. Members of the losing minority can accept majoritarianism as a fair procedure even when it yields incorrect results because it respects their status as political equals. The results of majority rule are legitimate because the procedure is fair, not because the results are right. Of course, majorities may believe that their political views are right, but the proceduralist defense of majoritarianism (or any of its variations such as plurality rule) does not presuppose the truth of that belief. Numerical might does not make a decision morally right. Majorities have a moral right to govern only because minorities do not.

Some procedural democrats go further in their defense and deny that there are any correct substantive moral conclusions in politics. They argue that there are no "fundamental values" that should be shared by all citizens.[37] But the defense of procedural democracy does not require this moral skepticism, and indeed it would undermine the defense. If there is no reason to believe that any moral claim is valid, then there is no reason to count anyone's moral claim at all, and no reason, therefore, to defer to the claims of the greatest number.[38] The strongest justification for majoritarianism does not rest on moral skepticism. It assumes only that citizens cannot collectively agree on the solutions to many moral conflicts, and (in light of the sources of moral conflict) should not be expected to do so. The value of political equality stands behind this assumption. Thus, the very basis for establishing that the disagreement cannot be resolved—our collective incapacity to find a conclusion justifiable to each citizen who is bound by it—presupposes that the conflicting moral claims of each citizen deserve respect.

If proceduralism presumes this substantive value, then we must ask whether majority rule adequately protects it. The answer, as a simple example will make clear, is that it does not. Proceduralists need to qualify their majoritarianism in ways that move procedural democracy in the direction of constitutional democracy. (Constitutionalists, as we suggest later, need to qualify their claims in ways that move constitutional democracy in the direction of deliberative democracy.)

Imagine a new director of Arizona's health system who is faced with the rapidly increasing costs of organ transplants in the state's health care budget. (Although the example is fictitious, the resemblance to the real characters in the case we present in Chapter 6 is not accidental.) Suppose further that the director calls on five citizens, chosen at random from the state's jury lists, to decide whether or not to impose a tax surcharge, which most citizens will have to pay, in order to continue providing organ transplants to terminally ill citizens like Dianna Brown. After selecting the jurors, the director simply asks them to vote, yes or no, on whether to continue funding organ transplants. Since he and his staff are divided about what to recommend, and so is the state legislature, the jury's decision is likely to be decisive.

All four of our sources of moral disagreement manifest themselves in this case: scarcity (the state's budget is under pressure), limited generosity (the citizens of Arizona are not altruists), incomplete understanding (the jury cannot know all the risks and benefits of the options at issue, or what the indisputably correct moral judgment should be under the circumstances), and incompatible values (some who may need an organ transplant in the future will believe that the certainty of having more expendable income is preferable to a lower risk of dying prematurely). How should the conflict be resolved by the jury?

Since citizens could offer good reasons in favor of either option, majority rule seems a natural choice. As Brian Barry shows, "the existence of relevant principles does not seem to offer a sound basis for resistance to a majority decision."[39] To strengthen the case for majority rule, Barry asks us to imagine someone claiming the right to decide the question "on the basis either of his social position or . . . of his presumptive expertise in casuistry." If his claim is accepted by all the other citizens, then no decision-making problem arises because there is agreement. If some of the citizens reject his claim to moral authority, it is again difficult to see how the question can be settled except by a vote. If the assertive citizen finds himself in the minority, it must be because he has failed to convince enough of his fellow citizens that he is right, or at least that he has the right to decide. He may continue to insist that his view should have been accepted, but in the face of actual rejection of the minority views, the case for deferring to the majority still looks strong.[40]

The defense of majority rule is not so simple if we fill in more detail in the case, however. Suppose that the first juror assumes, contrary to fact, that liver transplants like the one denied to Dianna Brown do not save lives. Out of ignorance he thinks that such transplants are a waste of taxpayers' money and he therefore votes against funding. The second and third jurors join him in voting against funding for a different reason. They believe one should prefer the satisfaction of greater disposable income to the security of a lower risk of premature death. They have this preference themselves even though, like Dianna Brown, they are at risk of premature death if the government does not fund organ transplants for people who are or who may become poor. Their preference would go against funding organ transplants no matter how effective they may be in extending life. These jurors also believe that voting one's personal preferences is the most democratic way of making the decision. The fourth and fifth jurors think that it is wrong for any democracy to deny any citizen life-saving medical care so long as the cost is not prohibitive. The fourth juror is uncertain about both the costs and the efficacy of organ transplants. The fifth juror knows a lot about the medical issues in question but little about the perspective of her fellow citizens. The vote is taken, and paying for organ transplants loses by a vote of 3 to 2.

Does the case for deferring to the majority look as strong as before? Whether it does surely depends in part on the cost of organ transplants and their efficacy in enabling people to live normal lives. If we assume that organ transplants are prohibitively expensive and ineffective in saving lives, then the case for accepting what the majority decided in this case still looks strong. But if we assume that the life-saving potential of organ transplants is great and the cost to individual taxpayers small, then the majority's decision looks less justifiable. Our confidence in the results of a majority decision against transplants declines as our confidence increases in the cost-effectiveness of transplants in enabling citizens to secure basic opportunities of life.

This inverse relationship reveals the most significant of several background conditions that we implicitly take for granted when we accept majority rule as the best way to deal with a particular moral conflict.[41] A majority vote alone cannot legitimate an outcome when the basic liberties or opportunities of an individual are at stake. Here the basic opportunity to live a normal life is at stake for people who, like Dianna Brown, will die young if they are denied access to an organ transplant.[42] If all the majority can say is, "We represent the popular will, and therefore our decision is legitimate, whatever its basis," then they have not said nearly enough to justify their decision to people like Dianna Brown.

The procedural defense of majority rule as the manifestation of popular will does not satisfy even the most minimal understanding of reciprocity. Dianna Brown and people like her have much more than their self-interest to invoke in reply: decisions violating the basic liberty or opportunity of any person cannot be justified simply because they result from majority rule or, for that matter, from any other generally acceptable voting procedure.[43] As we suggest later, it is plausible to claim that the chance to live a normal life by having access to organ transplants is a basic opportunity, provided that their funding is compatible with securing other basic liberties and opportunities of individuals. This constraint on proceduralism should be acceptable to all citizens since its purpose is to respect and protect each citizen's basic liberty and opportunity. Of course, the claims of liberty and opportunity also have their limits, but all the reasonable limits entail rejecting the proceduralist claim that majority rule is legitimate, whatever its outcome.[44]

Most procedural democrats accept that procedures should be constrained by some substantive values, but they try to restrict those values to those that are necessary to preserve the democratic process itself.[45] They agree that the majority must respect politically relevant rights such as freedoms of speech, the press, and association, the rule of law, and universal adult suffrage. But if the aim is to find a reciprocal perspective for resolving moral conflict, why limit ourselves to these procedural constraints? The simple example of the jury suggests that some decisions consistent with these constraints—such as denying life-saving health care to some people for the sake of satisfying majority preferences—cannot be justified merely by majority rule. The substance of the moral conflict affects the justifiability of the procedure and its results. If majoritarianism must be qualified by values internal to the democratic process, then why should it not also be qualified by values external to the process, especially if those values include a basic liberty or opportunity of individuals?

Even those basic liberties and opportunities, such as free speech, religious freedom, and education, which are (arguably) necessary conditions of a fair democratic process, are not valued only for this procedural reason. Whether or not religious freedom, for example, is necessary for a fair democratic process, it remains a basic liberty of individuals and therefore a moral constraint on majority rule. Procedure and substance are too intertwined here to mark a clear distinction between constraints on majority rule that should be part of a reciprocal perspective and those that should not. Just as proceduralism recognizes limits on majority rule in order to respect individuals as equal citizens, so it must also admit limits to protect basic liberty and opportunity in order to respect individuals as equal persons, each with his or her own life to lead.

Acknowledging the limits of majority rule does not deny it a prominent place in a deliberative perspective. Quite the contrary, procedures are necessary for the peaceful resolution of moral conflicts, and no one has yet proposed a decision-making procedure that is *generally* more justified than majority rule (and its variations).[46] When we qualify majority rule by saying that it should respect basic liberty and opportunity, as they are best understood at any particular time, we do not conclude that any other voting procedure is generally more justified. When majorities constrain their own decision making in the name of reciprocity, they qualify majority rule and justify it at the same time. On matters of health care (and many others involving basic opportunities), majority rule may generally yield morally better results than minority rule. But in so defending democracy, we have moved beyond procedural democracy. We are now invoking a nonprocedural standard by which to judge majoritarianism: its relative capacity to respect the basic liberty and opportunity of individuals.

Another reason why proceduralism is driven beyond procedures is that it is incomplete—and with respect to precisely that which it should know best: procedures.[47] To decide whether majority rule or some other procedure is justified, citizens have to deliberate about the substantive value of alternative procedures. Proceduralists therefore need to incorporate deliberation as a precondition for adequately resolving political disputes about procedures. The need for such deliberation undermines an important aim of proceduralism, which is to avoid substantive moral disagreement in the political realm. Proceduralists end up putting moral substance back into decision-making rules, thereby moving political debate in the direction of deliberative democracy. No procedural principle—not even majority rule—can morally afford to do without deliberative content.[48] There is no substitute for substantive moral deliberation in resolving conflicts over procedures.

The consequence of the incompleteness of proceduralism can be brought out by continuing the story of the Arizona citizen jury. Let us assume that the fourth and fifth jurors object to voting before they hear more about the pros and cons of funding organ transplants and the views of their fellow citizens. They do not reject majority rule as the ultimate decision-making rule, but they disapprove of voting before the members of the jury have carefully discussed the merits of the issue, tried to justify their positions to one another, and in general shown more respect toward the positions of those with whom they disagree than the simple act of voting allows. These two jurors want to defend deliberation as a supplement to voting.

This objection to the simple act of voting reminds us that majority rule and its procedural rivals are similarly silent about an aspect of decision making that is of critical moral importance to any contemporary democracy: the nature of the moral claims and the quality of the moral arguments that are made before a vote is taken. To assess the justifiability of a procedure in particular instances, even a procedure as widely accepted as majority rule, we need to know what kind of discussion took place, who participated, what arguments they presented, and how each responded to the claims of the others. This is the deliberation that is an essential part of any democratic perspective that seeks to resolve moral disagreements from a reciprocal perspective.

Some procedural democrats do not so much reject as ignore deliberation. They seek to resolve moral disagreement mainly by avoiding it: they try to make do with few substantive moral constraints, and they neglect the need for substantive moral discussion. When the silence of proceduralists is simply an oversight, the deliberative perspective can fill the void. But sometimes the proceduralist silence accompanies a view of politics as the aggregation of interests, usually by means of interest group bargaining. This view denigrates deliberation by reducing moral argument to expressions of self-interest in the way that we criticized earlier, and suffers from the deficiencies of bargaining that we shall point out later. It also neglects the internal processes of groups. The interests over which groups bargain can themselves result from a process of deliberation in which members develop and modify their own interests and their views of the interest of the group. But in whatever form, procedural democracy is at best incomplete, because it neglects the values that constitutional democracy stresses and because it ignores the processes that deliberative democracy emphasizes.

CONSTITUTIONAL DEMOCRACY

Constitutional and procedural democracy both protect individual rights against majority rule, but constitutional democrats give some rights priority over majority rule that procedural democrats do not. Procedural democrats recognize two kinds of rights that limit majoritarianism: rights such as voting equality that are *integral* to democratic procedures; and rights such as subsistence that, though *external* to the democratic process, are necessary for its fair functioning.[49] They take notice of a third kind of right but deny it priority over majority rule: rights such as protection against cruel and unusual punishment that are *external* to the democratic process and (at least arguably) not necessary for its fair functioning.[50] The view that this third kind of right should constrain democratic procedure is what distinguishes constitutional from procedural democrats.[51] Proceduralists give priority only to rights whose primary purpose is to make the democratic process fair, whereas constitutionalists give priority to some rights whose primary purpose is to produce justified outcomes by protecting the vital interests of individuals.

We have already seen the intuitive appeal of constitutional democracy. A basic opportunity was arguably at issue in the citizen jury's decision to deny organ transplants to individuals. It is true that the opportunity for an organ transplant is not typical of those that many Americans associate with constitutional democracy. But precisely for that reason the example reinforces the point that one main purpose of constitutionalism—to limit majoritarianism by moral constraints based on nonprocedural considerations—does not necessarily depend on a written constitution and judicial review. The "adjudicated constitution" is not the same as the "full constitution."[52] Some basic liberties and opportunities (as well as outcome-oriented rights) may be better protected by deliberative majorities themselves. As we suggest in the next section, courts are not the only or necessarily the primary province of deliberation.

By considering cases in which majority rule (or any other purely procedural rule) threatens basic liberties and opportunities, we come to recognize that outcomes of fair procedures are not justified unless they respect basic liberties and opportunities. A reciprocal perspective for resolving moral conflicts must make room for moral judgments not only of procedures but also of their results. Constitutional democrats are therefore right to broaden the search for substantive values that can resolve moral disagreements in politics.

Broadening the search in this way, however, creates difficulties for constitutional democrats parallel to the difficulties faced by their procedural rivals. One difficulty is the same for both. Constitutionalists no less than proceduralists insist that citizens need morally justified procedures for arriving at politically binding decisions. Constitutionalists also often turn to majority rule in some form to meet this need. John Rawls, whose theory we take as an exemplar of constitutional democracy, writes: "Some form of majority rule is justified as the best available way of insuring just and effective legislation. It is compatible with equal liberty and possesses a certain naturalness; for if minority rule is allowed, there is no obvious criterion to select which one is to decide and equality is violated."[53] Constitutionalists also have to decide what *form* of majority rule is the most justifiable way of securing just legislation. To decide what form majority rule should take, constitutionalism in this respect moves, just as proceduralism does, in the direction of deliberative democracy.

Constitutional democrats face an additional difficulty. Because constitutional democrats go further than procedural democrats in constraining democratic processes by substantive standards, the moral perspective they propose to resolve disagreements becomes even more contestable. Constitutional standards seem compelling when stated abstractly: few would deny that majorities should not violate the basic liberty of their fellow citizens. But abstraction purchases agreement on principles at the price of disagreement about their interpretation. The more abstract the constitutional standard, the more contestable its interpretation. For resolving moral conflict in politics, the interpretation matters just as much as the principle. It is therefore necessary to find a way to deal with these interpretive disagreements before the role of constitutional standards in both the theory and practice of democratic politics can be secure.

Rawls does not offer his theory as a solution to moral disagreements in what we call middle democracy. By focusing on the basic structure of society and proposing principles for a nearly just society, he avoids confronting the apparent indeterminacy of many moral conflicts that arise in contemporary politics. But Rawls no less than other constitutional democrats recognizes that conflicts over issues such as abortion, preferential hiring, and health care are central to the question of justice in democratic societies as we now know them. The task of interpretation therefore remains—to determine whether and how a theory of constitutional democracy can inform our political practice in a way that helps resolve the moral conflicts that are left open by abstract principles of liberty and opportunity designed with a nearly just society in mind.

To illustrate the difficulties of interpretation, consider the constitutionalist search for principles to govern social and economic inequalities. What policies would satisfy, for example, Rawls's principle of "fair equality of opportunity" or his "difference principle"? Does fair equality of opportunity—which requires that all members of society have an adequate chance of attaining offices and positions—permit (or demand) preferential hiring for blacks and women in the United States today? Does the difference principle—which stipulates that social inequalities be to "the greatest benefit of the least advantaged"[54]—require universal access to health care? Constitutional democrats who use these or similar principles to constrain the democratic process need to provide answers to such questions, and at a level of specificity sufficient to resolve the conflicts they manifest, or else they need to admit more deliberation into their conception of how moral disagreements should be resolved in a democracy. To fulfill the promise of constitutional democracy in resolving moral disagreements, absent an explicit commitment to deliberation, the answers must show that outcome-oriented principles in some meaningful sense take priority over a deliberative democratic process. This seems a more than Herculean task.[55]

In his later writings, Rawls in effect addresses this difficulty by suggesting that fair equality of opportunity and the difference principle are not among the morally necessary elements of what he calls the constitutional essentials and basic justice, which take priority over the results of the democratic process.[56] "These matters are nearly always open to wide differences of reasonable opinion," he writes, and they "rest on complicated inferences and intuitive judgments that require us to assess complex social and economic information about topics poorly understood."[57] He concludes that "freedom of movement and free choice of occupation and a social minimum covering citizens' basic needs count as constitutional essentials while the principle of fair opportunity and the difference principle do not."[58]

Rawls thus escapes this problem of interpretation in the cases of fair equality of opportunity and the difference principle because he gives up these principles as constitutional essentials or matters of basic justice. But a "social minimum covering citizens' basic needs" remains a constitutional constraint on democratic decision making, and therefore raises a similar issue of interpretation. Furthermore, many, perhaps most, of the large moral conflicts in contemporary politics fall within the territory that would be governed by the principle of fair equality of opportunity and the difference principle. The question therefore persists, on what basis should moral conflicts about these issues be resolved? Rawls relies on "established political procedures [being] reasonably regarded as fair" to resolve these substantive disagreements.[59] If we follow him, we find ourselves either back at the door of proceduralism, with all its attendant problems, or, alternatively, driven to make more room for deliberation.

If we take the first route, back to proceduralism, the problem of resolving moral conflicts over social and economic inequalities again becomes the problem of justifying a set of political procedures. Yet neither constitutional nor procedural democrats suggest how this can be done, or why we should even think it desirable to resolve all the remaining substantive disagreements over social and economic inequalities merely by procedural means, which may neglect the need for moral deliberation about the merits of the issues involved.

The second route leads to deliberative democracy. Rawls himself argues cogently for the value of citizenship and participation in politics. In the spirit of John Stuart Mill, he writes that democratic self-government enhances "the sense of political competence of the average citizen." Citizens are expected to vote and therefore "to have political opinions." He echoes Mill in declaring that the democratic citizen is "called upon to weigh interests other than his own, and to be guided by some conception of justice and the public good rather than by his own inclinations." Citizens must "appeal to principles that others can accept." Political liberty "is not solely a means" but also a valued way of life for citizens.[60] All of this suggests a morally robust political process.

Yet, like many proceduralists and other constitutional democrats, Rawls stops short of arguing that a well-ordered democracy requires extensive deliberation to resolve moral disagreements. This is puzzling. If democratic citizens are to value political liberty not merely as a means of pursuing their self-interest or group interest, if they are to weigh the interests of others and to guide their actions by a sense of justice, then democratic societies must encourage the give-and-take of moral argument about the substance of controversial political issues, of which there are bound to be many. Forums for deliberation should abound. Citizens and their accountable representatives should continually confront their moral conflicts together, in collective efforts to find justifiable ways of resolving their political disagreements. The lack of these forums in both theory and practice—the deliberative deficit it reveals—should be a matter of great concern to constitutional democrats.

When Rawls considers how to make the principles of justice more specific, he does not propose that citizens or their representatives discuss moral disagreements about these principles in public forums. Although his theory of constitutional democracy leaves room for such discussion, it emphasizes instead a solitary process of reflection, a kind of private deliberation. He suggests that each of us alone perform an intricate thought experiment in which a veil of ignorance obscures our own personal interests, including our conception of the good life, and compels us to judge on a more impersonal basis.

Here is how the solitary deliberation goes, as each of us alone tries to develop a reciprocal perspective by making the principles more specific.[61] Having agreed on the Rawlsian principles of justice, we first enter a constitutional mode of thinking. We imagine ourselves as delegates at a constitutional convention trying to design institutions and procedures that will yield results in accord with the principles of justice. Having created the best possible constitution for our social circumstances, we recognize that it does not address most of the controversial issues in contemporary politics. Lifting the veil of ignorance further so that we can know more about the current circumstances of society, we move to a legislative mode of thinking and try to decide what laws and policies would be just for our society. Even after we have gone through all the stages of thinking in this solitary process, we are likely to find that "this test is often indeterminate . . . When this is so, justice is to that extent likewise indeterminate. Institutions within the permitted range are equally just, meaning that they could be chosen; they are compatible with all the constraints of the theory . . . This indeterminacy in the theory of justice is not in itself a defect. It is what we should expect."[62]

To take Rawls's theory (or any other theory of constitutional democracy) down a more deliberative road, one must reject the idea that the indeterminacy of justice begins just where the determinacy of our solitary philosophical reflection leaves off. Deliberative democrats also rely on solitary reflection in two ways. First, solitary philosophical reflection should inform the deliberation that in turn helps resolve moral disagreements in democratic politics. Second, it should help produce a defense of deliberative democracy itself. But deliberative democracy rejects the idea that the indeterminacy of justice begins where the determinacy of solitary reflection leaves off. Solitary reflection supplements rather than substitutes for deliberation.

Rawls is surely right to say that we should expect considerable indeterminacy in any theory of justice. He is also right to suggest that we should think through principles of justice on our own as best we can before we enter into public deliberations. But the point at which our solitary thinking about justice becomes indeterminate does not mark the point at which our ability to find a reciprocal perspective to resolve moral disagreements about social justice becomes incapacitated.[63] This is so even if social justice is understood to refer only to constitutional essentials or the basic structure of society. If we are to increase our chances of resolving moral disagreements, we must not check our deliberative dispositions at the door to the public forum.

This conclusion is more compatible with the requirement of Rawls's own theory that democratic citizens and their representatives achieve a high degree of moral and political competence and maintain a stable commitment to principles of justice. Such competence and commitment are not likely to be sustained without extensive deliberation in public forums about the meaning of constitutional principles and their implications for specific decisions of government. Even if we cannot philosophically establish principles specific enough to determine justifiable policies, we should not dismiss the possibility of developing more conclusive moral reasons through public discussions in a process informed not only by the facts of political life but also by conceptions of the good life, and inspired by the ideals of deliberation. "Discussion," Rawls recognizes, "is a way of combining information and enlarging the range of arguments. At least in the course of time, the effects of common deliberation seem bound to improve matters."[64] In his later writings, Rawls moves significantly further toward deliberative democracy by emphasizing the role of reciprocity as a guiding principle of public discussion. His idea of public reason now includes all moral arguments that in due course can be shown to be consistent with reciprocity, even if those arguments express comprehensive moral philosophies rather than distinctively political conceptions of justice.[65] His theory remains constitutionalist, however, in the priority it gives to principles of justice over processes of deliberation. It also says little about the role of actual deliberation in non-ideal conditions. Although Rawls implies that deliberation is important, he does not pursue the implication.[66] In the next chapter we develop a principle of reciprocity that welcomes a wider range of moral arguments and at the same time imposes obligations on citizens to seek moral accommodation when their comprehensive conceptions differ.

The Need for Moral Deliberation

How far, then, do procedural and constitutional democracy move toward a deliberative perspective for resolving moral disagreements in politics? Both procedural and constitutional democrats rightly agree that the fundamental values of democratic institutions, such as equal political liberty, must be justified by moral arguments that are at least in principle acceptable to citizens who are bound by them. Both seek to show that democratic institutions protect the equal right of citizens to participate in political processes and to enjoy basic freedoms. The justifications typically appeal to a moral conception of the person. Constitutionalists and proceduralists agree that individual citizens should be regarded as moral agents who deserve equal respect in any justifications of the basic structure of government. For both, fundamental moral ideals that are or should be widely shared in contemporary democracies thus lie at the foundation of democratic institutions.[67]

Procedural and constitutional democrats also agree that democratic institutions are not justified unless they generally yield morally acceptable results. Democratic institutions that produce policies that deny some citizens freedom of speech or others the basic opportunity to live a decent life should be rejected on moral grounds. The precise content of the criticisms that proceduralists and constitutionalists make against such results may differ, but both have ample resources at their disposal to sustain a substantial moral appraisal of the public policies that emerge at the end of democratic processes.

Moral argument thus plays an important role in warranting both the foundations and the conclusions of these leading conceptions of democracy. Although such argument dominates both the beginning and the end of the democratic process, these theories assign it at best a small role within the ongoing processes of everyday politics—in middle democracy. If moral arguments are essential to justify the foundations and results of democracy, then why should they not also be essential within the ongoing processes of democracy? On this question—the place of moral argument within democratic politics—both procedural and constitutional democrats are surprisingly silent.[68] This is puzzling in a way that has not been sufficiently appreciated. If democracy must be moral at its foundations and in its outcomes, then should it not also be moral within its everyday processes?

It is in middle democracy that much of the moral life of a democracy, for good or ill, is to be found. This is the land of everyday politics, where legislators, executives, administrators, and judges make and apply policies and laws, sometimes arguing among themselves, sometimes explaining themselves and listening to citizens, other times not. Middle democracy is also the land of interest groups, civic associations, and schools, in which adults and children develop political understandings, sometimes arguing among themselves and listening to people with differing points of view, other times not. It is a land that democrats can scarcely afford to bypass. A democratic theory that is to remain faithful to its moral premises and aspirations for justice must take seriously the need for moral argument within these processes and appreciate the moral potential of such deliberation.

Given the limited generosity and incomplete understanding of both officials and citizens, what goes on in these processes generally falls far short of what our moral ideal would call for. Perhaps that is why so many democratic theorists seem to ignore the possibility, or downplay the significance, of principled moral argument within the democratic process. The everyday operation of the democratic process is imperfect, to be sure, but so are its structures and so are its outcomes. It is hard to see how we gain anything, morally speaking, by limiting ourselves to only some of its imperfect parts. It is more likely that neglecting the possibility of moral argument in any part will only multiply the imperfections in the whole. Amorality is rarely the weapon of choice in the battle against immorality. The amorality of a political process is surely more troubling than its imperfection. Imperfection is endemic to the human condition; amorality need not be.

Democratic deliberation addresses the problem of moral disagreement directly on its own terms. It offers a moral response to moral conflict. It thus seems the natural and appropriate response, one that could be part of a reciprocal perspective in politics. But exactly why is it desirable in democratic politics to respond morally to a moral problem?

The case for deliberation is best made by looking at its application to specific issues, seeing how it works in practice and how it might work better. That is what we undertake in the rest of this book. But four general reasons in favor of deliberative democracy are worth emphasizing at the outset. Together they provide a rationale for extending the domain of deliberation within the democratic process. This rationale justifies granting deliberation the authority to deal with the moral conflicts that procedural democracy and constitutional democracy fail to resolve. It also justifies rejecting the assumption shared by constitutional and procedural democrats that we must give priority either to process or to substance. The four reasons parallel the sources of moral conflict that we identified earlier. Each points to a way in which deliberation deals with an important aspect of moral conflict.

The first reason corresponds to the first source of moral disagreement, the problem of scarce resources. Deliberation contributes to the legitimacy of decisions made under conditions of scarcity. Some citizens will not get what they want, or even what they need, and sometimes none will. The hard choices that democratic governments make in these circumstances should be more acceptable even to those who receive less than they deserve if everyone's claims have been considered on their merits rather than on the basis of wealth, status, or power. Even with regard to political decisions with which they disagree, citizens are likely to take a different attitude toward those that are adopted after careful consideration of the relevant conflicting moral claims and those that are adopted only after calculation of the relative strength of the competing political interests. Moral justifications do not of course make up for the material resources that citizens fail to receive. But they help sustain the political legitimacy that makes possible collective efforts to secure more of those resources in the future, and to live with one another civilly in the meantime.

Creating more deliberative forums brings previously excluded voices into politics. This is one cause of the risk of intensified conflict that greater deliberation may bring. But the positive face of this risk is that deliberation also brings into the open legitimate moral dissatisfactions that would be suppressed by other ways of dealing with disagreement. Deliberative democracy seeks not consensus for its own sake but rather a morally justified consensus. Citizens strive for a consensus that represents a genuinely moral perspective, one they can accept on reciprocal terms. They usually continue to disagree, often intensely, on many politically relevant matters. A deliberative consensus can never be complete, and perhaps never completely justified.

The second reason for valuing deliberation takes into account the second source of moral disagreement in politics, limited generosity. Deliberation responds to this problem by creating forums in which citizens are encouraged to take a broader perspective on questions of public policy than they might otherwise take. John Stuart Mill presented one of the earliest and still most cogent accounts of such a deliberative process. He argued that by participating in political discussion, a citizen is "called upon . . . to weigh interests not his own; to be guided, in case of conflicting claims, by another rule than his private partialities; to apply, at every turn, principles and maxims which have for their reason of existence the common good."[69] We do not need to make the optimistic assumption that most citizens will suddenly become public-spirited when they find themselves deliberating in the public forum. Much depends on the background conditions: the level of political competence (how well informed citizens are), the distribution of resources (how equally situated they are), and the nature of the political culture (what kind of arguments are taken seriously). All we need to assume is that citizens and their representatives are more likely to take a broader view of issues, and to consider the claims of more of their fellows citizens, in a process in which moral arguments are taken seriously than in a process in which assertions of political power prevail.

The third reason for encouraging deliberation confronts the third source of moral disagreement: incompatible moral values. Deliberation can clarify the nature of a moral conflict, helping to distinguish among the moral, the amoral, and the immoral, and between compatible and incompatible values. Citizens are more likely to recognize what is morally at stake in a dispute if they employ moral reasoning in trying to resolve it. Deliberation helps sort out self-interested claims from public-spirited ones. Among the latter, deliberation helps identify those that have greater weight. Through this kind of deliberative process citizens can begin to isolate those conflicts that embody genuinely moral and incompatible values on both sides. Those that do not may then turn out to be more easily resolvable: citizens might discover that a conflict is the result of misunderstanding or lack of information, or they might come to see ways to settle a conflict by bargaining, negotiation, and compromise. In this way, deliberation can put bargaining in its place in a democratic society.

For those moral conflicts for which there is no deliberative agreement at present, ongoing deliberation can help citizens better understand the moral seriousness of the views they continue to oppose, and better cooperate with their fellow citizens who hold these views. Deliberation promotes an economy of moral disagreement in which citizens manifest mutual respect as they continue to disagree about morally important issues in politics.

The fourth reason for conceiving of democracy deliberatively responds to the incomplete understanding that characterizes moral conflict in politics. Compared to other methods of decision making, deliberation increases the chances of arriving at justifiable policies. More than other kinds of political processes, deliberative democracy contains the means of its own correction. Through the give-and-take of argument, citizens and their accountable representatives can learn from one another, come to recognize their individual and collective mistakes, and develop new views and policies that are more widely justifiable. When individuals and groups bargain and negotiate, they may learn how better to get what they want. But unless they also deliberate with one another, they are not likely to learn that they should not try to get what they want. When they deliberate, they move beyond the conventional patterns of group politics that characterize the standard conceptions of interest group bargaining.

The main sources of movement in middle democracy as conventionally portrayed are not changes of mind but shifts in power, as groups and individuals bargain and negotiate on the basis of preferences and self-interests. Power shifts may bring improvement, but only accidentally. Changes of mind are responsive to reasons that at least direct our attention toward improvement. When majorities are obligated to offer reasons to dissenting minorities, they expose their position to criticism and give minorities their most effective and fairest chance of persuading majorities of the justice of their position. Encouraged by both Aristotle and Mill, one may hope that views better than those held by either the majority or the minority will emerge from such a process. But even when deliberation fails to produce a satisfactory resolution of a moral conflict at any particular time, its self-correcting capacity remains the only consistently democratic hope for discovering such a resolution in the future.

It may be feared that extending the domain of deliberation has the risk of creating even greater conflict than it is intended to resolve. Once the moral sensibilities of citizens and officials are engaged, they may be less willing to compromise than before. More issues come to be seen by more citizens as matters of principle, creating occasions for high-minded statements, unyielding stands, and no-holds-barred opposition. There are moral fanatics as well as moral sages, and in politics the former are likely to be more vocal than the latter.

These are real risks. Moral sensitivity may sometimes make necessary political compromises more difficult, but its absence also makes unjustifiable compromises more common. Moral argument can arouse moral fanatics, but it can also combat their claims on their own terms. Extending the domain of deliberation may be the only democratic way to deal with moral conflict without suppressing it. No democratic political process can completely avoid the risks of intensifying moral conflict. It is a hollow hope that any one particular institution, even the Supreme Court, could be relied on to reach the right conclusion, and to convert that conclusion into effective political action, were it to do all our deliberating for us.

Other common ways of dealing with moral conflict are clearly worse. Some of the extremists in the abortion debate turn to violence outside the political process. Others try to manipulate citizens into supporting their cause rather than reasoning with them. Moral extremists must assume that they already know what constitutes the best resolution of a moral conflict without deliberating with their fellow citizens who will be bound by the resolution. In the land of middle democracy, the assumption that we know the political truth can rarely if ever be justified before we deliberate with others who have something to say about issues that affect their lives as well as ours. By refusing to give deliberation a chance, moral extremists forsake the most defensible moral ground for an uncompromising position.

Many constitutional democrats focus on the importance of extensive moral deliberation within one of our democratic institutions—the Supreme Court.[70] They argue that judges cannot interpret constitutional principles without engaging in deliberation, not least for the purpose of constructing a coherent view out of the many moral values that our constitutional tradition expresses. The fact that this process itself is imperfect—that judges disagree morally, even about the relevance of morality in the process—is not thought to be a reason to diminish the role of deliberation. On the contrary, the failures of moral argument in the judicial process are rightly thought to make the quest for successes all the more important.

Deliberative democracy extends this recognition to the rest of the democratic process. It calls into question the contrast between the principled decision making of courts and the prudential lawmaking of legislatures in which a judge seeks to "give meaning to our constitutional values . . . perhaps even [is] force[d] to be objective—not to express his preferences or personal beliefs, or those of the citizenry, as to what is right or just . . . Legislatures . . . see their primary function in terms of registering the actual, occurrent preferences of the people—what they want and what they believe should be done."[71] This contrast is problematic both empirically and normatively.[72]

Empirical evidence about the behavior of judges and legislators is almost never offered to support the contrast. The argument proceeds entirely by way of a kind of deductive institutionalism, relying on certain incentives of presumed self-interest. Because of the incentives built into the legislative role (such as the necessity of standing for election), legislators, it is assumed, will consider only the preferences of their constituents. Because of the incentives built into the judicial role (such as the need for professional respect), judges will have more regard for well-reasoned principles that are capable of discounting morally suspect preferences.

The trouble with such arguments, even in their a priori form, is that institutional incentives have a way of canceling out one another. Because legislators must defend their policies to many different groups, they may be forced to formulate generally acceptable policies, and justify them by general principles. Because judges must resolve particular cases, they may lose sight of the larger social implications of their decisions and frame their principles too narrowly, fitting only the facts of the instant case.

Without much more empirical analysis than anyone has yet undertaken, no one can say, even if the contrast exists in some form, whether either the motives or the decisions of legislators are more or less principled than the motives or decisions of judges. It is true of course that courts usually give reasons for their decisions, and legislatures do not, but that difference does not take the contrast very far. Individual legislators can and do give reasons for their decisions, and would be expected to do so more often if they and other citizens were not under the influence of democratic conceptions that downplay deliberation outside the judicial process.

The normative basis of the contrast between judges and legislators is even more questionable. The implication is that legislators need not, and perhaps even should not, justify their decisions on the basis of principle. Their *ideal* function is, like that of Benthamite calculators, to aggregate the preferences of citizens, correcting them where necessary to promote social utility. Since laws sometimes *should* reflect preferences in this way, it is useful to have institutions that can perform this function. But to prescribe that legislatures should be assigned this task exclusively is to press the idea of the separation of powers beyond its legitimate purposes. If citizens ought to make political decisions on the basis of reasons and principles that they can mutually affirm, then all those who govern in the name of the citizens—legislators as well as judges—also ought to give reasons and principles for the policies that they support.[73]

To relegate principled politics to the judiciary would be to leave most of politics unprincipled. Judges review only a small proportion of public policy, and much of what they do consider they accept mostly in the form that it was made by legislators and administrators. Furthermore, the moral reasons and principles to which judges defer do not stand above those of other members of society. Judges find their principles in the experience of their own society, and they must justify those principles to other members of their society. If citizens and their representatives deal only or even primarily in preferences, judges sooner or later will find themselves doing the same, or defending principles that no one else shares.

Some constitutional democrats portray judges as engaged in a "dialogue" with society,[74] in which judges listen to all sides of a controversy and speak to principles that all members of society can share. Insofar as such a dialogue takes place, it should go some way toward extending deliberation beyond the courtroom. But judges listen only to citizens who happen to appear as parties in the cases before them. They do not, except incidentally, seek parties who might better speak to the political issues that the cases raise. They are not supposed to listen to voices beyond the instant case because their office seems to requires a kind of independence that prevents them from taking into account much of the normal controversy of political life. They are not encouraged to listen because the judicial office protects their judgments from many of the normal challenges of political action, such as the challenge of publicity. A different and genuinely two-sided public conception of dialogue might require making some changes in the judicial role, but it would certainly require acknowledging the possibility and desirability of extensive deliberation in the other roles of public life. Deliberative democracy does not favor legislative over judicial deliberation or vice versa. Its principled defense of deliberation favors forums for deliberation wherever they can further the aim of resolving moral disagreements in a way that can be justified to the people who are bound by the resolutions.

The fragments of moral arguments that began this chapter and the more extended examples that will emerge in later chapters show that moral deliberation, however imperfect it may be, is already present in public life in many different forums. Legislators, at their best, make moral arguments, often quite capably, especially when one takes into account the conditions under which they work (which can themselves be subject to deliberative criticism). Consider the way the Congress discussed the controversial issue of federal subsidies for abortion. In 1976 Congress adopted the so-called Hyde Amendment to Medicaid provisions of the Social Security Act. The Medicaid provisions subsidize health care for citizens below the poverty line, and the amendment prohibited federal subsidies for Medicaid abortions except to save the life of the mother. A year later rape and incest were added as exceptions. In 1980 the Supreme Court in a 5-to-4 decision upheld the constitutionality of the Hyde Amendment.[75] Neither Congress nor the Court has yet found a satisfactory solution to this problem. But Congress continues to debate the issue regularly and at length, whereas the Court has considered the case only once so far.

The controversy over subsidizing abortion for poor women has many of the features of the various moral disagreements that make their way through our imperfect legislative and judicial processes. The sources of the controversy include not only the scarcity of resources and the limited generosity of citizens, but also incompatible values and incomplete understanding of how best to weigh the many factors that would help decide among the values. The issue is undeniably one in which moral principles are at stake, not merely personal preferences or group interests. Citizens and officials on both sides of the issue credibly invoke basic constitutional principles—in effect confirming the claim of constitutional democrats that justifications of public policy depend on moral considerations that go beyond the fairness of political procedures. But the controversy also provides evidence against the view that courts are *the* forum of principle in our democratic system, and that legislatures are incapable, or demonstrably less capable, of considering moral principles in the making of policy. Congressional debates over the Hyde Amendment have been replete with (good and bad) principled arguments, indeed on this issue more than the opinions of the Supreme Court, even though both institutions collectively have reached the same result.

Deliberative democracy is open to the possibility that many decisions affecting the basic liberties and opportunities of citizens should be reviewed by public officials who stand outside the ordinary political process, specifically the judiciary. But the rationale for such reviews in deliberative democracy goes beyond that of constitutional democracy and encourages us to seek forums of principle within our everyday politics. If the judiciary turns out to be better able to protect some or all basic liberties and opportunities, then a deliberative perspective will grant the judiciary special authority to review those rights. But this is a question of institutional design, not fundamental principle, and it remains more open to empirical investigation than constitutional democrats typically suggest.

The constitutional principles of deliberative democracy are robust, and they can be effectively recognized and respected in middle democracy, without giving priority to constitutional principles over and above the democratic process, as a final variation on the example of the citizen jury shows. Suppose that the two citizens who favor deliberation persuade the other three to deliberate before voting. In the course of discussing whether to fund organ transplants, the third juror (one of the two who preferred having more disposable income to protecting against the relatively low risk of a life-threatening disease) changes his mind. Impressed by the arguments of the two jurors who favor funding organ transplants, he casts his vote with them. He still has a personal preference for more disposable income. The arguments have not changed his *desire* in this regard. He still even thinks that it is in his self-interest not to fund organ transplants. But the deliberations have changed his mind about another politically relevant matter. He now thinks that he cannot justify satisfying the preference for more disposable income in a situation where the preference entails denying someone like Dianna Brown a life-saving organ transplant. When the vote is taken again, a majority favors funding organ transplants; some members of the majority have taken it upon themselves to constrain their votes by what they consider a constitutional right of individuals.

If a majority of citizen jurors had still rejected funding organ transplants in the face of life-threatening health risks to individuals, the director could have reviewed their decision himself. He might have criticized it for violating the constitutional rights of citizens like Dianna Brown. Or else he might have been convinced by arguments we have not yet considered that it is morally better not to fund organ transplants. The director could even take the dispute beyond the state legislature to a court to adjudicate. But in a deliberative democracy the question of who should enforce basic liberties and opportunities remains open to argument, itself a subject of deliberation.

We have offered some general reasons why deliberation should be extended beyond the boundaries established by procedural and constitutional democracy. Both need but neither provides a way of arriving at provisionally justifiable resolutions of moral conflicts with sufficient specificity in the political life of middle democracy. Extending deliberation could thus fill a moral gap in a way that would be consistent with the aspirations of both.

Moreover, the conflict between these conceptions of democracy itself is not likely to be resolved without giving deliberation greater scope. If all democratic institutions including courts are imperfectly just, and all democratic institutions including legislatures depend on the give-and-take of moral argument to correct injustices, then procedural and constitutional democrats can find some common ground. They can find it if each pays more attention to the need for deliberation within all democratic forums. The principles we develop in later chapters to define the conditions of deliberative democracy may be seen as expanding the standards for fair process that proceduralists emphasize. Likewise, the principles that constitute the content of deliberative democracy play a role much like the fundamental rights that constitutionalists stress.

Critical to finding this common ground is acknowledging the equal status of both the conditions and the content of deliberative democracy. Neither the conditions nor the content should be permitted to have the priority that their proceduralist or constitutionalist friends respectively claim for them.[76] At any point in time, deliberative democracy may appear to be giving priority to process when its conditions provisionally justify outcomes that may violate basic liberties and opportunities; and at other times it may appear to be giving priority to policy when its content offers reasons for refusing to be bound by procedurally correct results that violate those basic rights. But any general assignment of priority is misleading. Deliberative democracy aspires to a politics in which citizens and their accountable representatives, along with other public officials, are committed to making decisions that they can justify to everyone bound by them. This commitment entails the integration of substantive moral argument into democratic processes that manifest the equal political status of citizens. The political processes of middle democracy must be as morally defensible in their content as in their conditions.

We need not choose between proceduralism and constitutionalism if we can construct a conception of deliberative democracy that respects the merits of each while avoiding the failings of both. In the chapters that follow, we develop the principles and pursue the practical implications of such a conception. We venture into the land of middle democracy in order to develop a deliberative perspective that can inform the theory and practice of political argument in the future. We offer arguments about specific moral conflicts in contemporary American politics, and we develop a conceptual framework for continuing to deliberate about them. We analyze disagreements over distributing health care, legalizing surrogate parenting, and hiring preferentially, among other issues.

Neither the framework nor the claims we put forward represent final destinations or ultimate foundations. They can be only a beginning because deliberation must proceed in a spirit that invites others to improve on the arguments that any one offers along the way. It is *not* a beginning in the sense that it marks a point in a process that has an end. So long as democratic government endures, the search for a deliberative perspective will never be complete. The resolution of many disagreements will be provisional, ever subject to new moral challenges and always open to fresh settlements. "In democratic politics," Michael Walzer writes, "all destinations are temporary. No citizen can ever claim to have persuaded his fellows once and for all."[77]

Our own conclusions, like those of deliberative democracy itself, can be no more than way stations on the rough-and-tumble journey of deliberative democratic politics. Yet they are no less significant for that. The way stations of democracy are, after all, where citizens live nearly all of our political life. If the theory of deliberative democracy that we develop came to be more fully realized in the practice of democratic politics, the decisions that citizens and their representatives make would be more morally legitimate, public-spirited, mutually respectful, and self-correcting. Deliberative democracy promises only provisionally justified decisions, but they are justifiable to all citizens who are bound by them. That is more than democracy in America now offers most of its citizens most of the time. By making democracy more deliberative, citizens stand a better chance of resolving some of their moral disagreements, and living with those that will inevitably persist, on terms that all can accept.

—2—

The Sense of Reciprocity

DELIBERATIVE DEMOCRACY asks citizens and officials to justify public policy by giving reasons that can be accepted by those who are bound by it. This disposition to seek mutually justifiable reasons expresses the core of the process of deliberation. More specifically, the disposition implies three principles—reciprocity, publicity, and accountability—which are the subjects of this and the next two chapters. Each addresses an aspect of the reason-giving process: the *kind* of reasons that should be given, the *forum* in which they should be given, and the *agents* to whom and by whom they should be given.

Reciprocity is the leading principle because it shapes the meaning of publicity and accountability and also influences the interpretation of liberty and opportunity. It is not that these other principles can be derived from reciprocity or that they are subordinate to it in any formal way. The principle expresses a sense of mutuality that citizens and their representatives should bring to the public forum as they consider the other principles. It is as much a family of general dispositions as a set of specific obligations. Nevertheless, we can give it a more definite shape by developing the elements of reciprocity that were introduced in Chapter 1, and by contrasting the principle of reciprocity with its two rivals. These alternative approaches to moral disagreement—prudence and impartiality—pose challenges to reciprocity. It is necessary to overcome these challenges to make sense of reciprocity and give it the place it deserves in democratic politics.

The foundation of reciprocity is the capacity to seek fair terms of social cooperation for their own sake.[1] Because the results of democratic deliberations are mutually binding, citizens should aspire to a kind of political reasoning that is mutually justifiable. From a deliberative perspective, a citizen offers reasons that can be accepted by others who are similarly motivated to find reasons that can be accepted by others. Of course, some reasons that can be accepted in this sense are often not in fact accepted because the social and political conditions are not favorable to the practice of reciprocity.[2] Reciprocity does not always produce agreement even when specific social and political conditions are favorable. The more general features of society discussed earlier—scarcity of resources, limited generosity, incompatible values, and incomplete understanding—sometimes preclude deliberative agreement. But even in the face of what we call deliberative disagreement, reciprocity calls on citizens to continue to seek fair terms of cooperation among equals.

Reciprocity stands between prudence and impartiality, its challengers for the title of the regulator of reasons in democracy. As the diagram indicates, not only the justification but also the motives, processes, and goals of reciprocity differ from those of its rivals.

Principle	Justification	Motive	Process	Goal
Prudence	mutually advantageous	self-interest	bargaining	modus vivendi
Reciprocity	mutually acceptable	desire to justify to others	deliberation	deliberation agreement/ disagreement
Impartiality	universally justifiable	altruism	demonstration	comprehensive view

We have already met—and subdued—prudence in its most ambitious form: the general claim that all disagreements in politics must be governed by self-interest. Prudence returns now with a more modest claim: many if not most political disputes do not involve moral disagreement at all, and they are therefore more appropriately settled by bargaining, the distinctive method of prudence, than by deliberation. Furthermore, bargaining is the best and perhaps only method for dealing with the remaining moral disagreements that cannot be removed from the political agenda.

The reasons that prudential citizens give are intended to show that a policy is mutually advantageous: the policy is to everyone's advantage as far as possible under present or foreseeable circumstances. Reciprocity sets a different standard: the reasons must be mutually acceptable in the sense that they can be acknowledged by each citizen in circumstances of equal advantage (even by citizens who disagree with the conclusions that the reasons are intended to justify). Prudence aims at only a modus vivendi whereby self-interested citizens can deal with their disagreements through various forms of bargaining. Reciprocity aims at deliberative agreement, whereby citizens are motivated to justify their claims to those with whom they must cooperate.

The other rival principle—impartiality—demands more in this respect than reciprocity. Like reciprocity, impartiality prescribes that reasons must be general in the sense that they must be acceptable to anyone who is similarly situated in morally relevant respects. Reasons based only on social or economic status, for example, are precluded. This is simply the criterion of generality described in Chapter 1, which expresses a rudimentary characteristic of the moral point of view. But impartiality goes further: it demands that reasons be *impersonal,* requiring citizens to suppress or disregard their partial perspectives and individual projects when making policies and laws.[3] (The prime example of an impartialist approach is utilitarianism, some forms of which we criticize in Chapter 5.)

The motives to which an impartialist approach appeals are altruistic in the sense that its justifications refer to the general good, not the good of any specific individual. Individual citizens do not have to act on altruistic motives, but institutions should be designed to produce collective results that are justifiable by altruistic reasons. The preferred method of impartialists is neither bargaining nor deliberation but demonstration, which aims insofar as possible to establish the truth of a comprehensive moral view. In the face of moral disagreement, impartiality tells citizens and officials that they should affirm the view most consistent with true morality as determined by impersonal justification. There is then no further moral need for actual political deliberation.

In this chapter we show that reciprocity can deal with moral disagreement better than prudence or impartiality can. We acknowledge that prudence and its political ally bargaining play an important role in resolving many moral controversies in politics, but they should be constrained by the principle of reciprocity. We also make room for the comprehensive moral views that impartiality seeks, but they too are best constrained by reciprocity. Since in a pluralist society citizens are likely to continue to hold competing comprehensive views, the principles of democracy must provide some guidance for living with fundamental moral disagreement, not simply resolving it. Reciprocity, as we develop the idea, provides this guidance by setting standards for practices of mutual respect, which we call principles of accommodation.

Reciprocity and Its Rivals

In its most general form reciprocity involves "making a proportionate return for good received."[4] This is a basic moral concept, but it has special force in democratic politics, in which citizens must cooperate to make their lives go well, individually or collectively. In deliberative democracy the primary job of reciprocity is to regulate public reason, the terms in which citizens justify to one another their claims regarding all other goods. The "good received" is that you make your claims on terms that I can accept in principle. The "proportionate return" is that I make my claims on terms that you can accept in principle. Deliberative reciprocity shares with prudence this basic concept of mutual exchange but gives it moral content that formally resembles impartiality.

WHAT RECIPROCITY REQUIRES

Deliberative reciprocity expresses two related requirements, one primarily moral and the other primarily empirical. When citizens make moral claims in a deliberative democracy, they appeal to reasons or principles that can be shared by fellow citizens who are similarly motivated. The moral reasoning is in this way mutually acceptable. The qualifying phrase "similarly motivated" indicates that a deliberative perspective does not address people who reject the aim of finding fair terms for social cooperation; it cannot reach those who refuse to press their public claims in terms accessible to their fellow citizens. No moral perspective in politics can reach such people, except one that replicates their own comprehensive set of beliefs. And since that perspective would entail rejecting entirely the comprehensive beliefs of their rivals, it would not help reduce, let alone resolve, moral disagreements.

When citizens deliberate, they seek agreement on substantive moral principles that can be justified on the basis of mutually acceptable reasons. Deliberative arguments for universal health care, for example, would appeal to a mutually recognized principle of basic opportunity for all citizens or to another such principle that serves a similar moral purpose. Whether there are such principles, and how they should be interpreted, can often be discovered only in the process of deliberation itself. Insofar as moral reasoning in politics succeeds in finding such principles, the conclusions of deliberation become mutually justifiable. Insofar as it fails, reciprocity continues to make demands on citizens. It prescribes accommodation based on mutual respect.

The other requirement of reciprocity refers to the empirical or quasi-empirical claims on which moral reasoning often depends to achieve its practical purposes. When moral reasoning invokes empirical claims, reciprocity requires that they be consistent with relatively reliable methods of inquiry. Such methods are our best hope for carrying on discussion on mutually acceptable terms. The claims need not be completely verifiable, but they should not conflict with claims that have been confirmed by the most reliable of available methods. Even when moral reasoning does not explicitly rely on empirical evidence, its premises should not be implausible. Plausibility is no doubt partly subjective, but at the extremes at which the requirement comes into play, we can usually find a sufficiently objective test. We can at least distinguish, among beliefs that we regard as false, those that could be true without requiring us to reject reliable methods of inquiry from those that could be true only if we abandoned such methods.

Consider the claim that miscegenation is wrong because God says so in the Bible. We cannot prove or even logically refute the claim that God forbids mixing of the races. But we may ask: If God speaks literally through the Bible, why does so much of the Bible defy a literal reading? Many of its claims are implausible if taken literally, not only according to well-established scientific standards but also according to the more general beliefs and practices of those who rely on the authority of the Bible. Virtually all contemporary fundamentalists subject biblical claims to interpretation, accepting some as literally true and revising the literal meaning of others. To reject moral claims that rely on implausible premises is therefore not to repudiate religion. An appeal to divine authority per se is thus not what creates the problem for a deliberative perspective. The problem lies in the appeal to *any* authority whose conclusions are impervious, in principle as well as practice, to the standards of logical consistency or to reliable methods of inquiry that themselves should be mutually acceptable.

Religious fundamentalists may reply that they accept the requirement of reciprocity because their moral reasons, far from being impervious, are readily accessible to anyone who is willing to live a spiritual life as they do. All those who live such a life can gain similar access to the moral mandates of divine authority. How, then, can deliberative democrats claim that these religious appeals are any less accessible than other claims about public policy that draw on the personal experience of some citizens? The answer, which does not exclude religious appeals per se, is that any claim fails to respect reciprocity if it imposes a requirement on other citizens to adopt one's sectarian way of life as a condition of gaining access to the moral understanding that is essential to judging the validity of one's moral claims. This requirement stands in contrast to the many moral claims in public life that can be assessed and accepted by individuals who are con-scientiously committed to any of a wide range of secular and religious ways of life.

In the face of moral disagreement in politics, the principle of reciprocity tells citizens to appeal to reasons that are recognizably moral in form and mutually acceptable in content. Prudence questions the need for morality in this sense, while impartiality challenges the need for mutual accepta-bility. If political reasoning is mutually acceptable, the prudential critic asks, why does it have to be moral in any further sense? The impartialist critic asks the opposite question: If political reasoning is moral, why does it have to be mutually acceptable in any other way?

WHAT PRUDENCE PRESCRIBES

The prudential critic reminds us that much of everyday democratic politics consists of various forms of bargaining—deal-making, log-rolling, pork-barreling, coalition-building, and the like. Much of this bargaining takes place over matters that raise no moral issues, either because no significant moral values are at stake or because the significant disagreement is not about values but about the means to achieve them. Under such circum-stances it would seem that moral deliberation is entirely out of place and interest group bargaining perfectly in order. Furthermore, even when moral issues are at stake, bargaining may be the only process that citizens who hold different moral views could find acceptable. The motivation it requires—enlightened self-interest—makes relatively modest demands on human nature. If we assume that all the parties could reasonably accept the procedures governing the bargaining, then we may conclude that the practice is mutually justifiable. The prudential method in this way offers a kind of reciprocity, based on self-interest rather than direct moral reasoning, but intended to yield terms of fair cooperation. The rules of the game of politics thus could be mutually acceptable.[5]

Deliberative democracy must make room for political bargaining of the kind that its prudential critics favor, and we suggest later how it might do so. But the principle of prudence cannot be the principle that ultimately governs disagreement in a democracy. From a deliberative perspective, the problem with relying on bargaining as a substitute for moral reasoning, even within political institutions that are fully just, is that it rests on too thin a conception of what citizens owe one another in an increasingly interdependent society. On a bargaining conception citizens do not have any reason directly to promote the well-being of other citizens. This conception authorizes citizens to try to maximize their own or their group's advantage even at the expense of the well-being of other citizens. Furthermore, it provides no principled limitation on taking advantage of other citizens, and no principled basis for giving others an advantage at no gain to oneself. If all we have in common are the rules of the game, we are likely to confront one another more as adversaries than as cooperators. Even if citizens were to bargain under conditions of approximate equality, the results might still fail to meet the minimal standards of sociability that a reciprocal perspective would specify.

Under the conditions of inequality that characterize non-ideal societies such as ours, the objection to bargaining is even more serious.[6] Some citizens have far greater bargaining power than others, and they would be authorized to use that power in a self-interested or group-interested way to gain still more benefits for themselves or their group. Without a moral standard to appraise the baseline from which the bargaining begins, the proponents of prudence cannot justify the outcomes to those who are at a disadvantage from the start. What can they say to Dianna Brown, whose bargain with the state does not cover the transplant she needs to save her life? It would seem that all they can suggest is either that she got the best deal she could in light of her relative bargaining power, or that she and her fellow citizens failed to use all the power they actually had.

Dispensing with moral justification, prudence not only runs the risk of producing results that would be regarded as unjust from almost any perspective, but it also undermines its own claim to offer reasons that are mutually acceptable. By rejecting the moral form of reasoning, prudence ends up disabling the moral content that provides the basis for mutual justifiability. As a standard for dealing with moral disagreement in democratic politics, prudence is inadequate.

WHAT IMPARTIALITY IMPLIES

In contrast to prudence, the principle of impartiality affirms that political reasoning should be moral but denies that it must be mutually acceptable in the way that reciprocity prescribes. If a moral claim is correct from an impersonal perspective, then that is all the justification it needs. A moral claim does not call for confirmation by any process of democratic deliberation (though such a process might be useful or necessary for other reasons, such as maintaining political stability).

To require that reasons be acceptable to each citizen in some way beyond impersonal demonstration seems to imply that there are multiple perspectives, equally moral but mutually contradictory. Impartialists can recognize the existence of moral disagreement, even fundamental and temporarily irresolvable moral disagreement, but they regard it as a sign that moral reasoning has failed. At least one of the reasoners has erred, one or more have not carried the reasoning far enough, or else the problem itself is beyond the capacity of mortals to resolve. In the face of disagreement, impartiality tells us to choose the morally correct view and demonstrate its correctness to our fellow citizens, who, if they are rational, should accept it.

The goal of this process is to establish shared moral views that are comprehensive not only in the sense that they cover a wide range of human activities, but also in the sense that they include a single set of assumptions about the foundations of morality and understandings of human nature. At least potentially, the reasons citizens should give are impersonal all the way down. This does not mean that citizens must at every moment in their daily lives act like impartial judges, that they can never give preference to their families or friends. But it does mean that any such preferences must be justifiable from an impersonal perspective that embraces both principles and their foundations.

The goal of establishing a comprehensive morality is not confined to impartialists. Some theorists—for example, some communitarians—seek a comprehensive morality from within a partial perspective, that of a particular community. (The morality is comprehensive but not impersonal.) Although the content of their moralities may differ from that of the impartialists, the approach that communitarians who seek comprehensive moralities take toward moral disagreement has more in common with that of impartialists than with that of the advocates of reciprocity. For both impartialists and communitarians, persistent moral disagreement is mainly a practical problem, one to which their theories in principle offer a definite solution. For impartialists, the persistence of moral disagreement signals that citizens are too enmeshed in their own personal perspectives, which they should learn to transcend to arrive at a more impersonal perspective. For communitarians, moral disagreement is simply a reflection of the fact that different communities have different fundamental values. But both would argue that this disagreement poses a much more serious problem for proponents of reciprocity. It shows that on many important issues in democratic politics, we have to abandon the principle of reciprocity because there are no moral reasons that could be mutually acceptable from any perspective other than one that is completely impartial either generally or with respect to a particular community.

The political conflict over abortion, for example, seems to call for a more comprehensive kind of moral reasoning than reciprocity admits. It does not seem possible in this conflict to find conclusive reasons that can be accepted by all citizens who are motivated to find fair terms of social cooperation. Some citizens reasonably claim that the fetus is a constitutional person with rights that trump those of the pregnant woman. Other citizens believe that the fetus is only a potential person, and therefore has no such constitutional rights. If we insist on reciprocity, it seems that we have to abandon any hope of reaching a collective conclusion for collectively we would have no coherent moral view at all, only a multitude of conflicting moral views. The output of the democratic process would seem to be the same as the input: moral disagreement.

Persistent moral disagreement comes in various forms. In some cases citizens hold conflicting reasonable beliefs (about the status of the fetus, for example), which their best efforts at moral understanding cannot resolve. In other cases different citizens balance competing moral considerations in different ways (for example, in appraising the relative risks to the guilty and the innocent in the practice of capital punishment). In both kinds of cases our best efforts at moral reasoning in the spirit of mutuality produce no uniquely correct solution. On a variety of issues, such as abortion and capital punishment, two or more views stand in conflict, and there is no mutually acceptable position from which either can be rejected. The result is not agreement but what may be called fundamental deliberative disagreement. In such cases it may seem that we have to give up any hope of reciprocity and simply adopt the more familiar mode of impartiality.

The proponents of impartiality (and comprehensive doctrines in general) are right to insist that moral disagreement of these kinds is a serious problem. But it is a problem for any moral perspective in politics, including those that embrace impartiality and those that seek to establish comprehensive views on any basis. We suggest later how the principle of reciprocity can be extended to deal with this problem. But first we need to show why impartiality and comprehensive moralities do not adequately address it.

Suppose that a majority of citizens have concluded that from an impartial perspective their position on abortion is correct. They believe that it follows from a comprehensive view of morality and can be justified in accordance with the most general form of moral reasoning. How should they treat other citizens who do not accept either their view or their reasons for it? Historically, majorities who reject reciprocity have often tried to suppress minorities who hold different moral views. The instruments have been manifold (crusades, inquisitions, censorship, ostracism, social discrimination), but the attitudes have been remarkably similar (intolerance, contempt, antipathy). Most contemporary proponents of impartiality and comprehensive doctrines in democracies reject these instruments and these attitudes. They are able to do so because they adopt a principle of toleration or its equivalent. Toleration requires majorities to let minorities express their moral views in public and practice them in private. Religious toleration is the paradigm.

As liberal societies exclude religion from the jurisdiction of political action because citizens could never agree on religious truth, so, impartialists argue, should they ban abortion from the political agenda because citizens do not agree on the relevant moral truths. Governments should stay neutral in such disputes. Roger Wertheimer presents what is perhaps the clearest example of this argument, which in various forms is often invoked in public debate.[7] The argument essentially has three steps: (1) governments may not restrict freedom unless they can justify their restrictions rationally; (2) neither of the two sides in the debate is more rationally justifiable than the other; (3) therefore, the government cannot legitimately restrict the freedom of women to have an abortion.

Whether or not a neutrality argument will work for religious toleration,[8] it should be clear that it will not solve the abortion controversy. By the same form of reasoning that Wertheimer uses to conclude that the government should not act, one could reasonably reach the opposite conclusion, that legalizing abortion is illegitimate. From the perspective of those who believe that the fetus is a person, legalization permits its deliberate killing and therefore restricts its freedom absolutely. Unless we already accept one of the competing views of the fetus, we cannot assume that this restriction on freedom is any more or less justified than a restriction on the freedom of women.

Wertheimer's argument depends on giving decisive moral weight to the fact that the government need not act to make abortion legal. But we do not in general assume a presumption against the use of governmental co-ercion if taking a human life is arguably at stake. The argument could be recast by adopting a stronger version of the first step of the argument: governments may not restrict freedom unless they can rationally justify the restriction to *already rational* beings whose freedom is to be restricted. But this stronger claim also begs the question in favor of the pro-choice position. Why assume that all we need to show is that the restrictions can be justified to those who are already rational? It is of course true that we cannot justify the restrictions *to* fetuses or any beings who cannot appre-ciate the force of reason. But we do not in general assume that all the moral justifications we owe must be addressed to those who are currently capable of appreciating them. We are morally accountable, for example, to young children and future generations (as we discuss in Chapter 4).

More generally, it is doubtful that the neutrality argument for toleration itself can be justified even from an impartial perspective. If a moral view is correct, why not simply impose it? One might be tempted to answer that doing so would violate some principle of liberty, the priority of which could be demonstrated from an impartial perspective. But it is not plau-sible to assume that liberty should take priority over all other values, such as life itself, which is what is at issue in the dispute over abortion. Nor can we pretend that, if the government does not legislate on the issue of abortion, it remains neutral. We have already seen that we cannot avoid taking a position by removing the issue from the political agenda. Leaving a matter to private discretion decides it in favor of one side or the other. A policy that lets each woman decide the question of abortion for herself already presupposes that certain claims of pro-life advocates are wrong.

Even if a principle of toleration could be justified on impartial grounds, it would not go far enough for the purposes of deliberative democracy. It provides no positive basis on which citizens can expect to resolve their moral disagreements in the future. Citizens go their separate ways, keeping their moral reasons to themselves, avoiding moral engagement. This may sometimes keep the peace (though often only temporarily, as the violent confrontations over abortion show). But mere toleration also locks into place the moral divisions in society and makes collective moral progress far more difficult. Deliberative democracy offers a more robust kind of citizenship that avoids these problems without requiring people to devote their lives to political participation. Later in this chapter we defend an extended principle of reciprocity which supports this kind of citizenship by affirming the value of mutual respect. But even without that positive case for this principle, the negative case against impartiality and compre-hensive moral doctrines provides reason to look for an alternative. Both the negative and positive cases can be advanced if we consider how reciprocity and its rivals would deal with an actual example of moral disagreement.

Reciprocity in Practice

The state of Tennessee requires public schools to help students "become good citizens in their school, community, and society."[9] In Hawkins County in 1983 the board of education unanimously adopted a Holt, Rinehart, and Winston basic reading series for the use of all public school students in kindergarten through eighth grade. The aim of the reading curriculum, recommended by the board's textbook selection committee, was to teach both reading skills and the values of democratic citizenship. When the textbooks were issued, a group of fundamentalist Christian parents asked that their children not be required to use them. The parents maintained that the content of the books conflicted with their religious convictions. They objected to exposing their children to information about other ways of life unless the information also included a statement that their own way of life is the only true one. The parents also said that their children should not be taught to make critical judgments, to use their imagination, and to exercise choice "in areas where the Bible provides the answer." Among the specific parts of the curriculum to which the parents objected (and the grounds of their objections) were:

- a short story describing a Catholic Indian settlement in New Mexico, on the grounds that it teaches Catholicism;

- a reading exercise picturing a boy making toast while a girl reads to him ("Pat reads to Jim. Jim cooks. The big book helps Jim. Jim has fun"), on the grounds that "it denigrates the differences between the sexes" affirmed in the Bible;

- an excerpt from Anne Frank's *Diary of a Young Girl,* because Anne

Frank writes that nonorthodox belief in God may be better than no
belief at all; and

· a passage describing a central idea of the Renaissance as "a belief in the
dignity and worth of human beings," because such a belief is incompatible with true religious faith

The school board discussed the parents' objections and acknowledged
the sincerity of the parents' religious beliefs. But in the end it rejected their
request to exempt their children from reading the textbooks.

Neither prudence nor impartiality offers a satisfactory way of understanding, let alone resolving, this controversy over the curriculum. The
bargaining that prudence would recommend suggests two different outcomes, depending on what background conditions are assumed. If the
existing conditions are taken as the baseline, the parents (who represent
a minority in the county) have little bargaining power, and will have to
accept whatever the board decides. Even though (as we shall suggest) this
outcome turns out to be the correct one, bargaining seems an inappropriate basis on which to resolve a dispute about fundamental values. From
the parents' point of view, their way of life and their children's spiritual
salvation are threatened. Is bargaining on the basis of power the best that
democracy has to offer?

If we assume instead that the bargaining takes place under conditions
of equality, the outcome is indeterminate. What would be rational to agree
to would depend on the strength and intensity of one's interests, and the
likely effects of alternative policies on these interests. Since the parents are
in the minority, they still might lose. But they might win, if they could
(say) convince the board that they care so much about this issue that they
would continue to agitate for an exemption, making it difficult for the
board and the school administrators to concentrate on other educational
matters. What is missing in the calculation of relative bargaining power
is any consideration of the merits of each side's claims.

A principle of impartiality does consider the claims on their merits, but
the outcome it produces is the same fundamental moral disagreement that
began the controversy. In this case two comprehensive moral views face
each other in a standoff. On the one side are the parents whose religious
beliefs dictate their views about almost all aspects of life, including the
way their children should be educated. On the other side stand other parents whose moral views may be no less comprehensive. They believe that
their own values, including their religious values, are best served by a

school system that chooses textbooks on the basis of the judgment of educational experts. Nor is there any morally neutral position in this case. Neither exempting the children from the reading classes nor upholding the school board's right to require the children to use the textbooks is morally or politically neutral.[10]

What does the principle of reciprocity recommend in this case? It does not consider the relative bargaining power or intensity of interests on either side, and it does not seek a completely neutral position. Nor does it demand that the parties actually reach a consensus. What it requires are reasons that can be justified to all parties who are motivated to find fair terms of social cooperation.

Consider the parents' objections to the curriculum. They imply a willingness to grant an exemption to any children whose parents have religious beliefs that are similarly offended by the textbooks. The objections are thus general in form, and in this respect count as a moral claim. But their reasons do not meet the tests of reciprocity. The parents' reasoning appeals to values that can and should be rejected by citizens of a pluralist society committed to protecting the basic liberties and opportunities of all citizens. Keep in mind that the parents are trying to prevent schools from teaching their children to make critical judgments, to use their imagination, to exercise choice "in areas where the Bible provides the answer," and to consider the merits of the idea that all human beings have dignity and worth. If the parents were successful, their children (and perhaps others) would fail to receive the education that is necessary for developing their capacities as democratic citizens. The parents would deny the school board the authority to teach future citizens the skills and knowledge that are necessary for protecting the liberties and opportunities of all citizens, including the parents and their children themselves. Among those skills and knowledge is the capacity for critical reasoning—the ability to justify one's own actions, to criticize the actions of one's fellow citizens, and to respond to their justifications and criticisms. Since this capacity is a prerequisite for making reciprocal claims, its denial cannot itself be the basis for such a claim. If accepted, the claim would undermine the opportunity for (at least some) citizens to make reciprocal claims in the future.

The same kind of argument also defeats the parents' objection to teaching that each human being has dignity and worth. This belief too is necessary for basic liberty and opportunity. It, furthermore, underlies the principle of reciprocity itself. If each citizen were not regarded as having dignity or worth, then reciprocity would lose much of its moral point.

Beings who lack dignity or worth might not be morally obliged to find mutually acceptable terms of social cooperation. At the least, social cooperation among creatures without dignity or worth would be radically different from the kind of interactions among free and equal citizens to which most forms of democracy are committed.

In its civic education deliberative democracy goes even further than most other forms of democracy. It would teach children not only to respect human dignity but also to appreciate its role in sustaining political cooperation on terms that can be shared by morally motivated citizens. It would be pedagogically self-defeating if schools were to teach this lesson dogmatically or through indoctrination. But they are not bound to remain neutral on a question that affects the nature of democracy itself. To accept the fundamentalist parents' objection to teaching a commitment to "the dignity and worth of human beings" would therefore undermine a fundamental feature of deliberative democracy—a feature that makes possible the making of reciprocal claims on behalf of any moral or religious view.

The empirical claims that the fundamentalist parents make also fail to meet the test of reciprocity because they cannot be sustained by reliable methods of inquiry. When teachers require children to read stories describing a Catholic Indian settlement in New Mexico, the effect is not to inculcate belief in Catholicism. There is no reliable evidence that children who are required to read about different religions or different ways of life are likely to convert to those religions or choose those ways of life for themselves. The assumption that this is the effect of education ignores a simple distinction between teaching students about a religion and teaching them to believe in a religion. The parents, of course, may well deny the significance of this distinction: they may claim that merely teaching about other religions undermines their own religion by implying that religion is a matter of rational choice or subjective opinion. But the distinction is important not only as a matter of logic but also as a basis for a civic education that helps citizens understand the diverse ways of life of their fellow citizens. Without such an understanding, citizens cannot sustain an educational policy that respects all religions on terms that all morally motivated citizens can share.

It might be argued that the exercise that pictures the boy cooking while the girl reads is intended to change attitudes and may very well do so to some modest degree. Here the first response to the parents would point again to the prerequisites of citizenship. The exercise is seeking not to "denigrate" differences between the sexes but to eliminate differences in their basic liberties and opportunities. A more complete response would have to address the question of who should have the ultimate authority for the education of future citizens. If the fundamentalist parents object to the story because it portrays boys in a role that the Bible would not endorse, then they retain their right as parents to teach their children that boys should not have fun cooking because the Bible says so.

But if the parents insist on going beyond what they teach in their home, they would have to claim an unconditional authority over the education of some future citizens. That kind of claim cannot be the basis for resolving disagreement about educational policy on fair terms of cooperation. In a democratic society schools share educational authority with parents. As representatives of all citizens, school officials have a legitimate responsibility to teach children "to become good citizens in their school, community, and society." There is a public interest in educating good citizens, and no citizen can fairly claim that what constitutes good citizenship is whatever happens to conform to his or her particular religion.

What if the parents reject the principle of reciprocity itself? They might argue that it is biased against fundamentalism, and in favor of religions that conform to deliberative views of civic education and prevailing modes of empirical inquiry. The parents would be correct if they claimed that the principle is not neutral among religions or ways of life. The case for reciprocity, and more generally for the deliberative perspective, must be defended on substantive moral grounds, and there is no reason to expect that such a defense would have the same (positive or negative) implications for all moral positions.

But the value of public reason expressed by the deliberative perspective is not just another morality. It is offered as the morally optimal basis on which citizens who disagree about moralities and religions can act collectively to make educational policy. The principle of reciprocity is not privileged in the sense that it needs no moral defense. But the defense it needs and the objections to which it is vulnerable are different from those of moral and religious claims that do not take into account the problem of moral disagreement in politics. The principle proposes a basis on which those who morally disagree can cooperate, and it can be appropriately criticized only by proposing an alternative basis, not simply by reaffirming the moral or religious claim that constitutes the disagreement. The fundamentalists do not offer an alternative. Moreover, they themselves need some form of a principle of reciprocity even to make their own case. Even the objection that reciprocity is biased must be stated in a form that appeals to a sense of fairness that is assumed to be accepted by other citizens as a basis of social cooperation.

Do the claims of the board of education better satisfy the principle of reciprocity? The reasons the board gave to justify its decision are general in the sense that the policy applies to all parents, whatever their objections to the curriculum may be. No children receive exemptions on religious or moral grounds. In this respect the board's arguments, like those of the parents, constitute a moral claim. But the board's arguments against the fundamentalist parents accept the distinction between teaching a religion and teaching about a religion, which as we have seen is critical to the reciprocal perspective on educational policy. "While it is true that these textbooks expose the student to varying values and religious backgrounds," the superintendent of schools said, "neither the textbooks nor the teachers teach, indoctrinate, oppose or promote any *particular* value or religion."[11] The board's version of the distinction contrasts *particular* values and *public* values. Schools may not teach particular values, such as the doctrines of Catholicism, but they should teach public values, such as human dignity, which are essential to democratic citizenship. Public values of this kind should not be rejected by parents who are motivated to find fair terms of cooperation with their fellow citizens. The curriculum that the Hawkins County school board adopted was one reasonable, even if not uniquely correct, way for a public school system to teach democratic values.

The empirical assumptions on which the board relied also satisfy the standards of inquiry that reciprocity sets. Whether students were taught, rather than merely taught about, any particular religion could be discovered through reliable methods of inquiry if anyone doubted the board's claim. Those assumptions that do not lend themselves to empirical inquiry were also plausible in a way that could be generally accepted. The assumption that all human beings have dignity and worth, though not subject to ordinary empirical investigation, is consistent with an extensive set of social practices that are essential to democracy, including rights of religious freedom and other basic liberties and opportunities.

The Sixth Circuit Court of Appeals decided in favor of the school board, finding that "mere exposure" to ideas did not violate the free exercise of religion.[12] For broader reasons, the principle of reciprocity leads to the same conclusion. The claim that the parents make is not justifiable to citizens who themselves are motivated to present claims that can be justified to citizens with whom they morally disagree. The claims that the school board offers come closer to meeting this test. The principle of reciprocity in cases of this kind yields a determinate resolution.

At the Edges of Reciprocity

Unlike the case of the controversial curriculum in Hawkins County, many political disagreements cannot be resolved through reasoning that satisfies only or mainly the requirements of reciprocity. Trade policy and abortion exemplify the kinds of disagreements that the proponents of prudence and impartiality contend reciprocal deliberation cannot handle. Although reciprocity cannot resolve such controversies, it can provide standards for regulating the processes by which they may be resolved, and for sustaining practices of accommodation when they cannot be resolved.

BARGAINING IN ITS PLACE

Will a free trade policy with Mexico lead to more or less employment in the United States? More or less employment in Mexico? Better or worse protection of the environment? These and similar questions divided adversaries in the debate in 1993 over the North American Free Trade Agreement (NAFTA). The moral stakes were high, but the disagreement was not primarily moral.

The moral claims about NAFTA fell into roughly four categories: arguments from general welfare, basic opportunity, democratic development, and environmental protection. On grounds of general welfare, proponents claimed that NAFTA would help consumers by lowering prices and increasing the variety of products; benefit workers by increasing employment; promote economic growth; and facilitate the making of other trade agreements, such as GATT, thereby contributing to further beneficial increases in world trade. Opponents of NAFTA made the same arguments in reverse. They raised questions about the impact of NAFTA on product quality. They argued that NAFTA would lead to a net loss of jobs in the United States as corporations took advantage of the lower wages in Mexico. And, they said, the U.S. tax base would suffer, worsening the budget deficit and shrinking the resources available for social programs.

The disagreement over NAFTA's effect on vulnerable workers in the United States and Mexico, democratic development in Mexico, and the environment took the same form: consensus on the moral values but conflict about whether NAFTA would serve them. Senator Bill Bradley argued that rejection of NAFTA would make things worse for the most vulnerable workers, American as well as Mexican, while Senator Frank Lautenberg argued that implementation of NAFTA would exacerbate the problem of unemployment in the United States, imposing even more hardship on "the most vulnerable members of our economy."[13] Lautenberg even offered a quasi-Rawlsian argument against NAFTA: "The people who will lose their jobs are workers with the lowest incomes and the least-developed skills. The workers least able to survive even a brief period of unemployment."[14] The proponents of NAFTA did not take issue with the Rawlsian principle, or any other principles of justice that Lautenberg implicitly invoked. They disputed his empirical claim that NAFTA would harm vulnerable workers, arguing that both Mexican and American workers would benefit from the free trade that the agreement would promote.

The controversy followed the same pattern when the antagonists turned to the goal of democratizing Mexico and protecting the environment. Advocates argued that NAFTA would facilitate both goals, while opponents found it deficient in both respects. Some of the empirical assumptions were no doubt more plausible than others, and some of the disagreement no doubt resulted from the different weights and priorities that the parties assigned to the various values. But none of the major positions could be dismissed simply as rationalizations of economic or political interests, and only one expressed fundamental moral values that were in conflict with those of its opponents.

The one exception was the argument of Senator Phil Gramm, who relied on a principle that advocates of NAFTA did not share. He appealed to the value of liberty, but in a way that went beyond what most NAFTA proponents (and indeed most citizens) could accept. He suggested that free trade is a birthright of all Americans: "Who gives the Government the right to say that, if Mexico can produce a better shirt, I as a free person do not have a right to buy it? Too often Government tries to say that . . . It happens every day, but I do not accept it as being right. I object to it."[15] Had Gramm been successful in arguing that restrictions on free trade violate the basic liberty of individuals, then he would have settled morally the entire debate over NAFTA. But his claim about individual liberty goes beyond what even most libertarians would claim, and cannot be successfully defended on libertarian grounds, as we shall show in Chapter 6. In any case, the Grammian understanding of liberty did not play a prominent role in the NAFTA debate. The salient moral values were shared by both sides.

The antagonists in the debate were prepared to employ reliable methods of empirical inquiry to establish their non-moral claims, but those methods themselves did not yield definitive results, at least not on enough of the questions at issue in the dispute. The disagreement may have been largely empirical, but the empirical resources to resolve it were inadequate.

Disagreements over issues like NAFTA, in which political adversaries agree on the moral ends but still reasonably disagree about the most effective means to achieve them, seem ripe for resolution by bargaining, as the principle of prudence recommends. Even if moral considerations lurk in the background of such conflicts, they should not dominate the deliberations that resolve the conflict. In a deliberative democracy it is just as important that citizens recognize when they do *not* have a fundamental moral disagreement as when they do. On many political matters, moral standards should not be the final court of appeal for the simple reason that the controversy is not primarily moral in nature. Must we therefore leave reciprocity behind when we enter into political controversies of this kind?

Deliberative democracy makes ample room for bargaining. So long as all sides in a political controversy accept moral reciprocity as a constraint on their reasons for action, bargaining is a deliberatively legitimate way of resolving political conflicts that would otherwise remain unresolved. Bargaining thus constrained is completely consistent with deliberation. Understanding bargaining in this way, we can reject some of the criticism that is often leveled against political deals. Many commentators, even some supporters of NAFTA, criticized the bargaining that helped it pass. Senator John McCain declared that "every Member of Congress should have had the courage and wisdom to vote for NAFTA" on the merits, and he condemned "the politics as usual vote buying and selling that had little to do with free trade or a vision of a mutually prosperous hemisphere, and a lot to do with pork barrel pursuits."[16]

To appraise the practices of politics as usual, we should distinguish a broader and narrower objection to bargaining. The broader objection rejects any kind of bargaining as violating reciprocity; every piece of legislation should be supported on its merits, and its merits alone. This seems to be Senator McCain's view of how the politics of NAFTA should have been conducted. The narrower objection rejects bargaining only when the parties fail adequately to consider the merits of the collective results of their individual deals. Since these collective results affect the fair terms of cooperation, the proponents of reciprocity are obliged to look closely and critically at this kind of bargaining.

The problem with the broader objection is that well-informed people reasonably disagree over the merits of much legislation, just as they did over NAFTA. Only a false sense of certainty (NAFTA is "so clearly in the interests of our Nation") could lead one in disputes like this to dismiss all one's opponents as "narrow-minded," as Senator McCain seemed to do.[17] When one's opponents are not narrow-minded, one may have to make some broad-minded concessions—on other issues as well as on the policy under debate. The goal of bargaining in such circumstances is to forge majority coalitions on legislation that itself satisfies the principle of reciprocity at least as well as any alternative, when no single alternative can gain majority support simply on its own merits. If bargaining were ruled out, these coalitions could not form, and most new legislative proposals would remain in the committee room—if they advanced that far. To insist that each proposal gain majority support on its individual merits would be to ensure that relatively few new proposals would become law. The effect would be to privilege the status quo—a result that would be difficult to justify on the principle of reciprocity or for that matter on any adequate principle of justice.

The principle of reciprocity permits bargaining under conditions of empirical disagreement, provided that legislators and citizens properly consider the moral merits of the whole bargain.[18] Reciprocity thus puts constraints on log-rolling and pork-barreling, but it does not entirely rule out their use. The moral justification of a bargain should take into account not just the merits of the main legislation but the merits of the side deals as well. (In the case of NAFTA, these side deals became even more important because Congress could not alter the terms of the treaty.) Guided by reciprocity, adversaries in this conflict would have devoted less attention to their differences over the merits of the main agreement and directed more energy to considering the moral merits of side deals that were evidently necessary to win its approval. Had union supporters, for example, followed this approach, they might have been more effective in protecting the interests of vulnerable American workers. And they might have exacted greater concessions on other issues, such as job training programs, which could have been defended from a reciprocal perspective. Far from rejecting all bargaining, reciprocity suggests that sometimes it is morally better to bargain than not to bargain.

Reciprocity also permits bargaining in some circumstances even where deliberation would be morally preferable. Individuals and groups are not obligated to deliberate if others refuse to do so, and if doing so would put them at a further disadvantage. Citizens engaged in cooperative institutions do not have moral obligations to do their share unless they have reasonable assurance that others will not take advantage of them. This point has been elaborated at great length, sometimes in quite technical form, by political theorists since Hobbes, but the intuition that it expresses is a quite familiar and widely accepted assumption in ordinary moral argument in politics.

Excuses based on this assumption are easily abused. They may be appropriate for practices such as campaign finance (where candidates should not be expected to refuse PAC contributions unless their challengers also refuse them, even if the elimination of such contributions would be best for the system). But we should not be so tolerant of a candidate who excuses his lying to voters on the grounds that other candidates are also liars. Nor should the excuse allow advantaged citizens and officials to take further advantage of their position. In any case, even when the excuse is valid, citizens and officials are still obligated to criticize the obstacles to deliberation, and to try to create conditions that would make possible deliberation without unfair disadvantage. When bargaining is necessary because deliberation would be unfair, reciprocity prescribes institutional change. The sense of reciprocity is not only a disposition of individuals but also a quality of institutions.

DEALING WITH DELIBERATIVE DISAGREEMENT

At the opposite edge of the domain of reciprocity, far from the land of bargaining, we find deliberative disagreement. Instead of controversies to which moral reasons seem irrelevant, we find conflicts in which moral reasons so deeply divide citizens that no resolution seems possible on any fair terms of cooperation. A deliberative disagreement is one in which citizens continue to differ about basic moral principles even though they seek a resolution that is mutually justifiable. The disagreement persists within the deliberative perspective itself. It is fundamental because citizens differ not only about the right resolution but also about the reasons on which the conflict should be resolved.

A deliberative disagreement may be irresolvable because the best moral understanding that citizens can muster does not show them which position should be rejected from a deliberative perspective. Or it may be irresolvable because the competing moral claims in some controversies are inherently incompatible. Whether the ultimate source of such conflicts is epistemic (caused only by our limited understanding) or metaphysical (rooted in the moral values themselves), we have to face up to the fact that reciprocity is currently powerless to resolve them. Yet deliberation must go on, and reciprocity should not be left behind. We can see better how reciprocity might guide deliberation under these conditions by exploring more fully the nature of deliberative disagreement.

The public controversy over legalizing abortion is the paradigm of a deliberative disagreement. Both pro-life and pro-choice advocates argue from fundamentally different but plausible premises to conflicting public policies. Both make generalizable claims that are also recognizably reciprocal in their moral and empirical content. Pro-life advocates believe the fetus to be a human being—a person in the generic sense, with rights that should be constitutionally protected. The strongest general reason on which they base their opposition is the principle that innocent persons should not be killed. Pro-choice advocates believe the fetus to be only a potential constitutional person. The principle they invoke for defending legalized abortion is that women should have the liberty to decide whether to bear a child. Such a decision is a matter of personal integrity, as important to a woman's liberty as any other decision she makes in her life.

Pro-life and pro-choice advocates can agree that innocent people should not be killed, and that women have a basic liberty to live their own lives and control their own bodies. But they arrive at radically different conclusions about abortion because they cannot agree on whether the fetus is a full-fledged constitutional person, whether a woman's right to control her body takes priority over any claims the dependent fetus may have, and what responsibility a woman has to realize the human potential of a fetus that lacks consciousness and sentience. The claims on both sides of all these disagreements fall within the range of what reciprocity respects.

Insofar as empirical evidence is relevant to the abortion controversy, both sides make claims that are susceptible to normal methods of inquiry. Pro-life advocates appeal to established scientific facts about the gradual development of a fertilized egg into a viable, sentient fetus; they observe that the fetus has the biological characteristics of a human infant, and that its normal development culminates in a sentient and conscious human infant. The pro-choice advocate refers to testable claims about the effects of unwanted pregnancy and childbearing on women. Some of the claims on both sides are not empirical; further research is not likely to determine whether the fetus is a full-fledged human being entitled to constitutional protections. But neither side can show that these claims or assumptions are implausible on their face.

Different plausible beliefs about the personhood or constitutional standing of the fetus thus lie at the base of the strongest arguments for and against the legalization of abortion.[19] Although pro-life advocates sometimes invoke a religious conception of human life, the belief that the fetus is a human being with constitutional rights does not depend on a distinctively religious conception of personhood. A pro-life belief may also derive its plausibility from secular considerations such as the similarity of successive stages in the natural development from fetus to infant. The pro-choice view gains some credibility from the striking differences among a zygote, a five-month-old fetus, and an infant.[20] In these respects both pro-life and pro-choice positions seem reasonable. But reason itself, as one philosopher reminds us, does not "point in either direction: it is *we* who must point it, and *we* who are led by it. If you are led in one direction rather than the other, that is not because of logic, but because you respond in a certain way to certain facts [about the fetus]."[21]

In the long debate over abortion, many philosophers and theologians as well as citizens and public officials have sought to show that the controversy can be rationally resolved, that there is a single correct conclusion that is now knowable to any reasonable person. But the effect of reading and listening to the arguments on both sides, at least for citizens who are open to opposing views, has been to conclude that neither side has yet refuted its rival.[22] The effect simply confirms that the disagreement is fundamental and irresolvable, at least within the limits of our present moral understanding. But, more recently, some philosophers have sought to resolve the disagreement by arguing that there is some common ground that both sides share, and that if citizens recognize it, they can reach a mutually acceptable conclusion. The most important such argument is by Ronald Dworkin, who believes that the conclusion must be that legalized abortion is morally justified.[23]

Dworkin acknowledges that the fetus is human life—perhaps even a person in some philosophical sense. But he argues that because it has no consciousness or sentience (at least before five months), it cannot have interests. Without interests, it cannot plausibly be considered a constitutional person. Dworkin therefore believes that pro-life and pro-choice advocates should not disagree about either the question of the humanity of a second trimester fetus or its constitutional rights. Pro-choice advocates should not reject the claim that the fetus is a human life. Pro-life advocates should not reject the claim that the fetus has no constitutional rights to compete with the basic liberty of women. The abortion controversy can be resolved on common ground in favor of the pro-choice position—even though part of the common ground is the premise that pro-life advocates most passionately affirm, that the fetus is a human life.[24]

If Dworkin is right, the abortion controversy is not an instance of deliberative disagreement. It is rather merely an example of faulty logic, a failure to make certain distinctions and accept their implications. The crux of the argument is the claim that human beings cannot have constitutional rights unless they have prior sentience or consciousness. If Dworkin could show that this claim is justifiable to pro-life as well as pro-choice advocates, then he would indeed resolve the controversy—and on terms that are consistent with the principle of reciprocity. But he does not succeed in defending this claim on mutually justifiable grounds.

What reasons justify the claim that only human beings with prior consciousness or sentience can have constitutional rights? Constitutional rights protect human interests, and human beings do not have interests until they have sentience or consciousness. But these reasons can be rejected by pro-life advocates on the grounds that they presuppose the pro-choice conclusion in the abortion controversy. By itself, this pro-choice argument does not demonstrate that prior sentience or consciousness is a necessary condition for constitutional rights in the specific case of fetuses. The opposing claim is reasonable (though it too can be reasonably rejected): fetuses are an exception precisely because they are human beings with a future life to lead if they are not aborted. Pro-life advocates do not have to claim that *any* living being without sentience or consciousness has constitutional rights. They need assert only that a fetus has constitutional rights. They could do so on the grounds that the fetus, unlike other forms of life, is already a human being (as Dworkin acknowledges) and will naturally develop the sentience and consciousness of an infant if it is not killed. Dworkin gives no reason that should be compelling to pro-life advocates to reject the claim that the capacity to develop sentience and consciousness in this way is a basis for constitutional protection. The claim applies uniquely to fetuses, and this restriction would not necessarily violate the requirement of generality in moral argument since there are good reasons for singling out fetuses. At the same time, pro-life advocates may still claim that the fetus is not yet sufficiently like a constitutional person to deserve the same protection that infants and women should enjoy.

Thus, despite Dworkin's heroic efforts at arbitration, the two sides in the controversy still seem deadlocked. The difficulty is not that his arguments are internally inconsistent or that his analysis is incomplete, but that even pro-lifers who seek a mutually acceptable justification need not accept them. His arguments constitute a strong defense of the pro-choice position, but from a reciprocal perspective they do not provide reasons for rejecting the pro-life position.

Neither does the deadlock result, as some commentators suggest, from the fact that it has been framed in the language of individual rights. Perhaps the emphasis on "women's rights" has made pro-choice advocates appear "selfish," and has further polarized the debate, causing women to become "needlessly divided against each other."[25] No doubt the morality of abortion depends on many contextual factors that are distorted by forcing the disputants to speak in the language of rights. But replacing the question of "whether the self's rights have been invaded" with a "substantive question of virtue" (or some other contextual approach) will not eliminate the moral conflict.[26] The same deep disagreements about the status of the fetus and the relative weights of values will simply reappear as disputes about what virtues (or other moral qualities) are appropriate under various conditions. The debate may become deeper, but will be no freer of discord.

In the face of deliberative disagreement, what should democratic citizens do? They have to make some collective decision, even if the decision they make is not the only justifiable one from a reciprocal perspective. Deliberative democracy recognizes that the government must take a stand on questions involving such disagreement, even if reciprocity and its other constitutive principles do not determine the answer.

The fact that democracies must finally make a decision may tempt one to think that basic moral disagreement should not be treated differently from any other kind of moral or political conflict. What we have been calling deliberative disagreement, it may be said, creates no special problem for resolving moral disagreements in politics.[27] Citizens may— and perhaps should—be more uncertain about the truth of their own position when they find themselves locked in such a conflict. Certainly they should not be dogmatic about their view; they should recognize that they may be wrong, and that their opponents may be right. Citizens should also recognize degrees of uncertainty. They have good reason, for example, to be more certain about the injustice of slavery and racial discrimination than about the injustice of restrictions on second-trimester abortions or the imposition of capital punishment. But, having paid their respects to these limitations of moral knowledge, they must finally come to a conclusion.

On this view of moral conflict, then, all citizens can and should do is reach their own best judgment under the conditions of uncertainty, and argue (and vote) for the position they believe is right.[28] The uncertainty gives them no reason to change their beliefs or actions in any way. The fact that both sides have grounds for reasonably rejecting the position of their opponents should not make a difference in the way they think or act in the public forum. The moral strength of their opponents' case (whether pro-choice or pro-life) should be irrelevant to their political actions. Thus, on this view, reciprocity could not ask any more of citizens than does impartiality or any other general moral principle. Its counsel is simply to consider all the relevant factors from a moral point of view, choose the course of action according to one's own best judgment, and defend that choice to others as best one can.

This approach to moral conflict makes sense as far as it goes, but it does not go very far. The problem is that it fails to distinguish between generic uncertainty, which characterizes all moral judgments, even those that can be reasonably rejected by one's opponents, and conflict-specific uncertainty, which obtains only in the case of deliberative disagreement. In circumstances of generic uncertainty, it is usually sufficient simply to reject dogmatism. All that may be required is to acknowledge that sometime in the future reasons may be found to reject the position one now has the strongest available reasons for holding. Perhaps in the future someone will discover compelling reasons that would show that slavery or racial discrimination is morally justified, but at present one has good reasons to be confident that anyone making such a claim is morally wrong.

The circumstances of deliberative disagreement are different. There are mutually acceptable reasons, accessible *now* that not only call into question our best judgment but also permit other citizens to reject our judgment and defend opposing ones. From the perspective of reciprocity, the presence of such reasons makes a significant moral difference. Unlike ordinary moral conflict, deliberative disagreement places some citizens in opposition to others who are no less committed to finding fair terms of cooperation, and who are offering reasons that cannot be shown to violate those terms. The circumstances are quite different from those of moral disagreement in which one side does not have reciprocal reasons for rejecting the other, and thereby signifies that it is not motivated to find fair terms of cooperation (at least with respect to the policy at issue). The difference between these situations marks the distinction between deliberative and nondeliberative disagreement.

This distinction is clearly manifested in the difference in attitude that many liberals have toward someone who argues for racial discrimination in education or employment, and someone who argues for capital punishment or for the prohibition of abortion. Provided that all parties are committed to their own position on moral grounds, liberals are more inclined to respect the person who favors capital punishment or opposes abortion than the person who favors racial discrimination. They could show this respect even if they believed that capital punishment and a ban on abortion are just as wrong as racial discrimination. They could believe that all these wrongs are equally serious but still be more certain about the grounds for believing discrimination to be wrong. They in effect acknowledge that the reasons their opponents could give for favoring capital punishment or opposing abortion have moral standing in a way that the reasons for favoring racial discrimination do not. The latter fail to satisfy the test of reciprocity.

Granting that there is an important moral difference between deliberative and nondeliberative disagreement, one may still ask what political difference it should make. Since the principle of reciprocity does not resolve the conflict in either case, how can it prescribe that citizens act differently in one case than in the other? To answer this question, we need to extend the principle of reciprocity. In the rest of this chapter we develop some standards to guide the way in which citizens deal with deliberative disagreement—what we call the principles of accommodation.

The Meaning of Moral Accommodation

The principles of accommodation are based on a value that lies at the core of reciprocity and deliberation in a democracy—mutual respect.[29] It is what makes possible cooperation on fair terms. Like toleration, mutual respect is a form of agreeing to disagree. But mutual respect demands more than toleration. It requires a favorable attitude toward, and constructive interaction with, the persons with whom one disagrees. It consists in an excellence of character that permits a democracy to flourish in the face of fundamental moral disagreement.[30] This is a distinctively deliberative kind of character. It is the character of individuals who are morally committed, self-reflective about their commitments, discerning of the difference between respectable and merely tolerable differences of opinion, and open to the possibility of changing their minds or modifying their positions at some time in the future if they confront unanswerable objections to their present point of view.[31]

Mutual respect not only helps sustain a moral community in the face of conflict but also can contribute toward resolving the conflict. One way in which it can do so is simply by keeping open the possibility of a different, more accommodating solution in the future. If we publicly recognize that a policy adopted by the government may be justifiably rejected by other citizens who accept the requirements of reciprocity, we are more likely to remain open to proposals for alternatives that would be mutually accept-able, and more dedicated to changing the social and economic conditions to make those alternatives practicable.

Mutual respect can also help resolve moral disagreements by discour-aging other kinds of moral rigidity. Citizens who respect one another as moral agents are less inclined toward the moral dogmatism, and its ac-companying attitude of arrogance, that is common among those who take moral opposition as a sign of ignorance or depravity. ("Either you're for killing babies or you're against killing babies," declared Nellie Gray, the leader of a March for Life in Washington.[32] "Either you're for the freedom of women or you're against it" would be the analogous dogmatism on the pro-choice side.) Citizens who distinguish between deliberative and non-deliberative disagreements may also be less inclined toward the opposite kind of rigidity—excessive moral skepticism, which discourages serious moral discussion ("You have your opinion and I have mine, and who's to say who's right?"). Disagreements are then left to be settled only through political bargaining or by political force, immune from moral challenge now or in the future.

Mutual respect can fulfill its promise only if it can be translated into practices that guide actual political life. The principles of accommodation provide the standards for regulating those practices. They suggest how citizens who, after deliberation, still fundamentally disagree about an issue should treat one another with regard to that and related issues—even when their deliberations result in legislation that favors one side of the dispute. The principles make two general kinds of demands on citizens; one concerns how citizens present their own political positions, and the other how they regard the political positions of others. Although the prin-ciples refer to the manner in which moral opinions are held and expressed, they refer not mainly to style or rhetoric but rather to attitudes as mani-fested in public action. They seek not only a kind of speech but also action, and not only action but also action in cooperation with others over time.

The virtue of mutual respect that they aim to foster comprises a family of moral dispositions that support the principle of reciprocity.[33]

CIVIC INTEGRITY

The first principle of accommodation calls on citizens to affirm the moral status of their own political positions. This involves a kind of moral integrity in politics, which we call civic integrity. Citizens and officials demonstrate civic integrity in three ways. The first is by *consistency in speech*. We expect citizens and officials to espouse their moral positions independently of the circumstances in which they speak. This is a sign of political sincerity: it indicates that a person holds the position for reasons of morality, not (only) for reasons of political advantage. There is of course no completely reliable way to tell if such a principle is satisfied. It is difficult enough in private life to judge sincerity. In the more distant relations of public life, sincerity becomes so hard to confirm that we assume (perhaps too easily) that hypocrisy is all there is. But we can find some reliable criteria for recognizing, or at least providing good grounds for suspecting, insincerity. Politicians who continually shift their positions according to political fashions give us good grounds for doubting that they honestly accept the positions they espouse on moral grounds.

A second and familiar form of civic integrity is *consistency between speech and action*. The pro-choice advocate who prevents his daughter from having an abortion over her strong objection and the staunch opponent of legalized abortion who helps his daughter obtain an abortion fall short of acting in ways that command the respect of their fellow citizens. It is sometimes possible to point to differences that would legitimately distinguish the speech and action (perhaps, in these examples, a belief about special obligations to family). But apparent inconsistencies call for careful and candid explanations. Public officials have even greater responsibilities in this respect because their words may be reasonably taken as a commitment to carry out certain policies. Furthermore, their culpability for failures to act is probably greater. We do not admire politicians who in a campaign emphasize their concern over abortion but, once elected to office, fail—whether from laziness or lack of leadership—to work for the policies implied by the position they advocated.

The third form of civic integrity is what may be called the *integrity of principle*. This consists in the acceptance of the broader implications of the principles presupposed by one's moral positions. Those who oppose abortion out of respect for fetal life should advocate policies that would ensure that children are adequately fed. There may be good reasons for denying the apparent implications of one's principles (if, for example, other more weighty principles block the inference that would otherwise be warranted). But even when there are such reasons, the burden should fall on those who would deny the implications. If pro-life advocates oppose the program of Aid to Families of Dependent Children on grounds that it is inefficient and mismanaged, then they should seek alternative public policies that would go at least as far in protecting the health and welfare of poor children.

CIVIC MAGNANIMITY

The second principle of accommodation calls on citizens and officials to acknowledge the moral status of the positions they oppose. This principle also has three parts, which parallel the three aspects of civic integrity. Since this principle looks outward toward one's judgments of others, it may be thought of as expressing forms of civic magnanimity.

Acknowledging the moral status of a position that one opposes requires, first, that one treat the position as expressing a moral rather than a purely strategic, political, or economic view. This *acknowledgment in speech* begins by recognizing that an opponent's position is based on moral principles about which people may reasonably disagree (both sides satisfy the requirements of reciprocity described earlier). A striking example of this kind of acknowledgment can be found in a debate on the funding of abortion that took place several years ago in the House of Representatives. A member argued against a motion to deny government funding for abortions in the case of rape and incest:

> Let me at the outset say that I understand the depth of feeling of those who support the motion and who feel that abortion should be permitted only when the life of the mother is in danger. I understand the sincerity with which those who advocate that position come to the floor . . . Now, I know that obviously [our] position [in favor of funding abortions in cases of rape and incest] is one that morally is inconsistent with the position of those who are supporting the motion, but I suggest to you it is certainly an understandable, defensible position, and one which I would hope those who do not like abortion would nonetheless understand . . . *I would hope that they would at least acknowledge that there is . . . moral controversy.*[34]

In the discussion that followed, many members did in fact acknowledge through the tone and content of their arguments the moral nature of the controversy.[35]

This debate stands in contrast with an earlier one—also in the House and also on abortion funding—in which members manifested markedly less respect for the moral seriousness of their opponents. At one point in that debate, a member argued against funding abortion on the grounds that it would lower the birthrate and thereby increase the federal deficit: "If we are going to pay off this debt, somebody has got to be born to pay the taxes to pay it off."[36] This prompted the next speaker to throw away her prepared remarks and attack him for ignoring the moral issue: "I am shocked to hear that American women are meant to be breeder reactors to sustain civilization and pay off the deficit. I am insulted—insulted—by the use of the language that was used here in this debate . . . To refer to American women as fertile females that need to sustain the civilization is an affront to us. I think American women do more than breed; I think that American women do more than pay off the deficit . . . We are talking about *matters of life*."[37]

There are of course many other ways to impugn the moral status of an opponent's position. One of the most prevalent—and corrosive—is to claim that a position is politically motivated. This is an all-purpose argument which can be used to discredit any position, whatever its moral merits.[38] What all such arguments have in common is a refusal to give moral reasons for rejecting the position. Contrary to the practice of imputing ulterior motives, we manifest mutual respect by joining with our fellow citizens in serious and sustained moral discussion on the substance of the issues that divide us. In such discussions we not only state publicly our reasons for rejecting an opponent's position but also invite and consider responses to our objections.

A second component of magnanimity (paralleling the requirement of integrity in action) calls for the simple virtue of *open-mindedness*. Cultivating this disposition maintains the possibility that citizens can be convinced of the moral merits of their adversaries' position. Open-minded citizens try to break personal and institutional habits that would discourage them from accepting an opposing position at some time in the future, or at least from modifying their position in that direction. Both the political mind and the political forum should be kept open to reconsideration of decisions already made and policies already adopted.

To commend a disposition toward openness is not to imply that an open mind is the only important or admirable quality of a democratic citizen. Magnanimity in action should also make room for affirming one's own moral views strongly and consistently. The aim is to seek a balance between holding firm convictions and being prepared to change them when one encounters objections that, on reflection, one cannot answer. Maintaining this delicate balance is no doubt psychologically as well as intellectually demanding, but the personal and political dangers of a simpler path—succumbing to moral dogmatism on the one hand or moral skepticism on the other—are greater.[39]

Although the disposition toward openness is elusive—especially in politics—we can sometimes detect it or its absence even in the statements of public officials. Consider the difference in emphasis in these two statements by prominent public officials, both of whom personally opposed abortion but administered a public policy of legalized abortion. Writing about his struggle with the issue during his tenure as secretary of Health, Education and Welfare, Joseph Califano commented: "I concluded that it was not sufficient simply to express my view clearly and consistently, but that it was also essential *to communicate the certainty with which I held it.* Any hedging would only encourage those who disagreed, to hope for a change that would not be forthcoming."[40] In a nationally publicized speech at Notre Dame, Mario Cuomo, then governor of New York defended his position on the legalization of abortion this way: "I . . . [am] eager for enlightenment, eager to learn new and better ways to manifest respect for the deep reverence for life that is our religion and our instinct. I hope that the public attempt to describe the problems as I understand them will give impetus to the dialogue in the Catholic community and beyond, a dialogue which could show me a better wisdom than I've been able to find so far."[41]

At least on its face, Cuomo's speech shows a greater commitment to openness than does Califano's comment. Cuomo seems more inclined to consider the possibility of changing his mind on some aspects of the abortion question. His speech invites further discussion and calls for continuing the dialogue on the issue. He holds open the possibility of moral change, and thus manifests moral regard for the position that it opposes.

Cuomo's speech is characterized not only by openness but also by a commitment to finding a mutually acceptable value—"reverence for life"—that could help resolve moral differences at the level of policy. Ronald Dworkin invokes a related value—the sacredness of life—in a similar effort to find common ground among adversaries in the abortion conflict.[42] Both of these are instances of the third component of magnanimity, the disposition to seek what we call the *economy of moral disagreement.* In justifying policies on moral grounds, citizens should seek the rationale that minimizes rejection of the position they oppose.[43] While the corresponding component of integrity calls on citizens to accept the broader implications of their positions, this form of magnanimity tells citizens to avoid unnecessary conflict in characterizing the moral grounds or drawing out the policy implications of their positions. A similar point applies to empirical disputes in moral argument: citizens also have an obligation to seek an economy of factual disagreement.

Seeking an economy of moral disagreement at both foundational and policy levels of political argument should not be confused with compromising one's moral convictions solely in the interest of agreement. Rather, the aim is to search for significant points of convergence between one's own understandings and those of citizens whose positions, taken in their more comprehensive forms, one must reject.[44]

THE ECONOMY OF MORAL DISAGREEMENT IN ACTION

This search for convergence is not so rare as is often assumed. Some of the best work in practical moral philosophy can be interpreted as seeking such an economy of disagreement. In a well-known philosophical analysis of the abortion controversy, Judith Jarvis Thomson narrows the range of reasonable disagreement between pro-life and pro-choice advocates to cases in which pregnancy results from largely voluntary sexual intercourse.[45] By means of several hypothetical examples, she shows that even people who believe the fetus to be a constitutional person should acknowledge that abortion may be justified in circumstances where pregnancy is the result of forced intercourse. That is part of the point of her example of the unconscious violinist. Thomson asks you to imagine an unconscious violinist who suffers from kidney failure, and who, against your will, has been plugged into your circulatory system to save his life. The violinist's survival depends on his remaining plugged into you for nine months. No one would want to claim that he has a right to remain attached to you if you object.[46] The example is meant to suggest that sometimes it may be morally permissible (though not admirable) to kill an innocent person even if one's own life is not at stake. The example should convince even people who perceive the fetus to be a full-fledged person that to permit abortion is not obviously wrong in the case of a woman who becomes pregnant through no fault of her own (for example, by rape).

Even if such hypothetical examples succeed in their aims, the moral and political distance remaining between pro-life and pro-choice advocates is still great. In the vast majority of cases in which women seek abortions, where pregnancy is not the result of force, Thomson's arguments leave pro-choice and pro-life advocates radically opposed. Yet even in this treacherous territory of deliberative disagreement, there is still some prospect for further accommodation. The grounds on which the government decides the question should comply with the standard of the economy of moral disagreement. If the government decides to legalize and fund abortion, it should be on grounds that acknowledge as far as possible the moral legitimacy of the pro-life position.

To a remarkable extent, the Supreme Court in *Roe v. Wade* did just that. Although the Court did not admit as a constitutional argument the claim that fetuses are persons, the majority opinion emphasized that the state has an interest in protecting potential life.[47] This emphasis moved the rationale for the decision closer to the conclusions of a pro-life position, particularly as they apply to the later stages of fetal development. Moreover, the Court shifted the emphasis in this way without abandoning the premise that fetuses are not constitutional persons. The Court allowed states to ban abortion in the third trimester, on the grounds that the state's interest in potential life is compelling once the fetus is viable. On this logic, if medical technology advances and viability extends to earlier stages of pregnancy, then the Court's rationale should give increasing protection to fetal life (with the aim of equalizing the risks of abortion and normal childbirth).

Yet the Court did not follow its own logic to this conclusion, and therefore did not move as far as it might have in the direction of moral accommodation. In its discussion of the second trimester of pregnancy, the Court introduced a consideration that is required neither by pro-life nor by pro-choice premises. It appealed to a paternalistic claim that the state has a compelling interest in protecting the health of pregnant women even against their own will.[48] The only rationale that the Court gave for this claim is that second trimester abortions are riskier than normal childbirth. But in subsequent cases the Court has not itself consistently followed this rationale. It has declined to judge restrictions on second trimester abortions according to whether they are necessary to equalize the risks of abortion and normal childbirth. Furthermore, having granted the state's interest in protecting potential life, the Court failed to offer a credible moral (or legal) argument for giving it lower priority than the state's interest in protecting maternal health.

This failure came back to haunt the Court in the *Webster* decision.[49] Relying on the paternalistic claim for regulating second trimester abortions rather than a claim based on the value of prenatal life, the Court encouraged states to invent dubious medical rationales to justify their restrictions on abortion. Since then, the states have had to try to show that the restrictions would protect maternal health, even when their actual purpose was to protect prenatal life.[50] The Court's reliance on a paternalistic rationale for restricting second trimester abortions has thereby rendered its judgment more divisive and less open to change through deliberation than principles of accommodation would prescribe.

In contrast to *Webster,* a later opinion *(Planned Parenthood v. Casey)* offers a more positive example of the economy of moral disagreement. In the later case the majority of the Court reaffirmed the liberty of women to obtain abortions that *Roe* established. But it also upheld some state restrictions on first and second trimester abortions (such as a twenty-four-hour waiting period), provided that the restrictions do not impose an "undue burden" on a woman's liberty. The majority argued that the state's interest in protecting potential human life is sufficiently strong to permit restrictions that do not pose "substantial obstacles" to women who want to have an abortion. The meanings of "undue burden" and "substantial obstacle" are of course contestable and subject to manipulation. But the use of these terms in the majority's opinion illustrates one way in which pro-choice citizens can move a small but significant way toward accommodating pro-life concerns without giving up the commitment to protecting the basic liberty of women.[51] These citizens could accept the standard even without accepting the Court's specific conclusion in this case (since they may very well believe that the waiting period in fact poses a substantial obstacle for poor women). The "undue burden" standard has been recognized as acceptable from a variety of moral perspectives and is therefore a promising way of seeking an economy of moral disagreement on abortion.[52]

In a deliberative democracy not only judges and legislators but also citizens should practice the economy of moral disagreement. Citizens ought to be able to agree, for example, that someone's views on abortion should not affect how she is treated with respect to other public policies. A pro-lifer ought not to favor denying a woman who has an abortion access to other essential medical care. A pro-choicer should not refuse pro-lifers the right speak against abortion even in front of an abortion clinic.

In a similar spirit of accommodation, some philosophers would go even further. George Sher argues for a "moral compromise" that would permit abortions but deny government funding for elective ones.[53] This has been essentially the policy that (with some exceptions) has prevailed in this country since the Hyde Amendment was adopted in 1976. The policy has been generally unpopular with both pro-choice and pro-life advocates, but Sher contends that both have good reason to accept it, or something like it. A moral compromise is appropriate if the "grounding" of one's principles is "problematical," if the opposing view is supported by "plausible-sounding arguments," and "if thoughtful and intelligent people are unable to agree about the issues."[54] The abortion controversy meets these criteria, and each side, according to Sher, should therefore be prepared to modify its position in a way that would not be appropriate in ordinary policy disputes. Pro-life advocates should give up "more extreme responses" that might be justified in the face of an "officially sanctioned policy of murder."[55] Because of the presumption against government interference that both sides should appreciate, pro-choice advocates should not have to give up legalization, but they should give up policies that would increase the number of abortions. A policy of government-subsidized abortion is likely to do just that. Moreover, such a policy "amounts to an implicit government endorsement" of abortion, and it also forces pro-lifers to support through their taxes a policy they regard as murder.[56]

Although moral compromise may sometimes be permitted or even required by principles of accommodation, Sher's proposal—like current policy—is not warranted. His argument depends critically on the premise that the failure to subsidize abortion violates no one's rights.[57] It is true that from the fact that one has a right to abortion it does not follow that one has a right to government funds to exercise the right. As we shall argue in Chapter 6, basic liberties do not carry with them any automatic guarantee of public subsidy for the opportunity to exercise them. Thus, in the fragment of the argument cited at the beginning of Chapter 1, President Carter's implicit claim that denial of funding for abortion is not unfair cannot be easily dismissed. Nonetheless, the refusal to fund abortions for poor women, when childbirth is funded, creates an almost irresistible pressure on indigent women to carry a child to term. The government in this way could be said to violate the basic liberty of indigent women to choose between these alternative courses of action. The government does not force a woman to choose childbirth in exactly the way that a criminal law against abortion would; but given the special financial circumstances of Medicaid-eligible women, they cannot, except at unacceptable risk, choose the option of abortion. It might be said that "the government literally makes an offer the indigent woman cannot afford to refuse."[58]

Although this kind of argument may not finally establish a case for funding abortion, it does suggest that under current circumstances the bare claim that not subsidizing abortion violates no one's rights need not be accepted from a reciprocal perspective. Therefore, even if reducing the number of abortions is a legitimate end of a moral compromise, refusing to fund abortions may not be a justifiable means.

Other approaches are more promising. Accommodation calls on citizens to try to minimize the range of their public disagreement by promoting policies on which their principles converge, even if they would otherwise place those policies significantly lower on their own list of political priorities. Thus, pro-choice advocates may think that publicly funded programs that help unwed mothers care for their own children are less important than pro-life proponents do, but the pro-choicers should join in actively promoting these programs and other policies that are similarly consistent with the principles they share with opponents. By trying to maximize political agreement in these ways, citizens do not end serious moral conflict, but they affirm that they accept significant parts of the substantive morality of their fellow citizens to whom they may find themselves deeply opposed in other respects.

Even in the case of abortion funding, there is room for some further accommodation. Taking up one line of argument that Sher mentions but does not pursue, a pro-life advocate might argue that, although in a democracy she may have to allow others to perform actions that violate her fundamental moral principles (even acts that she regards as murder), she should not be forced to contribute to those actions with her own funds through taxes. If her fellow citizens truly acknowledge the moral seriousness of her views, they should find some way to reduce her complicity in actions she regards as murder. The plea is powerful, and from a reciprocal perspective her claim seems justified. The difficulty is to find a fair means of satisfying her claim. The argument for reducing complicity does not imply that a pro-life advocate's overall tax burden should be reduced. All citizens should still pay their fair share of taxes, but the tax monies of pro-life advocates should not contribute to subsidizing abortion, against which they have a legitimate conscientious objection on deliberative grounds. Although we permit conscientious refusal in military service, we do not extend the permission to taxes. The taxes of conscientious objectors, however, could be directed toward other morally acceptable policies that are funded by democratic government.

A better alternative for accommodation, one that reduces the complicity of pro-lifers but not their tax burden, would be voluntary contributions through the tax system to subsidize abortions—a simple check-off on income tax forms, like the three-dollar contribution to the Presidential Campaign Fund that citizens now may make.[59] Citizens who favor funding abortion would check the appropriate box, and three dollars of their taxes would go for that purpose. Pro-lifers would not check the box. It might be objected that if we institute a check-off for abortion, we would have to allow it for an indefinite number of other causes—from defense expenditures to environmental protection, animal rights, National Public Radio, and the like. This objection is not decisive. The abortion controversy has some special features—the conditions of deliberative disagreement—that would justify special treatment. Most of the other causes that might be proposed would probably fail to satisfy those conditions. Those causes that did would similarly deserve a box on the 1040 form, too. Some states already have various check-offs, even on less morally controversial issues. Colorado permits voters to donate money to the state domestic abuse fund, the wildlife program, and the U.S. Olympic Committee. If such a check-off for abortion failed to raise enough money, other voluntary sources might be tapped. But even if additional public funding turned out to be necessary, the continuing effort to find ways of accommodating pro-life moral objections would be valuable in promoting mutual respect.

The politics of mutual respect is not always pretty. The deliberation that takes place among citizens and officials under the principles of accommodation may be quite robust. Citizens may find it necessary to take extreme and even offensive stands. They may find it necessary to refuse to cooperate with opponents, and even threaten retaliation. These strategies may be justified when, for example, they are required to gain attention for a legitimate position that would otherwise be ignored, and thereby to promote mutual respect in the long term. Although it does not promise a comprehensive common good, a politics of mutual respect does seek agreement on substantive moral values for the society. By thus raising the moral stakes of politics, it may even increase moral conflict in politics in the short term.

Mutual respect, as expressed through the two principles of accommodation, thus extends the principle of reciprocity by encouraging citizens and public officials to appreciate the moral character of the positions of people with whom they disagree. But no less important than the obligations that reciprocity places on individual citizens are the demands it imposes on political institutions. To fulfill these demands, we are likely to have to make changes in our institutions, and to create some new forms of governance. We may have to bring our informal practices as well as formal rules regulating political speech and action more into line with the principles of accommodation. Those principles would not justify social or legal prohibitions on what citizens may say in the public forum. In this respect they are intended to be consistent with conventional liberal doctrines of free speech. But the principles—and reciprocity more generally—not only permit but may in fact require changing the balance of institutional influences on public deliberation.

The principles imply that the forums in which we conduct our political discussion should be designed so as to encourage officials to justify their actions with moral reasons, and to give other officials as well as citizens the opportunity to criticize those reasons. Legislators, for example, might act more like judges by assuming a regular responsibility to explain in writing, in principled terms, the basis for their decisions. To encourage the habit of openness, we could create more incentives for reconsidering important moral decisions and policies at regular intervals. Although unlimited opportunities to reopen questions would of course paralyze government, some of the existing barriers to fundamental changes may be too high. The procedures for amending the Constitution, for example, make the possibility of future change in some major policies seem hopelessly remote. To promote an economy of moral disagreement, we might fashion more broad-based political organizations that permit citizens who hold different moral positions to work together on other causes whose goals they share. In this respect a fluid and open party system would be more desirable than a political structure dominated by single-issue groups.

The merits of these particular institutional proposals would have to be considered in the context of the relevant political factors. Other changes may serve the same goals, and some may be more effective.[60] The point of these suggestions is to emphasize that the principles of accommodation not only impose duties on individuals but also carry implications for institutions. Mutual respect is a *political* virtue that supports reciprocity, and as such it is shaped by the political institutions in which it is practiced.

Democracy within the Limits of Reciprocity

A deliberative democracy governed by reciprocity flourishes neither in a society of self-centered citizens nor in a society of saints.[61] Yet it finds a place for the self-centered in a morally constrained process that permits, and under certain circumstances encourages, bargaining on the basis of mutual advantage. It welcomes saints, or at least their political accomplices, those who pursue impartial ideals that express comprehensive moral visions. Citizens in a deliberative democracy also recognize that such ideals may create fundamental moral conflicts, with which they deal under the influence of principles of accommodation.

With this understanding of reciprocity, we do not face the stark choice that is often posed in contemporary political theory. We do not have to choose between modeling democracy on procedural principles or founding it on comprehensive conceptions of the good. Deliberation governed by the principle of reciprocity goes beyond procedural democracy. Unlike procedural theories that tend to minimize the moral content of politics, reciprocal democracy accepts the need to promote substantive moral principles in politics—principles that could become part of a public morality for the society as a whole. Although the policy prescriptions of reciprocity are less comprehensive than those of most public moralities, its prescriptions for political reasoning and deliberation are more comprehensive—and more demanding—than those of procedural democracy. In cultivating the virtue of open-minded commitment among citizens and in encouraging an economy of moral disagreement in politics, reciprocity orients citizens and public officials toward a deliberative perspective that is compatible with continuing moral disagreement. This perspective is constituted partly by those substantive rights and obligations on which many moral philosophies converge and partly by a public search for further moral agreement.

But the search does not aim at the kind of common good that many communitarians seek.[62] Such an aim underestimates the significance and legitimate persistence of moral disagreement. In a pluralist society comprehensive moral conceptions neither can nor should win the assent of reasonable citizens. A deliberative perspective for such societies must reject the unqualified quest for agreement because it must renounce the claim to comprehensiveness. This is part of the point of extending reciprocity to include the principles of accommodation—to recognize that the political agenda is never likely to be free of fundamental moral conflict. Just because citizens deliberate together about substantive moral values does not mean they shall—or should—come to agree collectively on a coherent set of those values.

To reject comprehensiveness as an aim does not lead to skepticism—moral or metaphysical. On the contrary, it reflects the core commitment to a conception of politics that is conducive to deliberation and to a conception of persons whose convictions are also guided by deliberation. Just as Lockean liberals insist that religious belief should not be commanded, so deliberative democrats affirm that moral decisions about public policy, and in particular collective moral decisions, should be made deliberatively. In opening the forums of political decision making to a wide range of legitimate moral disagreement, and defending practices that cultivate mutual respect among citizens within those forums, the principle of reciprocity supports a political process that promotes moral learning. Citizens put their moral beliefs to the test of public deliberation, and strengthen their convictions or change their minds in response to the arguments presented in a politics governed by reciprocity.

The aim of such a process is not necessarily to induce citizens to change their first-order moral beliefs. It is rather to encourage them to discover what aspects of those beliefs could be accepted as principles and policies by other citizens with whom they fundamentally disagree. Since it is this second-order agreement that citizens should seek, they do not have to trade off their personal moral views against public values. Deliberative reasoning is not correctly represented if it is described as giving more weight to the value of mutual respect or deliberation than (for example) to the sanctity of life. A citizen may still believe that the sanctity of life is more important, but recognize that under current conditions her understanding of the value is not yet sufficiently appreciated by her fellows citizens and therefore cannot yet become the basis of public policy that is justified from a reciprocal perspective. Such recognition expresses the idea that the only mutually justifiable route to gaining collective acceptance of individual moral beliefs is through mutually respectful deliberation.

The perspective of deliberative democracy, then, does not require a consensus on public policy or even on constitutional law. At its center stands instead an appreciation of principles that set the conditions of political discussion—reciprocity and its companions publicity and accountability. This shift in focus of what democratic citizens should share is significant, theoretically and practically. Theoretically, a deliberative perspective expresses as complete a conception of a common good as is possible within a morally pluralistic society. Recognizing that politics cannot be purged of moral conflict, it seeks a common view on how citizens should publicly deliberate when they fundamentally disagree. Practically, this perspective encourages the cultivation of a set of civic virtues that can guide citizens through the maelstroms of moral controversy in a pluralistic society. It can help citizens resolve moral conflict with fairness and, when they cannot resolve it, enables them to work together in a mode of mutual respect. This is the counsel of the principles of accommodation, and ultimately the sense of reciprocity.

_3_

The Value of Publicity

THE REASONS that officials and citizens give to justify political actions, and the information necessary to assess those reasons, should be public. This principle of publicity is a fundamental requirement of deliberative democracy. It is also a principle that would seem to be readily justifiable from almost any moral perspective. It was Kant who first emphasized the close connection between morality and publicity: "All actions which relate to the right of other men are contrary to right and law [if their] maxim . . . does not permit publicity."[1] From the very different perspective of utilitarianism, Bentham also insisted that publicity is essential to ensure that government promotes the greatest happiness of the greatest number. "Let us place at the head of [the political assembly's] regulations the fittest law for securing the public confidence, and causing it constantly to advance towards the end of its institution . . . [the] law . . . of publicity."[2]

Politicians, too, declare their commitment to the principle. In the best-known proclamation of a publicity principle, Woodrow Wilson called for "open covenants . . . openly arrived at . . . Diplomacy shall proceed always frankly and in the public view."[3] Earlier he had affirmed that "publicity is one of the purifying elements of politics."[4] Today many American political institutions embody this commitment to publicity. "Sunshine laws," freedom of information acts, investigative journalism, and a robust First Amendment ensure that U.S. citizens have access to more information about, and reasoning by, public officials and public agencies than ever before in our history.

But the principle of publicity is not as easy to sustain, either in theory or practice, as at first it might seem. Kant himself adopted only a weak, hypothetical form of the principle (though it applies well beyond politics). He requires only that justifications *could* be made public, not that they actually must be made so. In this form the principle expresses only "an experiment of pure reason."[5] Bentham was prepared to abandon the principle when a secret scheme would better serve the greatest happiness. His proposal to simulate executions of criminals, for example, would work only if the practice were kept secret.[6] Woodrow Wilson made sure that the foreign leaders with whom he dealt understood that he did not mean to rule out the possibility of "confidential diplomatic negotiations involving delicate matters."[7]

Even in what is probably one of the most open governments in the world, secrecy persists. According to the Information Security Oversight Office, which keeps watch over the U.S. government's secrets, 6,408,688 new official secrets were created in 1993.[8] (That works out to 17,558 new secrets a day.) No doubt many more secrets were not even recorded. Until recently, even the rules and criteria for classifying and declassifying secret information were themselves secret.[9] Studies of some of the most serious abuses of power in recent years—Watergate and Iran-Contra—remind us how successful secrecy can be even as they tell the stories of those officials who were finally exposed.[10] Other abuses, such as the dangerous radiation experiments on human subjects conducted during the 1950s, which were not revealed until the 1990s, come to light only many years after they occurred, too late to punish the perpetrators or to do much for most of the victims.[11]

These discrepancies between the ideal of publicity and the practice of secrecy are not necessarily evidence of a failure of moral nerve. The problem is not mainly that politicians lose the courage of their convictions in the face of political pressures. No doubt some do, and institutions of democracy should protect citizens against the temptation of officials to forsake publicity for the sake of expediency. But the deeper problem lies within the realm of political morality itself. It arises from the conflict between two values—publicity and its opposite, secrecy—and also from the conflicts between publicity and other democratic values—in particular, liberty, opportunity and deliberation itself. It is these conflicts that this chapter explores. The aim is to locate the place of a principle of publicity in deliberative democracy—to establish the basis for a presumption in favor of publicity and the authority of claims of secrecy and other values that could rebut the presumption. Publicity has its moral limits, but those limits themselves must be publicly affirmed.

The Principle of Publicity

Utilitarians and Kantians converge not only in defending publicity but also in defending it on the basis of democratic values.[12] Bentham's reasons are all consequentialist, but all the consequences he catalogs refer to the needs of democratic government. Publicity is valuable first and foremost because it is a friend of democratic accountability.[13] It motivates public officials to do their duty. It also encourages citizens to deliberate about public policy and enables officials to learn about and from public opinion. Bentham also adds amusement value to the list of benefits of publicity—the enjoyment citizens receive from watching some public officials make fools of themselves.

To oppose publicity, Bentham argues, one must assume that citizens are less competent than officials and also that officials are more trustworthy than citizens. Both of these are dubious assumptions. Many citizens may be less politically competent than some officials, but it is the competence of politically active citizens that is relevant. These citizens are capable of judging as well as officials, and if they are less informed, it is the fault of the officials who conceal critical information. Bentham exposes the faulty logic of those partisans of secrecy who say to citizens: "You are incapable of judging, because you are ignorant; and you shall remain ignorant, that you may be incapable of judging."[14] In this way, secrecy aggravates a problem partly of its own making.

To deny that officials are more trustworthy than citizens, we do not have to assume that their moral character is worse. The reason why citizens are justified in their distrust is that officials work in circumstances that would tempt one of even average moral character to neglect the public interest. "Whom ought we to distrust," Bentham asks, "if not those to whom is committed great authority, with great temptations to abuse it?"[15] Their duties involve "the affairs of others" which are often complicated and difficult, and in which they naturally take less interest than in their own affairs. Their personal interests often oppose the public interest, and they "possess all the means of serving themselves at the expense of the public, without the possibility of being convicted of it." What can overcome these "dangerous motives"? Only the "respect for public opinion—dread of its judgment—desire of glory?—in one word, everything which results from publicity."[16]

In the spirit of Bentham, modern democracies have found that publicity can be a powerful sanction. Beyond prominent hearings and dramatic exposés of official misconduct, there are many routine procedures that bring decisions and the reasons for them to public light before they are finally made. For example, the practice of requiring agencies and companies to issue environmental impact statements before proceeding with major development projects is often more effective, according to one study, than other methods of enforcement, such as administrative sanctions or economic incentives.[17] Agencies and companies pay closer attention to environmental matters when they know they will have to defend their actions in detail in public. Another less obvious but equally important reason why these statements are effective is the influence of the analysts who prepare them. Hired by the agencies and companies to specialize in this work, the analysts develop their own strict professional standards and tend to become advocates within the agencies and companies for environmental causes. The general practice of requiring officials to justify their decisions by issuing impact statements could have similar effects in many other areas of policy, such as arms control and human rights, where established statutory goals are inadequate to guide or constrain the actions of officials.[18]

This practice has a further advantage. Because it forces officials and citizens to focus on specific risks *and* benefits, it is less likely to discourage desirable risk-taking by public officials than more general and diffuse forms of publicity. As utilitarians themselves are the first to recognize, the threat of publicity can deter officials from taking controversial positions or making bold decisions. One of the strongest arguments for secrecy, as we shall see later in this chapter, appeals to its capacity to counter this effect. The argument does not rebut the presumption in favor of publicity, however; it only qualifies it. Publicity requirements should be carefully tailored to specific circumstances and should be accompanied by other measures to ensure that officials who take desirable risks are rewarded and those who fail to take them are not.

Bentham's argument for publicity is powerful on its own terms, but it is significantly incomplete. He rightly ties publicity to democracy, but wrongly detaches it from morality. On his consequentialist account, publicity has no (nonutilitarian) moral value in itself; its efficacy depends entirely on non-moral motives. Publicity is just a mechanism to make the self-interest of officials coincide with the general interest. On this view officials have no *moral* reason to favor publicity over secrecy (unless they happen to be utilitarians). They may keep secrets if they can get away with it. There are of course consequentialist reasons to seek moral sanctions.

Laws against secrecy are not likely to be sufficient to constrain powerful officials, who "possess all the means of serving themselves at the expense of the public," including the means of evading the law. Even when officials are caught, the damage is often already done. Innocent citizens may already have suffered. But beyond these consequentialist considerations, we need a rationale for publicity that could be accepted by public officials themselves. A deliberative perspective should offer officials some reason— other than their presumed lack of trustworthiness—to accept the publicity principle. Kant provides such a reason.

Kant presents the publicity principle as a test that any policy must pass in order to be just. A policy is unjust if making it public would defeat its purpose. Kant's own examples come mainly from international politics. A large state could not publicly declare that its policy is to conquer small states; if it did, small states could unite in self-defense and overpower the large state. The policy is morally wrong because it can succeed only in secret. The point is not that such a policy would not work. Even if its consequences would be on balance beneficial, the policy would still be wrong because it cannot be disclosed to those who are affected by it. The obligation to justify policies to those whom it affects provides the moral basis of the publicity principle.

Kant's argument holds at least as strongly for domestic politics. Here the policies not only affect but also bind citizens and are enacted on their behalf. Bentham's scheme for faking executions would not be justifiable, even if the bogus victims consented to play their part. The policy enacted in the name of all citizens could not be revealed to all citizens without defeating its purpose. It would therefore lack a necessary means of securing moral legitimacy in a democracy. Public policies, then, must be transparent in this way. They should be justifiable to the citizens who are bound by them. This adds moral content to the utilitarian case for the publicity principle.

Kantians point out that utilitarianism itself may not be able to pass the publicity test. The utilitarian justification for moral rules, such as "do not kill innocent people," must be kept secret. Otherwise, using a utilitarian calculus, public officials might authorize the killing of innocent people even when it was not justified on utilitarian grounds. Because it is so easy to misuse utilitarianism in practice, it is better, many utilitarians themselves argue, to conceal the real (utilitarian) reasons for political decisions. Moral reasoning that must be kept secret is self-effacing. It is also self-defeating, Kantians maintain, and therefore not morally acceptable at all.

Philosophers disagree about whether the self-effacing nature of utilitarianism makes it self-defeating. We do not have to settle this question in order to determine the place of publicity in a deliberative perspective. At least in public, utilitarians can join Kantians in defending the presumption in favor of publicity, and also defending it on *moral* grounds. Utilitarians may secretly believe that the *real* justification is strictly instrumental. (It is moral only in the sense that it promotes utility.) But this belief is of little or no consequence for their politics. In public the sophisticated utilitarian embraces the publicity principle, acting as if publicity had more than merely instrumental value.

In another respect, however, the utilitarian version of the publicity principle is stronger than the Kantian one. Since Kant's principle is merely hypothetical, it does not govern the actual process of making a public policy, but rather governs only the conduct of a thought experiment.[19] The actions and policies of public officials pass the publicity test whenever they would be accepted if they were made public, even if they actually remain secret. Utilitarians can rightly object that this interpretation of publicity is too permissive. Public officials would justify acting in secret whenever they convinced themselves in a private thought experiment that their actions satisfied the publicity test. To be sure, Kantian officials would not be justified in keeping a secret if they were self-serving, careless, or otherwise mistaken in the way they conducted the thought experiment. The thought experiment does come with critical standards, but publicly justifying political actions is not one of them.

From a deliberative perspective, the more fundamental reasons why the test should require actual rather than hypothetical publicity rest on democratic deliberation itself. They express the four values of deliberation presented in Chapter 1. To fulfill the purposes of deliberation in a democracy, it is not enough that the policy could be justified. The political process of justification itself shapes in several ways the nature and validity of the reasons that officials give.

First, only public justifications can secure the consent of citizens, whether it be tacit or explicit. Such justifications help sustain a sense of legitimacy that makes political cooperation possible in the face of continuing moral disagreement. Second, making reasons public contributes to the broadening of moral and political perspectives that deliberation is supposed to encourage. As John Stuart Mill suggested, "The best side of their character is that which people are anxious to show, even to those who are no better than themselves . . . People will give dishonest or mean votes . . .

more readily in secret than in public."[20] Third, reasons must be public to fulfill the potential for mutual respect that deliberation seeks by clarifying the nature of moral disagreement. Finally, the self-correcting character of deliberation—its capacity to encourage citizens and officials to change their minds—would be undermined if reasons for policies could not be openly discussed. In a deliberative democracy, then, the principle of publicity requires that government adopt only those policies for which officials and citizens give public justifications.

Yet this principle is acceptable only as a presumption. Publicity is undoubtedly a democratic good for all the reasons that utilitarians and Kantians suggest. But so is secrecy, also for utilitarian and Kantian reasons.[21] Some policies and practices that all citizens desire cannot succeed without secrecy. Privacy and confidentiality, which rely on secrecy, are essential to basic liberty. Relationships of love, friendship, and trust depend on secrecy. Some secrecy, or at least lack of candor, may be necessary to protect the opportunities of citizens who suffer discrimination. Even deliberation itself is not always enhanced by complete openness. In settings insulated from the glare of publicity, deliberators may be more likely to change their mind in response to compelling arguments. This chapter explores each of these bases for claims of secrecy—necessity, liberty and opportunity, and deliberation. Under what conditions and for what reasons can the presumption of publicity be rebutted by the claims of secrecy?

THE NECESSITY OF SECRECY

Publicity is necessary to justify any policy, but secrecy may also be necessary to effect some policies. This argument for secrecy turns the Kantian test on its head—or at least on its side. On this view a policy is justly secret if making it public would defeat its purpose. The Open Market Committee of the Federal Reserve Board, which is responsible for controlling interest rates in order to maintain a healthy economy, holds its meetings behind closed doors, exempt from the sunshine laws.[22] The committee releases a summary of its deliberations, but not until six weeks after each meeting. The summaries, which do not refer to comments of individual members, have been described as "boilerplate reports on the economy that anyone could copy out of Government and newspaper reports."[23] Federal Reserve Board chairman Alan Greenspan and other members of the committee have argued that greater publicity would make monetary policy "suffer, and the economy along with it."[24] If the views of members of the Open Market Committee were made public, members could be subject to "intense lobbying efforts . . . [which] would undermine decades of effort to insulate the central bank from short-term political pressures."[25]

More generally, this basis for rebutting the publicity presumption is that secrecy is necessary to accomplish the primary purpose of the policy or practice in question. Publicity remains the rule, but some exceptions are justified on grounds of necessity. As Greenspan put it: "The Federal Reserve makes its decisions public immediately, except when doing so could undercut the efficacy of policy, or compromise the integrity of the policy process."[26] This is a kind of justification that utilitarians are likely to offer, since it treats publicity and secrecy as values that can be traded off against each other. But the justification is appealing from other perspectives as well. If the primary aim of the policy is beneficial and would be defeated by publicity, and if the costs of the required secrecy do not exceed the benefits of the policy, why should anyone object to the secrecy?

OBJECTIONS TO NECESSITY

One difficulty with permitting this very broad exception to the publicity principle is that it assumes that a group of officials, without benefit of public review, will consistently choose the most beneficial policy. On subjects as complicated as monetary policy there is bound to be a wide range of acceptable policies, and also a wide range of disastrous ones. Without public review of the process of decision making, citizens cannot know, and the officials themselves cannot be confident, that the officials chose the best of the acceptable policies. That the results of the policy were satisfactory does not mean that another policy might not have worked even better. Independent review and criticism of the reasoning that led to the policy may reveal alternative policies that would produce better results in the future. In the case of disastrous policies, citizens can hold secret bodies such as the Open Market Committee accountable for the results, but again they cannot suggest improvements in the process of decision making that led to those results.

Another difficulty becomes clear when we ask why publicity would defeat the primary purpose of the process or policy that officials wish to keep secret. If the reason is that many citizens would object and try to block the policy, this justification for secrecy is democratically suspect. The Iran-Contra affair is replete with decisions and policies which, if they had become public, would have been opposed and probably overturned. President Reagan approved a plan to send arms to Israel, which would ship them to Iran.[27] Iranian officials had indicated that in response to gestures of this kind they might release some of the American hostages they were holding. Reagan evidently persuaded himself that this policy did not constitute trading arms for hostages. But if the policy had become public, most people in the United States and abroad probably would have interpreted it as doing just that, and the ability of the United States to secure the release of other hostages, or to prevent the taking of hostages in the future, would have been undermined. One part of the conclusion is probably right: the secrecy was necessary to protect the policy. But the reason why publicity would have frustrated the policy reveals a fundamental moral flaw in the policy itself. The publicity would have clearly exposed that the policy involved trading arms for hostages, an action the president had said that he, along with most Americans, opposed.

Yet another difficulty with the argument from necessity is that it neglects the contribution of publicity to the desirability of the policy itself. Or to put it another way: the costs of secrecy are not, as the argument tends to assume, independent of the benefits of the policy. Even if officials choose the best possible policy, citizens lose the chance to participate in that choice, even vicariously. Secrecy of the kind practiced by the Open Market Committee deprives citizens of opportunities to understand the reasoning that led to the policy, and to decide on their own the merits of the policy. The secrecy also prevents citizens from judging the decision-making abilities of individual officials and therefore their competence for future public service. To the extent that the process is secret, the policy and the policymakers remain disconnected from a broader democratic public.

NECESSARY EXCEPTIONS

Despite the problems with the argument from necessity, some policies are necessary, and some secrecy may be necessary for their success. Can we narrow the range of exceptions so as to allow some secrecy while as far as possible avoiding its problems? Some of the costs of secrecy cannot be avoided if we wish to adopt certain policies. Citizens cannot know in advance where police have decided to deploy unmarked cars, and how to identify them. Here not only some secrecy but even some deception seems justified. But notice that it is the details of the policy, not the policy itself, that is secret. Equally important, the fact that the details of the policy are secret is not itself secret. Citizens have a chance both to decide in advance whether the policy is justified and to review the details of the policy after it is implemented. The secrecy is justified not only because it is necessary for the policy, but also because the question of whether and in what form it is necessary is itself the subject of public deliberation. This element of public accountability for the secrecy itself is what is missing from the argument from necessity.[28] Greenspan (belatedly) honored this requirement by appearing before the House Banking Committee, giving reasons for the secret practices of the Federal Reserve Board, responding to questions that challenged those reasons, and agreeing to abide by the outcome of these and other public deliberations.

Public accountability enables citizens and their representatives not only to discuss the reasons for the secrecy but also to find ways to limit its scope. Even when some secrecy is necessary, officials tend to insist on more than they need. But when challenged in a public forum, they may find that they can do just as well with less. Under questioning by the House Banking Committee, several Federal Reserve Board members conceded that the details of the committe's deliberations did not have to be kept secret indefinitely. The practice had been to transcribe the discussions at the meetings but to keep the transcripts secret in perpetuity. So secret were the transcripts that until Greenspan was called to testify before the Banking Committee, some members of the Open Market Committee did not know of their existence. Challenged by the Banking Committee, board members could not justify the permanent secrecy. Nor could they defend continuing this practice in preference to the alternative that the congressional committee proposed: releasing the transcripts after five years.

In the original version of the Freedom of Information Act, Congress included a general exemption for confidential information of a financial nature.[29] Similarly, in designing provisions of the Sunshine Act, Congress exempted meetings that would prompt speculation in financial markets. But these and other similar exceptions to the publicity principle are not set once and for all. For example, Congress retains the authority to reassess the Federal Reserve Board's claims to secrecy. Its committees, and through them the general public, can continually assess how well the Federal Reserve Board's secretive practices serve its public purposes. Thus, if exceptions to the publicity principle are fully discussed, approved in advance, and regularly reviewed, they are more likely to be acceptable from a deliberative perspective. We may think of them as only first-order exceptions to publicity, since they are justified by second-order rules that are consistent with the publicity principle.

This way of reconciling secrecy and publicity works best for ongoing practices and policies. It is less suitable for one-time exceptions, decisions that respond to crises, or unforeseen problems. When Joycelyn Elders, former U.S. surgeon-general, was the director of the Arkansas Health Department, she learned that four batches of the condoms the department had distributed to health clinics and schools had a higher-than-acceptable failure rate.[30] Her staff told her that the increased risk would affect relatively few users (95 percent of the condoms in the worst batch were still effective). She ordered the condoms recalled, but some had already been distributed by the clinics. She did not tell the public. She said later: "We felt making an announcement would be creating a major scare that would make everyone afraid to use condoms." If the risk was judged to be low (and an independent authority confirmed that judgment), her decision to keep the recall secret could be justified at least for a short period of time. But once the department had determined that the condoms then available in the clinics and schools were safe, a public announcement about the recall would not have left fearful users without recourse. Because of the announcement, some might have decided to discard their condoms without replacing them. But the greater risk was that if the recall were discovered later (as in fact it was), the coverup would cause citizens to distrust even more state programs of this kind, and lead to even less use of condoms. In any case, as Bentham would remind us, the balancing of these risks is too delicate to be left solely to those whose political reputations could weigh in the calculation.

Preventing publicity from defeating policies is thus a more limited justification for secrecy than it at first seems. Even in those relatively rare cases in which it is valid, citizens are right to insist that the secret-keepers give an account of the reasons for the secrets, and respond to demands to limit their scope. If first-order secrecy is sometimes necessary, second-order publicity should not be far behind. Publicity about secrecy, appropriately arranged, is the only form in which a deliberative perspective can accept the necessity of secrets.

Secrecy in the Service of Liberty and Opportunity

The claims of secrecy go beyond the need to prevent desirable policies from self-destructing. Secrecy may be justified to protect the constitutional values of basic liberty and opportunity. Publicity can threaten these values both by frustrating some policy or practice that supports them and by violating them directly. Unrestrained publicity can violate the personal integrity, and therefore the basic liberty, of officials as well as citizens, and can also obstruct their basic opportunities.[31] How can deliberative democracy protect these values while preserving a presumption in favor of publicity?

The boundaries of publicity cannot be completely specified in advance, but some simple distinctions may help map its legitimate territory. First, we should distinguish between general and particular secrets. General secrets deal with policies that refer to indeterminate groups and categories of individuals, whereas particular secrets primarily contain information about specific and identifiable individuals. The former make weaker claims against publicity than the latter.

GENERAL SECRETS

Some policymakers invoke the value of personal integrity to argue that entire subjects or methods of decision making should not be made public.[32] A case in point is the policy on public financing for the treatment of kidney disease. The discussions were carried out mainly within the inner circles of the medical community. The final decision to fund all renal dialysis was, in fact, made with little deliberation at all.[33] Both opponents and proponents were reluctant to have this issue openly discussed because it involved calculating the costs and benefits of saving lives. Some political scientists defend secrecy in cases of this kind. One suggests this scenario: "Imagine the perfectly rational congressman trying to justify the legislature's decision to limit expenditures for medical care: 'Mrs. Jones, I share your grief about the plight of your husband, but we simply cannot afford to spend $30,000 per year to keep him alive when people are dying elsewhere who could be saved for much less.' " Such candor, this political scientist concludes, "threatens the life-preserving norm that decent societies should respect."[34]

Notice that this is a utilitarian claim in favor of secrecy that runs counter to Bentham's argument (as well as to Kant's). The claim assumes a gap in political understanding between citizens and legislators. But such an assumption is implausible and undesirable. It is implausible because there is no evidence that legislators are any better able than ordinary citizens to decide rationally how much a life is worth. And assuming such a gap is undesirable because not letting citizens hold policymakers accountable for decisions that critically affect their lives is not a means of respecting personal integrity, but is itself an affront to it. We may disagree about whether citizens should consent to let legislators or bureaucrats put a price on their lives. That is a disagreement we should have in a public forum, and then hold officials accountable to the provisional resolution we reach. But the argument for secrecy here does not leave any opening for accountability at all, and so cannot even get off the democratic ground.

On some policies the problem is not a dispute about a gap between citizens and officials but the result of divisions among citizens themselves. When there is deep disagreement on moral issues, publicity may make agreement on the right policy more difficult to achieve. Some commentators argue that making moral disagreement public is part of the cause of our difficulties in reaching a satisfactory policy on abortion in this country. They claim that before the reform movements in the 1960s, abortion, though outlawed, was available at the discretion of individual doctors. Because the "fundamental ideological differences . . . were hidden from the public (to be weighed in individual cases by individual doctors), this kind of compromise worked reasonably well for many years."[35] But once the issue rose to prominence, courts, legislatures and political parties had to take explicit positions on the question, and opposition to women's rights grew. The government stopped funding abortions for government employees and members of the military and their dependents. Some states passed laws that restricted the opportunities for abortion. Opponents firebombed abortion clinics. The basic liberties of women, so it is argued, were better protected before the issue gained such public attention. The "lesson to be learned from this case," one political theorist concludes, is that "it is morally better to leave certain things unstated."[36]

There are at least two difficulties with this kind of argument. First, when disagreement is as deep and extensive as it is on the abortion issue, implicit compromises are not likely to be sustained indefinitely.[37] The reform movement was not the only source of pressure to make abortion a major public issue. The growing federal role in medical care and child support, the increasing strength of religious groups in politics, and the changing role of women in the work force, among other factors, were bound to put abortion, along with a wide range of reproductive issues, high on the public agenda. Neither does it appear to be true that the basic liberties of women were better protected before abortion gained in public attention. There is now evidence that the highly public litigation strategy pursued by the pro-choice movement before *Roe v. Wade* may have been the most effective way to secure access to abortion for women.[38]

The other difficulty is that the argument assumes that the morally correct position is that abortion should be legal. The assumption is necessary to the claim that "the morally superior outcome was arguably better served by leaving certain things unsaid."[39] But it is precisely this assumption that is at issue in the moral disagreement. To argue against the publicity principle on these grounds is to beg the question that the principle is intended to address. It would decide in advance a question that the publicity principle rightly maintains should be decided only after public deliberation. If citizens had already resolved the moral disagreement, they would of course have less need to subject it to public discussion. But in the absence of a reciprocal resolution, democratic deliberation continues, and properly under the direction of the principle of publicity.

Some citizens, and some political scientists, look nostalgically back to the nineteenth-century Congress, whose leaders "put a lid" on divisive questions, especially those concerning race and religion.[40] They praise the Rules Committee in the House of Representatives for keeping questions such as public aid to Catholic schools off the agenda in the 1960s, and wish the same could be done for abortion funding now. No doubt there are some issues that at certain times simply should not be discussed, if it is really the case, and can be known to be the case, that public discussion would be more harmful to basic liberty and opportunity. Yet preventing public discussions of these issues, however politically divisive, may also prevent our having good grounds for knowing and agreeing that public discussion would make matters worse.

Democratic leaders in Congress tried to keep race off the political agenda for many years, thinking it best that the subject not be discussed, at least not publicly. This silence probably slowed down progress toward racial justice. Sexual harassment and homosexual rights also were subjects about which politicians did not talk publicly until relatively recently, and many still think they are too divisive for democratic deliberation. But it is doubtful that we could make political progress on any of these questions without open public deliberations. Covertly racist messages, for example, are frequently communicated in American politics. Open public deliberation about race does not guarantee moral progress; but unless citizens explicitly confront the covert racism in many political messages, such progress comes only inadvertently.[41] Moreover, some experimental evidence suggests that covert racist messages are significantly more effective in promoting racist attitudes in politics than overt racist messages, to which citizens can consciously and critically respond.[42]

Even if there is rarely adequate justification for excluding whole subjects from discussion, might there be particular occasions on which a subject such as sexual harassment or race should not be publicly discussed? Some argue that the Senate hearings on Anita Hill's charges of sexual harassment against Clarence Thomas reinforced racist attitudes in this country, and that this effect could have been foreseen. If as a society we are not capable of responsibly deliberating about some subjects, this argument goes, then we should not try. At least we should wait until we can handle sensitive and divisive subjects more maturely.

The trouble with this argument—even if its questionable claim about the effects of the hearings is true—is that the argument may be self-fulfilling. If citizens do not try to deliberate about issues such as sexual harassment, homosexual rights, or racial justice, they may never learn how to do so responsibly. Sexist, homophobic, and racist messages will not thereby disappear from American politics; they will retreat between the lines. We can and should carefully consider how to design the forums for discussing such issues. We may legitimately decide that the need to protect basic liberty and opportunity requires some degree of secrecy in these forums, or at least some limits on the scope of the discussion. But the case for keeping quiet about disagreement on general policies can rarely be sustained, politically or morally.

PARTICULAR SECRETS

Particular secrets about individuals have a stronger claim. As Bentham insists, publicity should not "unnecessarily injure innocent persons."[43] The medical records of individuals, for example, should generally not be subject to public scrutiny, even if the medical care that citizens receive is paid for by the government. Dianna Brown, the Arizona woman who sought a liver transplant, should not have to reveal the details of her personal life in order to make a successful claim. Publicity about such intimate matters may rightly be regarded as an assault on one's personal integrity. Furthermore, information that is less closely tied to personal integrity may still injure individuals through its effects on their basic opportunities. The test scores of individual women and blacks who won promotions at AT&T in the case we consider in Chapter 9 should not be publicized if the effect is to reinforce prejudices against them and impede their efforts to succeed in their new jobs. In both of these cases, the public interest in the issue could be satisfied by releasing information in a general form, as in statistical analyses or anonymous case studies.

Public officials may reasonably ask that their claims of basic liberty and opportunity be respected, too. Failing to honor the legitimate claims of public officials is likely to discourage many highly qualified citizens from serving in public office. Indeed, it may discourage just the sort of person who, once in office, would be most sensitive to the rights of privacy of ordinary citizens. In this way the privacy of officials supports the privacy of citizens. But public officials make legitimate claims of their own as well. Their personal integrity, perhaps even more than that of ordinary citizens, depends on their keeping some secrets. Public officials also value relationships of love, friendship, and trust, which would be impossible to maintain were they denied the right to keep secrets. Respect for the dignity of those who have lost their lives in public service places some other limits on what the public should demand to know. For example, citizens do not necessarily have a right to hear the audio tape of the conversation of the crew during the last minutes of the space shuttle *Challenger* disaster.

Secrecy also supports the basic opportunity of officials to be given fair and equal consideration in competing for public office. If politically irrelevant information or misinformation about officials is publicized, they are far less likely to be judged on the basis of their qualifications for office. Yet, unlike other citizens, public officials voluntarily assume a public role, and therefore much more of what would otherwise be their private life becomes a matter for legitimate public interest. The general principle should be that only information relevant to the performance of one's office should be publicized. This relevance standard can be made more particular only by considering specific examples in context. A brief examination of a few examples reveals that the ordinary distinction between public and private life does not necessarily coincide with the morally appropriate distinction between information that is relevant to performance in office and that which is irrelevant.[44]

Some of the most complex cases for the publicity principle involve information that we commonly take to be part of a person's private life for reasons that aim to protect the personal integrity of individuals. What otherwise might be a publicly irrelevant part of a politician's private life becomes relevant when the politician uses the information to gain political advantage.[45] A politician who, like Gary Hart, uses his private life as a campaign ploy, claiming that he is a faithful family man and inviting the press to follow him, thus invites public scrutiny of what would otherwise be protected. And when otherwise intimate information is invoked to try to influence our political judgment, we as citizens have a right to find out more about it.

Partly for this reason Senator Bob Packwood was not justified in resisting the Senate Ethics Committee subpoena of his diary in 1993 during its investigation of sexual harassment charges against him.[46] He himself had first introduced the diary as evidence, and used it selectively in his own defense. The diary, moreover, had been typed by a secretary who had been paid with either government or campaign funds. Absent these factors, Packwood's case for privacy would have been stronger. Even when the Ethics Committee is investigating serious charges of clear relevance to a member's conduct in office (as in this case), it is still obliged to respect the privacy of members, including genuinely private papers such as diaries. (That the committee probably has a legal right to subpoena *any* relevant documents does not mean that it was morally right to do so.)

Sometimes the ordinary distinction between public and private life coincides with the distinction between relevant and irrelevant information. President Reagan's withholding of information about the Iran-Contra deal was relevant to assessing his performance in office and should have been open to public scrutiny. By contrast, rumors about the sexual orientation of Reagan's son were not relevant, and whether true or not should not have been publicized without his son's consent. To the extent that Reagan made family values a campaign issue, however, he strengthened the case for publicizing what would otherwise be a protected part of his intimate life. Information about strained relations with his daughter, for example, became relevant to the extent that he publicly claimed that the government has a legitimate interest in influencing and assessing family values.

The boundaries between public and private activities are not as sharp for officials as they should be for ordinary citizens. Some kinds of otherwise private immorality may indirectly affect an official's capacity to do a job. When an attorney general belongs to a private club that discriminates against blacks and women, when the president's "drug czar" is addicted to cigarettes, when the enforcement chief of the Securities and Exchange Commission is accused of wife-beating, the public rightly takes notice. The officials in these cases recognized, or were forced to recognize, that their private conduct had too close a relation to their public role to remain private: Griffin Bell quit his club, William Bennett evidently stopped smoking, and John Fedders resigned from the SEC.

CONFLICTING CLAIMS OF SECRECY

The boundaries of publicity become more difficult to determine when the privacy of more than one individual is at stake, and public consequences of great moment are involved. A dramatic illustration of the difficulties can be found in the dilemmas faced by some of the leading participants in the process of confirmation of Judge Clarence Thomas for the U.S. Supreme Court. Although the issue of sexual harassment has generally received the most attention, this case also raises important issues of privacy that bear on the principle of publicity.

While the Senate Judiciary Committee was holding nationally televised hearings on Thomas's nomination in early September 1991, behind the scene members of the committee's staff were receiving some highly damaging information about him. Anita Hill, a law professor at the University of Oklahoma, told staff members, in confidence, that Thomas had treated her in ways that could be regarded as sexual harassment while she was working for him from 1981 to 1983 at the Department of Education and the Equal Employment Opportunity Commission.[47] Hill said that Thomas frequently asked her out, and though she refused, he continued to talk to her in vivid detail about sex. Thomas would typically "turn the conversation to discussion about his sexual interests," often describing films he had seen depicting group sex and women having sex with animals.[48]

Although the events that followed these allegations were extraordinary, the kind of clash they created between the values of secrecy and publicity is common in political life. Both Hill and Thomas had plausible claims of secrecy. Hill initially had made her statements on the condition that they be treated as confidential. Thomas believed that a public hearing on the allegations (which he denied) would be a humiliating and degrading intrusion into his private life even if he could prove that the allegations were false.

Was the Senate committee justified in making Hill's charges public? Thomas's claim was certainly understandable. The allegations struck at the core of his personal integrity: simply publicizing them would cause him irreparable harm. But they were also relevant to one of the most important questions that Congress decides: who is qualified to sit on the Supreme Court. Thomas did not have a right to this job. Nor was this a criminal trial, contrary to what some comments of the chairman of the committee implied. Thomas's basic liberty and opportunity could be adequately protected if he were given a fair chance to defend himself in the proper forum.

Also on the side of secrecy was Hill's claim that her basic liberty as a citizen would be violated if her request for confidentiality were not honored. She had come forward only reluctantly, out of a sense of duty to provide the information so the committee could investigate. If the chief counsel of the Judiciary Committee reasonably understood Hill to be insisting on a degree of confidentiality that included not revealing her identity to the nominee, then the Judiciary Committee had a strong reason to keep her allegations secret.[49] But respecting her request confronted the committee with a dilemma. The committee could ignore the charges, in which case they would fail in their constitutional duty to examine Thomas's qualifications thoroughly. Or they could consider the charges without telling Thomas, in which case they would violate Thomas's right to confront his accusers—a basic liberty. The committee could escape this dilemma only by persuading Hill to accept a lesser degree of confidentiality than she had initially requested.

The claims of publicity would not have required a full public hearing. Closed-door hearings, for example, might have been acceptable to Hill, fairer to Thomas, and consistent with the committee's constitutional responsibilities. As in the case of the Open Market Committee of the Federal Reserve Board, the hearings could have been confidential, with full records to be released at a specified future date. This kind of deliberative forum seems in principle the optimal way to balance the various claims in this case. But in practice it is often not a stable solution. In this instance too many people already knew too much about the case, and too many stood to lose or gain too much by its outcome: the committee could not reasonably expect that the hearings would be kept secret. The option of closed-door hearings was therefore never seriously considered. After a reporter telephoned Hill and read her parts of her own supposedly confidential statement, Hill spoke with the reporter and held a press conference. The committee then proceeded to bring her allegations to the attention of one of the largest national audiences in the history of congressional hearings.[50]

The decision to enter the public forum does not remove all limits on the publicity principle. The committee rightly refused to pursue some lines of investigation that risked even greater exposure of the personal lives of the witnesses. They did not permit Thomas's supporters to introduce testimony about Hill's past relationships with men. They did not seek some evidence that would have involved even greater intrusions into his personal life (for example, records of videos that Thomas rented for his personal use). Arguably, some of this information would have been relevant to the committee's deliberations, at least to assessing the credibility of witnesses. But having respected publicity by opening the hearings, the committee could now incline toward respecting basic liberty by limiting their scope.[51] The public hearings let citizens judge for themselves whether the inquiry into the allegations had been extensive enough. The very openness of the hearings reduced the need to broaden the inquiry. Ironically, if the committee had held closed hearings, it would have been less justified in narrowing the inquiry.

Thus, the value of secrecy—its role in protecting basic liberty and opportunity—does not override the publicity principle. It only limits its scope in certain circumstances and for certain reasons. Within these limits secrecy is no less important than the publicity it constrains. The limits are justified by the same values that support publicity—the values that constitute deliberative democracy. The justification of deliberative democracy (as we suggested in Chapter 1 and argue further in later chapters) requires respect for the basic liberty and opportunity of all citizens. Consistent with the demands of democratic deliberation, public officials may keep most secrets about those aspects of their lives that are not relevant to their duties of office. Public officials themselves must respect an even greater realm of privacy in the lives of ordinary citizens. These limits to publicity are consistent with the democratic ideal that informs it. The principle of publicity is in this way self-limiting without being self-effacing.

Secrecy in the Service of Deliberation

One of the strongest moral bases for the publicity principle in government is that it promotes democratic deliberation. Specifically, it encourages officials to give reasons for their decisions and policies and to respond to challenges to those reasons from citizens. It is therefore not surprising that one of the strongest challenges to the principle comes from the claim that secrecy itself sometimes better supports deliberation than does publicity. We call secrets that do so deliberative secrets.

Commenting on the procedures of the Constitutional Convention, James Madison made just such an argument for secrecy: "No Constitution would ever have been adopted by the Convention if the debates had been public."[52] The members presumably agreed with Madison, and so did many citizens. But Thomas Jefferson, who had followed the proceedings from France, where he was serving as the American ambassador, strongly objected to the secrecy: "I am sorry that they began their deliberations by so abominable a precedent as that of tying up the tongues of their members. Nothing can justify this example but . . . ignorance of the value of public discussion."[53]

Despite their disagreement, both Madison and Jefferson appeal to the values of deliberation. Madison points to the outcome (the Constitution), but he is also assuming that the process that produced it was better because it was secret. Members could speak candidly, change their positions, and accept compromises without constantly worrying about what the public and the press might say. Jefferson may have agreed that the secrecy improved the quality of the deliberations (though he does not say so), but he gave more weight to the value of exposing the deliberations, whatever their quality, to the wider public.

Even though the publicity principle seems more attuned to Jefferson's view, it does not endorse his claim that "*nothing* can justify this example [of secrecy] but ignorance of the value of public discussion." What could, and to some extent did, justify the secrecy was the ratification of the Constitution, a form of retrospective accountability for the process as well as for its results. Prospective accountability would have been better, letting citizens approve the secret proceedings when they authorized the convention in the first place. But the legal status of the convention was already in doubt, and under the circumstances approval after the fact may have been the only course available.

In ongoing governments, however, such exceptions to the publicity principle should require prospective as well as retrospective accountability. If deliberative secrets meet those tests, they can make valuable contributions to policy-making. They encourage deliberation in which officials may take more risks at the earlier stages of the formulation of policy, and therefore reduce the chance that a well-grounded policy that could later survive public scrutiny will be rejected because it is now unpopular.

For many years the House of Representatives followed the practice of keeping the names of the members who signed a discharge petition secret until a majority had signed. The petition is the chief means by which a majority can bring to the floor for action a bill that would otherwise remain in committee. Spurred by radio talk shows, a remarkable grassroots campaign in 1993 drew attention to this previously little known procedure, and forced the House to agree to disclose the signatories in the future. Much of the debate turned on the question whether the secrecy promoted democratic deliberation. Those who favored the change, seeming to declare their allegiance to the publicity principle, argued that disclosure would serve deliberation. As one advocate of the change wrote: "Those barons who bother to argue in defense of keeping the names on discharge petitions secret say this: Publicity would mean 'plebiscitary' government and the end of the House as a 'deliberative' body. But the secrecy is really part of a scheme to *prevent* deliberation about important measures."[54]

But the defenders of the traditional practice could argue that it was deliberative secrecy, a justifiable way of encouraging better discussion and fuller consideration of legislation. Publicity increases political pressure on legislators to bring a popular bill to a vote before it has received thorough discussion in committee. In cases of unpopular but desirable bills, it discourages members from signing the petition. A member runs the risk of going on record in favor of a bill that will never gain the support of enough members even to come to a vote. Secrecy also serves another deliberative purpose: legislators remain freer to change their minds about a bill in response to ongoing discussions. As one of the defenders of secrecy wrote, "The House may become more responsive [to direct public pressure], but only at the cost of its *deliberativeness*. The detailed scrutiny by committees, which has been the House's pride and joy, will more often be omitted in the rush to bring issues to a vote."[55]

In this case the defenders of the traditional practice seem to have the better of the argument. The deliberative costs of publicizing the names are clear, while it is hard to identify any specific benefits at all. Furthermore, most of the costs of the secrecy are temporary, since the signatories are disclosed as soon as the petition achieves a majority. Since the ongoing practice containing this element of secrecy evidently can withstand public scrutiny, then it appears to be acceptable.

In many other cases the secrecy cannot be justified. Consider the deliberations of the Clinton administration's Task Force on National Health Care Reform, which brought some five-hundred experts together in four months of meetings in 1993 to design a comprehensive plan to guarantee health care. For more than two months the meetings were closed, and even the identities of the experts were kept secret. After a federal district court ordered the names disclosed and part of the meetings opened, a public hearing was held, but the administration continued to resist releasing many records of the proceedings.[56]

Although some administration officials tried to justify the secrecy on grounds similar to those cited in favor of the discharge petition practice, the claim is weaker here. There are several important differences between the cases. The period during which the secrecy of the discharge signatories was maintained was short, and was followed by open debate on the specific matter at issue. The secrecy of the task force, by contrast, lasted several months (and for some records even longer), insulating the plan from public debate during the critical phase of development and conveying the impression that it would be closer to a final presidential proposal than to a preliminary one.

Not only did the task force block public deliberation on the merits of its views on health care reform, but it also never asked citizens or their representatives to consider whether the secrecy was necessary to serve a deliberative purpose. The absence of either prospective or retrospective accountability makes the secrecy all the more suspect on democratic grounds. Even at the time, critics pointed out that public support for the administration's plan would ultimately be harder to achieve if the policymakers did not show that they were responding to criticisms and taking into account diverse interests in the process of formulating the plan.[57] In the end, the plan failed—no doubt for many reasons. But it is difficult to argue that the secrecy served the plan well. Even if secrecy improves the quality of a deliberation, it may reduce the chances that a well-reasoned proposal will ever become law.[58]

It is less important to adjudicate the arguments about whether secrecy is justified in either of these particular cases than to identify the terms under which disputes like these should be conducted. A secret or a set of secrets is not justified merely if it promotes deliberation on the merits of a public policy; citizens and their accountable representatives must also be able to deliberate about whether it does so. A fully justified secret is in this way doubly deliberative.

Some secrets by their nature never reach this second order of deliberation. They are therefore almost never justified, whatever their potential contribution might be to first-order deliberation. They block accountability from the start. Two kinds of secrets are especially damaging—what may be called deceptive secrets and deep secrets.

DECEPTIVE SECRETS

An official who conceals information with the intention of causing citizens to believe something the official knows is false creates a deceptive secret. The rare occasions on which such secrets are justified usually involve practices directed against criminals or enemies in wartime. But that the immediate target of the deception is someone who does not have a right to the information is not a sufficient justification because other citizens too will be deceived. An operation by the Drug Enforcement Administration illustrates the difficulty.

The DEA acknowledged in 1988 that it had pursued a policy of allowing local police officials to claim that they had seized illegal drug shipments, even though the shipments were brought into the country by DEA's own undercover agents. The practice was designed to protect the identity of the agents, who were acting as middlemen for South American drug traffickers, and allow the investigations to continue, but to stop the drugs from reaching distributors in the United States. News executives protested that this policy created what we call deceptive secrets, which misled the public about the number and nature of drug arrests. DEA officials argued that the practice was carefully limited, that it served an important goal that Congress had approved, and that all the details of the seizures would eventually come out in court proceedings. Assuming that there were no less deceptive means available to achieve the same purpose, the DEA's argument goes a considerable way toward justifying the policy. But the absence of any prospective accountability for the method (as distinct from the goal) of the policy is troubling. Some form of prior approval, at least confidential consultation with a congressional commmittee, should have been sought.

Most deceptive secrets serve less worthy goals. They are typically the cover that officials create to hide particular actions that would be criticized or reversed were they to be disclosed. Officials sometimes use deceptive secrets to cover up mistakes that would make them look bad, but—more insidiously—officials also use them to protect questionable policies that they believe are right. CIA Director Richard Helms was asked by a congressional committee in 1973 whether the agency had tried "to overthrow the government in Chile" and whether it had had "any money passed to the opponents of Allende," the Chilean president. To both questions Helms answered, "No, sir." His answers were literally correct but misleading. In offering only a simple negative, Helms encouraged the committee to infer, as did Senator Stuart Symington, without correction by Helms, that "the stories [that the CIA was] involved in the war are wrong."[59] The CIA had in fact been actively involved in trying to defeat President Allende, but Helms believed that his oath as a CIA official bound him to keep this involvement secret.

In the Iran-Contra affair of the mid-1980s, many officials kept their actions and their policy secret by giving misleading answers to Congress. Lieutenant Colonel Oliver North, the national security aide who ran much of the operation, admitted later that he had deliberately misled Congress. When asked, "But these operations were designed to be secrets from the American people?" he responded: "I'm at a loss as to how we could announce it to the American people and not have the Soviets know about it." Admiral John Poindexter, the national security adviser, withheld information not only from Congress but also from President Reagan. "I decided to insulate the President from the decision [to divert funds from Iran to aid the Contras] and give him some deniability," he later testified, "and so I decided . . . at that point not to tell the President."[60]

The justifications that these officials offered are forms of the argument from necessity, and they all fail. The secrecy was designed to prevent citizens and their representatives from challenging the premise of the argument—the assumption that the policy itself was justifiable. It is important to take note of the justifications here not because they fail in principle but because they illustrate a kind of secrecy that is likely to succeed in practice. This kind of high-minded deception is so insidious precisely because it is more apt to be effective than the blatantly self-interested kind. Acting on principle for what they believe to be higher causes, perpetrators are better able to enlist the help of others in their plans. North probably would not have been able to mobilize so much support for his projects had he been acting mainly for personal gain. What is remarkable is how long his elaborate schemes were kept secret. Iran-Contra did not become public until it became clear that its policies were foundering. Furthermore, prosecuting and therefore deterring this kind of secrecy is difficult. After Richard Helms pleaded "no contest" to a criminal charge of misleading Congress he was merely fined $2,000 and given a suspended sentence; he wore his conviction like "a badge of honor."[61] Although many participants in Iran-Contra were indicted, few were convicted, and most of those were pardoned.

The sympathy that high-minded secret-keepers sometimes arouse should not blind us to the fact that their secret-keeping does grave damage to deliberative democracy. Perhaps they are not such contemptible characters as those who deceive for personal gain, but their actions may be even more dangerous for democracy. In recent years the criminal law has been used more often than in the past against officials who have deployed deceptive secrecy.[62] Some commentators criticize this trend, arguing that it relies on overly broad standards that are inconsistent with the rule of law, and that it has turned what should be treated as political differences into criminal offenses.[63] But if the standards are clarified, the criminal law could be an appropriate instrument to protect democratic deliberation. Along with other protections, it may be required to support deliberation. Punishing the makers and keepers of deceptive secrets should not be seen as criminalizing political differences. Quite the contrary. It is a means—perhaps a necessary means—of ensuring that serious political differences are debated in open political processes.

Why not just let the voters discipline the secret-keepers by removing them (or their elected superiors) from office? After all, it is not always clear in advance what should count as a deceptive secret, and determining whether it is justified is a matter of political judgment. Who is better placed to make such judgments than the voters themselves? No doubt the electorate has an important role in making these judgments, but the electoral process itself is vulnerable to deceptive secrets. Unless citizens have some assurance that candidates are not using secrecy to mislead them, citizens cannot effectively hold officials accountable. Citizens can of course vote against officials who have deceived them—if they find out. But why should they believe that the opponents of deceptive politicians will be any less deceptive once in office? Citizens can have reliable grounds for this belief only if there are institutional protections against deception that go beyond the electoral process. In any case, the responsibility of elected officials itself goes beyond standing for election, and beyond just giving an account to their electoral constituents. As we discuss in Chapter 4, representatives have obligations to citizens in other districts and other states, as well as to their colleagues and to the institution as a whole.

A more radical challenge to the effort to promote publicity comes from those critics who brand it as naive. Secrecy is inevitable, they say, and the attempt to eliminate it just makes matters worse. The criticism may be given a moralist twist by arguing that measures to increase publicity bring about *less* honesty in government. Since the power of legal and political sanctions to regulate deception and secrecy is limited, we can expect some officials to continue to engage in these practices. Officials who refuse to use deceptive secrets would then be at a serious disadvantage in political and bureaucratic competition. Few will deny themselves these techniques, and those who do will be likely to lose out in the competition. As a result, government will come to be ever more populated with officials who have few scruples about creating and keeping deceptive secrets.

The logic of this argument is tempting but treacherous. It is tempting because the obligations of politicians, like those of ordinary citizens, sometimes depend on what other people are willing to do in return. If a good politician's competitors are unwilling to act honestly, the critic asks, then why should he be obligated to do so? Indeed, according to this logic, he should be obligated to act deceptively so as to bring about the best outcome for the electorate. The logic is treacherous because it leads to the conclusion that the more deception exists in politics, the more *morally* desirable it becomes. Specifically, the more that bad politicians deceive citizens, the more desirable it is that good politicians should do so. If good politicians decline to do so, we will be governed by worse politicians, those who have no reluctance to use immoral means. The best therefore should become like the worst. They must be willing to get their hands dirty, keeping secrets and deceiving citizens in order to prevent less moral politicians from winning. The argument recalls Machiavelli's admonition that politicians should "learn how not to be good"—to serve not mainly their own but the public interest.[64]

The argument justifies far less deception than most modern-day Machiavellians assume.[65] It is not enough for politicians to justify their deception by claiming that their competitors are acting deceptively. The upshot of this logic undermines democracy, and fails to reciprocate the trust that citizens place in public officials by virtue of granting them the substantial power of representation. The argument defending competitive deception among politicians therefore cannot be justified on moral grounds. Nor can politicians credibly claim that they have no acceptable alternative but to respond in kind to their competitors' deceptive practices. Politicians often have the knowledge and power to expose the deception of their competitors, and therefore have even less excuse to jump on the bandwagon of unjustified deception.

The partial truth of this Machiavellian argument is better captured by the principles of a deliberative perspective. Deceptive secrets in ongoing democratic practices can be justified only if they can be shown to be necessary to safeguard the democratic values of basic liberty, opportunity, and deliberation, and only if this showing can meet the test of accountability. By these criteria, which are the same ones that license secrecy in general, few deceptive secrets will ever be justified.

DEEP SECRETS

A second form of concealment that also damages the deliberative process is what has been called a deep secret.[66] This is a secret the very existence of which is hidden from citizens. In contrast, a secret is shallow when citizens know that a piece of information is secret but do not know what the information is. Citizens at least have the opportunity to challenge the keepers of shallow secrets, and ultimately to decide whether the secret should be kept. With a deep secret, they are entirely at the mercy of the secret-keepers. Some of the radiation experiments that the government conducted on human subjects during the 1940s and 1950s were deep secrets, at least as far as most citizens and their representatives were concerned. The most successful deep secrets are so deep that they do not cause citizens, and sometimes even other public officials, to suspect anything in particular. Rather, they often cause a more general belief that there is nothing to worry about, that there is no reason to raise questions about a policy or even a whole range of policies.

Deep secrets can be deceptive when their purpose is to mislead in specific ways (for example, by causing citizens to believe falsely that the CIA is not conducting covert operations in a certain country). In recommending confirmation of President Clinton's nominee for secretary of the navy in 1993, the Senate Armed Services Committee praised the nominee for his "extensive business and managerial experience." The committee knew but never reported that "the nominee's longest managerial tenure had been as the head of a Texas savings and loan . . . that failed at a cost to taxpayers of at least $100 million" and led to a settlement with federal regulators in which the nominee was charged with violating state and federal laws and committing "gross negligence."[67] Moreover, the nominee's résumé, as issued by the White House, did not include any reference to his position as head of the failed savings and loan, thus concealing from senators who were not on the committee some important information that might have led to them to suspect a problem that required further investigation.

Because deep secrets are often mistakenly assumed to be less deceptive than other forms of concealment, politicians resort to them to avoid suspicions of deception. A deep secret is often the refuge of a politician who seeks to escape charges of deception. In one month in 1990, President Bush was subjected to a barrage of such charges in the press. He or his aides, reporters said, had denied making plans for a summit, even as the administration was working hard to arrange the Malta summit. The White House and the State Department denied any high-level contact with China while sending two secret missions there. Bush denied having any plans for a four-power conference on a unified Germany, even though arrangements for such a conference were announced the next day. Shortly after these stories appeared, Bush lashed out at reporters, declaring that because they were always calling his answers deceptive, he would now follow a policy of nondisclosure. "I hate to be secretive, to say nothing of deceptive, but I'm not going to tell you that," he said in response to a series of questions about foreign policy. "I'm not going to discuss [that] because I'm not going to be burned for . . . doing something deceptive." He gave a similar reply even to the question whether he had had a good night's sleep: "I can't go into the details of that, because some will think it is too much sleep and others will think it's too little sleep." Finally, asked about this new policy toward the press, he said, with a grin, "I can't comment on this new relationship," thus deploying a (semi)-deep secret to avoid being charged with deceiving the press about his deception.[68]

If officials avoid deception by keeping deep secrets, they remove their actions even farther from the reach of accountability. Deep secrets often block not only discussion of their own content but also evaluation of related information. An example of this use of a deep secret occurred during the hearings held by the House Human Rights Committee on the conduct of the Iraqi military in Kuwait during the Persian Gulf war. The star witness testified that the Iraqi soldiers had removed respirators from infants in the neonatal units in Kuwaiti hospitals. One of the co-chairmen of the House committee knew, but did not make public, that the star witness was the daughter of the Kuwaiti ambassador to the United States.[69] The chairman also did not disclose that he himself had a business relationship with the Washington public relations firm that was representing Kuwait in the United States.

Deep secrets of this kind are damaging to deliberation because they corrupt political judgment on policy matters that go beyond their own content. If the chairman of the House Human Rights Committee had said merely that he could not reveal the source of the information about the removal of respirators, then citizens could have known enough to question the impartiality or reliability of the source. The deep secret allowed citizens (and other representatives) to assume that the witness was an impartial observer. Had her family connection been revealed, or had it even been known to be a secret, her testimony would have been scrutinized with more care. (Subsequent investigation showed that her account was at least exaggerated and probably largely false.)

Are there *any* deep secrets about public matters that should be treated as deliberative secrets, justified on the grounds that they are necessary to protect the quality of democratic discussion? The most likely candidates are secrets about the private lives of public officials. We have already noted that some information about public officials should be kept private in order to protect basic liberty, especially if the information does not bear significantly on an official's performance in office. But even if the information is relevant, and even if its disclosure violates no one's basic liberty, there still may be good deliberative reasons on the side of keeping the information secret. Some kinds of information—notably, revelations of sexual activities of prominent officials—tend to corrupt the public debate.

The press and the public find the subject irresistible. The respectable press and serious commentators are scarcely immune: they spread the information while analyzing how the less respectable press and less serious commentators cover the story.

Public debate is not corrupted simply because private lives are discussed. The problem is that public attention tends to dwell on the titillating to the neglect of the tedious. Allegations of Senator John Tower's excessive drinking and womanizing deserved some discussion during the hearings on his nomination to be secretary of defense, but they reasonably deserved no more than his activities as a consultant for defense contractors.[70] Yet citizens heard little about these financial dealings, which probably would have revealed much more about his capacity to head the Department of Defense.

Suppose we grant that reports of Bill Clinton's alleged extramarital affairs were relevant to judging whether he would make a good president, and were therefore a legitimate subject for discussion during the 1992 campaign. Or suppose we grant the more sophisticated version of the relevance argument favored by the respectable press: that even if Clinton's alleged extramarital affairs were not germane, how he handled the accusations was relevant to judging how well he would perform under the pressures of public office. Accepting these suppositions, we should still criticize the prominence they enjoyed in the campaign. Even if relevant, details about Clinton's private life did not warrant the attention they received during the primary campaigns, compared to his track record in public office (including politically relevant aspects of his character revealed by that record) or his positions on tax reform, education, crime, or foreign intervention. There are already enough pressures toward superficiality in political campaigns. There is no reason to encourage the further distortions that concentrating on revelations about private immorality causes. A political version of Gresham's law operates relentlessly in American democracy: cheap talk drives out quality talk.

The quality of deliberation would be less strained if we talked less about the private immoralities of public officials. Such immoralities are rarely the most relevant information for assessing a person's performance in office. Democracy might even be better served if most of these secrets were kept deep. Would a democratic society therefore be justified in banning or regulating public discussion in order to protect deep secrets of this kind? The justification on democratic grounds would take the form of collective self-imposed paternalism. Like Ulysses, citizens would bind themselves in order to resist the Siren's call that tempts them with sensationalism instead of substance in their political life. This self-constraining option, so considered, appears to be consistent with democratic accountability. After full deliberation, citizens would decide to restrict future deliberation by placing some limits on the publicity principle. To protect themselves from their own weaknesses, they would deny themselves certain kinds of information. They would restrict the flow of less important information so that they could make better use of more important information.

The difficulty with this argument for selective secrecy is that it requires some authority to select what should be kept secret. Ulysses knew in advance exactly what temptation he wished to resist, and he had a crew who would put wax in their ears so that they could resist the temptation and continue to sail the ship. Citizens cannot specify in advance what they do not want to hear, and they cannot easily appoint agents who will plug their ears. Whom can citizens trust to distinguish the less from the more politically relevant information? Not the elected public officials themselves, who have a strong interest in concealing some information we should know. Not regulatory agencies, such as the Federal Communications Commission, which have a strong obligation to respect freedom of the press, an important value in any deliberative democracy. Not the press itself, which is not politically accountable to citizens.

Journalists and newscasters, editors and publishers, and producers of television news nonetheless have a professional responsibility to attend to the quality of public discussion. In deciding what stories to pursue and what stories to play prominently, they have some discretion. Their decisions cannot be wholly determined by some objective standard of what is newsworthy, nor should their decisions be entirely governed by a market test of what the public wants. What the press prints shapes to some extent what the public comes to prefer. The marketplace of ideas is a misleading metaphor if it suggests that what the public demands is independent of what the press supplies. Markets are not suitable mechanisms for distinguishing between information that is more and information that is less important for discussing public policy. They do not provide effective forums for collective action based more on citizens' considered judgments than on their momentary preferences.

Although citizens may not legally bind the media to provide or suppress politically relevant information, they can reasonably ask that the media use their discretion to improve the quality of public discussion. A commitment to "all the news that's fit to print" implies that some news is not fit to print. Some news, furthermore, may be fit to print, but not on the front page. The need to concentrate on the politically important is perhaps even more critical in television news, which faces severe time limitations. The media can exercise self-constraint, recognizing a professional obligation to contribute to the quality of public deliberation.[71]

Laws cannot enforce this professional responsibility of journalists without threatening other even more important conditions of deliberation, especially the value of free speech. Without deliberative forums in which citizens can agree on what politically relevant information should be publicized, no one could claim to know what information citizens do not wish to hear. With deliberative forums, some citizens would surely dissent from the conclusions reached by the majority. They would legitimately decline to put wax in their ears. Respect for their basic liberty to receive politically relevant information is an essential part of deliberative democracy.

Thus, even in the face of some secrets that would promote better deliberation, the publicity principle should prevail. Democratic citizens ultimately cannot escape the responsibility for the quality of their own deliberation. Self-restraint may not work as well as we might wish, but it is the only kind of restraint that democrats can justifiably accept on the content of their public deliberation.

Beyond Publicity

Some of the friends of publicity ask too much of it. They believe that it will transform self-interested claims into public-spirited ones. One writes: "There are certain arguments that simply cannot be stated publicly. In a political debate it is pragmatically impossible to argue that a given solution should be chosen just because it is good for oneself. By the very act of engaging in a public debate—by arguing rather than bargaining—one has ruled out the possibility of invoking such reasons."[72] It may be ideally impossible to make such claims publicly, but it is not "pragmatically" impossible. Citizens and officials may be more reluctant to make claims on their own behalf in public than in private, but not so reluctant that they forgo the advantage of making them. Moreover, they often express their self-interested claims in terms of group interests, which convey some sense that at least they care about some other people besides themselves.

The constraint of publicity probably does rule out making arguments that one would not accept if others made them: argue unto others as you would have them argue unto you. But this does not preclude appeals to group interests. Indeed, it is quite consistent with ordinary log-rolling. It would not, for example, prevent this exchange, which occurred on the floor of the Senate during a debate on agricultural subsidies:

> *Mr. Langer (North Dakota):* We don't raise any tobacco in North Dakota, but we are interested in the tobacco situation in Kentucky, and I hope the Senator [from that state] will support us in securing assistance for wheat growers in our state.
>
> *Mr. Clements (Kentucky):* I think the Senator will find that my support will be 100 percent.
>
> *Mr. Barkley (Kentucky):* Mr. President, will my colleague from Kentucky yield [the floor]?
>
> *Mr. Clements:* I yield.
>
> *Mr. Barkley:* The colloquy just [heard] confirms and justifies the Woodrow Wilsonian doctrine of open covenants openly arrived at. *(Laughter).*[73]

The laughter may be reassuring. It may signal that such deals are not usually made so openly, and that publicity may after all provide some deterrent to a politics of pure self-interest.[74] But it should also be a sobering reminder that the main contribution of publicity is not to make politics public-spirited but simply to make it public so that citizens can decide together what kind of politics they want. The hope is that as they offer reasons for what they want, we will find common moral ground, even if the ground is not always on the high road.

That the reason-giving takes place in public is certainly not sufficient for developing a deliberative perspective. The temper of our political culture, the condition of our educational institutions, the character of our representatives are bound to shape the content of democratic deliberation. But the significance of these and the other forces that affect our ways of facing moral disagreement together are likely to be better appreciated the more open our political process is. In this way publicity provides the necessary means for transcending its own limits.

_4_

The Scope of Accountability

IN A deliberative forum, each is accountable to all. Citizens and officials try to justify their decisions to all those who are bound by them and some of those who are affected by them. This is the implication of the reason-giving process of deliberative democracy. Universal accountability is obviously difficult to realize in practice. It is also problematic in theory: it does not fit comfortably with political representation, a necessary and desirable process in deliberative democracy. Representation poses two challenges to universal accountability, one concerning *who* gives the reasons, and the other concerning *to whom* the reasons should be given.

The first kind of problem is the challenge of specialization, and it results from the division of political labor that any representative democracy creates. In a representative democracy some deliberate for all. As a result, not only may the deliberators come to different conclusions than do those for whom they deliberate, but they also may come to have different views about what reasons are important, and what should count as giving reasons. The gap between officials and citizens creates a problem of accountability in any democracy, but the problem is exacerbated in a democracy in which the account that officials give takes the form of moral reasons. Should representatives use the reasons that they find compelling or those that appeal to constituents? Neither alternative seems satisfactory. Both threaten deliberation—one by leaving too much of it to representatives, and the other by turning over too much of it to citizens.

The second kind of problem—the challenge of constituency—concerns the identity of those to whom the representative owes an account. Representatives are first of all accountable to voters, and to others with whom they have some special relationship (such as supporters of their party). By its nature, representation allows—indeed requires—legislators to give special consideration to those whom they represent. Yet this inherent partiality does not fit well with the moral point of view that deliberative democracy seeks. Universal accountability implies a comprehensive constituency, while representation presupposes a circumscribed one.

Both of these challenges arise because deliberative democracy raises the stakes of democratic accountability. It requires more than do procedural and constitutional democracy. A deliberative principle of accountability asks representatives to do more than try to win reelection, and more than to respect constitutional rights. In a deliberative democracy representatives are expected to justify their actions in moral terms. In the spirit of reciprocity, they give reasons that can be accepted by all those who are bound by the laws and policies they justify. Given the criterion of generality implied by the moral point of view, the reasons should also address the claims of anyone who is significantly affected by the laws and policies.

Both theoretical challenges show up in the practice of representation. The political controversy in South Dakota over legalized abortion is a case in point. As the abortion battle returned to the states in the 1990s, the South Dakota legislature took up a bill that would have banned abortion under most circumstances.[1] Pro-life forces were well organized and influential in the legislature, and public opinion in the state strongly supported the bill. Scott Heidepriem, the Republican state senator from the James River Valley district, was pro-choice and personally opposed to the bill. A majority of his constituents, holding pro-life positions, favored the bill. He saw his decision as posing the classic dilemma of a representative: Should he act on his own moral principles or on those of his constituents? He chose to act on his own principles, and in the final count voted against the bill, which was narrowly defeated. It was a difficult decision, and many saw his action as a "profile in courage." Yet the political picture was complicated in two ways, each of which reveals one of the challenges to accountability.

We can see the force of the first challenge by asking whether pro-life citizens could praise Heidepriem for doing his duty even as they object to the position he took. Abortion is not the kind of issue on which he is likely to have special expertise. Pro-life constituents do not have to accept his view even about constitutional law. His constituents might reasonably complain that they too have deliberated about this question, and that their conclusion should prevail. At the least he should try to convince them of his position. Such questions arise because in a deliberative democracy constituents should be able to give effect to their views not only by voting at election time but also by influencing the judgments that their representatives make in the legislative process. The electoral verdict itself, or even the campaign, should not carry the full burden of reason-giving communication in the political process. Some important issues do not receive sufficient attention either because they are not yet on the political agenda or because other issues dominate.

Yet at the same time, Heidepriem is himself obligated to deliberate. He must therefore have some freedom to consider reasons he finds significant, and some room to change his mind in response to discussions in the legislature. Even if Heidepriem's constituents are as competent as he to decide the abortion question, they do not have the experience or responsibility of a full-time legislator. It is, after all, part of his official obligation as a legislator to think about the issue of legalizing abortion, through discussion with his colleagues and also with his constituents, most of whom have not talked about the issue with as many different citizens as he has. If this experience and reflection have led him to conclude that legislatures do not have the right to restrict abortions, should he not be free—or perhaps even obligated—to act on this conclusion?

This conflict between Heidepriem and his constituents resembles the classic dilemma of representation: Should a representative be a trustee or a delegate?[2] But the issue of accountability here is importantly different. The question is not whether Heidepriem should follow the call of his conscience or the will of his constituents but rather a more fundamental— and prior—question: Whether it is desirable that Heidepriem justify his choice at all to his constituents. Why is it not sufficient that he stand for election and let his constituents judge him by his actions? The demand that he give reasons for his position seems to force him to choose between an account that will satisfy more qualified deliberators and one that would appeal to less qualified deliberators. His duty of accountability stands delicately poised between elitism and demagoguery.

Whereas the first challenge assumes that Heidepriem knows who his constituents are, the second challenge calls this assumption into question. Some of Heidepriem's pro-life colleagues in the Senate objected that "outsiders"—in particular, national feminist organizations—should not be trying to influence the outcome of an issue that the residents of South Dakota ought to decide on their own. But Heidepriem believed that abortion in South Dakota was not a question for only the citizens of his state to decide. It was a national question, concerning individual rights, which the Supreme Court should decide. Heidepriem may have also thought that he is accountable to all those who are significantly affected by his public decisions. His accountability might extend, for example, to teenagers who cannot vote but whose lives would be significantly affected by abortion legislation. It might even extend to unborn fetuses. If we reject, as deliberative democracy suggests that we should, the view that representatives are accountable only to those who can vote for them, then we face a formidable challenge in determining who should count as the constituents to whom they owe an account.

Some democrats might argue that we could avoid both of these problems if we embraced more participatory forms of government, such as direct democracy. They would claim that these problems are the result of the division of labor between elected officials and other citizens. If this division were eliminated or its importance in governing diminished, the problems it creates would also disappear or decrease. More participation in politics is generally desirable (as we have argued elsewhere),[3] but representation in some form is here to stay. For the foreseeable future, the scale and complexity of modern government, including any kind of democracy, requires a significant measure of representation.

From a deliberative perspective representation is not only necessary but also desirable.[4] The number of people who at the same time can have even a simple conversation, let alone an extended moral argument, is limited.[5] The more serious and sustained the moral argument—the greater the chance for the genuine public conversation that deliberative democracy seeks—the more stringent these practical limits become. This fact of democratic life has long been recognized. Aristotle believed that ordinary citizens deciding together could reach a better decision than experts acting alone, but he had in mind a relatively small assembly. He did not imagine a town meeting on the scale that would be necessary to govern a major American city by direct democracy, let alone a state or national government.[6]

Deliberative democracy does not specify a single form of representation. It searches for modes of representation that support the give-and-take of serious and sustained moral argument within legislative bodies, between legislators and the citizens, and among citizens themselves. Some forms may even combine direct and representative democracy, as in the citizen workshops discussed in Chapter 5. The main concern here, however, is a question that is prior to institutional forms: How can deliberative accountability be consistent with democratic representation? It is necessary to show how it is possible to maintain the scope of accountability that deliberative democracy favors while accommodating the process of electoral representation. Although the requirements of deliberative democracy make the problem of accountability more pressing, the resources of deliberation provide more justifiable ways of responding to the challenges of representation than do other conceptions of democracy.

The Problem of Specialization

Representation makes possible better or at least more sustained deliberation. But this benefit for deliberative democracy may have a corresponding cost: it may create a special class of political deliberators. Representatives become specialists in deliberation, while citizens become spectators. The first danger of this division of political labor is elitism, the tendency of those who deliberate to dominate those who do not. The second danger seems just the opposite—an excess of populism, the tendency of representatives to pander to their constituents. But this danger too has its source in the division of labor that representation encourages: it is simply the other face of the challenge that representation poses to deliberative accountability.

IS DELIBERATION ELITIST?

Some critics of deliberation argue that it is elitist because in various ways it favors advantaged citizens. Deliberation, the critics believe, requires discussion that is "rational, moderate, and not selfish." It therefore implicitly excludes "public talk that is impassioned, extreme, and the product of particular interests."[7] By itself this exclusion would not be elitist; it is only biased against the irrational, immoderate, and selfish. The critics must thus be assuming that members of disadvantaged and marginalized groups are more likely to be unreasonable in these ways. Why might the critics make such an assumption?

Critics may assume that the social and economic disadvantages of members of marginalized groups have diminished their capacity for deliberation, both as participants and as spectators. No doubt there are differences in deliberative ability among individuals, and these differences may very well correspond to social, educational, and economic status. But even if this is so, acting on a deliberative principle of accountability may help compensate for the differences. Disadvantaged groups have usually found representatives from within their own ranks who could speak for them, and who could articulate their interests and ideals, at least as reasonably and effectively as representatives of established groups. Martin Luther King, Jr., exemplifies this kind of representation at its best. But not every representative of the disadvantaged needs to be a Martin Luther King. The deliberative capacities of representatives who speak for the advantaged rarely reach that level.

In any case, when the representatives of disadvantaged groups are less successful in politics, it is rarely because of any disadvantage in deliberation. The lack of political success of marginalized groups stems not from a deliberative deficit but from a lack of power. They suffer the consequences of underlying inequalities in social and economic opportunities. To the extent that the political struggle takes place on the basis of deliberation rather than of power, it is more evenly matched. The deliberative playing field is more nearly level. Moral appeals are the weapon of the weak—not the only weapon, to be sure, but one that by its nature gives them an advantage over the powerful.

Another reason why critics may think that deliberation is elitist is that they assume that higher status is an advantage in most political discussions in the public forum. Even if the disadvantaged and their representatives are adept at deliberation in the approved manner, the dynamics of group discussion tend to favor people with higher social and economic status.[8] They simply talk more, and their views are taken more seriously by most members. The outcomes of deliberation are therefore more likely to reflect the initial views of the most advantaged deliberators.

But again it is doubtful that this effect is mainly due to deliberation. It is more likely that deliberation offers a better chance of overcoming the influence of status in the political process. Compared to bargaining, deliberation, properly structured, can diminish the discriminatory effects of class, race, and gender inequalities. Structuring group discussions to make them more deliberative also makes it less likely that the results will simply reaffirm the initial views of the most advantaged deliberators. Studies of jury deliberations, for example, suggest that when jurors begin by considering evidence instead of simply voting, they are more likely to discuss issues in an open-minded way, and presumably, therefore, to pay more attention to the merits of the arguments than to the status of their fellow jurors.[9]

Deliberation is of course not sufficient to overcome the background inequalities that taint the public forum and the public policies adopted there. Consider this familiar inequality: How can representatives discuss the merits of issues on anything like equal terms so long as their very status as representatives depends on private donations of money? Campaign contributions, which disproportionately come from wealthy citizens and well-organized groups, influence who runs for office, who is elected, and what policies successful candidates support. The system of financing campaigns through private contributions disadvantages already disadvantaged citizens. Public financing of campaigns would ameliorate this problem, as would a fairer distribution of income and wealth.

Those who benefit from the background inequalities are not likely to support the policies that would mitigate their effects. It is difficult to deliberate dispassionately about the laws that might bring about the end to one's own chance to deliberate as a lawmaker. The results of deliberative representation are skewed, but not therefore determined, by the very inequalities that the deliberative process of representation is supposed to correct. Deliberation must be part of any strategy to break out of the cycle of injustice created by background inequalities. In representative legislative bodies influence typically depends on factors other than the social status of representatives. Political skill, collegial loyalty, institutional seniority—and even a sense of reciprocity and a capacity to deliberate—count for more than social status. Some of these characteristics may be no more relevant to the merits of public policies than social status, but they do not necessarily reinforce prevailing injustices in the same way.

A third reason why critics may think that standards of deliberation are biased against marginalized groups concerns the style of argument they are assumed to need to use. If disadvantaged groups are to gain an effective voice in the public forum, the critics believe, their representatives must make passionate rather than rational appeals. They cannot be bound by the rules of rational discourse which favor the established order and perpetuate the privileges of the already advantaged.

In this form the objection lacks historical perspective. Much of the force of radical criticism of society in the past has relied on rationalist challenges to the status quo. Indeed, the complaint against radical critics has often been that they were too rationalist. Many of the most vigorous critics of society could have defended their positions most cogently in a dialogue subject to the constraints of moral reasoning. It was those who invoked tradition and authority who would have had difficulty in meeting the demands of the deliberative principle of accountability.

But perhaps the critics of deliberation are making a more qualified point: some appeals that do not meet the standards of deliberation may be necessary to get deliberation started in the first place. Deliberation cannot occur unless an issue reaches the political agenda. Nondeliberative means may be necessary to achieve deliberative ends. If this is the critics' claim, then it is consistent with the deliberative principle of accountability.

When the U.S. Senate in July 1993 took up the routine renewal of a patent on the Confederate flag insignia, Carol Moseley Braun, the chamber's only black member, took the floor with an "oratory of impassioned tears and shouts," and threatened a filibuster. Her passionate—some said extremist—rhetoric was probably necessary to provoke the Senate to take the issue seriously. With her rhetoric she turned the routine into the notable, and provoked deliberation that almost certainly would not otherwise have occurred.

Moseley Braun had first used conventional political methods in the Judiciary Committee to oppose the request by the Daughters of the Confederacy to renew their patent on the insignia, arguing that the insignia is a symbol of slavery. After she succeeded in persuading the Judiciary Committee to deny the request, however, Senators Jesse Helms and Strom Thurmond attached the patent renewal as an amendment to a national service bill. The patent had no relevance to national service, a measure that was expected to pass; the amendment was simply a way to get the patent approved without debating its merits. The Helms-Thurmond amendment passed overwhelmingly in a test vote, with almost no discussion. Only at this point did Senator Moseley Braun threaten a filibuster and resort "to high drama."[10] Not only did the drama attract media attention, but, more important, it also provoked deliberation in the Senate that probably otherwise would not have taken place. "On this issue," Moseley Braun argued on the floor, "there can be no consensus. It is an outrage. It is an insult. It is absolutely unacceptable to me and to millions of Americans, black and white, that we would put the imprimatur of the United States Senate on a symbol of this kind of idea."[11] Her speech stimulated a debate that changed senators' minds, or at least their positions. Over a three-hour period, twenty-seven senators reversed their earlier vote, defeating the amendment 75 to 25.[12]

This episode illustrates two ways in which deliberation can be consistent with impassioned and immoderate speech. First, even extreme nondeliberative methods may be justified as necessary steps to deliberation. The Senate had never taken this issue seriously in the past and was on the verge of treating it as routine once again. The legislative process is deficient if it neglects or excludes perspectives that deserve serious consideration and can contribute to a justifiable resolution of the issue. When reasonable perspectives are neglected, there is a strong argument from the premises of deliberative democracy itself to use any legal means necessary to get those views taken seriously.

Second, deliberation itself does not always have to take the form of a reasoned argument of the kind that philosophers are inclined to favor. Moseley Braun's speech may have been impassioned, but it made substantive points, to which members could respond with their own arguments. As one account put it, Braun "matched reason to passion."[13] Dispassionate argument that minimizes conflict is not always the best means of deliberation. Matching reason to passion can often be a more effective way of representing one's constituents, taking account of their well-being, and encouraging other representatives to do the same. Senator Howell Heflin of Alabama responded to Moseley Braun's arguments by saying that his ancestors "might be spinning in their graves," but he would reverse himself and join her in voting against the Confederate flag because "we must get racism behind us."[14]

Some critics who think that deliberation is elitist offer an alternative that they believe to be more egalitarian. They call it "testimony."[15] On one understanding, testimony is a statement or narrative that gives public voice to a critical stance of some individual or group, but does not seek a perspective that can be justifiable to other individuals or groups. This understanding of testimony explicitly rejects one of the chief requirements of moral argument, and therefore does not contribute to democratic efforts to resolve moral disagreements. But other understandings of testimony, closer to the way in which it is typically understood by both testifiers and their audience, could serve this end.[16] Senator Moseley Braun did not simply testify to her experience as a black American, hoping thereby only to criticize the perspective of senators and other Americans who saw the Confederate flag as a positive symbol. She intended her testimony to effect a change in the perspectives of other representatives and in the public policy of her government.

In this form testimony can serve as an important first step in a process by which representatives try to reach consensus on controversial issues. By listening to the testimony of citizens and colleagues whose perspectives differ from theirs, representatives are more likely to arrive at a mutually justifiable political agreement. Like a jury trial, the deliberative process often cannot even begin without the presentation of testimony. Properly given, testimony expands the horizons of both representatives and citizens.[17] To this extent the critics who suspect deliberation of elitist tendencies are right about the antielitist value of testimony.

But if the critics seek to replace deliberation with testimony, they lead us toward a political process that is likely to be even more elitist than that to which they object. Testimony alone does not move a political process forward. It may bring differences to the attention of others, but without deliberation it leaves the differences unresolved, the policies unchanged. In a society that suffers from injustice, the status quo is not the favored outcome for marginalized and disadvantaged groups. The different voices that testimony introduces into the democratic process should express values that citizens can and should share as a matter of social justice. Otherwise, testimony turns into a politics of futile gesture. Declarations of frustration and acts of protest for their own sake also have their political uses, but they do not benefit the disadvantaged unless they reach out to representatives who would give opposing testimony. Senator Moseley Braun did not simply affirm her identity as a black woman and her experience of racism. She related her outrage to experiences that her colleagues—including Senator Heflin—could understand and based her claims on values they could actually accept.

IS DELIBERATION TOO POPULIST?

The second criticism of deliberative accountability comes from the opposite direction: the principle gives too much weight to public opinion and too little to the moral and political expertise of representatives. The danger of excessive populism has its source in the same reason-giving requirement that leads other critics to worry about the elitist tendencies of deliberation. If representatives must justify their actions not only to one another but also to citizens, as deliberative accountability demands, then their justifications must appeal to the general public. Political rhetoric of this sort, these critics fear, tends to become simplistic and even demagogic. Because the reasons that representatives give also shape the kinds of policies that governments adopt, policies also tend toward the simplistic and demagogic.

Other forms of democracy, the critics imply, are not prone to this tendency. Procedural democracy avoids it because representatives are accountable for the policies they support and for the results of those policies. They are not primarily accountable for the reasons they may give for those policies. Because there is less need to explain the rationale for policies, there are fewer constraints on the kinds of policies that representatives can adopt. Constitutional democracy is also assumed to avoid the excesses of populism, but in a different way. There are constitutional constraints on the policies that representatives can adopt, and these constraints may be imposed by other elites—notably judges, who give reasons for their decisions in a forum relatively insulated from popular pressure. Deliberation occurs in constitutional democracy, but primarily among well-insulated elites.

Because deliberative accountability requires representatives to give reasons to citizens and to respond to the reasons citizens give, critics object that it not only degrades public discourse but also impedes representatives in the exercise of their own best judgment. Deliberative accountability would make political life much more difficult for a representative who, like Senator Heidepriem, wished to oppose the pro-life views of most of his constituents. Unlike his constituents, Heidepriem had studied constitutional law and chaired the Senate's Judiciary Committee. He had good reason to think that the bill to ban abortions in South Dakota was unconstitutional and that mounting a test case would be a waste of the state's resources. (Several test cases in other states were already making their way through the courts.) Even if the bill passed, it would probably be challenged in court and "embroil South Dakota in legal turmoil for years to come," costing the state up to as much as a million dollars in court fees and producing no real benefits to the citizens of the state. Furthermore, South Dakota already had a law on the books that would ban abortion in the event that the Supreme Court overturned *Roe v. Wade.*[18] Heidepriem did not need to take a condescending attitude toward his constituents to recognize that they were unlikely to have thought through the legal, moral, and political dimensions of the abortion issue as carefully as he had.

Would the deliberative principle of accountability have forced Heidepriem to defer to his constituents against his better judgment? It certainly would have encouraged him to explain as carefully as he could the reasons for his pro-choice position, and in return to listen to his constituents' reasons. This is hardly excessive populism. Without engaging in this kind of process, representatives are likely to assume that they know better than their constituents, even when they cannot respond adequately to their arguments. Representatives who do not engage in this deliberation are also less likely to find ways of accommodating those aspects of their constituents' positions that could be accepted from a reciprocal perspective. Although some people are better at moral argument than others, and some arguments can be shown to be superior to others, the moral judgments of each citizen deserve respect when consistent with a reciprocal perspective.

Heidepriem did try to present his case to his constituents. From the start of his political career, he had made public his position on abortion and his reasons for supporting a woman's right to abortion prior to fetal viability. "My view," he told the press, "is that there is no perfect answer, but I've read *Roe v. Wade* a number of times, and I'm amazed at how close [Justice Harry] Blackmun gets it right."[19] Heidepriem thought that any bill that proposed restricting a woman's right to abortion in most situations was clearly unconstitutional, and he said so publicly, immediately after the antiabortion bill was introduced in the South Dakota legislature. He also tried to make arguments that he thought might appeal to pro-life citizens. That was presumably one purpose of his points about the test cases in other states and about the existing state law that would ban abortion if *Roe* were overturned. Heidepriem himself believed these arguments, and he did not try to simplify or distort them for political purposes.

If Heidepriem is to be criticized on this score, it is not for failing to defer to his constituents but for relying too heavily on legal arguments. Even if legally correct, these arguments did not definitively determine what state legislators should do, and to the exent that Heidepriem implied that they settled the issue, he gave the moral arguments that are central to his constituents' concerns too little weight in the debate. Still, he acknowledged that the issue is a moral one, and he presented his own position fairly and openly. In a case as difficult and controversial as that of abortion, Heidepriem showed that a representative can satisfy the reason-giving principle of deliberative accountability without resorting to demagoguery.

Not only was Heidepriem's rural district conservative, but it also "contained the highest concentration of anti-abortion organizations in the state."[20] He was under no illusion that he could change constituents' minds on abortion, and he did not. Thus the question persists: To what extent does accountability require him to defer to his constituents? More specifically, after he presented his best reasons as effectively as he could and his constituents continued to reject them, should he instead have offered reasons that he thought specious but that his constituents might have found more persuasive? And if even those attempts failed, was he finally obliged to defer to their judgment?

In this case Heidepriem's primary reason for opposing the bill contains the answer. He believed that a bill restricting abortion would violate the basic liberty of women. Deliberative democracy recognizes constitutional liberties and opportunities as constraints on majority will, and authorizes representatives to resist majority will if it threatens to violate these liberties and opportunities. Accountability does not require representatives to defer to constituents under these circumstances. But of course pro-life constituents may also believe that basic liberties are at stake, and if they give reciprocal reasons for their belief, they do not have to defer to Heidepriem. They would have reasonable grounds to oppose him in the next election. It is not enough that representatives or their constituents believe that a basic liberty is at stake, and not enough that the Constitution currently protects that liberty. They must have good grounds, consistent with the principle of reciprocity, for believing that the liberty is basic and should be protected by the Constitution.

What about disagreements that do not involve basic liberties and opportunities? If accountability requires representatives to defer to constituents in all such cases, it might still seem to leave too little room for representatives to engage in deliberation. But there are other grounds on which representatives may decline to follow a majority of their constituents. What they might be and how they can be consistent with accountability can be seen by considering some other cases in which the reasons that representatives gave appealed to special knowledge.

The first is set in the mid-1980s in Tacoma, Washington, where, for the sake of "expanding the opportunities for its residents to experience art in public places," the city council had decided to set aside 1 percent of the city budget to spend on public art.[21] An art commission—advised by an expert jury—had selected a bold neon sculpture for Tacoma's new sports and convention facility. Most members of the city council wanted to support the commission, but in the face of widespread public criticism of the design, they were reluctant to approve the commission's decision without further discussion. The council held a public hearing to solicit the views of citizens. Few people attended, and no consensus emerged. The county auditor declared that a public vote on the sculpture, forced by an initiative petition, would be only advisory to the council. The advisory vote went overwhelmingly against the sculpture. The council then voted, 7 to 2, "to abide by voter wishes" and reject the design. Less than two months later the council held another public meeting ("so Council members could learn why citizens dislike the piece"). Of some five-hundred citizens who attended, more than two thirds favored the sculpture. Five days later the council reversed itself, voting 6 to 3 to retain the sculpture. "Tacoma is not a democracy any longer," said one opponent. "It is an oligarchy."[22]

Although the art commission and the jury were well qualified to judge sculpture, it would be difficult to claim that their choice was the only correct one for the sports facility. The opposition was not all, or even mainly, unsophisticated. Some critics of the design thought that it would be better to choose a piece of art more in keeping with the city's traditions (for example, one that used wood and other materials from the region). Was a neon sculpture an appropriate adornment for a facility constructed of local lumber and crowned by the largest freestanding wooden dome in the world? Some also argued that the cost of the sculpture could not be justified in a city that was suffering from an economic recession. Although members of the commission responded to these criticisms, the responses did not show, and mostly were not intended to show, that the critics of the design were lacking in civic spirit, or that the criticisms were without aesthetic merit.

What does the principle of accountability tell members of the city council to do in the face of such persistent yet reasonable public opposition? One city councilman attacked his colleagues who had changed their position in response to the referendum (the first advisory vote). He branded this behavior cowardice and warned that it threatened to turn city government into a pure democracy, claiming that "every time [the council] made a decision they'd go out and have people vote on that decision."[23] This councilman was not speaking on behalf of deliberative democracy. The principle of accountability permits a representative under these circumstances to defer to his constituents.

The justification for deferring to popular opinion in this case is stronger than in the case of the abortion bill. From a reciprocal perspective, it is unreasonable to deny that a woman's basic liberty is at stake in the case of abortion (although people may reasonably disagree over whether fetuses have interests that limit women's liberty). Basic liberties are not at stake in the neon sculpture case. The best reasons that representatives could give against popular opinion in Tacoma's "neon war" were not morally or aesthetically compelling in the same way. Even if we could say that one side was correct about the sculpture, that side would not deserve the same deference as the correct side in the abortion dispute (and this is so no matter which side we believe to be the correct one).

Thus, those members who changed their votes even if they did not change their minds were not violating the principle of accountability. (One member in fact opposed the sculpture for reasons similar to those that most citizens gave, and some members may have been influenced by the discussion at the previous public meeting.) Constitutional rights were not at stake, and expert opinion was uncertain and divided. But even in this case, where deference to constituents may be justified, accountability does not require it. After the kind of sustained interchange that the council encouraged, a member who had good reasons for his view was justified under the circumstances in voting for the sculpture. Council members made their best case to citizens, listened to their views, and responded to their criticisms.

The council appropriately resisted a proposal to decide the question formally by referendum. Such a procedure, standing alone, denies the importance of public deliberation. Voting en masse is no substitute for deliberating in forums that permit representatives to challenge and respond to the views expressed by citizens and allow citizens to engage with representatives and with one another. Thus, when the deliberative principle of accountability justifies or allows deference to popular opinion, it does so with a difference. Deliberation precedes deference.

Except when basic liberties and opportunities are at stake, deliberative accountability does not instruct representatives how to vote in the face of opposition from their constituents. The principle does imply that some reasons should have more weight than others, and some should not count at all. But any rule that purports to tell representatives in all cases when to defer to constituents will almost certainly misrepresent their responsibility. On many public policies the balance of the reasons, considered in good faith in a deliberative process, is likely to vary in ways that cannot be determined in advance of current circumstances and actual discussion. That deliberative democracy makes room for this variability is one of its virtues.

Heidepriem and the Tacoma city council confronted specific decisions—whether to ban abortion, and whether to purchase a piece of sculpture. Voters could listen to their reasons, present their own, and hold officials accountable at the next election, if necessary choosing new representatives to reverse the decision. Many public policies, however, do not take the form of reversible, single decisions. Policies allocating resources to health care, for example, consist of a set of complicated decisions, subject to continual revisions, the effects of which do not track electoral cycles. How can citizens hold representatives accountable for policies of this kind, which are increasingly common in modern government?

Here a further advantage of deliberative democracy becomes evident. Instead of the arbitrary moments of accountability that elections offer, deliberative democracy provides an ongoing process. Deliberation continues through stages, as officials present their proposals, citizens respond, officials revise, citizens react, and the stages recur.[24] This is what we call the reiteration of deliberation. The potential strengths (and weaknesses) of this kind of deliberation can be seen in the process that the state of Oregon adopted in the early 1990s to set priorities for its publicly funded health care under Medicaid.[25] In the face of the mounting financial crisis in the state's Medicaid budget, legislators and health administrators sought to extend coverage to more citizens (especially the uninsured poor) by eliminating coverage for some treatments (the least cost-effective).

In May 1990 a publicly appointed Oregon Health Services Commission developed a ranked list of 709 medical conditions paired with treatments, ordered mainly according to utilitarian cost-benefit calculations. The list provoked much justifiable criticism (capping a tooth ranked much higher than an appendectomy). The commission then began an elaborate process of consultation, which included a random sample telephone survey of state residents to see how individuals would rate the quality of life resulting from the various conditions and treatments, and held forty-seven community meetings throughout the state involving more than a thousand citizens to identify community values on health care. Run by a nonprofit organization with experience in facilitating public discussion of ethical issues in health care, the meetings were designed to encourage participants "to think and express themselves in the first person plural . . . as members of a statewide community for whom health care has a shared value."[26] The commission asked other groups to examine the results of the surveys and meetings, and finally, after more discussion among themselves, presented a revised list for the governor and the legislature a year later, in May 1991.

Both the process and the outcome have been severely criticized, and no doubt both are flawed. The most serious problems result from a fact beyond Oregon's control—that the plan directly covers only poor citizens. Many critics rightly point to the injustice in making some poor citizens sacrifice health care that they need so that other poor citizens can receive health care they need even more urgently, while better-off citizens can get whatever treatment they need.[27] This basic injustice may have adversely influenced the surveys and community meetings, which in any case fell short of the deliberative ideal.

Nevertheless, the process forced officials and citizens to confront a serious problem that they had previously evaded—and to confront it in a cooperative ("first person plural") spirit. As a result, even the basic unfairness in the policy was somewhat lessened in a way unexpected by the critics of the plan (and probably by its proponents as well). When the legislators finally saw what treatments on the list would have to be eliminated under the projected budget, they managed to find more resources, and increased the total budget for health care for the poor.[28] Beyond the budget, the final list itself seemed to reflect better the considered judgments of most health professionals as well as ordinary citizens. Although some observers saw little connection between the earlier debate and the content of the revised list, the commission did correct most of the priorities that had been widely criticized. The year-long deliberations evidently helped citizens, legislators, and health care professionals arrive at an improved understanding of their own values—those they shared and those they did not. The experience enabled citizens and their representatives to undertake, in a more reciprocal spirit, what was likely to be a long and difficult process of setting and adjusting priorities that could eventually affect the quality of health care for all residents of the state and even in other states.

Reiterated deliberation encourages public officials to learn from their mistakes and to correct them. It enables citizens to hold their representatives accountable for making better decisions in the future. This kind of process comes closer to the deliberative principle of accountability than does the electoral process alone. Reiterated deliberation, punctuated by periodic elections, is the best hope for the principle of accountability. Only by such means can we hope to ameliorate the pernicious effects of the political division of labor without sacrificing its beneficial ones.

The Problem of Constituency

So far we have been concentrating on what may be seen as the vertical dimension of the challenge of representation: the division of labor between representatives and those they represent. The possibility that each may give and respond to different kinds of reasons raises doubts about realizing the principle of accountability from top to bottom in the political structure. Now we turn to the horizontal dimension and confront the challenge of realizing the principle across the boundaries of constituency. The principle requires that representatives justify their actions from a moral point of view, which implies that they owe an account not only to their electoral constituents but also to what we may call their *moral* constituents—citizens in other states and other nations, groups of disadvantaged citizens, and citizens yet to be born.

Who are a representative's moral constituents? To whom does a representative owe an account? The decisions made by Oregon legislators about their health care plan affected not only the residents of the state but also citizens in other states. The residency requirements generally denied coverage to citizens from out of state, even though some of the funding came from the federal government. Should the legislators give any weight at all to the claims of nonresidents? The health care plan would affect some groups more than others—for example, poor African Americans or Hispanics and poor women. Should any or all legislators take responsibility for representing these or other disadvantaged groups? Finally, decisions about funding prenatal and postnatal care affect future citizens—who they will be and how they will live. How can legislators be accountable to those who are not yet born?

This set of questions poses a formidable moral challenge to deliberative accountability. If representatives are accountable only to those who elect them, then many people whose well-being is significantly affected by their decisions are denied adequate representation, and their claims are likely to be neglected. But if representatives are accountable to every individual—and group—whose well-being is significantly affected by their actions, then electoral constituents may reasonably object that they are denied the special consideration they deserve from their representative. Universal accountability seems to drain all moral meaning out of the electoral connection between public officials and the citizens who elect them.

To address the challenge that the problem of constituency poses to the principle of accountability, we consider three categories of potential moral constituents, people who should be represented but are not present in the electoral process. The challenge of constituency spans space (nonresidents), identity (groups), and time (future generations). Each dimension introduces increasingly difficult problems.

BEYOND THE DISTRICT

The Oregon legislators did not explicitly consider the claims of nonresidents, but Arizona officials did during their debate on funding organ transplants. Dr. Donald Schaller, head of Arizona's health care program, argued against public funding of heart transplants in part because he thought it would encourage people from Idaho and California to come to Arizona for treatment.[29] It is not fair, Schaller said, to tax Arizonans to subsidize expensive medical treatment for Idahoans and Californians. So much for the claims of nonresidents: they count for so little that the possibility that they might be satisfied becomes an argument against a policy of funding a treatment for residents. Perhaps Arizona should not subsidize the health care of citizens in other states, but the claims of those citizens deserve more, and a different kind of, consideration than they received in the Arizona debate.

To defend deliberative accountability, we do not have to deny that representatives should attend to the claims of those who elect them. Electoral accountability is an important instrument with which democracies try to ensure that public officials look after the interests of all citizens. But electorally based representation by itself, taken as a sufficient standard of accountability, focuses the attention of representatives too narrowly on the claims of voters in their own district. The parochial focus is justified only on the assumption that each citizen has (at least) one representative, and the claims of all citizens are effectively expressed in a legislative body at some appropriate level of the political system. The member from Phoenix does not have to worry about the residents of Tucson because they have their own member who effectively represents their interests. Neither need be concerned about the residents of Idaho, who have their own representatives, both in the state and in the federal government.

But this assumption relies on a kind of invisible hand to bring the political system into moral equilibrium: the well-being of all affected citizens is best served by letting each jurisdiction look after only its own. That is not an assumption that representatives or citizens in any actual democracy can reasonably accept. If the political system does not work this way, then representatives should weigh this fact in the accounts they give to citizens.

Neither procedural nor constitutional democracy provides an adequate response to this challenge. Procedural democrats tend to say that if a representative's electoral constituents happen to care about the interests of nonresidents, then the representative should also care about them, and to the same extent. If voters choose to ignore the interests of nonresidents, then their representatives need not—indeed should not—attend to them either. Constitutional democracy offers a better but still insufficient answer: representatives should respect the claims of citizens who are not their constituents when those claims express basic liberties or opportunities. The difficulty with this response is that in many cases the claims of nonresidents do not rise to the level of constitutional protection but may nevertheless merit consideration. No one can reasonably object that the

Arizona legislature violates the constitutional rights of Californians by denying them access to transplants in Arizona. Yet many might maintain that the Arizona legislature should consider the effects of its policies on the well-being of nonresidents. It is an argument that deliberative democracy tells representatives to take seriously.

Because deliberative democracy requires legislators to give moral reasons for their actions, it expands the conventional forms of accountability, and thereby offers a more adequate theoretical response to the challenge of constituency. In addition to responsiveness to constituents and respect for constitutional rights, deliberative accountability asks representatives to give reasons for their actions that could be accepted from a reciprocal perspective. That perspective embraces nonresidents as well as residents.

To be sure, Arizona's legislators may have good reasons for deciding to exclude nonresidents from coverage. The legislators may argue that their first obligation is to the citizens of their own state, who are contributing to the costs of health care in the state; and that, given limited resources, the state cannot subsidize care for nonresidents without denying treatment to needy residents. This is a position that is potentially consistent with the principle of reciprocity. But even if most states cannot be expected to provide adequate health care coverage on their own for outsiders, the obligations of the Arizona legislators do not stop at the state line. They have a responsibility to support national policies that would provide health care to residents of other states as well as Arizona. The legislators themselves should take steps to help forge a national health plan that would give all citizens the kind of health care that they believe is due to Arizonans.

The implications of extending accountability in this way apply not only to representatives but also to citizens. Representatives still have to face voters at the next election, and however broadly they may construe their own responsibility, they must give an account that satisfies their electoral as well as their moral constituents. If voters consistently decline to consider the well-being of nonresidents, representatives cannot consistently prefer their moral constituents to their electoral ones. That is a truth emphasized by procedural democracy. But the truth expresses only a political necessity, not a moral virtue. In deliberative democracy, representatives are justified in appealing to political necessity only insofar as they continue to try to persuade their electoral constituents to take seriously the claims of their moral constituents.

On a deliberative conception of accountability, representatives should not always take the views of their constituents as given. The deliberative response to the problem of specialization is also part of the response to the problem of constituency. By giving reasons and responding to criticism, representatives try to persuade their constituents to take a broader view of the responsibilities of government. Unlike Dr. Schaller, they will not treat the claims of nonresidents as a reason to deny the medical claims of their own residents. Like the Oregon health care officials, they can ask their constituents to think more often in the "first person plural." Like Senator Heidepriem, they can urge them to look beyond the borders of their state and consider the national implications of local legislative action.

How far beyond the borders should deliberative accountability take the representative? Moving from a local to a national perspective is a familiar and often necessary journey of justification. For policies such as health care that call for major commitment of resources, have significant effects across state lines, and require little variation by region, the reasons representatives give should certainly take account of the claims of national constituencies. Some of these same considerations also argue for broadening the scope of accountability beyond national boundaries. To what extent should the citizens of other societies also count as the moral constituents of representatives in this country?

Representatives need not always, or even generally, pay as much attention to the welfare of citizens of other countries as they do to the welfare of the citizens of their own country. Representatives have enough trouble making public policies that deal adequately with our problems. For most of the policies of the welfare state—from health care to unemployment insurance—representatives are probably justified, for reasons of both competence and fairness, in giving priority to citizens of their own country. But it is necessary that they be able to justify this priority in each case (and that may be less easy to do than is usually assumed).

To the extent that representatives accept this burden of justification, foreigners become moral constituents. Our representatives may ignore their welfare only for reasons that foreigners can also accept. In this significant sense, foreigners stand under the protection of reciprocity. But if we accept this implication of deliberative accountability, there are likely to be some policies to which foreigners might morally object. Perhaps they do not have any claim on Americans to give them health care on an ongoing basis, but surely they have some right to object to policies that harm their health. They may, for example, take exception to U.S. policy on exporting hazardous products, especially toxic wastes, to their country.

Until recently, the United States exported large quantities of waste designated as hazardous by the Environmental Protection Agency.[30] Some went to Canada and Mexico, countries that ship about the same amount here, but some (including toxic chemicals that were mixed into fertilizer) went to developing countries such as Bangladesh and South Africa. The United States participated in negotiations that produced the Basel Convention of 1989, which limits international trade in waste, but declined to sign the pact. In 1994 Carol Browner, the new EPA administrator, sought to bring U.S. policy into line with the convention by banning most such exports. Her proposal reversed the policy of previous administrations, which let U.S. companies send waste to any nation that agreed to receive it. This earlier policy in effect denied that U.S. representatives must justify their policies to foreign citizens: our representatives should concern themselves only with what is good for Americans and the American economy, and let foreign governments and the free market take care of the well-being of their own citizens. Two kinds of arguments could be offered in support of this position, and if either were valid, it would justify limiting the scope of accountability of our representatives.[31]

One set of reasons refers to the fact that foreign nations voluntarily accept our exports. This constitutes an argument from consent, but it mistakenly identifies the consent of the government, or in some cases the consent of certain business groups, with the consent of citizens. The kind of individual or even collective consent that might justify the practice is not usually present. Many countries to which the United States exports hazardous products are not representative democracies. Their citizens have thus not consented, either collectively or individually, to the health risks that the hazardous wastes impose. Even in those countries that are democratic, we cannot assume that a majority of citizens consent to the policy in any meaningful way unless they are well informed about the life-threatening risks that the wastes pose. It is not likely that most citizens know about the policy, let alone appreciate its risks. Even if they do, they may not be able to avoid exposure to the risks without sacrificing their livelihood or some other basic opportunity. If U.S. officials took seriously the argument from consent, they would have to reject the practice or else support extensive political reforms that would educate the citizens of foreign countries (as well as the U.S.) about these risks and enact rules that would permit exports only when genuine consent could be established.

A second set of reasons is intended to show that exports actually benefit citizens in other countries, offering products that are less hazardous than those otherwise available, and generally improving their standard of living. For many products, however, it is not clear that this kind of claim can be established. Some of the hazardous wastes are made into fertilizer, but it remains an open question whether the benefits from the fertilizer outweigh the risks to health. In the case of carcinogenic pesticides (such as heptachlor, DBCP, and dioxins), the risks are high.[32] Moreover, they tend to fall on the most disadvantaged citizens rather than on those who benefit most from improvements in the economy through international trade. The effects on the welfare of citizens in these countries are at the least uncertain, and anyone who relies on an argument for welfare needs to provide more evidence about those effects than is usually available.

But more than the argument from consent, this argument brings citizens of foreign nations into our moral framework. A representative who appeals to the welfare of these citizens, even for the purpose of justifying the export of hazardous waste, is already acknowledging these citizens as moral constituents. This kind of appeal recognizes the broader scope of deliberative accountability. The representative is giving an account to which citizens of other countries can respond; its defect is that it is one that they have good moral reasons to reject. The problem, then, is less the absence of moral deliberation than the deficiency of its content. The reasons are deficient mainly because they assume without adequate evidence that the policy actually improves the welfare of foreign citizens.

Because even representatives who acknowledge the demands of deliberative accountability sometimes give deficient accounts, deliberative democracy does not guarantee that the claims of foreigners will receive the attention they deserve. Nor does it provide any formula for determining how to balance the claims of our fellow citizens against those of foreigners when they come into conflict. Some institutional changes might help achieve a more justifiable balance. For example, forums could be established in which representatives would speak for the ordinary citizens of foreign countries, presenting their claims and responding to the counterclaims of our representatives. Such a process could help correct the bias of the commercial and government-to-government negotiations that dominate policy-making on these issues. Environmental impact statements might also be required to consider effects on citizens of other countries.

The purpose of such practices would be not only to inform representatives about the claims of foreigners but also to educate citizens about their circumstances. As in other cases in which deliberative democracy extends accountability, the process depends on the moral capacities of voters as well as on those of representatives. No representative can champion the cause of moral constituents for long without winning the support of electoral constituents. The more closely the perspectives of electoral constituents track those of moral constituents, the more nearly the deliberative principle of accountability can be realized.

THE STATUS OF GROUPS

In the spring of 1993, President Clinton withdrew his nomination of Lani Guinier to be assistant attorney general for civil rights.[33] He said he had recently read some of her law review articles, and found that he disagreed with her views on group representation. Specifically, he disagreed with her proposals for changes in the electoral system that would give blacks more weight in the legislative process.

Guinier's critics portrayed her views on group representation as extremist. They charged that the reforms she proposed would be divisive, antimajoritarian, and undemocratic. (These charges came even from senators who on other occasions had shown no hesitation in using the antimajoritarian procedure of the filibuster.) Modifying electoral systems to facilitate group representation is far more common and widely accepted than her critics imply. But both the critics and defenders of group representation are correct in believing that it raises important theoretical and practical difficulties for a democracy. Our primary concern here is whether group representation helps or hinders deliberative democracy—in particular, whether it is consistent with deliberative accountability.[34]

The reasons that deliberative accountability requires are given to and by individuals. The individual is the only kind of agent who can judge whether a reason should be accepted as a basis for fair cooperation, in accordance with reciprocity. That individuals should finally make this judgment is a basic premise of any democracy that grants the right to vote only to individuals. To this extent the principle of accountability is inescapably individualist. But to accept the premise that reasons must be given to and by individuals is not to determine the question whether the reasons must refer only to individuals. Individuals may decide to express their own claims in terms of the interests of groups, and representatives may choose to respond to the claims in the same terms. Furthermore, both citizens and their representatives may decide to design their electoral systems so as to facilitate the expression of group interests in this way. The question is to what extent such designs are compatible with deliberation.

Group representation in a general form is familiar enough. Citizens identify with various social groups, and see their own prospects as depending on those of their group. When a legislator represents an individual who identifies with a group in this way, the legislator represents the group as well as the individual. Rather than requiring any special institutional design, this kind of group representation occurs as a matter of course. Legislators succeed in representing groups without even trying. Perhaps because it seems so natural and because it serves established groups, group representation in this form has few critics, and President Clinton is not among them.

What Clinton (and others) evidently object to in this instance are changes in the electoral system deliberately designed to give some groups a political advantage over others. Since these changes are intended to benefit groups that are otherwise disadvantaged in the political process, they implement what may be called compensatory group representation. The rationale for such changes is based partly on claims of justice. A majoritarian electoral system that does not provide special protections for disadvantaged minorities is likely to produce unjust results because the interests of advantaged groups will continue to be more effectively represented. Judicial protections are not enough because they protect only some basic liberties and opportunities. Many of the actions of government that critically affect some of our basic liberties and opportunities—such as policies on education, health, and employment—remain largely in the province of legislatures, not courts. In Chapter 9 we examine the general form of this justification when we consider the case for preferential hiring. Much of the logic of that analysis applies here insofar as compensatory group representation is seen as a way of protecting the basic opportunities of disadvantaged citizens. But even if such representation could serve social justice in this way, we need to ask whether, and to what extent, it serves the democratic process. Specifically, is it compatible with deliberative accountability?

The answer depends in large part on exactly what institutional form the representation takes, and what the alternatives are. Guinier's most controversial proposal is "proportionate interest representation," a system of cumulative voting, which establishes multimember districts and gives multiple votes to each citizen so as to increase the chances that blacks will be able to elect at least one representative.[35] For example, in Chilton County, Alabama, instead of casting one vote in each of seven contests for county commissioner as in the past, county citizens now elect the entire county commission in one election, each citizen having seven votes to use however he or she chooses.[36]

Guinier does not present this scheme mainly as a way of improving political deliberation. Her own theory, she implies, is as much "interest-based" as "deliberative."[37] But multimember districting has the potential to enhance, at least in some respects, the process of deliberation in the legislature. It could encourage "cross-racial coalitions," as voters try to elect more than one candidate, and as candidates try to broaden their support and improve their chances of election and reelection. Once in office, candidates would continue to have an incentive to address the concerns of citizens of more than their own racial, religious, or ethnic group. The favorable effects of such a scheme would of course depend on the particular configuration of political forces in the district, and also on its political culture. Multimember districts are probably less conducive to deliberation during elections than districts that produce closely contested elections across racial and other politically relevant lines. But they are probably more conducive to electoral deliberation, as well as legislative deliberation, than the racial gerrymandering that Guinier wishes to avoid.

A system gerrymandered by race (or religion or ethnicity) may bring more diverse representatives into legislatures—more in the spirit of traditional group representation. But it is also more likely to be racially (or religiously or ethnically) divisive than intradistrict electoral reform of the kind advocated by Guinier, and therefore usually less conducive to deliberation in the long run. Representatives from racially gerrymandered districts have greater need to speak exclusively for the groups that predominate in their district, and to distinguish themselves sharply from representatives from other districts where different groups predominate. Some exclusiveness in representation may be desirable if it is the only way that the long-standing grievances of black citizens can be effectively addressed. But as a permanent mode of representation, it is likely further to divide citizens and discourage deliberation.

Deliberative accountability calls for more extensive representation in the public forum. To this extent, advocates of compensatory group representation are right to urge that "a democratic public should provide mechanisms for the effective recognition and representation of the distinct voices and perspectives of those of its constituent groups that are oppressed or disadvantaged."[38] But sometimes the advocates seem to suggest that their aim is to certify or encourage group identity for its own sake, and sometimes simply to increase the number of representatives of certain groups in positions of power. Whatever the merits of these objectives, they do not alone satisfy the moral standards of deliberative accountability.

It is not sufficient (and not always even necessary) to show that a procedural reform gives more political power to disadvantaged groups or that it increases the number of representatives who identify with and are identified by a disadvantaged group. In the first place, there are difficulties in deciding which groups are entitled to such representation.[39] Many of the lists of "oppressed groups" in need of special representation turn out to include the vast majority of Americans. Even theorists sympathetic to differentiated citizenship do not favor a system that recognizes every such group.[40] To guard against balkanizing citizens into so many distinct groups, any form of group representation should be carefully tailored to the context. Guinier's argument for disadvantaged group representation is specifically addressed to overcoming the problems of racism in the United States, arguably the most urgent domestic issue of social justice. Group representation schemes that are designed primarily for black Americans may be justified even if group representation for every disadvantaged group would be impracticable.

There is a second and more general reason why greater political power or recognition should not be the main goal of group representation. Increasing the political power of some disadvantaged groups may be a necessary condition for better deliberation, but some ways of increasing the political power of groups also damage deliberation. Representatives who speak in the name of groups do not always speak for the good of their members. If they do not reach out to work with representatives of other groups, seeking policies that can be justified from a reciprocal perspective, they are less likely to forge the coalitions necessary to sustain policies that will serve their constituents, electoral as well as moral.

Before justifying compensatory group representation in a deliberative democracy, then, we should determine whether it encourages more representatives to pay more attention to the voices of neglected citizens, fosters cooperation between representatives of those citizens and representatives of other citizens, and stimulates all representatives to give reasons and invoke moral principles that cut across racial and group divisions. Group representation is not itself a moral end, but electoral schemes that satisfy these conditions may be justifiable means to better representation, especially in a society that is still plagued with racism and other forms of discrimination against disadvantaged minorities. At the same time, we should continue to search for systems of representation that will enhance deliberation for all citizens. That was part of the aim of the system of the single transferable vote (a form of proportional representation) that John

Stuart Mill advocated.[41] It should also be a primary aim of any changes we make in our current system of representation.

Like other proposals that seriously address the problem of representation in a pluralist society, Guiner's should not be dismissed simply because it may require major changes in our current practices of representation. These practices do not now typically come close to satisfying deliberative principles. To what extent the proposals offered by Guinier, Mill, and others satisfy the principle of accountability and other conditions of deliberative democracy is partly an empirical question, one on which the answers are likely to vary with circumstance and to change over time. Any assessment of the merits of these systems must therefore also continue over time, taking place in the same process of deliberation in which the merits of other public policies are discussed. This means that representatives deliberate about who is entitled to participate in their deliberations. Deliberation determines the identity of the deliberators. In a democracy there is no way to avoid this circularity completely. Representatives and citizens therefore need to establish and maintain strong standards for deliberation—in particular, a robust principle of accountability.

BACK TO THE FUTURE

Unlike citizens in other districts or other countries, and unlike members of disadvantaged groups, future generations do not yet exist. That creates a problem for the principle of accountability. The difficulty is not simply the gap between electoral and moral constituents. If that were the only problem, it could be addressed by treating future generations like nonresidents or groups, and finding ways to encourage representatives and their electoral constituents to take their presumptive claims seriously. Ultimately that approach must be part of any solution, but a prior problem must be overcome first: the policies that we adopt now affect *who* will live in the future.[42] Public policies influence the pattern and timing of marriages and births, and thereby determine which people will populate the future. It follows that members of future generations cannot object that they are harmed by any policies we adopt now. They cannot claim that they would have been better served by a different policy because, if a different policy had been chosen, they would not have existed.

The implication of this fluid status of future generations is that the principle of accountability cannot refer directly to claims or interests of future citizens. If representatives are to give reasons that could be accepted by future generations, they will have to take a different form from the reasons they give to electoral and even other moral constituents. Why this is so, and what kinds of reasons might be necessary can be clarified by considering several different responses to the problem of representing future generations.

In a newspaper column chiding "Generation X" (the "despairing twenty-somethings"), a political commentator asks: "Why should one group of people—the current generation—sacrifice anything at all so that a different group of people—the next generation—can be better off, when the second group will be better off than the first group in any event?" His answer (based "less in logic than in emotions") invokes "the desire of parents to see their children prosper and of patriots to see their country thrive."[43] Leaving aside the assumption that the next generation will in fact be better off (to which we return later), this answer is probably the most commonly accepted reason for respecting the claims of future generations. The answer is plausible as far as it goes, but it does not go very far. Given the fluidity problem just described, emotional attachments cannot extend beyond two or three generations. Forced to rely on "logic," we would still lack reasons to attend to more remote future generations.

A second response takes this logic all too seriously. It simply abandons the idea that representatives should have to justify their actions to future generations in any way. On this view public officials do not owe anyone— even their constituents—an account of how their actions will affect future citizens because future generations have no claims or interests that can be represented. An exception may be made for those likely to be born in the near future, insofar as their interests can be closely identified with the interests of those living now, such as parents and grandparents. But representatives have no reason to try to justify their actions to those who will live in the more distant future.

This response may be tempting because of the difficulty of finding a way to express why representatives should care about future generations without falling back on the mistaken claim that public policies harm people who would not otherwise exist. But the response might also be appealing for another reason. It may seem to be warranted by the practice of discounting future claims in the manner familiar to economists and policy analysts. On this approach representatives should take into account the (assumed) preferences of future generations but give them less weight than the preferences of the present generation.

The most important justification for discounting future claims is based on the idea of opportunity costs. Resources allocated to public policies that benefit future generations, such as pollution controls on carbon dioxide, must be diverted from other uses. To favor the future, we must forgo present opportunities; the cost of doing so is measured by the rate of return that these resources would otherwise have earned. If the rate of return is assumed to be 10 percent (a typical discount rate for government projects), then the value of the benefits to future generations will be equal to their present value reduced by 10 percent per year. At this rate, however, the value of a government policy quickly declines the further in the future its benefits are expected to be enjoyed. The claims of the generation that will live, say, one hundred years from now will have little if any weight in a calculus carried out now at any plausible discount rate. A discount rate of this kind would permit representatives to ignore completely some of the most serious risks of radioactive wastes governments are now burying, since they will fall on generations many centuries in the future.

Although the case for using some kind of discount rate in choosing public policies is compelling, the case for any particular rate is controversial. No actual rate of return in the market accurately reflects even the current generation's preferences about how much should be distributed to succeeding generations. Actual rates are skewed by the inequalities in current income distribution, and also by the failure of the market to measure some values that citizens care about. Some policy analysts suggest that, instead of expressing opportunity costs, the discount rate should be "a conscious value judgment as to the rate at which society wishes to trade off future for present resources."[44] But, this approach, still rooted in the preferences of the current generation, provides no basis for assuming that the claims of future generations receive their due.

Another justification for discounting the future is based on uncertainty. Because we have less confidence about what citizens will want in the future, and what risks they will face fifty years from now, we are warranted today in valuing the claims of those who will be alive tomorrow more than the claims of those who will live fifty years from now. Uncertainty is not generally regarded by policy analysts as a reason to increase the discount rate.[45] But the effect on the status of the claims of future generations is similar: uncertainty reinforces the tendency to count the claims of future generations much less than those of the current generation, and those of remote generations not at all.

Representatives should of course take uncertainty into account. But uncertainty about the limits of uncertainty itself allows its influence to expand without limit. It spreads a fog over the future that prevents representatives from seeing clearly any claims of succeeding generations beyond the next two or three. If the future is so uncertain, representatives do not need even to ask whether our generation is justified, for example, in risking irreversible damage to the environment by depleting fossil fuels and polluting the atmosphere. Other damage, such as that resulting from the disposal of nuclear waste, is even less likely to be considered. These so-called "sleeper effects" remain dormant for many generations but then may cause catastrophic damage. The appeal to uncertainty often becomes "an excuse for myopia."[46]

A related justification for discounting the claims of future citizens has more moral content. Later generations benefit from the accumulated capital of society—the store of knowledge, the experience of social cooperation, and other factors that are not fully captured by the market or any other measure. We are justified in shifting more burdens to our successors than would be morally warranted in relations with our contemporaries because we are also providing our successors with some of the resources they will need to cope with the burdens. This justification explicitly addresses the issue of fairness, but its implications are ambiguous. Indeed, when we recognize that future generations may also face more difficult problems than we face, it is not clear on balance whether the discount for the future should be negative or positive.

Thus, the standard ways of considering the needs of future generations would justify representatives' not merely discounting but actually dismissing the claims of distant future generations. In varying degrees and with varying moral bases, they justify a response to the problem that would permit representatives to believe that they do not owe any account at all to the distant future.

A third response takes the needs of future generations seriously—so seriously that their value goes beyond what representatives should legitimately consider. According to Ronald Dworkin, "Our concern for future generations is not a matter of justice at all but of our instinctive sense that human flourishing as well as human survival is of sacred importance."[47] Ascribing sacred importance to future generations seems to elevate their status: if representatives justify their actions in such hallowed terms, what more can we ask? Future generations could ask no more accountability than this even from God.

The appeal to human flourishing expresses an important part of the justification that representatives should give in a deliberative democracy. But in this form it presents a serious difficulty. Justifying laws on the basis of sacred value comes close to legislating religion, and any democracy that values basic liberty must be wary of encouraging that kind of legislation. Dworkin himself suggests that beliefs about one sacred value—the inherent value of human life—are *"essentially* religious."[48] He argues that under certain conditions (notably those that apply in the case of abortion), the government may not curtail liberty to protect an intrinsic value, and that to do so is "tantamount to establishing one interpretation of the sanctity of life as the official creed of the community."[49] Most views about the value of future generations, at least when their policy implications are specified, are likely to express "differing interpretations of a shared belief in the sanctity of human life."[50] On Dworkin's view and that of many liberals, these interpretations would therefore be suspect as reasons for justifying any form of coercive government action. They would not be readily available for representatives seeking to satisfy the principle of accountability.

It is of course possible that interpretations about the sacred value of future generations could converge. If so, representatives could appeal to that value in justifying their actions. When the community is "not seriously divided about what respect for intrinsic value requires," and basic liberties are respected, liberals such as Dworkin do not object to legislation to promote that value.[51] But the turn toward the sacred in public deliberation is not a promising route to a reciprocal perspective. It is more likely to lead citizens to think in religious terms and thus to encourage them to affirm their moral differences rather than their agreements. Given that risk, we should at least look for alternatives. A better strategy for deliberative accountability would be to seek a less spiritual basis for respecting future generations.

Yet finding a mundane justification may not be so easy. The most systematic search for a place for future generations in a completely secular theory of justice—exemplified in the work of John Rawls—shows how difficult the task is. In the initial full-length version of his theory, Rawls had trouble formulating within the "original position" a justification for a just savings principle, which requires earlier generations to save for later generations. In the original position we are to reason on the basis of our self-interest but behind a "veil of ignorance" that prevents us from knowing who in particular we are, or in what generation we happen to live.[52] Under these conditions, the reasons individuals give would not be biased in their favor, but the reasons would not appeal to any moral considerations.

What role could future generations play in our reasoning in these circumstances? As part of our self-interest, we could take into account the interests of our immediate descendants but we would have no reason to consider the interests of more remote generations. The veil of ignorance leads people to maximize their interests (and those of their immediate descendants). Thus, "since nothing can be done to change the past," one critic points out, "there is no advantage to the people in the original position in choosing a principle that requires any net savings (or indeed, one might add, prevents them from running things down) unless they actually care about the welfare of the next generation."[53] Even if we assume that people in the original position care about the well-being of their children and their children's children, their concern for future generations must diminish rapidly as they contemplate each succeeding generation. From a moral point of view, the concern diminishes too rapidly. But there is no way to prevent its premature expiration without introducing into the original position the same moral considerations it is designed to do without.

In a later version of his theory, Rawls lets some of these moral considerations come back into the original position. To choose a just savings principle for future generations, individuals are now to apply a kind of golden rule to savings: Do unto future generations as you would have past generations do unto you. A just savings principle is necessary "because society is a system of cooperation between generations over time." The parties in the original position "can be required to agree to a savings principle subject to the further condition that they must want all *previous* generations to have followed it."[54] This argument, and the kinds of reasons it tells representatives to give, moves quite a distance from the self-interested reasoning of the original version of the original position. The newer version is thus much closer to the reciprocal moral reasoning required by deliberative accountability.

The course of Rawls's journey—from constrained self-interest to generational reciprocity—carries a lesson for deliberative democrats. Future generations are not adequately represented if representatives are held accountable only for pursuing the interests of their constituents. To be sure, if these interests are defined to include "moral interests" and constituents are said to have a moral interest in the well-being of future generations, then accountability to the interests of constituents will ensure that public officials care about future generations. But this move either smuggles in a moral argument under the guise of self-interest or else treats our concern for future generations as purely contingent on the interest we take in them.

The deliberative principle of accountability holds representatives accountable not only for satisfying the interests of their constituents but also for acting in a way that can be justified to future generations.

"Do unto future generations as you would have past generations do unto you" thus provides a good starting point for political deliberation. But it may still encourage citizens and representatives to focus too much on interests and similar claims that individual constituents may make on their own behalf. The representation of future generations should not take the form of trying to prevent harms or provide benefits to particular persons. What needs to be represented are not the claims of future individuals but the moral value of human flourishing.

What that kind of value might mean in practice, and what kind of hard choices it might force if taken seriously, can be illustrated by briefly considering the debate over the international Biodiversity Treaty. At the Earth Summit held in Rio de Janiero in 1992, President Bush was branded a "foot-dragger" for failing to take the lead in protecting the international environment.[55] He declined to sign the treaty because he saw few benefits and many significant costs for U.S. citizens, to whom he considered himself primarily accountable. He may have been right that the costs included a moderate decline in the standard of living for some members of the current generation of U.S. citizens.[56] Yet scientists largely agree that future U.S. citizens will suffer if some steps are not taken now to protect the world environment, even at the cost of some serious sacrifices by current citizens. How can public officials in this country justify such sacrifices to those to whom they are directly accountable?

Members of the Clinton administration took a more positive stance toward international environmental cooperation. Reversing the Bush position, they signed the Biodiversity Treaty. Officials gave many different kinds of reasons to justify this change, but the most sustained argument is to be found in the writings of Vice President Albert Gore, Jr., who had long been a champion of environmental causes. Gore acknowledges that environmentalism may require some sacrifices now, but he does not try to justify them by arguing that his environmental policies will benefit our own generation, our children, or even our children's children. His argument is more general. In addition to appealing to an "environmentalism of the spirit" that evokes sacred values, Gore also puts a more secular question to citizens: What will future generations say about what we have done to their world?[57]

This is just the kind of question that deliberative accountability should pose to citizens and their representatives. If we imagine that future generations will answer this question by saying that our neglect drastically reduced the possibilities for human flourishing in their world, we will now have reason for reconsidering the direction of our policies. Although the future citizens we imagine cannot say that they themselves would have been better off, they can say that the human world would have been better off had we adopted better polices. Ways of life would have been better; the world would have enjoyed more intrinsic value. Such answers are powerful precisely because they do not express some self-interested complaint of future generations. Because they do not say that "we as individuals would be better off had our predecessors shown more concern for our interests," they make a moral argument that avoids the fluidity problem and ultimately transcends generations. It is an argument that citizens and representatives of our generation can make as convincingly as future generations. They can make it convincingly if they accept the responsibility to broaden their constituency to embrace the value of human flourishing in the future.

Yet there is no complete escape from the present. In any electoral democracy representatives must confront citizens who live now, not in the future. Deliberative democracy holds out hope that representatives will appeal to principles that transcend the present, but only if representatives and citizens come through mutual discussion to understand their significance in the present. To encourage this common understanding—to bring the minds of representatives and citizens back to the future—some institutional reforms may help. Some of the changes could take advantage of quite immediate political interests. Changes in tax laws and lobbying regulations could increase the incentives for citizens to organize groups that speak for future generations. Broadening the requirements for environmental impact statements—requiring a "future generations impact statement"—could focus public attention on the longer-range effects of our current policies. Bestowing public honors and in other ways giving more recognition to citizens and public officials whose actions show exceptional concern for future generations could shift the perspective of public debate in small but significant ways. Exploiting the "love of fame after death"— a motive that even Hobbes thought influenced political leaders[58]—could extend the temporal horizons of the democratic process.

In addition to its own distinctive difficulties, extending moral constituency temporally to embrace future generations poses some of the same fundamental challenges as does broadening the idea of constituency spatially to include nonresidents and disadvantaged groups. In both these dimensions the theory and practice of democracy depends on the capacity of citizens and their representatives to take a moral point of view. In both, democratic deliberation serves to encourage representatives to give reasons that transcend the boundaries of electoral constituency.

The principle of deliberative accountability does not purport to offer a determinate answer to the question of what representatives should do in all cases when the claims of their electoral constituents conflict with those of their moral constituents, whether nonresidents, groups, or future generations. Indeed, we should be suspicious of any theoretical principle that offers simple rules for the complex cases of moral conflict that representatives and their constituents confront. But deliberative accountability can help us avoid the mistaken tendencies of the forms of accountability favored in procedural and constitutional democracy.

Had Senator Heidepriem acted as a purely procedural representative, he would have simply deferred to his constituents instead of deliberating with them. In fact, up to a point Heidepreiem did act in the spirit of deliberative democracy: he explained his reasons for taking a pro-choice position, and he responded to his constituents' reasons for favoring the pro-life bill. Deliberative accountability also provided him with a cogent response to those who claimed that South Dakota politics should not be influenced by "outsiders"—in particular, national pro-choice organizations. Since abortion legislation in South Dakota affects the basic liberty of citizens, it is a legitimate matter of concern not only to the voters of South Dakota but also to nonvoters and nonresidents as well.

But Heidepriem came close to making a mistake that some constitutional democrats encourage: he relied too much on what the Supreme Court says the Constitution says. In its strongest form, constitutional democracy tells representatives to consider how the Constitution should be interpreted, not simply to accept how the courts have so far interpreted it. Deliberative democracy goes further. To satisfy its demands, a representative such as Heidepriem must consider, and encourage his constituents to consider with him in public discussion, what basic liberties should be protected by the Constitution. Without engaging in deliberation about this question, neither he nor his constituents can regard their conclusions about constitutional liberties as warranting the respect of their fellow citizens. They may be convinced that they are right—they may even be right—about what the Constitution requires or should require. But if they are deliberative democrats, they will submit their constitutional conclusions to the critical scrutiny of their fellow citizens, conducted in accord with principles of reciprocity and publicity. They will regard the capacity to survive such scrutiny as a necessary condition and a substantial reason for making their conclusions the law of the land.

The problems of specialization and constituency are not completely resolvable.[59] They result from conflicts inherent in the process of representative democracy itself, and they are intensified by the reason-giving demands of deliberative democracy as it broadens the scope of accountability. But these same demands also point toward both a better way of understanding those conflicts and a better approach to living with them than do conceptions of accountability that neglect deliberation. Deliberative accountability makes democracy more justifiable to those who enjoy, and sometimes suffer, its consequences.

—5—

The Promise of Utilitarianism

THE THREE PRINCIPLES that constitute the conditions of deliberation place some limits on the content of deliberation, but they leave a lot of democratic discretion unconstrained and therefore a lot of moral disagreement unresolved. Some theorists have thought that they could do better, and have proposed principles designed to eliminate or at least greatly diminish the domain of moral disagreement in politics. The approach that seems most promising for this purpose is utilitarianism, which (in the version most relevant for public policy) holds that government should seek to maximize the welfare of the greatest number of citizens.

Utilitarianism is the most influential—and still most widely accepted—way of attempting to resolve moral conflicts that arise in the making of public policy.[1] Although it is a species of the impartialist approach criticized in Chapter 2, it has some features that give it a special appeal in politics, and call for further critical examination. In ordinary political debate, utilitarianism usually appears in the form of calls to consider the effects of a policy on the welfare of all citizens. A citizen claims, for example, that the benefit of a new environmental standard is outweighed by the harm it causes to those who will lose their jobs. In administrative agencies and on legislative staffs, it exerts its influence by means of welfare economics and, in a more practical form, policy analysis.[2] The utilitarian way of thinking, known by many different names and seen with many different faces, pervades the public forum in middle democracy.

The strongest and most sophisticated forms of utilitarianism appear in the work of several contemporary moral philosophers.[3] Although we draw on some of these theories, we do not treat them here as candidates for principles to guide deliberation in politics, and therefore do not direct our criticisms primarily at them. The proponents of these theories generally seek foundations for morality rather than frameworks for political argument. Even if utilitarianism were to turn out to be the most acceptable foundation for morality, it would not necessarily be the most satisfactory basis for dealing with moral conflict in politics. Our primary interest here is in the characteristic strengths and weaknesses of modes of utilitarianism in discussing moral conflicts in politics. We are mainly concerned with the reasons that utilitarians give to justify public policies, and thus with the vocation of utilitarianism in action in middle democracy.

Unlike majoritarianism and constitutionalism, utilitarianism puts morality directly into the political processes of middle democracy. It offers a perspective from which to give moral reasons in politics, and by which to evaluate them. It does so by positing a single sovereign principle that would enable decision-makers to compare competing values and arrive at a uniquely correct answer to the question: How should citizens and officials resolve moral conflict over public policy? We argue that utilitarianism fails to provide a satisfactory answer to this question because it either neglects moral claims that should have a place in deliberation or abandons its own claim to provide a distinctive resolution to conflicts.

To assess the role of utilitarianism in democratic politics, we use a case of moral disagreement of a kind that seems especially amenable to its method: a dispute about environmental regulation in one metropolitan area in the 1980s. Amid growing public concern about the environment, Congress passed a series of laws in the early 1970s intended to protect the quality of air, water, and other natural resources throughout the United States. This landmark legislation, which included the Clean Water and Clean Air Acts, won widespread support, and has been widely praised.[4] The remarkable consensus on an issue bristling with moral and political conflict was achieved in part by a strategy of avoidance: legislators used broad language and indefinite standards that left many of the specific problems to be resolved later by administrators, state and local officials, and ordinary citizens. This approach differed from more recent and more immediately contentious measures such as the bill establishing the Superfund, which includes administrative regulations that run to more than five-hundred pages. In contrast, the Clean Air Act simply authorizes the Environmental Protection Agency (EPA) to set emissions standards that provide an "ample margin of safety" to protect the public health.[5]

The broadened language did not quell the controversy for long. When the EPA tried to specify what should count as an "ample" margin of safety for hazardous air pollutants, the familiar conflicts broke out again. All four sources of moral conflict are plainly present here in full force: scarcity of clean air, employment, and profits; the limited generosity of employers, employees, and other citizens threatened by industrial pollution; the incompatible ends of minimizing health risks and maximizing job opportunities and corporate profits; and the incomplete understanding of the complex questions of health risks and industrial alternatives. The Clean Air Act offers little guidance in resolving these conflicts because its approach, like that of much environmental law, implies that there is only one goal that policymakers should pursue.

In 1983 EPA administrator William Ruckelshaus directly confronted the conflicts created by the act and sought to formulate a policy that went beyond satisfying its single goal of environmental safety. In the broadest terms, his aim can be seen as reaching a resolution of the conflicts that could be morally acceptable to all citizens. But he began with the more limited question left for his agency by the language of the Clean Air Act: What margin of safety is ample for a hazardous substance such as inorganic arsenic? His search for an answer produced a public debate that brought national attention to the American Smelting and Refining Company (Asarco) in the tiny town of Ruston, population 636, just outside Tacoma, Washington.[6]

The only producer of industrial arsenic in this country, Asarco had long been regarded as "one of the major polluters in the Northwest."[7] Even small amounts of airborne arsenic increase the risk of cancer, and EPA experts estimated that the large quantities Asarco was releasing into the air were causing at least four cancer deaths a year within a twelve-mile radius of the plant. If Asarco were required to use the "best available technology" to reduce arsenic pollution, the death rate could be cut to one a year. The cost, EPA said, would be $3.5 million in additional capital outlays, which was likely not only to reduce Asarco's profits but also to force the layoff of some workers. The cost of eliminating cancer deaths entirely within that radius would be far greater. Asarco said that it would have to shut down if the EPA decided to enforce the most stringent (zero-death) standard. Asarco employed approximately 575 workers on an annual payroll of $23 million, paid $3 million in state and local taxes, spent $12 million locally, and indirectly supported another $13 million worth of local business.

Public opinion in the area was divided over what should be done. Most residents of Ruston, who depended on Asarco for their livelihood, opposed the stricter emission controls, fearing that the plant would have to close. The former mayor of Ruston, a longtime Asarco employee, said: "I've worked in the plant all my life. So have my brothers, and so have my neighbors. We're not sick . . . Now the government's . . . trying to take our children's livelihood away."[8] Other Asarco employees argued that the stresses of unemployment would probably cause more loss of life (through other illnesses and suicide) than the disputed effects of inorganic arsenic emissions.

Most residents of Tacoma and nearby Vashon Island, a middle-income community across the bay from Ruston, favored the stricter emission standards, even at the risk of causing Asarco to close. As one homeowner said: "I'm not for the loss of jobs. [But] . . . people who staked their life savings on a place and a home are finding they can't enjoy the land because of the emissions of the Asarco plant."[9] Other nearby residents resented being "the dumping grounds for these pollutants without any benefits such as jobs or Asarco tax payments." A member of the Tacoma city council likened the effects of Asarco's pollution to "somebody standing on the other side of the city line with a thirty-ought-six and firing it into Tacoma." Another resident put it more simply: "I'm concerned about getting lung cancer." As the controversy intensified, the conflict of values was starkly captured by the newspaper headlines: "Smelter Workers Have Choice: Keep Their Jobs or Their Health," and "Tacoma Gets Choice: Cancer Risk or Lost Jobs."[10]

The Asarco dispute has several features that lend themselves to the kind of analysis that utilitarianism favors. First, as a public official representing all citizens, Ruckelshaus sought a method that would enable him to take into account all the conflicting claims that citizens were making, not just the single goal of protection from air pollution. At the same time, utilitarianism would also permit him to challenge some of those claims. With utilitarian methods, he could include all the preferences in his calculations, but he could also criticize those that were not based on adequate information. Second, as utilitarians urge, Ruckelshaus wanted to concentrate on the consequences of the policy, not the motives of the various parties to the dispute. Nor could he allow himself to let the immediate harms distract him from the long-term effects of the policy that utilitarians would tell him to keep in view. Third, Ruckelshaus had to find a way to compare the conflicting values in this case—the choice between jobs and health. These values were often already expressed in quantitative terms in the public debate, and therefore seemed fit for translation into a common measure—utility, or its more familiar surrogate, money. Some of Ruckelshaus's staff, trained in the techniques of policy analysis, were prepared to carry out the translation. Whatever the difficulties of this translation might be, it seemed to offer more hope of finding some common ground than the discourse of rights, which would have had the effect of blocking further comparison of the competing claims. Thus, to the extent that utilitarianism succeeds in dealing adequately with the Asarco dispute, it looks promising as a way for guiding debate not only on the issue of environmental protection, but also more generally on a broad range of public policy problems with similar features.

Elements of Utilitarianism

In these features of the Asarco problem that Ruckelshaus faced, we can see the three characteristic elements of utilitarianism in politics. First, utilitarianism offers a single *inclusive* end—utility—that is intended to accommodate all other ends citizens may have, insofar as they can be made compatible with one another. Unlike the other preeminent political ends that political theorists propose—Hobbes's security, Locke's life, liberty, and property, or Rousseau's community, all of which exclude other ends—utility is intended to include all of these and more. In the classical utilitarianism of Bentham, any end that anyone pursues counts as a kind of utility.[11] Utilitarianism commends itself as a method that—at least initially—welcomes all claims.

Contemporary utilitarians define utility in terms of some form of well-being, most commonly as a form of the satisfaction of preferences. The end is understood as a state of affairs that best satisfies revealed preferences (as indicated by actual behavior) or informed preferences (as indicated by hypothetical behavior). These understandings could in theory yield different results, but they tend to converge in practice. On either approach, policymakers may decide not to count some expressed preferences. They may reject, for example, those that are not stable or those that are not consistent with some other preferences. By the same token, in order to justify a decision to discount some preferences on either approach, policymakers have to appeal ultimately to preferences that people actually are expected to have, at least in the future. On both approaches utility remains an inclusive end.

In this spirit utilitarianism promises to be democratic. The original utilitarians were democratic reformers, fighting to extend the franchise and denouncing the privileges of the aristocracy. Everyone counts for one, Bentham is reported to have said, and no one for more than one.[12] A utilitarian policymaker tries to give people as much as possible of whatever they want. In this respect Ruckelshaus was more faithful to utilitarianism than he might at first appear. Faced with the difficult moral conflict, he took his staff to Tacoma to find out what citizens' preferences actually were, and also to give citizens information that might change their preferences.

His strategy did run counter to two types of utilitarianism. He did not behave like a "Government House utilitarian," calculating costs and benefits with a method that citizens could not comprehend and assuming rational preferences that they might or might not hold.[13] "For me to sit here in Washington, and tell the people of Tacoma what is an acceptable risk would be at best arrogant and at worst inexcusable," he said.[14] Neither did he act like what we might call a Caesarian utilitarian, taking preferences "as given," correcting only for conflicts with other preferences.[15] In an editorial titled "Mr. Ruckelshaus as Caesar," the *New York Times* accused Ruckelshaus of pandering to public opinion like a Roman emperor "who would ask the amphitheater crowd to signal with thumbs up or down whether a defeated gladiator should live or die."[16] But Ruckelshaus had no such intention. The citizens of Tacoma "know that the right to be heard is not the same thing as the right to be heeded."[17] Furthermore, Ruckelshaus hoped that giving citizens more information might alter some of their preferences. Neither of these two positions (either counting only rational preferences or taking preferences as given) is essential to utilitarianism.

Ruckelshaus followed a different approach, one that was consistent with this first element of utilitarianism and—up to a point—with the conditions of deliberative democracy. Part of this approach consisted in holding a series of public workshops in which EPA officials presented information from epidemiological studies, risk calculations, and dispersion models. The information was designed to help citizens understand the costs and benefits of the alternative policies that EPA was considering, particularly the tradeoffs between risks to health and jobs. After presenting the relevant facts about these alternatives, EPA officials answered questions and listened to comments. A series of public hearings followed the workshops, during which hundreds of people, some speaking for themselves, others representing groups, expressed their views and the views of those whom they represented. Because these hearings followed the workshops, the preferences that citizens expressed, EPA officials could assume, were better informed. The EPA could now take these self-corrected preferences and try to formulate a policy that would maximize the welfare of all the citizens in the region.

The second important element of utilitarianism is its *consequentialism:* the preferences that define utility should refer primarily to states of affairs, not to actions, motives, or character. This element "requires that we check to see whether the act or policy in question actually does some identifiable good or not . . . [It] demands of anyone who condemns something as morally wrong that they show . . . how someone's life is made worse off."[18] To be sure, the motives, moral beliefs, or character of public officials may have important consequences for policy, and when they do, the utilitarian stands ready to consider them. But they have no independent moral weight.

Utilitarians rightly remind us that attacks on motive and character distract citizens from the substance of issues. In Bentham's relentless inventory of political fallacies, "imputation of bad motive" is branded one of the "weakest" forms of argument.[19] The fallacy consists in inferring from the alleged bad motives of the person who proposes a policy that the policy is also bad. This is a mistake, Bentham notes, because "(1) motives are hidden in the human breast, and (2) if the measure is beneficial, it would be absurd to reject on account of the motives of its author."[20] This fallacy, like its companion "imputation of bad character," is an expression of a general "distrust": citizens are encouraged to oppose otherwise desirable policies on the grounds that "there lurk *more behind them* of a very different complexion."[21] Talk about motive and character in this way produces a political discourse that is accessible only to those who can see what is "hidden," what is "behind" policies, rather than what is in them. This is not a discourse that would promote democratic deliberation.

The controversy in the Asarco case evidently was remarkably free of imputations of bad motive and character. Although Ruckelshaus was "highly regarded for his integrity," this did not prevent some environmentalist leaders from at first suspecting his motives. Their suspicion was understandable: the administration he represented had shown little commitment to their goals, and his predecessor at the EPA had failed to enforce many of the laws already on the books.[22] Ruckelshaus had to win the confidence of leaders and citizens by conducting a fair process and making well-supported arguments. Insofar as he succeeded in this aim, it was on the consequentialist terms that utilitarians recommend.

Another way in which the consequentialism of utilitarianism supports a broader perspective on moral conflict lies in its sensitivity to long-range effects. Closing the Asarco plant would be extremely painful for many people, probably more painful in the short run than allowing Asarco to emit cancer-causing pollutants, the harmful effects of which would not be evident until much later. Utilitarianism, however, would not permit the EPA to consider only short-term effects, a perspective that often offers the path of least political resistance. It tells Ruckelshaus to set emissions standards that would produce the best consequences over the long-run, taking uncertainty into account. The moral universe of utilitarian policymakers is expansive: they must consider the moral claims even of those who may not be able to make them now—those who will become sick but do not know it, and those who may be born with birth defects.

The third element of utilitarianism addresses the question: How should the consequences be calculated? The answer seems to follow almost analytically from the first two elements of utilitarianism. If utility is the inclusive end of political morality, and only consequences that produce utility count, then decision makers should try to produce as much utility as they can. Utilitarianism tells policymakers to translate all claims into utility and maximize it.[23]

This element of utilitarianism promises a way to overcome the problem of incompatible ends. Utilitarians do not deny that values may conflict. The EPA cannot simultaneously minimize the risks of cancer and of unemployment. But utilitarians face up to the fact that the EPA must make a political decision that sacrifices one of the values, or some of each, making tradeoffs between them. This kind of decision requires that utilitarians translate all relevant values into the common currency of utility. With this currency, they have a single goal that includes all other values, and can make rational choices among seemingly incompatible values.

The approach that this understanding of utilitarianism recommends—and that Ruckelshaus generally followed—thus considers seriously the moral claims of all citizens. It gives citizens the chance to change their preferences as they learn more about alternatives, and to try to find a policy that can be justified to all concerned. To the extent that this approach succeeds in these aims, it helps fulfill the promise of utilitarianism to provide a perspective for resolving moral conflict, and comes closer to meeting the demands of deliberative democracy.

Yet utilitarianism cannot completely keep this promise. Even in the deliberation-friendly form in which we have tried to present it, utilitarianism falls short. Each of its elements creates problems for a condition of deliberation. First, the democratic promise of utilitarianism may encourage officials to take seriously the informed preferences of all citizens, but it offers a constricted view of democratic accountability. Utilitarians must assume that citizens prefer only utilitarian methods for resolving moral conflicts within the democratic process—an assumption that they cannot consistently maintain. Second, the consequentialism that utilitarians urge broadens the perspective of citizens and officials, but at the same time distorts the meaning of some claims that citizens legitimately make, inducing utilitarians to retreat from the demands of the principle of publicity. Finally, utilitarianism promises to overcome incompatible ends, but its method reintroduces moral conflicts as great as those it claims to resolve. To the extent that it does resolve conflicts, it is at the expense of the fundamental values of liberty and opportunity, which any reciprocal perspective must recognize.

Obstacles to Accountability

Take utilitarians at their word and grant that their method includes the claims of all citizens in the calculation of both the costly and the beneficial consequences of a policy. A policymaker who, like Ruckelshaus, adopted such a method could then plausibly assert that he was accountable to all citizens: he considered all their preferences in his calculations, and gave reasons to those whose preferences he would modify or reject. What he could not justify in this way is his decision to use the utilitarian method itself. It is difficult for citizens to hold utilitarian policymakers accountable for their method because any account these policymakers give presupposes the method.

Utilitarianism puts two obstacles in the way of deliberative accountability. First, utilitarians do not take adequate account of the fact that citizens' preferences can be changed by the political process. Most utilitarians recognize—indeed some insist—that providing more and better information can and should change the preferences of citizens. Utilitarians could approve at least one of Ruckelshaus's aims in Tacoma: to help the citizens of Tacoma become better informed about the risks and benefits of various policies. To this extent utilitarians do not have to take preferences as given, and can permit, even encourage, processes that would cause preferences to change. But the point of democratic deliberation goes beyond changing preferences by providing more information. The preferences of citizens vary not only or even mainly with the amount of information they receive and absorb, but also with how they receive and absorb it—including how their preferences are influenced by participating in politics.[24]

In a democratic process that encourages genuine deliberation, preferences can change not only as citizens are offered more information about policy alternatives, but also as they come to understand the preferences of other citizens and learn to work with one another to discover policy options that they had not previously considered. Deliberation in a public forum is therefore quite different from informed political decision making carried out in private. A deliberative political process may encourage citizens to form views not merely of what they want for themselves but also of what they want for their society. Aggregating what citizens want individually, which is what utilitarian policy analysis does best, does not necessarily produce the same result as asking citizens to consider together what they want collectively.[25]

Citizens have ideals of the good society just as they have ideals of the good life. In addition to wanting good jobs and cleaner air for themselves and their children, they also may care about the social good of more job opportunities or a healthier environment for everyone. At least there is no reason to assume that they do not, so long as their concerns are expressed in a political process that asks them mainly what they want for themselves. Political processes are not neutral with respect to the kind of ideals they encourage: some are more favorable than others to the development of public ideals. Utilitarians can take note of this fact, but their own assumptions stand in the way of taking advantage of it to promote deliberative improvements. Treating all values as individual preferences, utilitarians are not in a strong position to criticize citizens who fail to develop and express social ideals.[26]

Had Ruckelshaus been faithful to this kind of utilitarianism, he would have sought only to inform the citizens of Tacoma about the risks and benefits of each of the policies he was considering. If this were his only aim, he might simply have distributed an informational brochure or perhaps a dramatic video to workers at Asarco and residents of the area. Instead, he held the public workshops, at the cost of considerably more time, money, and controversy. The process his staff designed, whatever the final judgment about its value, evidently had a significant effect on the preferences and, more broadly, the public views of citizens who participated. Ruckelshaus observed that "even the residents of Vashon Island, who were directly exposed to the pollution and yet had no employment or financial stake in the smelter[,] began to ask whether there was a means of keeping the smelter going while reducing pollution levels. They saw the workers from the smelter—encountered them in flesh and blood—and began incorporating the workers' perspective into their own solutions."[27] Even most of Ruckelshaus's critics, some of whom had at first thought he was "copping out," changed their minds after participating in the process. One concluded that "in becoming involved, the public begins to appreciate the difficulty attendant on making regulatory decisions. . . , and the inadequacy of simply identifying 'heroes' and 'villains' in environmental protection."[28]

Yet the critics were right to be wary. Public officials who act as Ruckelshaus did set out on a precarious course. In the spirit of deliberative accountability, their aim is to respect and enlighten citizens at the same time. But the respect can turn into demagoguery and the enlightenment into hegemony. On the one side an official risks pandering to citizens, and on the other manipulating them. Ruckelshaus tried, evidently with some success, to steer a middle course, leading without commanding, attending without following, hearing without heeding. As these metaphorical phrases indicate, there is no formula for the proper exercise of leadership in a deliberative democracy. It calls for a subtle and elusive rendering of role. But the challenge of identifying, encouraging, and assessing better performances of this role—the core of the problem of leadership—is not likely to be a central concern of any approach that, like utilitarianism, is satisfied with public officials who merely inform citizens.

The success of this kind of leadership, and more generally the success of deliberative accountability, is not to be measured by the extent of consensus it produces. Our criticism of utilitarianism for neglecting the way political processes shape preferences does not assume that somehow moral conflicts would be resolved if only the right political processes were put in place. Quite the contrary. Even the most justifiable processes are likely to leave public opinion seriously divided on many issues. The many days of well-led democratic deliberation in Tacoma produced no consensus. Although the process was far from perfect, even a far better process would probably not have produced agreement. So long as citizens can only argue with, not overpower, one another—so long as deliberation is more common than domination—complete consensus on public policy will be rare in democratic politics.

The second utilitarian obstacle to deliberative accountability even more directly involves conceptions of the democratic process. Utilitarianism does not adequately recognize that citizens have views about the political process itself—not only preferences but also ideals of what the process should be. Many of these ideals cannot be easily accommodated within a utilitarian calculus since they implicitly assume a process that is in significant respects anti-utilitarian.

Citizens care about how political discussion or its absence influences their views about policy and politics more generally. Furthermore, they argue about whether they should have more or fewer opportunities for such discussion. A significant part of the debate in the Asarco case was about the process of discussion itself: questions were raised about whether Ruckelshaus was paying too much attention to public opinion, and about whether the workshops and hearings were fair. Controversies over process are endemic to democratic politics and a legitimate focus of moral argument among democratic citizens. We care about not only what is decided but also how it is decided.

More and more Americans are dissatisfied with political campaigns that avoid substantive issues or reduce discussion to sound bites.[29] Utilitarians no doubt share this dissatisfaction, and would favor more substantive campaigns that would help citizens become better informed. But the public dissatisfaction goes further. The widespread interest in the EPA's public workshops shows that at least some citizens were looking for processes that could provide opportunities for genuine debate. Politicians and the public are looking more favorably on deliberative forums, such as town meetings and juries with a representative sampling of citizens. Political theorists, as we noted in Chapter 1, are also exploring the possibilities of creating better forums for deliberation. These are controversial proposals, and they themselves have to be discussed in a democratic process that may not yet be as deliberative as it ought to be. But any democratic process that would make officials fully accountable must also make room for challenges to its own structures. We suggested in previous chapters how deliberative democracy can accept challenges to the process of deliberation itself. Deliberative democracy can also include utilitarian considerations in political decision making. But even a deliberation-friendly utilitarianism cannot so easily accommodate comprehensive challenges to its way of making political decisions.

Suppose that most citizens, after well-informed and thoughtful discussion, come to the conclusion that utilitarian principles should not govern the making of public policy. They believe that utilitarian approaches distort their own moral views and discourage public discussion that would help them understand the moral views of others. How should utilitarian policymakers respond? They could ignore this view, on the grounds that it is not likely to maximize social utility. This would preserve their utilitarianism but cast doubt on their commitment to democracy. They could accept the anti-utilitarian conclusion, on the grounds that it represents the informed preferences of most citizens. This would preserve their democratic commitment but put their utilitarianism at risk. (This second option could be consistent with utilitarianism if the policymaker made the further judgment that accepting nonutilitarian preferences is likely to maximize utility. But, as we shall see, this approach threatens to make utilitarianism politically irrelevant.)

In general, the views of citizens about the role of utilitarianism in the political process cannot themselves be placed in the same utilitarian calculus that public officials use to arrive at the optimal social policy. That calculus presupposes these views; the calculus cannot even get started without accepting the principle of utility in some form. Utilitarians could of course try to carry out a second-order calculus to show that the principle is the most useful way to make policy decisions. But any such conclusion would still presuppose that utilitarianism is the proper decision-making procedure, at least for reaching conclusions about what the proper decision-making procedure should be. Citizens who oppose utilitarian methods could still reasonably object.

The comprehensive claim that many utilitarians make—treating utility as the sovereign principle for resolving moral conflict in politics—thus cannot be sustained. What about more modest claims? Some utilitarians who analyze public policy assign policy analysis a more limited role. They would let the normal democratic processes decide many issues, including the role of policy analysis itself. They grant that "not . . . every important social value can be represented effectively within the confines of cost-benefit analysis" and that "we cannot make a cost-benefit analysis decision concerning which values should be included and which should be treated separately."[30]

In this way, by giving up its comprehensive claims, utilitarianism could make its peace with democratic accountability. Policy analysis would remain firmly under the control of citizens and officials who are accountable for when and how they use it. This modest view of its contributions is consistent with deliberative democracy, so long as officials, like Ruckelshaus, encourage citizens to help decide when policy analysis should and should not be used. On this view utilitarianism becomes one method or principle among many, any of which citizens may deliberatively choose to deal with moral conflict. This role is less than many utilitarians promise, but it is as much as deliberative democrats should desire.

Retreats from Publicity

Utilitarian methods also pose problems for the principle of publicity. One of the elements that makes utilitarianism so useful for policy analysis—its tough-minded investigation of all the consequences of choices among values—has the danger of creating a gap between policymakers and citizens. The way that utilitarians understand this consequentialism produces a general tension between the utilitarian methods and public attitudes toward fundamental values, and confronts utilitarianism with a dilemma. If utilitarians believe that citizens cannot be persuaded to adopt more utilitarian habits of mind, either they will have to keep citizens in the dark about the methods they really use to make decisions, or they will have to abandon their utilitarianism as a general method of political decision making.

Even from the perspective of deliberative democracy, the resistance to utilitarian thinking is not always justified. For example, some citizens in Tacoma, especially those workers who might lose their jobs if the EPA closed the plant, evidently saw a big moral difference between the government's deciding to close the plant and the government's doing nothing. Whether or not the consequences of inaction would be worse, no one (certainly not the government or citizens collectively) intended or directly acted to bring about the cancer deaths. The loss of jobs seemed a much more direct and deliberate result of government action. In this case the utilitarian approach seems a useful corrective. Ruckelshaus and his colleagues would be justified in trying to persuade citizens that the consequences of the government's failure to act here should be considered as seriously as the consequences of any government decision to close the plant. Neither is an act of nature.

A different kind of case is illustrated by the public resistance to putting a price on the value of life. We noted in Chapter 3 that some utilitarian policymakers are reluctant to go public with calculations that make explicit the monetary value of life in public policy. Perhaps candidates running for office or members of legislatures cannot talk openly about trading lives for dollars; their political future may depend on their letting constituents cling to the sentimental notion that human life is priceless. But in the executive branch, in the offices of other governmental agencies, and on the staffs of legislative committees, putting a price on the value of saving a life is a standard practice in policy planning and program evaluation.[31] Although there is disagreement about what methods should be used, there is widespread agreement among policy analysts that good policy-making in many areas—from traffic safety to public health—requires some estimate of the "value of life." When citizens agree to set the speed limit on public highways at 65 mph rather than 55 mph, they should know that a certain number of lives will be lost. But they evidently value the convenience and economic benefit over the risk to life, and judge the tradeoff worthwhile. Utilitarianism would not require citizens to do anything that they do not already implicitly accept. Perhaps citizens believe that some values are incommensurable; but, utilitarians argue, this belief is an illusion, one that public officials cannot afford to indulge, and in any case one that citizens' own behavior belies.

In this kind of case deliberative democrats would urge utilitarians to go public with their argument, as indeed some would be quite prepared to do. It is possible that citizens could be persuaded to face up to the consequences of policies in just these terms. But unlike the citizens in the Asarco case who gave more weight to the consequences of government action than to those of inaction, the citizens who object to policies that put a price on life may have a point. Insofar as their point expresses the more general view that not all values should be understood in terms of tradeoffs, it is a view that falls within the range of claims that a reciprocal perspective should encompass, as we show in the next section. Here we focus on the form of this conflict between utilitarianism and the attitudes of some citizens, because that is what makes the problem for the principle of publicity so acute.

It is to the credit of utilitarianism that it faces up to the fact that we must sometimes trade some of one value to get more of another. Such tradeoffs are the stock in trade of policymakers, and no method of dealing with moral conflict in politics can go far without recognizing their necessity. But utilitarianism goes further. It claims that all values are candidates for such trades; no values are incommensurable.[32] It therefore denies that there are some goods so precious that they should not be sacrificed for any amount of some other good. This denial goes beyond the claim that intrapersonal and interpersonal comparisons are possible. It implies that such comparisons are possible over the whole range of human values. Moreover, commensurability is meant to govern even the informal ways of making these comparisons. If all values are commensurable, it makes no sense to take any position that implies that there are some goods that one should not trade for any amount of money.

The view that all values are commensurable runs against the moral intuitions of many citizens, and the intuitions are not without foundation. Most people value money because it is exchangeable for so many goods, but most would not agree to trade any amount of money for some harms to themselves, their family, or their friends. This attitude is reflected in the fact that some goods are customarily excluded from the market: there are some things that money cannot buy.[33] The idea of a market in children, for example, strikes most people as abhorrent. It is a degradation of human life in much the same way that slavery is a violation of basic liberty. Life and basic liberty are in this sense ultimate values. They are incommensurable with money and lose an essential part of their value if they become objects of monetary exchange. (In Chapter 7 we consider the question whether practices such as contract parenting, in which a woman is paid for bearing a child, violate basic liberty.)

Many other goods, such as sports cars and stereo systems, are commensurable with money and are not degraded by market exchange. The value of such commodities is at least partly (though of course never wholly) reflected in their price. Many other goods, such as education and health care, fall somewhere in the middle: they are not primarily commodities, and they are not generally degraded by monetary exchange, but money does not come close to compensating for their loss. Given the range of goods and the variety of ways of valuing them, neither the utilitarian nor anti-utilitarian positions on this question could be accepted in advance of actual deliberation. Any conclusion, even one that adopts utilitarian modes of valuation for some goods, would have to meet the test of publicity.

A third case, yet another kind of conflict between utilitarian methods and public attitudes, calls for yet a different response. Here the problem arises not because citizens resist utilitarian claims but because they accept them. The utilitarian arguments or principles themselves tend in practice to produce results that from a utilitarian perspective are undesirable. In the Asarco case perhaps it would have been better if Ruckelshaus had believed and acted on the belief that his primary obligation was to save jobs and lives immediately at risk, since he could do much more about them than about the long-term consequences that could result from his decisions. An impartial concern for all consequences (even appropriately discounted for uncertainty) might lead him to neglect some of the short-term harms that he could actually prevent, and thereby fail to produce as much net utility as he might otherwise. More generally, it is often better if most citizens, and especially most public officials, believe that it is always wrong to lie, break promises, or kill innocent persons, even if exceptions are sometimes justified, so that they will be less likely to commit these acts when they are not justified.

These kinds of cases are familiar enough in political life, indeed so familiar that some utilitarians are inclined to argue that political morality should for utilitarian reasons not be utilitarian. This is so even for less familiar cases, such as the perplexing problem of future generations we considered in Chapter 4. There we argued that none of the arguments that base a concern for future generations on the rights or interests of individuals is adequate. One advantage of utilitarianism is that it does not use such arguments, and therefore seems to offer a more promising way of dealing with the problem of future generations.

But utilitarianism also has the consequence of undermining the reasons that many citizens find most persuasive for respecting future generations, and thereby causes citizens to give them less than their (utilitarian) due. It is a utilitarian, Derek Parfit, who has posed the problem most incisively. Risky or depletive energy policies, Parfit argues, are not against the interests of people in the distant future.[34] This argument refers to what we called in Chapter 4 the fluid status of future generations. Any significant change in energy policy changes the identity of the persons who will live in the future. Different policies would cause different people to marry and conceive different children, (as these and other effects multiplied over time), causing the world of the future to be populated by different people. Those members of future generations who would be harmed if we kept our present policy would not exist if we adopted a more benign policy. They could hardly complain that our present policy was worse for them. No matter how depletive our present policy, it does not make anyone in the distant future worse off.

To oppose depletive energy policies, then, we must either: (1) deny Parfit's argument that future persons could be made worse off by present policies; (2) discover an argument that does not appeal only to the interests of future persons; or (3) suppress Parfit's argument. Most commentators on Parfit generally try to avoid challenging (1), pinning their hopes on (2).[35] That is also Parfit's own preferred strategy. He believes that we could justify less depletive policies on the principle that "it is bad if those who

live are worse off than those who might have lived."[36] The principle is
congenial to utilitarianism, and it is also consistent with the view that we
suggested in Chapter 4 could be a basis for deliberative accountability for
future generations. But Parfit does not try to defend this principle, and he
concedes that it violates some people's intuitions.

In the end, Parfit comes close to recommending (3), at least for those
people who do not share his intuitions. He concludes that if people could
not accept the principle that satisfies (2), he would be tempted to suppress
his own argument that future persons cannot be made worse off by present
policies.[37] This strategy obviously poses a problem for deliberative publicity. The problem partly consists in denying most citizens access to politically relevant knowledge that a few possess. This problem persists even
if we share Parfit's intuitions and accept his justification for respecting
future generations. For Parfit allows that the most convenient argument
against depletive policies may still be the claim that the policy is against
the interests of people in the distant future. It is permissible to make this
claim because, though it is false, it is "not seriously misleading."[38] But
again, public officials who make the claim to citizens who do not know
that it is false are withholding knowledge that citizens may rightly regard
as relevant to judging the policy.

Since the most troublesome cases for utilitarians are those in which their
own criticism or their own principles have consequences that produce a
decrease in net utility, some utilitarians are thus prepared in those cases
to abandon the use of their own arguments and principles in the public
forum. Because the range of such cases may be great and its limits difficult
to predict in advance, some utilitarians would go further. They suggest
that utilitarian reasoning should not be generally used at all by citizens
and public officials in making personal or public decisions. Utilitarianism
should be regarded not as a "decision-procedure" but only as a "standard
of rightness."[39]

The idea that utilitarianism should not be used as a decision-making
procedure in politics is a surprising development in a theoretical tradition
whose founders saw the principle of utility as an instrument of political
reform. They certainly would have resisted the idea that their theory provides only an abstract standard of rightness, not a method for making
practical decisions. Not only did the classical utilitarians expect their
theory to be practiced in politics, but also contemporary utilitarians, including many economists, public officials, and ordinary citizens, continue
to use the theory in some form directly as a method for making political
decisions.

The argument that utilitarianism should not be used directly takes some subtle turns, but its basic claim is simply that decision makers are more likely to come closer to maximizing utility if they follow nonutilitarian principles than if they try to follow the principle of utility in deciding on particular actions or general rules.[40] They would do better, in utilitarian terms, if they simply kept promises or protected innocent lives than if they tried to calculate whether keeping promises or protecting innocent lives would maximize utility in the long run. Nonutilitarian thinking generally produces better consequences, the right outcomes for the wrong reasons.[41]

How can utilitarians show that utilitarian thinking should not be used to resolve moral conflicts within democratic politics? Presumably they would determine that the net benefits of using utilitarian decision making are greater than the net benefits of other decision-making procedures. Yet it is hard to imagine how anyone could establish by sound utilitarian methods whether utilitarianism is the optimal way of thinking in politics. A utilitarian calculus on this scale would be likely to be even less conclusive, or at least less generalizable, than the already complex policy analyses of the kind that EPA officials employed. The problems of incommensurability and indeterminacy that afflict utilitarianism in its more familiar applications to specific problems would be exacerbated in such a far-ranging undertaking.

Nevertheless, let us assume that utilitarians could somehow demonstrate that nonutilitarian modes of thinking work better than utilitarian ones to resolve moral conflicts in politics. The demonstration would do utilitarianism little good. Its effect would be to undermine the promise of utilitarianism to serve as a perspective for resolving moral disagreements in politics. If utilitarianism is counterproductive in practice, then on its own terms utilitarianism should not serve as that perspective. Public officials and citizens should not rely on it in trying to resolve moral conflicts. Utilitarianism wins a theoretical victory at the price of practical utility. Furthermore, the victory is so complete that even the value of believing its theory is put in doubt. Utilitarians would have to recommend against believing in utilitarianism if, as seems likely, such beliefs tend to cause people to use counterproductive decision-making procedures. Whatever its truth value, utilitarianism on its own terms would lack moral value as a view that citizens could actually believe and on which they could act. No one could believe in it or act on it without violating utilitarian commitments.

In these ways, then, utilitarians have a tendency to retreat from the principle of publicity. But this response is appropriate only in some circumstances or only on some understandings of utilitarianism. Only when utilitarianism puts forward comprehensive claims to be the sovereign principle of political morality, and only when utilitarian reasoning would produce nonutilitarian results, is the conflict between utilitarianism and publicity irresolvable. In other cases, when utilitarian arguments against popular attitudes are completely or partially justifiable, utilitarians can make their peace with the principle of publicity. To do so, however, they must enter into the public debate on the same terms as everyone else, and in the process scale down the scope of their promise to provide a single sovereign principle for resolving moral disagreement.

Ambivalence toward Reciprocity

How should the EPA deal with the conflicts among the informed preferences of citizens in Tacoma? Utilitarianism tells officials to translate the preferences into a common currency and add. What sounds simple in theory becomes problematic in practice. The method creates problems for any effort to find a reciprocal perspective from which to assess moral conflict in politics. The problems arise for both the translation of claims into utility and its maximization, each of which we now consider in turn.

The project of translating values into a common currency runs into two difficulties. The first is that individual preferences do not come already expressed in a common currency. People do not ordinarily use even the most common currency, money, as the main measure to evaluate competing claims in their lives—career versus family, work versus leisure, health versus more lucrative or satisfying employment. They do not usually even think in terms of preferences, let alone "utiles," when they compare the value of gainful employment, good health, a loving family, and other things that matter in their lives. The workers did not take their jobs at Asarco after calculating that the pay and other benefits compensated them adequately for the extra health risks. Some no doubt accepted work at Asarco because it was the only job open to them, others because they wanted to live and work near their families in the Tacoma area, some perhaps simply because they liked the work. These reasons are consistent with their also believing that Asarco is not adequately compensating them for the health risks the job imposes.

A method that forces the claims of citizens into a framework that they would not normally use should be suspect in deliberative democracy. It raises doubts about whether the claims in this form are ones that citizens can themselves accept, and thus whether they are in this sense reciprocal. But utilitarians may still argue that citizens would, or even actually do, accept their way of comparing values. Most citizens may not be able to think of all their competing values in terms of a common currency and then calculate the course of action that offers them the greatest net benefits. But the utilitarian policymaker can infer from citizens' behavior—from what choices they make in the market or in their daily life—how they rank various values, and what policy would best resolve conflicts among them. Utilitarians infer the logic of an internal calculus from "revealed preferences." That is, the behavior of citizens rather than their thinking reveals the relative prices they put on competing values. By choosing to stay with Asarco, the workers reveal their preference for doing this kind of work, even with all its risks.

Inferring the value that citizens place on competing ends from their revealed preferences is misleading in several ways.[42] Many people are not well informed about the risks of their work or place of residence. They may not have access to the information they need, or they may not have the time or expertise to make good use of it. If Asarco workers and other residents of the Tacoma area had already considered the major health risks before choosing where to live and work, they would have had less reason to attend the workshops and hearings held by the EPA. They would not have shown so much concern about the risks. From *this* behavior one might reasonably infer that they were at least having doubts about taking the risks. If preferences are to reveal anything about risks, they must be informed; but in this case, as in many others, the relevant information about the risks is not available to those whose preferences are taken to be revealed.

Even if the information is available, the risks may not be fully appreciated. Receiving information about risks is not likely to have the same effect as living with them: seeing a co-worker lose an arm in an industrial accident or a neighbor become ill from toxic chemicals in the back yard. Most people must choose where to work or live before they experience the costs and benefits of their choices. Therefore, they often cannot make the well-informed choices that would accurately reveal the value they place on competing ends. Furthermore, even if citizens were fully informed about the costs and benefits of alternative occupations and locations, they might have no choice but to take a risky job or to live in an unsafe environment.

In general, preferences reveal little about the conditions of the choice—how free workers are in choosing their place of work or citizens are in picking their place of residence. To take revealed preferences as a reliable indicator of preferences under such circumstances would be to ignore the value of basic liberty. The problem, then, is not merely that utilitarianism expresses citizens' claims in terms that they may not accept, but that the terms neglect basic values, such as liberty, that any reciprocal perspective should recognize.

The second difficulty with the way utilitarians translate preferences into a common currency arises when they try to compare the claims of citizens. How can Ruckelshaus know whether clean air versus employment for one citizen is worth as much as clean air versus employment for another? He has to make interpersonal comparisons, and he would welcome an objective or neutral measure that itself does not require moral judgement. If he had such a measure, he could legitimately say that he is respecting the claims of citizens, not imposing his own values on them. Utilitarianism purports to offer just what he needs: an objective method of interpersonal comparison that does not require the policymaker to apply any further moral assessment to citizens' preferences beyond what the principle of utility itself requires. In this way the moral conflict—the problem of incompatible ends—could be resolved from a perspective that should be acceptable to all citizens.

Yet controversy about what measure should be used, though expressed in more neutral-sounding technical language, is often no less fierce and no less morally loaded than the political disagreements utilitarianism seeks to resolve. For example, consider the various methods that have been proposed for measuring cardinal utility. The choice among some of them depends in part on whether one thinks that maximum utility or average utility is more just.[43] Why should anyone suppose that moral judgments can be avoided here?

The illusion that further moral judgments can be avoided may be partly the result of thinking that the problem is simply one of imagining what it would be like to be in another person's situation. We may be able without too much difficulty to compare what it is like to be in the shoes of Owen Gallagher, a longtime Asarco worker who opposed the stringent controls, with what it is like to be in those of Michael Bradley, a Vashon Island resident who favored them. This kind of comparison seems possible without making any moral judgments. But the comparison that utilitarians need to make goes further. They must be able to estimate how good or bad it is for Gallagher to be in his situation and Bradley to be in his, and compare the estimates. This kind of comparison is of course possible, but not without using a moral standard to make the estimate, and there is no reason to assume that the standard is consistent with utilitarianism.

Among contemporary utilitarians, especially those concerned with public policy, the most common way of dealing with the problem of interpersonal comparisons is to try to avoid making them. Many methods rely on some version of the concept of Pareto superiority, which ranks policies according to their independent effects on individuals.[44] A proposed policy is Pareto-superior to an existing policy if the proposed policy makes at least one citizen better off and no citizen worse off than they would be with the existing policy. For example, suppose that the government already buys surplus milk from farmers, and is considering a policy that would distribute the milk free to schoolchildren who cannot afford to buy it. Some people would be made better off, and no one worse off. To conclude that this policy is better than the status quo, we do not have to compare different people's utilities.

Used in this way, the Pareto criterion is consistent with the utilitarian commitment to counting preferences equally, but it does not support the goal of maximizing utility. It would not justify adopting any policy that makes some people worse off, even policies that would produce much greater total utility and make nearly everyone better off. More generally, the criterion simply does not apply to most policy choices. Most new public policies would make some people worse off than they are now. No budget plan for reducing the deficit, lowering unemployment, or stimulating the economy could pass in a Congress determined to make no one worse off. Even such an obviously beneficial policy as using surplus milk probably would have some losers.

None of the options open to the EPA in the Asarco case came close to satisfying the constraint that no one be made worse off. Enforcing the stricter emission standard to benefit some Tacoma residents would make Asarco workers and shareholders worse off than before. Even choosing the more lenient standard would probably make Asarco shareholders worse off. If the EPA waited until it found a policy that made (at least) someone better off and no one worse off, it would do nothing. This way of using the Pareto criterion privileges the status quo, preventing government from acting even when there are policies that would greatly benefit many citizens and slightly harm a few. Rather than a method of putting utilitarianism into practice, it turns out to be a way of preserving the status quo against utilitarian improvements.

To avoid this unhappy consequence, many utilitarian policymakers apply the Pareto criterion in a different way. On this approach, a policy is justified if its net benefits are great enough to make some better off and also to provide compensation to those who would otherwise be made worse off. Adopting this test, the EPA could have considered some new alternatives, such as a stricter emissions standard but with provision for compensating Asarco management and workers for their losses, or a more lenient standard with compensation only for the Asarco shareholders. If the potential losers could be compensated, then either of these policies would make some people better off and no one worse off.

But how can potential losers be compensated? The most common answer is: hypothetically. On this approach, a policy is justified simply if the total benefits exceed the total costs. Given the net increase, there is a pattern of compensation that *would* make everyone better off.[45] The policy is justified even if the losers are not actually compensated. How can hypothetical compensation satisfy anyone's preferences? Defenders of this approach assume that in the long run the losses are widely distributed, and nearly everyone gains. This is a heroic assumption, as hard to believe as it would be hard to sell to those who lose consistently in the political process.

Yet to provide actual compensation may be even more difficult—not only politically but also morally. If policymakers were to try to compensate citizens for losses in the way this approach requires, they would immediately face the difficulty of determining what constitutes fair or just compensation. Under the compensatory approach, individuals have the power to block socially beneficial policies by demanding very large side payments, claiming that it is their informed preference to refuse to settle for less. Individuals acquire a kind of bargaining power that borders on extortion. The bargaining situation created by a compensatory criterion encourages citizens to form preferences that depart sharply from what would be generally regarded as a fair baseline for determining gains and losses. It would not be consistent with any adequate principle of reciprocity. Yet utilitarianism does not provide any other standard for what a fair baseline would be.

Faced with the difficulties of making interpersonal comparisons in the strict manner of classical utilitarianism and the difficulties of avoiding making them, some contemporary utilitarians adopt a more informal approach. They point out that any moral theory that respects the interests of others must make interpersonal comparisons.[46] Almost any moral view has to make some estimate of the relative value of different people's interests. Furthermore, policymakers make such comparisons all the time; it would be "indecent" if they refused to do so.[47] At the least, we can go a long way with "negative utilitarianism": "As much as individuals differ in the tastes for goods, they all share roughly similar perceptions of and aversions to those things that cause them misery."[48]

This informal approach is sensible enough, but it purchases its good sense at the price of utilitarian purity. If making interpersonal comparisons involves assessing in some way how much different people value the same or different goods, then everyone does it, not only utilitarians. In this form interpersonal comparisons are ubiquitous. But many are also contestable. In general, they cannot provide the neutral premise the utilitarian needs to begin the chain of logic that would lead irresistibly to a utilitarian conclusion. Moral disagreement begins rather than ends with the comparison.

Sometimes the comparisons are controversial: extra income means as much to the rich as to the middle class. Sometimes they are not: extra food means more to the starving than to the well fed. But in either case moral conflict is present at the creation of the comparison. This is obviously so if the comparison is controversial: to decide even what would count as good evidence that the rich value extra income as much as the middle class is already to favor some conceptions of justice over others. If the comparison is not controversial, the reason is usually that many different moral perspectives converge in reaching the judgment that supports the comparison; there are nonutilitarian reasons for assuming that food matters more to the starving. Even so, the moral conflict breaks out again when we try to decide what action or policy this comparison calls for: Should the government provide the food, and if so who should be taxed— only the rich, the well fed, or all the nonstarving? How such questions are answered partly depends on the moral assumptions built into the original comparisons.

The other major part of the utilitarian method of aggregating preferences—maximization—gives rise to similar difficulties. On its face, the commitment to maximization seems more acceptable than the idea that all values can be translated into a common currency, and in fact probably is more widely accepted by citizens. Its appeal can be appreciated by looking again at policies that deal with the value of life, focusing this time not on the issue of putting a price on life but instead on the goal of maximizing the number of lives saved.

Maximization is based on a simple moral principle, so plausible on its face that it is hard to see how anyone could reasonably reject it: governments should try to save more lives rather than fewer, other things being equal. If the government has a certain amount of money to spend on saving lives, public officials (who should count all people equally) are obligated to save as many lives as possible. To fulfill this obligation, officials must maximize the number of lives saved. To see why this is thought to be so compelling, consider this hypothetical policy problem that a utilitarian might pose.

Imagine that you are the chair of a government task force on health and safety regulation with $100 million to spend on a new policy. To simplify your problem, you have only four options, and can choose only one. You are inclined to favor the option that would place more stringent limits on exposure to formaldehyde in the workplace because during the election campaign the president told workers in a plant in Ohio that he would do something about this problem. But then policy analysts in the Office of Management and Budget give you this chart showing, for each option, how much it would cost (in millions) to prevent one premature death.[49]

Fire protection in aircraft cabins	0.1
Use of electrical equipment in coal mines	9.2
Arsenic exposure in the workplace	106.9
Formaldehyde exposure in the workplace	82,201.8

Given your budget, you could not even come close to preventing one premature death by establishing a formaldehyde exposure limit for workers. You would need a budget 800 times larger to save even one life. If you chose an arsenic exposure limit, you could save almost one life. But if you strengthened electrical safety standards in coal mines, you could save approximately ten lives. You could save the most lives (1,000) by providing better fire protection in aircraft cabins—100 times more than the next best policy, 1,000 times more than the arsenic emissions policy, and over 800,000 times more than the policy you initially favored.

In the face of these great disparities in the cost of saving lives, how could anyone deny that policymakers should calculate the value of life and try to maximize the number of lives saved? Even while accepting that policymakers should sometimes calculate the value of life, one may still object to using the calculation to pursue the goal of saving the most lives possible. Because this goal is based on the view that all lives deserve equal consideration, it is morally attractive, and may even seem morally required. But if public policy were exclusively to follow its dictates, some other important moral considerations would be disregarded. A comprehensive commitment to impartiality, as expressed by some utilitarians, leads to a neglect of special relationships (such as family preferences) and special statuses (such as economic disadvantage) that deliberative democracy should take into account. A reciprocal perspective must make room for these considerations, but a thoroughgoing utilitarianism excludes them because it makes no distinctions among persons.

In practice, however, most utilitarian policymakers recognize special relationships of various kinds, at least when they can be shown to be socially useful. For example, they give priority to the lives of the citizens of their own government.[50] The OMB policy analysts did not try to calculate whether the same amount of money could be used to prevent more premature deaths, say, in Italy, India, or the Ivory Coast. In face of a devastating flood or a coal mine disaster, public officials do not stop to calculate how many more lives could be saved if the funds were spent on preventive measures (even though prevention is almost always more efficient).[51] Many other policies give preference to citizens on the basis of their age, family responsibilities, and past and potential contributions to society.[52]

In your role as chair of the regulatory task force, you might justifiably decide not to try to maximize the number of lives saved. You might choose the second option, improved safety in coal mines, even though it is only second best with respect to the number of lives it saves. The government arguably has a special responsibility to protect vulnerable and disadvantaged members of society. Coal mines are far more hazardous than airplanes. Coal miners on average are far less advantaged than airplane passengers. Few coal miners can choose a different line of work, whereas many airline passengers could choose alternative forms of transportation. The measure of cost per life does not tell policymakers anything about the voluntariness of the risk. For these and other reasons, deciding to spend more to save a coal miner's life may be a justifiable departure from the policy of maximizing the number of lives saved. If most citizens share your inclination to give preference to the coal miners, the departure could even be consistent with the utilitarian precept that each person counts for one and no one for more than one. But you would still have to consider the effects of the increased costs of the safety improvements. If they could not be funded in a way that avoids causing miners to lose their jobs, you may have to reconsider your preference.

Utilitarianism itself, then, would in practice neither prohibit nor require you to prefer the coal miners. Your decision would depend largely on forms of reasoning that are not committed to maximization and on factors such as moral intuition, political calculations, and the instructions of those whom you represent which may run counter to it. This kind of result is not peculiar to this case. It is inherent in any utilitarianism that permits, as any reciprocal perspective in politics must, policies that do not maximize the number of lives saved.

To see in its starkest form the implications of a strict policy of saving the maximum number of lives, consider this proposal for an organ lottery.[53] Suppose that transplant surgery has advanced to the point where most major organs can be transferred safely from one patient to another. Under these circumstances it is likely that two dying people could be saved if each received an organ from a single donor. Imagine that one needs a heart, and the other a kidney. When no usable organs come by means of natural deaths or voluntary donations, the government computer selects at random suitable donors from a pool composed of all healthy adult citizens. Each lucky winner would be required by law to give up his or her life so that two other citizens could live. (Some limits on the eligibility of recipients would be necessary: heavy smokers, for example, might be excluded, and younger citizens might have higher priority than older ones.)

Once adjusted for such factors, it would seem that the scheme ought to be acceptable to those utilitarians strictly committed to saving the maximum number of lives. For each healthy donor the lottery selects, at least two lives can be saved. A well-designed organ lottery would multiply considerably the number of lives that society could save—not just by two for one but by three or more for one. The multiplier would be limited only by the number of organs any one individual is able to "donate."

This bizarre hypothetical was first proposed not as a counterexample by the enemies of utilitarianism but as a positive illustration of its advantages by one of its friends. The lottery is intended to show that public policy could save even more lives if we recognized that the government's bringing about the death of one citizen is morally equivalent to its failing to save the life of another citizen, at least under conditions like that created by the lottery. The only basis for refusing to accept this moral equivalence, so the proponent of the lottery suggests, is a sentimental attachment to questionable moral distinctions between direct and indirect action, or killing and letting die.

Many other utilitarians of course reject the lottery, and do so on utilitarian grounds. Psychological distress, the potential for corruption, complexities of administration, moral hazards—these and other indirect consequences and side effects would provide ample utilitarian reason for rejecting the lottery. No doubt a strong case could be made against the lottery on such grounds, but citizens may doubt that these are the grounds on which their real objections are based. Is their objection to the lottery mainly that it would do more harm than good—simply that it would not work as promised? Surely the objection is deeper than that. Even citizens who believe that the government should save as many lives as possible could reasonably reject a policy that would force individuals to give up their organs for any purpose that maximized lives saved. They could see such a policy as a violation of their basic liberty. Although the boundaries of such a liberty are imprecise, they are clear enough to encompass this kind of forced sacrifice. The widespread distress that the organ lottery can be assumed to create is not accidental; it is grounded in this deeper moral principle. Utilitarians can reject proposals like the organ lottery, but their reasons for doing so miss the point of the moral claims that many citizens would wish to make. The objections that utilitarianism makes to schemes like this lottery show that it does not encompass the whole range of reasons that a reciprocal perspective requires.

Maximization is also deficient in another way. While telling utilitarian policymakers to choose the policy that maximizes total welfare, utilitarianism says nothing about how the welfare should distributed. This silence is the source of utilitarianism's neglect of another fundamental value, basic opportunity. A simplified representation of the utilities in the Asarco case illustrates the problem. Suppose that EPA analysts determine that (compared to no regulation) the stricter standard will produce total net utility worth $3.5 million over ten years, while the more lenient standard yields a total equivalent to $3 million in the same period. It is likely that the relatively well off residents of Vashon Island will be the major beneficiaries of the stricter standard, while the low-skilled workers suffer a much greater loss. Assume that the utilities are distributed like this:

Income Group	Lenient Standard	Strict Standard
Upper-middle (Vashon Island)	+1.0	+4.5
Middle (Tacoma)	+1.5	+2.0
Lower (Workers)	+0.5	−3.0
Net benefit	+3.0	+3.5

Looking only at the total net benefits as utilitarianism recommends, Ruckelshaus would have to conclude that the stricter standard represents the better policy. But then if he noticed the great differences between the policies in the benefits that each income group receives, he might not be so certain that he should select the first policy. Although that may be the right choice, the conclusion that it is right should not be reached without considering the possible injustice in choosing a policy that provides only a small extra total benefit over one that offers so much fairer a distribution of the benefit. Many more of the workers, already disadvantaged in comparison with the Vashon Island residents, are likely to lose their jobs under the stricter policy, and suffer further losses in their basic opportunities in the future. In making a choice, Ruckelshaus surely should consider the possibility that the policy that enhances basic opportunity is morally better than the one that maximizes total utility.

But the utilitarian might well ask: Who says the distribution is better? The preference for a more egalitarian distribution cannot rest on the mere opinion of Ruckelshaus or his staff. To impose their moral view on citizens would be arbitrary, inconsistent with democratic principles, unless it also expresses a view that most citizens accept or are likely to come freely to accept. Assume (what seems plausible enough) that this view is widely accepted, that if presented with these alternatives in this form, most citizens would choose the first policy. If the egalitarian preference is widely shared in this way, utilitarians could then argue that they can accommodate it simply by including it in their calculus. So long as the preference for the distribution of the first policy produces at least half a million dollars' worth of utility, policymakers could justify choosing it over the second policy.

This seems a happy solution. Utilitarians are pleased because Ruckelshaus chooses the policy with the greatest total net benefit, and those who care about distribution are assuaged because the policy satisfies their sense of fairness. The aims of both utility and opportunity are advanced. The difficulty is that the solution—or the way of arriving at it—reintroduces the moral conflict that utilitarianism promised to avoid. How much weight should the utilitarian give to the preference for a more egalitarian distribution compared to net benefits already included in the calculation? The conflict between preferences for maximizing utility and preferences for fairly distributing it continues, and the utilitarian offers no distinctive way of resolving the conflict. (Utilitarians fall into a confusing regress if they attempt to construct a meta-calculus that considers preferences about preferences. The conflict between the basic moral attitudes underlying maximization and distribution persists at any level of analysis.)

The strategy of simply adding an egalitarian preference to the calculus also fails to meet the reasonable concerns of citizens who care about fair distribution and equal opportunity. They do not regard their concerns as constituting a preference just like any other preference. They would object, with good reason, to granting their conviction the same moral status as mere preferences, which could include, for example, the preference of racially discriminatory policies. Even if preferences based on prejudices of this kind could be excluded on utilitarian grounds, the strategy would still misrepresent the meaning of the claims of citizens who care about equal opportunity. Those claims rest on a belief in human dignity that takes priority over the results of any aggregation of preferences.

The belief is prior in two ways. First, it rules out certain distributions of benefits even if they maximize welfare. Citizens deserve to be treated as equals, with a right to basic opportunity, no matter how the maximizing calculus comes out. Second, the maximizing calculus itself presupposes some kind of commitment to human dignity. Some utilitarians explicitly acknowledge this priority. Policymakers "must always give dignity and self-respect precedence over preferences and choices in cases of conflict," one argues, because these "feelings" provide "the whole *raison d'être* for utilitarian . . . schemes for respecting their preferences."[54] The concession is cogent and necessary for a reciprocal perspective, but again it deflates the utilitarian promise to deal with moral conflicts in terms of a single inclusive end.

Utilitarianism begins, promisingly, by recognizing that public policy cannot fully realize all at once all the values that citizens cherish, even ultimate ones such as life and liberty. No value is ultimate or absolute in the sense that it can never be subject to tradeoffs. Utilitarians argue that, at the very least, public policy cannot avoid trading lives for lives, or liberties for liberties. But even here, in the cases most favorable to its claim, utilitarianism delivers less than promised. Having told the policymaker to be prepared to sacrifice some lives and some liberties, utilitarianism offers surprisingly little advice about which lives should be sacrificed, or whose liberties should be forfeited, when some must be. The advice, if it does not threaten basic liberty, is indeterminate in the face of conflicts about how that liberty should be preserved. Deliberative democracy is also indeterminate in some cases, but, as we shall see, for good nonutilitarian reasons.

As a method of aggregating the preferences of the citizens of Tacoma, utilitarianism is bound to disappoint Ruckelshaus or any policymaker who seeks a standard that could be accepted by all citizens. If policymakers use utilitarianism as their sovereign principle, they are likely to ignore or distort the meaning of some legitimate claims that citizens make, in particular those that express the value of basic liberty and opportunity. Reciprocity suffers as a result. To the extent that policymakers qualify their utilitarianism to try to accommodate other moral claims, they make it less able to resolve moral disagreement in any distinctive way. Any resolution calls for further deliberation.

Beyond Utilitarianism

Despite its deficiencies, utilitarianism, in a modest and qualified form, deserves a place in deliberative democracy. Its attention to the claims of all citizens (including future generations) and its concern for long-range consequences are virtues that no democracy should ignore. Even its penchant for quantifying values is sometimes appropriate in the assessment of policies. It would be foolish, wasteful, and even unjust to try to choose among policies that aim mainly to save lives without comparing how many lives can be saved by alternative policies with a given amount of money.

In public arguments about how much various people value various goods, then, citizens may appeal to utilitarian considerations. But they may also appeal to other kinds of moral considerations, and then they argue about which kind should prevail in the particular circumstances. It is an ongoing argument, one in which utilitarianism can be only one method among many. If utilitarians are to remain deliberative democrats, then they must let deliberation put utilitarianism in its place. If the aim is to find a perspective that all citizens can accept, citizens should make sure that utilitarianism and its ally policy analysis remain under the firm control of deliberative democracy.

When policy analysts finished calculating the costs and benefits of the options open to the EPA, they left Ruckelshaus without a determinate solution. The options still stood in conflict. One option (the stricter emissions standards) would slightly lower the risk of cancer for everyone living in the area, while another option (the more lenient standards) would greatly lower the risk of unemployment for Asarco employees and maintain the standard of living of others whose livelihood depended on the company. Ruckelshaus recognized that policy analysis could not solve this problem.

Ruckelshaus hoped that if he took the options to the people, providing not only information but also opportunities to discuss the options among themselves, one would come to be seen as more acceptable. Or perhaps an even better policy would emerge from the discussion. To some extent that is just what happened. For many citizens, new goals emerged. They began to focus their attention on finding new jobs for the Asarco workers and new nonpolluting industry for the region. When the Asarco smelter finally closed (more as a result of international economic trends than from the effects of environmental regulation), Tacoma had already begun to diversify its economy in pursuit of these goals.[55]

To call for more public deliberation does not by itself offer an answer to any particular policy question that policymakers face. Nor does it alone provide content for a perspective that deals with moral disagreements in politics. It points us in the right direction—toward a democratic process that embraces a wide range of moral considerations and a wide array of occasions for discussing them. It also establishes some important conditions (reciprocity, publicity, and accountability) that help direct the discussion in that process. Yet without some further indication of what principles should constitute the content of deliberation, deliberative democracy is an incomplete alternative to utilitarianism.

Thus, even if the criticisms we have pressed undermine the larger promise of utilitarianism, utilitarians still may ask about deliberation in middle democracy, What alternative do you propose? A friend of utilitarianism offers these choices: "intuition . . . revelation, scripture, the Koran, or *Das Kapital,* or . . . an oracular figure of some sort (wiseman, holyman, soothsayer, shaman, king, or dictator) or . . . discussion and bargaining among competing groups or interests to achieve consensus, or, failing that, to arrive at compromises."[56] Without a framework for dealing with moral disagreement about public policies in middle democracy, officials and citizens may have to turn to some or all of these methods. The challenge to deliberative democrats, then, is to provide such a framework. The conditions of deliberation presented in the previous three chapters provide part, but only part, of the framework. We also need principles to assess policies themselves, and those principles should express basic values such as liberty and opportunity more satisfactorily than utilitarianism does. In the next chapter we accept that challenge, and further develop the constitution of deliberative democracy.

—6—

The Constitution of Deliberative Democracy

CAN A deliberative perspective provide a framework for moral argument in politics that is more accommodating than the principle of utility but yet more constraining than the principles of reciprocity, publicity, and accountability? The most promising candidates for principles that could guide the content of democratic deliberations are those that take seriously the two values that utilitarianism neglects: liberty and opportunity. In this chapter we consider perspectives that elevate each of these values into constitutional principles to guide democratic deliberations. We argue that both liberty and opportunity are necessary, though not sufficient, for a democratic perspective that adequately deals with moral disagreement. Appropriately ordered and interpreted, liberty and opportunity join reciprocity, publicity, and accountability as the constitutional principles of a deliberative democracy.

Constitutional principles refer to standards that public officials and citizens must not violate in the making of public policy in order that those policies can be provisionally justified to the citizens who are bound by them. These constitutional principles serve best as self-constraints. Democratic deliberators invoke and interpret these principles in the process of proposing and criticizing public policies in the everyday politics of what we have called middle democracy. (To designate a principle as constitutional, it will be recalled, is not to imply that courts are the primary—or even the ultimate—interpreters or enforcers of the principle.)

To illustrate the idea of a constitutional principle in deliberative democracy, we can say that if negative liberty is regarded as a constitutional principle, then public policies that violate negative liberty are not justifiable, even if they are enacted in a process that otherwise satisfies the conditions of deliberation. Libertarians make such a claim, and egalitarians say something similar about a more qualified understanding of liberty *and* opportunity. Both agree that some constitutional principles are morally necessary guides to democratic decision making, but they disagree about which principles are necessary.

We have already suggested that deliberative democracy needs principles that extend beyond the conditions of deliberation to its content. In the democratic search for provisionally justifiable policies, the content of deliberation often matters at least as much as the conditions. The deliberative perspective we develop here, then, explicitly rejects the idea, sometimes identified with deliberative democracy, that deliberation under the right conditions—real discourses in the ideal speech situation—is sufficient to legitimate laws and public policies. We open the door to constitutional principles that both inform and constrain the content of what democratic deliberators can legitimately legislate.

What, then, should be the substance of the principles that regulate the content of deliberation? To answer this question, we begin with a perspective that would constitutionally protect individual liberty against the claims of social welfare. Taken as a guide to moral argument in politics, libertarianism holds that citizens should be free to act as they wish, so long as their actions do not harm other citizens by means of force or fraud. Libertarians rightly give priority to liberty, and to some of the right kinds of liberty. But they grant the claims of negative liberty too much authority. Libertarians give citizens too much of a good thing.

The second perspective we consider—egalitarianism—respects liberty as a constitutional principle but limits it in order to make room for equal opportunity. We focus on the most influential and well developed defense of an opportunity principle, one presented in Rawls's theory of justice.[1] The understanding of Rawlsian egalitarianism is a vast improvement over libertarianism, but it is still incomplete in important ways. Its claims for equal opportunity have a tendency to expand without limit, and the theory provides little guidance about what the limits should be. Just as we defend basic liberty against libertarianism's more expansive principle of liberty, so we defend basic opportunity against a more expansive interpretation of the opportunity principle.

In keeping with the spirit of a deliberative constitution, we argue that citizens and public officials are responsible for setting limits to the liberty and opportunity principles, and they should do so through a deliberative process that satisfies the conditions of reciprocity, publicity, and account-ability. The constitution of deliberative democracy consists of these *conditions* of deliberation, taken together with the principles of liberty and opportunity, which inform the *content* of deliberation, all appropriately ordered and interpreted over time by the people bound by these principles.

Health care policy offers the most relevant and perhaps most challenging context for developing these constitutional principles. We focus on the decision of the Arizona state legislature to reduce funding for organ transplants and to increase support for health care for poor women and children.[2] Arizona was one of the first states to confront the problem of setting priorities for different kinds of health care. The way in which its legislature dealt with the problem was both less complex and less satisfactory than the course some other states (most notably Oregon) later followed. Partly for this reason, the Arizona case more vividly illustrates the central issues that health care poses for making hard choices in the context of moral disagreement.

It is doubtful that even the federal government can provide unlimited coverage of transplants without limiting coverage of some other expensive procedures, or else limiting effective access to some other expensive opportunity goods, such as education or police protection. Limiting effective access to certain goods is what some commentators call rationing, a term that most politicians try to avoid. We also avoid the term, but not because rationing is unpopular. Rather, the term is misleading, for what is generally at issue is not a ban on buying or supplying medical goods and services above a certain amount but rather limits on public funding of medical goods and services that most people cannot otherwise afford. It is therefore more accurate to refer to such practices as limiting coverage. As new high-cost therapies continue to appear on the medical scene and vie for a share of the increasingly limited medical budget, the issue of limiting coverage is likely to become more pressing.

Liberty

Shortly after the Arizona legislature eliminated public funding for liver and heart transplants in 1987, Dianna Brown, a forty-three-year-old woman who suffered from terminal liver disease, requested a liver transplant under the state system that provided health care for the indigent. Her request was denied, and a few weeks later she died. A transplant could have saved her life. Her personal physician said: "I don't think her death was unreasonably painful or prolonged, but in my mind it was unnecessary."[3]

To say that Dianna Brown's death was unnecessary is to imply that she had a claim on the state, and by extension on her fellow citizens, to help her obtain a liver transplant. What kind of moral claim could she reasonably make? We begin by considering whether she could claim that her liberty is violated if the state does not provide the transplant. Libertarians would say no. It might at first seem strange that a theory that values liberty so highly would refuse to count a preventable death as a violation of liberty. But this refusal is defensible when we recognize what granting priority to this kind of liberty would mean for the liberty of other citizens. To say that Dianna Brown does not have a claim based on liberty, however, does not decide the case against government funding of transplants, as many libertarians would have us conclude.

LIMITS ON LIBERTY

If Dianna Brown has a right to a transplant based on liberty, the state would have to provide the transplant by any means necessary, short of violating the same (or greater) liberty of other citizens. The state would not be warranted in sacrificing one person's life in order to obtain organs to save the lives of several others, as in the lottery scheme described in Chapter 5. But a modified version of the lottery might well be justified— for example, one that covers only certain kinds of procedures, such as kidney transplants, which do not require the death of the donor. Other policies that are objectionable from most moral perspectives might also be required. For example, the state could appropriate organs that do not cost people's lives, even without their informed consent. The government could authorize clinical drug trials that enroll patients without their consent, if not enough patients are expected to participate voluntarily, and if the drug has the potential to prevent deaths like Dianna Brown's in the future. That is, in order to protect the greater liberty of future Dianna Browns, the state could infringe the lesser liberty of other citizens now.

Such arguments come perilously close to the most objectionable feature of utilitarian reasoning in politics. The form of justification is the same: maximizing a social good even if it means violating the integrity of individuals without providing any direct benefit to them in return. That the social good is (thought to be) the liberty of many individuals rather than social welfare does not alter the fact that to promote that good, the state would be permitted to violate a basic liberty of individuals. When requests like Dianna Brown's are themselves treated as liberty claims, they tend to lead to violations of other liberties. Libertarians deny that they are liberty claims at all, and adopt a negative concept of liberty: freedom from interference. Citizens can claim a violation of liberty only if the state or other citizens use force or fraud against them.

Armed with this negative concept of liberty, libertarianism resists not only needy individuals who claim that their liberty would be violated unless they receive organ transplants, but also utilitarian governments that claim the authority to abridge individual liberty to promote social welfare even when collective goods (such as national defense) are not at stake. Libertarians object to admitting both kinds of claims into deliberative decision making, and for the same reason, one that a deliberative perspective that is committed to reciprocity should also respect. Both kinds of claims fail to take seriously the separateness of persons. Neither guarantees individuals a sphere of action protected from obligations to serve the good of others.

Individuals should not be treated as fungible for the purposes of achieving the greatest social good. As Robert Nozick argues: "No moral balancing act can take place among us; there is no moral outweighing of one of our lives by others so as to lead to a greater overall *social* good."[4] On libertarian grounds, no government may require me to act without my consent to satisfy the claims of my fellow citizens, no matter how worthy. A distribution is justifiable only if it is the product of the free choices of *all* the individuals involved: "From each as they choose, to each as they are chosen."[5] In the name of treating each of us as separate people with our own lives to lead, libertarianism replaces the single utilitarian principle—maximize happiness—with another single (and sovereign) constitutional principle: protect individual liberty.

Libertarians are right to suggest that any mutually acceptable perspective on politics must give priority to a liberty principle, and they are also right in two important respects about the kind of liberty that a deliberative perspective should protect.

First, some interventions to which libertarians object would count as violations of liberty from any moral point of view that is justifiable to the morally motivated citizens who are bound by it. Compulsory organ donations and clinical trials or medical experiments without individual consent are paradigms of such violations. The liberty at stake here is what we call *basic*. It protects the physical and mental integrity of persons, and is a precondition for the exercise of other liberties, as well as for the use of opportunities.

The boundaries of personal integrity are not easily demarcated, but the two paradigms we have cited—compulsory organ donations and involuntary clinical trials—clearly involve violations of personal integrity. Unless individuals have the right to refuse to donate their organs or to participate in medical experiments, they do not have the capacity to control their physical integrity. A similar standard holds for mental capacities. Unless individuals have the right to resist certain kinds of constraints on their personal beliefs (for example, on their religious or moral convictions), their mental integrity is in jeopardy. In such cases liberty trumps social welfare; it takes priority over other (noncollective) goods that public policy might promote. If personal integrity is to have any standing in a deliberative democracy, citizens and public officials must respect at least this form of personal liberty. Individuals should be protected from policies that would conscript their bodies for transplants and experiments, and their minds for religious and other causes.

Both these paradigm cases are significantly different from military conscription. National security is a collective good, which benefits all citizens if it benefits any. Because national security is a collective good, even citizens who do not conscientiously object to military service have no incentive to volunteer for it. Conscription is necessary if anyone is to benefit at all. The exception made for conscientious objectors nonetheless pays homage to a liberty principle that protects personal integrity.

Since personal integrity may extend beyond these paradigms (for example, to protection against military conscription when national security is not clearly at stake), a pressing question in deliberative democracy is the scope of basic liberty. By asking to what extent other violations of liberty resemble the paradigm cases, we seek to determine the extent to which they should count as basic and thereby enjoy the priority granted to basic liberty. The answer to this question turns out to be complex. As in later chapters we examine the conflicts between liberty and other values, we find that the borders of basic liberty are irregular, sometimes following the lines set by libertarians, but often expanding or contracting its domain. In the case of health care, the map is also more complicated than is usually assumed. On one side libertarians set an acceptable limit on the scope of basic liberty, but on the other they permit it to expand beyond mutually acceptable boundaries.

The mutually acceptable limit is the second respect in which libertarians correctly identify a characteristic of liberty that a deliberative perspective should acknowledge. Basic liberty should not be expanded to include positive claims on society for all those resources that one may need to pursue one's own way of life. We distinguish, as also do a wide range of theorists, between liberty and the worth of liberty or the opportunity to live a good life.[6] If a deliberative democracy were to broaden the scope of liberty to include the goods necessary to its exercise, it would set virtually no limit on justifiable intervention by government. Treated as claims of liberty, requests like that of Dianna Brown would give the government license to invade not merely liberty but the basic liberty of other citizens. We shall suggest later that Dianna Brown has a claim on her fellow citizens and on the government, but neither she nor those who defended her right to health care argued that her claims extended to permitting violations of basic liberty.

Another, partly theoretical, reason to resist broadening the scope of liberty has important practical implications as well. The broader concept would undermine distinctions between liberty and other morally important values such as opportunity. The theory of deliberative democracy would become a theory of liberty, and virtually all disagreements would turn on differences among kinds and degrees of liberty. This approach would not be likely to enhance the quality of moral deliberation in politics. Important conceptual distinctions would be disregarded and significant moral differences slighted. The distinct values of opportunity would be less likely to be recognized, and the priority of liberty itself could not be so strongly defended.

LIBERTARIAN EXPANSION OF LIBERTY

Although libertarians resist the expansion of liberty when a citizen is making demands on the government, they encourage its expansion when citizens are resisting the demands of democratic government. The consequences of this asymmetry can be shown by considering the libertarian response to a somewhat different version of Dianna Brown's problem—one closer to the actual case. Suppose that the advocates of Dianna Brown's claim argue not that a respect for liberty, but that a respect for opportunity, requires the government to act. On grounds of opportunity, they would argue, the government must fund organ transplants for those citizens who cannot afford them through no fault of their own. Can citizens who oppose this policy object that their liberty is indefensibly violated by a policy of taxation to fund organ transplants?

According to many libertarians, they can. All (negative) liberties are basic and therefore take priority over individual well-being and social welfare. Taxation by the majority is therefore an unjustified violation of the liberty of every citizen in the minority who opposes the tax. If you find yourself in the minority, you can claim that the government is acting illegitimately in forcing you to contribute your labor to the cause of social welfare against your will. As Nozick asserts, "Taxation is on a par with forced labor."[7] In this way libertarians extend the priority of basic liberty to all negative liberties, including freedom from taxation without individual consent.

The analogy between basic liberty and the liberty to keep one's pretax income cannot be sustained. Forcing you to donate an organ is not equivalent to forcing you to give up even half of your income, assuming you still would have enough to live a decent life. Nor is taxing your income the same as forcing you to work for the state. A doctor who opposes government funding of organ transplants because she believes taxation violates her liberty would surely experience it as a wrong of a different order if the government conscripted her to perform the transplants. Like compulsory organ donations and involuntary confessions, forced labor directly affects personal integrity, taking away control over one's body or mind. The effect of taxation on personal integrity is typically remote at best. We are not normally attached to the money we earn in the same way we are connected to our actions and beliefs.

The further that liberty is broadened beyond personal integrity, the weaker becomes the claim that liberty is the supreme human good, which must trump all others. The more contestable the claim that a liberty is basic, the more objectionable is the attempt to privilege it by denying a deliberative majority the legitimate authority to legislate in its domain. Citizens often disagree about the desirability of taxes because they disagree morally about the policies that the taxes would support. Giving absolute priority to negative liberty would preempt this disagreement by declaring deliberatively off-limits a wide range of policies that governments might legitimately enact. Many political disputes about authorizing taxation for social welfare purposes fall within the range of deliberative disagreements, and therefore should not be insulated from democratic decision making.

Libertarians must also allow room for democratic decisions about some redistributive policies. To reject any public policy that would redistribute income or wealth, libertarians must assume that the given distribution is just. But libertarians cannot justify this assumption, as Nozick and some other libertarians recognize.[8] The present distribution of income and wealth in the world is the product of (among other things) many past actions that libertarians must consider unjustified coercion. Libertarians therefore cannot object on libertarian grounds to the use of state coercion to change this distribution in the direction of aiding the less advantaged. Indeed, libertarianism in its most mutually acceptable form must grant government the authority to restore a just distribution, understood as one that would have resulted had there been no unjustified coercion in the past.[9] Nozick therefore speculates that a redistributive state may be necessary to get libertarianism going on its own terms. Yet libertarians do not provide any principles for rectifying past injustices, and it is hard to see how they could while at the same time claiming that redistribution is legitimate only if it is the product of actual free exchanges among individuals.[10]

Libertarianism thus cannot sustain the claim that taxation to fund organ transplants for people who could not otherwise afford them violates individual liberty. Citizens who oppose funding organ transplants must find some other basis for their position.

LIBERTY AND HEALTH CARE

A closer look at the debate in Arizona will show more clearly the significance of containing the claims of liberty. With the passage of Medicaid in 1966, health care coverage for the poor improved significantly in this country, but many citizens, including many of the "working poor," remain without health care coverage. Some states, including Arizona, do not provide Medicaid benefits to all citizens who would be eligible under federal guidelines. This is because Medicaid has been an optional cost-sharing program: the federal government has paid a share of the costs incurred by a state in providing health care for the poor, provided the state's plan met federal standards. Arizona's decision to defund transplants took place while the state was also trying to improve health care coverage for other poor citizens under its Medicaid-like program.

Before 1987 Arizona's health care plan for the indigent, the Arizona Health Care Cost Containment System (AHCCCS—pronounced "access"), did not cover basic health services for families of four whose income exceeded $3,354, even though the federal poverty level for a family of four was $13,750. AHCCCS thus denied access to approximately two thirds of Arizona's poor.[11] In 1987 the Arizona state legislature voted to extend the coverage provided by AHCCCS for some citizens in this income category: to prenatal care for pregnant women and pediatric care for all children under the age of thirteen. The basic features of this policy remained in effect for many years, although the eligible income levels were adjusted for inflation. Most of the working poor who were uninsured by their employers were still not covered by AHCCCS, and therefore did not enjoy the protection of Medicaid.

If a deliberative democracy were to accept the libertarian principle of liberty, it could not increase health care coverage for the poor beyond current policies, or even justify many of the improvements in coverage that have already been legislated. Nor could it defensibly criticize these policies. The fact that many poor residents of Arizona, unlike the more affluent, do not have access to basic health care is not unjust unless it can be shown that past coercion deprived them of an income that would otherwise be theirs by the workings of the free market. In light of the more ascertainable claim that taxing the affluent to provide AHCCCS for the poor is coercive, a libertarian principle is disposed to declare such redistributive policies illegitimate, "legalized plunder."[12] But, as we have seen, it cannot morally sustain its disposition to declare that negative liberty trumps opportunity.

In the actual debates in Arizona over funding health care, even Arizonans who inclined toward a libertarian position did not react to proposed increases in taxes as they would probably have reacted to a proposal of forced labor. No one (as far as we can determine) used the analogy with forced labor or any similar argument to oppose taxation, or to suggest that it would violate their individual liberty. Although the libertarian principle of negative liberty inclines libertarians to condemn most redistributive taxation, their inclination lacks justification even from their own moral perspective. Deliberative democracy should accept a principle of basic liberty, but should resist the libertarian tendency to favor an overextended conception of liberty and an underdeveloped conception of opportunity.

Opportunity

Dianna Brown's request for a transplant was not a claim of liberty against the state. She herself put her request in a different form: "If a transplant isn't necessary I don't want it. But if it is the only solution, I would like a *chance for a chance*."[13] This is the language of opportunity: she was asking for the chance to live a normal life, no more or less than the chance that healthy citizens have. A deliberative democracy cannot justifiably deny such requests on the grounds that taxation for these purposes violates the liberty of other citizens. But is there a reason for government to grant such requests? So long as basic liberty is protected, would it be mutually acceptable for the government simply to let citizens live their own lives in the way they see fit, making and taking their own chances? Or should a deliberative democracy restrain itself by means of more than a basic liberty principle?

THE ROOTS OF OPPORTUNITY

Dianna Brown's free choices did not create her plight; her need for a transplant and her inability to pay for this expensive procedure resulted from factors beyond her control. If she does not receive the transplant, she may object that she has been denied an opportunity that most other citizens enjoy. Unlike Dianna Brown, wealthy citizens could pay for a transplant if they needed one, and can cover their other health care costs. Egalitarians argue that such disparities are unfair, and at least prima facie constitute a denial of equal opportunity. This argument is based on a moral conviction that egalitarians claim all citizens should share: one's life chances should not be determined by factors that are arbitrary from a moral point of view.[14]

Should all citizens share this conviction? To answer this question, egalitarians might ask them to reflect on cases like that of Dianna Brown. Unlike Dianna Brown, many citizens were fortunate enough to be born to parents who could provide them with excellent health care from their early years and superior education that improved their chances of financial security in the event of illness. They can hardly claim that they did anything at birth to deserve their favored place in this natural social lottery. They just happened to be born into families able to provide them with the chance to live a good life. They may or may not have made the most of that chance, but they certainly did nothing to deserve the chance itself. Surely the luck of the natural lottery should not deprive some citizens of the life chances that others win through no merit of their own.

This is the intuitive core of the egalitarian defense of a principle of equal opportunity. Citizens do not deserve their place in the natural lottery. There is no reason to assume that the current distribution of resources is justified, and some reason to claim that the government is justified in acting to change that distribution. Equal opportunity supplies both the standard that libertarianism lacks to assess the current distribution of resources and the basis to claim that a deliberative democracy should constrain itself by respecting the value of equal opportunity. Egalitarians argue that all citizens, regardless of their class, race, gender, age, and ethnicity, should be treated as free and equal citizens, entitled not only to basic liberties but also to equal opportunity. As Rawls writes: "The expectations of those with the same abilities and aspirations should not be affected by their social class."[15] Equal opportunity is intended to give each citizen, as far as possible, an equal chance to develop his or her natural talents and to choose among the range of good lives available within society.

Egalitarianism does not demand equal results. A democratic government must respect basic liberty. Public policy therefore should not aim to make all citizens equal in all respects. Public policy need not even treat citizens equally in any respect to honor equal opportunity. Certainly it would be impossible to make everyone equally healthy. Egalitarians want to commit democratic governments to treating individuals as free and equal citizens. According to Rawls, this means that certain "primary" goods, such as the income and wealth that are necessary conditions for living a decent life, should be distributed so as to maximize the life prospects of the least advantaged members of society. Considerable inequality may be justified if it makes the least well off better off than they would be with a more nearly equal distribution. But any social institution or practice that falls short of maximizing the long-term opportunities of the least advantaged violates the "difference principle," which is the first of a two-part principle governing the distribution of opportunity goods. (The second part, which we will discuss shortly, is called fair equality of opportunity.)

Rawls does not ignore liberty. On the contrary, he gives a form of basic liberty priority over egalitarian values. This is a priority that any democratic perspective should respect. But in order to leave room for opportunity, egalitarians must adopt a more limited conception of liberty than that favored by libertarians—again, as must any adequate democratic perspective. The egalitarian potential of a democratic perspective would be undermined were the government to count, for example, freedom from taxation among the basic liberties. If the Arizona legislature enacted a new tax to pay for health care for the working poor and some residents objected that the tax unacceptably violates their liberty, a deliberative democracy should not accept their objection.

A democratic government should not, as Rawls points out, assign priority "to liberty as such, as if the exercise of something called 'liberty' has a preeminent value and is the main if not the sole end of political and social justice." Instead, it should focus "on achieving certain specific liberties and constitutional guarantees, as found, for example, in various bills of rights and declarations of the rights of man." The Rawlsian rationale for protecting particular liberties is based on a consideration of "which liberties are essential social conditions for the adequate development and full exercise of the two powers of moral personality over a complete life."[16] The two powers of moral personality are a capacity for a conception of the good life and a sense of justice.[17] These two distinctively human powers and their conditions are the foundation for what we have called personal integrity. They support a broad scope for claims of liberty, but not so broad as to preclude the claims of opportunity.[18]

THE GREATEST BENEFIT OF THE LEAST ADVANTAGED

Some egalitarians treat health care as a primary good, and then require that it be distributed according to the difference principle—promoting "the greatest benefit of the least advantaged members of society."[19] Rawls himself does not impose this requirement. For simplifying purposes, his theory assumes that no one suffers from disabling or life-threatening illness.[20] A deliberative perspective designed for a non-ideal society cannot afford to ignore the complexity that health care creates, but it has good reason to reject the difference principle as a constitutional constraint on distributing health care.[21]

Consider what the difference principle would imply if it treated health care as a primary good (along with income, security, and education).[22] It would require the state to distribute as much health care as is medically necessary (or its equivalent in insurance coverage) first to the sickest citizens and then to the next sickest, and so on, until no further expenditures could improve the health of the sickest group in society. (Or until the next-sickest group in society is more advantaged than the least educated, safe, or wealthy group in society, but this comparison opens up another can of worms for egalitarianism.) When there are many high-cost medical procedures that offer a reasonable chance of saving, extending, or otherwise improving lives, the difference principle creates a "bottomless pit" of medical needs into which vast amounts of social resources must flow, leaving little for other social goods, including primary goods as valuable as income, security, and education.[23]

The problem is far from hypothetical. Medical technology is rapidly expanding its capacity to keep people alive, but at great and growing cost. Kidney dialysis, among the first high-technology medical treatments to be publicly funded, dramatically demonstrates the life-saving and budget-breaking potential of modern medicine. In 1973 Congress voted to fund dialysis for every American who needed it, at a projected cost of about $75 million annually. But by 1992 the cost of dialysis had risen to over $2 billion.[24] Dialysis is now only one of many high-cost life-saving medical technologies, some of which are publicly funded but many of which are not. The pressure to fund those that are not now covered has grown, and at the same time so has the demand to provide basic health care for the millions of citizens who lack access to it.

The dilemma that the Arizona legislators faced grew out of pressures like these. Prior to 1986 the director of AHCCCS had the authority to approve or disapprove requests for organ transplants on an ad hoc basis. Because organ transplant technology was relatively undeveloped and its availability not yet well known, he received few requests and had no problem funding those that showed some promise of medical success. As transplants became more feasible, requests rapidly multiplied, and so did the cost of each transplant. By 1987 the estimated cost of treating one heart transplant patient was over $150,000, and one liver transplant patient over $230,000. At the same time, political pressure to extend basic health care coverage to the working poor increased. The cost of providing this coverage had also grown, but compared to the expense of transplants, the cost on an individual basis made it attractive. The cost of prenatal care for one normal delivery, for example, was estimated at $2,000.

Some public officials posed the issue as an explicit choice between transplants and basic care. They favored extending coverage to pregnant women and children among the working poor while reducing funding for organ transplants. Leonard Kirschner, the new director of AHCCCS, asked: "So where do you want to spend your money? Do I want to spend my money on doing eight heart transplants at a million and a half dollars? Or go out and get more of these poor people who are not getting prenatal care, and give them some prenatal care? That's about $2,000 a case. What's $2,000 into a million five? 700 cases? What about 700 deliveries for eight heart transplants?"[25] Public officials, Kirschner suggested, have a responsibility to use public resources where they can do the most good. His position rightly assumes that the legislators did not have the option of following the difference principle. They probably could not maximize the life chances of the least advantaged, the next least advantaged, and so on, even with regard only to health care. Once they tried to maximize the life chances of the least advantaged with regard to education, security, income, and wealth as well as health care, they faced at least two intractable problems: deciding who counts as the least advantaged, and justifying the maximization of their life chances in the face of competing values.

Kirschner's alternative to the difference principle sounds like a modified version of utilitarianism: given limited resources, maximize the number of lives saved.[26] But neither he nor anyone else in the Arizona debate actually presented the kind of analysis necessary to show what policy would maximize the number of lives saved or the net benefits to society. Dr. Jack Copeland, an eminent heart surgeon who headed the University of Arizona's heart transplant center, came closest to offering a cost-benefit analysis. He favored funding—especially of heart transplants. He pointed out that most of his patients returned to work within six months of the surgery and again became productive members of society. If such benefits were included in the calculation, he argued that the net cost of a heart transplant would be only $6,100. But, as most officials and citizens seemed to realize, utilitarian calculations, even if they could be carried through, would not finally decide the conflict between Kirschner and Copeland. The prospect of such a standoff should help resist the temptation to return to the principle of utility, even in face of frustration over the demands of the difference principle.

EGALITARIAN OPPORTUNITY

Egalitarians can offer an opportunity principle that is less problematic than both the difference principle and the principle of utility. It is exemplified by the second part of Rawls's opportunity principle—fair equality of opportunity—and it serves as the basis of the more promising approach taken by Norman Daniels.[27] In Daniels's view a democratic government should treat health care neither as a basic liberty nor as a primary good to be distributed according to the demanding dictates of the difference principle but rather as what we call a basic opportunity good. Such a good is to be understood as a condition for enjoying almost all other opportunities in life, including the ability to compete for valuable social positions.

Because health so greatly influences our other opportunities, the government, Daniels argues, should be bound to equalize opportunities for health care within the normal range of human functioning.[28] According to this approach, government must give all citizens whatever health care they need to maintain the opportunities that any normal citizen in their society with similar skills and talents would enjoy in the absence of disease or disability. This is an egalitarian principle of basic opportunity. Appropriately modified, the principle would also govern the distribution of other basic opportunity goods, such as education.

The case for treating health care as a basic opportunity good in contemporary democracies is compelling. But is it equally compelling to require that democratic governments provide each citizen with whatever is necessary for normal human functioning? This principle suffers from a version of the bottomless pit problem that plagued the difference principle. Although Daniels's principle does not demand maximizing the life prospects of the least advantaged, it does imply that democratic government must provide equal access to medical treatment for every disease and disability that interferes with the normal range of opportunities enjoyed by healthy citizens. While less than the difference principle asks, that is still much more than most governments can give if they expect to provide other social goods, including other basic opportunity goods.

To ensure that each citizen can enjoy the normal range of opportunities, Arizona's AHCCCS would be required to fund every organ transplant that was deemed likely to bring any citizen up to the baseline of normal functioning. Furthermore, AHCCCS would have to fund every other medical service (such as intensive neonatal care) necessary to secure, as far as possible, a normal range of opportunities for every person. It is difficult to estimate what the total cost of this kind of policy would be, but it is clear that it would absorb most of the state's budget even if taxes were significantly increased.

The problem with the principle is not only that it demands more resources than the government is likely to be able to command. It also demands so much investment in health care that governments could not provide equally important basic opportunity goods such as education, public safety, food, and housing. Funding health care in a way that would satisfy the egalitarian principle would leave too little to satisfy its own dictates with regard to other basic opportunity goods. By the same token, if government tried to fund education to normalize the life chances of all citizens, this would probably leave inadequate funds for health care.

The problem has yet another dimension. Suppose citizens agree on a standard for allocating resources among basic opportunity goods such as health care, education, public safety, food, and housing. Citizens could still reasonably object to the egalitarian opportunity principle. The principle would require the government to devote all its resources to basic opportunity goods, completely neglecting other social goods. In their private lives most people make room for things that are not, strictly speaking, needs. They buy stereo systems, cameras, VCRs, and sports equipment, and they spend money on concerts, movies, travel, sports events, and other forms of entertainment that could hardly be considered as essential as health care or education. Some people spend more of their income on these "quality of life" goods than others do. Regardless of the relative value one places on such goods, one can recognize that no reasonable conception of a good life would exclude them completely. People would question the sanity of someone who spent all his resources trying to make himself as healthy, as secure, or even as educated as possible. Similarly, in public life citizens may reasonably reject a policy of spending all their collective resources on needs and none on parks, sports, and the arts. Not everything in a good life or in a good society is a need.

In its strong form this egalitarian opportunity seems to wish away the problem of scarcity, one of the sources of the problem of moral disagreement that it claims to solve. A deliberative democracy therefore needs to limit the demands of egalitarian opportunity. Daniels recognizes the need to limit these demands so as to maintain the productive capacity of society and "important social institutions." Once such limits are recognized, Daniels believes, the "bugaboo of the bottomless pit is less threatening." But in making the bottomless pit less threatening Daniels has made his principle less determinate. "Deciding which needs are to be met and what resources are to be devoted to doing so," he writes, "requires careful moral judgment and a wealth of empirical knowledge about the effects of alternative allocations."[29]

If this is a call for continuing the democratic discussion, then it is quite compatible with deliberative democracy. But if Daniels's approach assumes that an opportunity principle can somehow overcome imperfect moral understanding and incomplete information, then it is misguided. There is no discernible group of experts who can be relied on to make such morally consequential decisions with careful moral judgment and a wealth of empirical information. Taken by itself, without deliberation as its ally, the egalitarian principle of opportunity would be unrealistic as well as undemocratic in its demands.

Deliberative democracy therefore needs an opportunity principle that makes more limited demands. Government cannot be constitutionally required to provide equal access to equal-quality medical treatment for every disease and disability that interferes with the normal range of opportunities enjoyed by healthy citizens. Nor can it be required to provide equal access to education, public safety, and every other basic opportunity good that serves a similar purpose of "normalizing" every person's life chances. Egalitarians such as Daniels admit that implementing these requirements in the real world is impossible. We have argued that even were it possible, under normal circumstances it would be undesirable.

An opportunity principle should make it legitimate for democratic governments to limit coverage and not pretend to provide determinate standards by which to do so. The boundaries of an opportunity principle are best set by well-informed moral discussion in the political process, as the conditions of deliberative democracy suggest. Such an opportunity principle would guide but not fully determine the policies that may legitimately be adopted by a democratic government. Citizens and public officials in a deliberative democracy recognize the need for their deliberation to inform, as well as be informed by, an opportunity principle.

A principle of egalitarian opportunity that requires (or appears to require) normalization across the entire range of basic opportunity goods should therefore not be part of the constitution of deliberative democracy. Just as libertarianism is indiscriminate in its defense of liberty, so egalitarianism is extravagant in its devotion to opportunity. Whereas libertarianism threatens to displace the value of opportunity, egalitarianism threatens to disregard the importance of deliberation. It is by the exercise of deliberation that accountable public officials and citizens best decide which opportunity goods in the range of egalitarian indeterminacy should have priority over others, and which opportunity goods should give way to quality of life goods.

The truth in egalitarianism is that all citizens, regardless of their position in society, should have effective access to an adequate level of basic opportunity goods. Confronted with the problem of the bottomless pit, citizens should not revert to libertarianism, which ignores the need for an opportunity principle. Governments are not morally free to neglect health care, education, security, and other basic opportunity goods which make it possible for people to lead normal lives and to compete for valuable social positions. A deliberative perspective cannot do without a principle of opportunity any more than it can do without a principle of liberty.

BASIC OPPORTUNITIES

What a deliberative perspective needs, then, is a principle of opportunity that reflects the constraints of scarcity and imperfect knowledge. Such a principle can both avoid the problem of the bottomless pit and address the problem of indeterminacy. The principle can deal with the first problem by scaling down its demands and with the second by delegating to the deliberative process the task of specifying some of its content.[30]

A deliberative perspective on opportunity consists of two principles that govern opportunities. The first, which we call the basic opportunity principle, obligates government to ensure that all citizens may secure the resources they need to live a decent life and enjoy other (non-basic) opportunities in our society. The second principle, which we call the fair opportunity principle, governs the distribution of highly valued goods that society legitimately takes an interest in distributing fairly among individuals. Prominent among these are skilled jobs, which are fairly distributed on the basis of qualification rather than need. Having a decent job is a basic opportunity because it is necessary for exercising equal citizenship and living a minimally good life, but having the job that you want, or even the job you deserve, is not.[31] Nevertheless, having the job that you want or deserve is an important opportunity in life, and determining whether highly valued jobs are distributed fairly, in a nondiscriminatory manner, is therefore an important function of any principled perspective on opportunity. Because the Arizona case does not directly raise the question of employment opportunities, we defer the analysis of the fair opportunity principle until Chapter 9, and focus here on the basic opportunity principle.

Basic opportunities are those goods and services that are necessary for living a good life and making use of other opportunities, such as the opportunity to compete for skilled jobs. What kind of good or service is to count as a basic opportunity is not likely to be as problematic a question as what level of support is necessary. Health care, education, physical security, housing, food, employment, or the equivalents in income, are all goods that are especially important to living a decent life and securing other opportunities in our society. It is possible to determine whether other goods (such as private property) should count as basic by considering whether they sufficiently resemble the clear cases. If it turns out that there is not a sharp line separating basic opportunities from some others, the principle will refer to goods that are more or less basic.

The more intractable problem for the basic opportunity principle arises when it is expected to determine the *level* at which any given good should be provided. If the principle is to preserve its egalitarian thrust, it should require that in some significant sense the level of basic opportunities must be equal for all citizens. Defining an adequate social minimum, a level that would enable any citizen to live a decent life and make use of opportunities that are generally regarded as valuable in our society, seems the most promising approach. Such a social minimum would not ensure that each citizen is at the same level; that would be impossible without abandoning the basic liberty principle, which would be undesirable. But a social minimum would give each citizen the same claim on public resources, and in this significant sense provide a form of equal opportunity.

Ronald Dworkin suggests a way, consistent with this approach, to determine collectively the level of adequacy for health care. His view, while remaining reliably egalitarian, has the potential to overcome the bottomless pit problem. He asks citizens to consider "what kind of medical care and insurance it would be prudent for most Americans to buy for themselves." He supposes that the question would be answered under conditions in which income and wealth were more fairly distributed, citizens had adequate information about health risks and medical technology, and insurance rates did not discriminate against people with preexisting conditions.[32] Dworkin's recommended method of reasoning admits a large measure of indeterminacy. Even well-informed citizens who reason carefully would be likely to arrive at different (but perhaps not wildly divergent) conclusions. But provided that the dependence of this method on the results of actual deliberation is recognized, it could furnish one of the more promising interpretations of the basic opportunity principle. It would advise citizens to deliberate collectively about the level and kind of health care insurance that they would buy were they spending their own (justly distributed) income rather than tax dollars. Their collective conclusion, guided by this basic opportunity principle, would constitute a provisionally justifiable level of health care for members of their society.

On any of the deliberative approaches to interpreting the principle of basic opportunity, the level of opportunity does not represent some immutable standard, objectively determined outside the political process. The basic level would vary with the trends in economic development and with changes in social expectations. The level would rise as the economy grew and as citizens came to have higher expectations. Just as citizens and public officials in the 1930s came to see social security for financial protection in old age as part of a social minimum, so in the 1990s the vast majority are coming to regard guaranteed health care as a basic opportunity. In a similar way their expectations about the level of support for these basic opportunities change over time, and in response to public deliberation.

Although the content of the basic opportunity principle is subject to changes in social expectations in this way, its moral authority is not dependent on public opinion. Social expectations should not be confused with responses to opinion polls, electoral results, or individual preferences that utilitarians would aggregate. The substance of social expectations must be morally defensible, and the process that shapes them should be deliberative, not coercive or manipulative. What counts as a basic opportunity—both the scope and the level at which it is funded—is to be determined through democratic deliberation. A standard for basic opportunities must be publicly defended on moral grounds, consistent with the requirements of reciprocity among citizens. Through public deliberation among accountable agents, a democratic government should aim at finding a level and a scope of basic opportunities that are mutually acceptable to morally motivated citizens, regardless of their differences in income or wealth, race or ethnicity, health or disability.

Until this kind of deliberation occurs, the full content of the opportunity principle remains partially indeterminate. But even in its rudimentary form, basic opportunity has some implications for policy choices that would move democratic politics in a more egalitarian direction while respecting the priority of basic liberty. Consider again the Arizona legislators. The basic opportunity principle requires them to ask whether prenatal care, pediatric care, and various organ transplants are necessary to provide even minimally decent life chances for citizens who cannot afford to pay for these kinds of care.

Routine prenatal and pediatric care are widely assumed to be basic opportunity goods. The empirical evidence for this assumption is (as we shall see) not as strong as is usually assumed. But even if it turns out that prenatal care makes a substantial difference in only a minority of cases, the basic opportunity principle could still require coverage of such care. It does not restrict coverage only to those basic opportunity goods that are "cost-effective" in some utilitarian sense.

Liver transplants like the one that Dianna Brown needed are not as widely regarded as opportunity goods. Once we recognize, however, that prenatal care is a basic opportunity good not because it is necessary to save or extend the lives of most children but because some children will not live even minimally decent lives without it, then the door is open to the claim that liver transplants should be considered a basic opportunity good, which a democratic government is morally bound to cover if it can. (*If it can* is an important proviso, to which we return in a moment.) Having opened the door in this way, the Arizona legislators would be obligated to examine the evidence about the effectiveness of liver transplants in extending the lives of people who would not otherwise be able to live what is reasonably considered a normal life. Liver transplants are vastly more expensive than prenatal or pediatric care, but governments may not refuse to fund them for this reason alone.

If scarcity of social resources permits, basic opportunity requires funding of liver transplants and other high-cost medical therapies if (but only if) they are necessary to provide people with decent life chances. Dianna Brown needed a liver transplant to provide her with decent life chances. She asked for a "chance for a chance," but she also added: "I can understand that you have to look at the overall picture. I always try to understand. I can't say I always do—Lord knows I don't—but I try."[33] Do scarce social resources permit Arizona to fund liver transplants and all other basic opportunity goods that are similarly essential to decent life chances?

This question is not easy to answer. The Arizona legislators were responsible for looking at the overall picture, and part of this responsibility was to try provide a basic level of opportunity for every citizen of Arizona. What does the picture look like from a deliberative perspective that takes basic opportunity seriously? It is certainly arguable that failing to fund liver (and similarly effective organ) transplants for Dianna Brown and others with equivalent needs denies them basic opportunities. Had Dianna Brown been rich, she would have been able to afford a liver transplant. Basic opportunity does not require equalizing opportunity between rich and poor, but it does imply that all citizens, rich or poor, enjoy some basic level of opportunity. By 1987 liver transplants were no longer experimental procedures. They were becoming widely available in the private market for those who could afford them, or whose insurance companies would pay for them. Those who, like Dianna Brown, could not afford them had no chance of living anything close to a normal life span, unless the state paid for them. With regard to their effects on other opportunities, transplants were thus as basic as any good can be, and they were not equally available. In defunding liver transplants, the Arizona legislators were therefore neglecting the demands of basic opportunity, and thereby discriminating against citizens who could not otherwise afford to stay alive.

The argument is not quite so simple, however, when one considers whether legislators had at their disposal enough resources to fund liver transplants and other basic opportunity goods that are equally (or more) essential to providing people with decent life chances. Could the legislators reasonably conclude that under the circumstances they should not fund such transplants? Suppose the legislators reasoned: Because each organ transplant is extremely expensive and the demand is rapidly growing (as the transplants become more effective), it is probably not possible to raise the tax revenues that are necessary to fund a policy that supports all transplants. Without additional revenues or greater assistance from the federal government, the state cannot even support transplants *and* prenatal and pediatric care, let alone all the other basic opportunity goods that deliberative democracy seems to demand. As legislators (or public officials to whom legislators have delegated the decision), they must decide how to distribute health care resources under conditions of scarcity. They cannot avoid hard choices between, say, liver transplants on the one side and prenatal and pediatric care on the other.

Although in fact most Arizona legislators were reluctant to confront explicitly the possibility of limiting coverage, the director of ACCCHS was not. Kirschner advocated a principle of "women and children first," which he called the "*Titanic* concept of medicine."[34] He meant not that only women and children should receive transplants, but rather that, given limited resources for health care, the state should support prenatal and pediatric care, which produce the greatest long-term gains for women and children. Neither did Kirschner mean that the state should fund such care for all women and children (a policy that would cover women and children from affluent families, who are not generally those most in need of medical care or other basic opportunity goods). If government declines to cover *all* effective life-saving medical care for women and children who cannot afford it, then it should not pay for medical care for those who could otherwise afford it.

Kirschner presumably had in mind a more refined version of the "*Titanic* concept": let the women and children with incomes below the federal poverty line and without coverage go first. In any application of the basic opportunity principle, this group would rank high on the list of people who are entitled to government aid. But some of those who need transplants fall in this same group. Why prefer prenatal and pediatric care over transplants? The assumption seems to be that choosing the former policy would produce the greater increase in basic opportunities—not only in the utilitarian sense of producing the greater aggregate of social welfare but also in a nonutilitarian sense of increasing the lifespans of poor children who would otherwise be the persons with the shortest lives. The utilitarian and nonutilitarian rationales for giving priority to prenatal and pediatric care for poor children seem to converge in this case. In its focus on extending the lives of the least advantaged, this moral reasoning is consistent with a basic opportunity principle. The individuals whose basic opportunities are to be extended are selected on the basis of the egalitarian considerations at the root of the concern for securing basic and fair opportunity for all.

The problem with this reasoning lies not in its moral but in its empirical assumptions and the conditions under which those assumptions are taken for granted. A decision to fund prenatal and pediatric care instead of organ transplants can be justified only if legislators are warranted in making two assumptions.

The first is that prenatal and pediatric care would be effective in saving or extending the lives of the least advantaged. Although this is a widely accepted assumption, the available evidence is tenuous.[35] In light of the evidence, legislators guided by a basic opportunity principle cannot simply assume that prenatal and pediatric care take priority over liver transplants and other effective, albeit expensive, procedures.

The second assumption is that legislators cannot raise taxes to fund organ transplants along with prenatal and pediatric care (or any other as yet uncovered basic opportunity good) without defunding some other equally or more important basic opportunity good. This assumption holds only if the constraint of scarcity is as severe as most officials and legislators believed in this case. If it is not, then defunding liver transplants, which are known to be effective in giving people like Dianna Brown a chance to live a normal life, violates the basic opportunity principle. If legislators can raise taxes, they are obligated to provide the funds for liver transplants in order to give citizens like Dianna Brown a "chance for a chance."

The principles of liberty and opportunity certainly cannot help citizens deal with the problem of moral disagreement if they ignore one of the sources of that disagreement—the scarcity of resources. But it would be a moral as well as an empirical mistake for legislators to take any given level of scarcity for granted, as if it were completely externally given rather than at least partially internally dependent, its level determined in part through deliberation. The basic opportunity principle shows just how hard some choices are, and it requires legislators who take it seriously to try to determine partly through deliberation the relative importance of the values at stake. When legislators discover how difficult it is to justify giving priority to prenatal and pediatric care over liver transplants, the basic opportunity principle encourages and guides their effort to secure greater resources to mitigate the problem of scarcity. This is one of the important roles of the basic opportunity principle in a deliberative perspective.

By itself, the basic opportunity principle cannot determine the level of resources that should be available for public support of health care. But it can tell Arizona officials that they cannot simply rest content with the present level of taxation. If they do not subject to deliberation the constraint of scarcity as manifest in limited tax dollars, then they are not fulfilling their obligation under the basic opportunity principle. To a significant degree, then, the fiscal limitations under which public officials operate as they seek to refine and follow the principles of liberty and opportunity are determined through the deliberative process itself.[36] When legislators fail to consider seriously whether taxes can and should be raised, they fail in their responsibility to respect the demands of an opportunity principle that promotes the life chances of disadvantaged citizens.

Public officials generally cannot know the limits of the resources at their disposal until they have exhausted their own resources of responsible leadership in a democratic process of deliberation. They cannot responsibly say that they do not have enough until they have asked for more. Those Arizona legislators who never tried to make the case for funding transplants to their constituents or their colleagues are in a weak position to plead the excuse of scarcity. The problem of scarcity is real, but its severity and its effects depend in significant measure on how officials and citizens come to see the competing moral claims that are made on the limited resources. In the process of deliberating about these hard choices, and becoming aware of their actual value in extending and improving the quality of human life (as many belatedly did in the case of Dianna Brown), citizens themselves may press officials to seek more resources, and officials may encourage citizens to favor more support.

Deliberation in the Service of Liberty and Opportunity

What the principles of liberty and opportunity require depends in two ways on deliberation. First, the content of the principles themselves is partly shaped by moral discussion in the political process. This kind of indeterminacy is probably inevitable, but in any case, as we have argued, it is also desirable. It leaves room for improvements in the level and mix of liberties, opportunities, and other goods that governments provide. Second, the constraints on the principles of liberty and opportunity themselves—in particular, limited resources—are less fixed than is often assumed. Moral debate in politics can reveal new possibilities and suggest new directions, making realization of the principles more feasible than was previously thought. Because deliberation has the potential for improving collective understandings of liberty and opportunity, the conditions of deliberation are an indispensable part of any perspective committed to securing liberty and opportunity for all.

Deliberation plays several important roles in the service of securing liberty and opportunity. It protects liberty and opportunity by requiring officials and citizens to justify their actions in terms that are consistent with these principles. This self-limiting quality of deliberation also comes to the aid of liberty and opportunity by helping citizens to specify and apply the principles in ways that less dialogical forms of justification concede they cannot. The principles that express the values of liberty and opportunity become more specific and more defensible in the course of the deliberative process. Deliberation is therefore not only self-limiting—as citizens and public officials who deliberate constrain themselves by constitutional principles—but also self-transforming, as the principles themselves are developed through the process of deliberation. When deliberation works well, citizens and public officials improve their own and one another's understanding of the content of constitutional principles.

Deliberation also has a role in developing standards of liberty and opportunity that lie beyond the basic principles. When moral conflict is not wholly resolved by these principles, and the constitutionality of a decision is therefore not at issue, citizens can still deliberate in order to discover morally better decisions and morally better ways to conduct the democratic process. More ambitious forms of liberty and opportunity have a place in deliberation at this stage, not as constitutional constraints but as deliberative guides, helping to identify new issues, setting priorities, and shaping the content of policies. Since the constitutional principles of liberty and opportunity in a deliberative perspective leave much more to the discretion of the democratic process than is usually supposed, there is considerable scope for stronger standards of liberty and opportunity to serve as deliberative guides.

Constrained by constitutional principles of liberty and opportunity, deliberation plays a large part in democracy. In the case of health care, it should have a starring role. How much money should government spend on high-tech medical care compared to preventive care? At what point should the satisfaction of medical needs be traded for quality of life goods?

How much should the government spend on health care relative to education and public safety? The principles of basic liberty and basic and fair opportunity rule out some answers to these questions (e.g., organ lotteries), and they may influence the answers to others (e.g., giving priority to life-saving organ transplants over other expensive but more experimental treatments). But they leave a vast range of decisions to the democratic process, where they are properly made, provided the process is deliberatively conducted.

The critical potential of the deliberative conditions presented in earlier chapters can be seen in the controversy over organ transplants in Arizona. Did the Arizona legislators satisfy the principles of deliberation when they decided to defund organ transplants? We suggested that even if there was not enough money to cover both prenatal and pediatric care *and* life-saving organ transplants, the legislature's decision to defund organ transplants was not justified. Even giving the legislators the benefit of the doubt and assuming that they could not have raised more tax revenues, we should still conclude that their decision suffered from a deliberative deficit. They could not justify their decision to citizens like Dianna Brown, whose opportunity to have normal life chances they were denying.

In the first place, the legislators simply did not deliberate enough. They did not seriously consider the relative contributions that health care alternatives could make to basic opportunity. Specifically, they did not even try to compare the contribution of funding organ transplants to those of prenatal and pediatric care. Second, and even more important, most of the legislators showed little respect for the principle of reciprocity. It is true, as we have noted, that a few officials in Arizona and some citizens did try to justify the decision to defund organ transplants in reciprocal terms. They saw the issue as a choice between transplants and prenatal and pediatric care, where both could not be supported, and argued that poor infants and their mothers should come first because this is where tax dollars could do the most good. But they said little about the standard of "good" they were using, and therefore even less about the potential of prenatal and pediatric care to produce this good. This moral argument was far less developed than it could have been on the basis of deliberation, and its empirical assumptions were not subject to even a modest degree of scrutiny.

Some critics of the decision argued that the legisature just did not "want to come up with the money, period."[37] If legislators had had the moral will to fund both, these critics claimed, they could have found a fiscal way.

Still other legislators who voted for defunding transplants said that they were not making a conscious trade-off, nor were they absolutely opposed to trying to find more funds. They simply accepted the expert opinion of the officials at AHCCCS, which they interpreted as concluding that a policy of funding transplants was not medically sensible. "You try to listen to medical experts in terms of what is reasonable and what is cost-effective and what makes sense from a medical standpoint," said one legislator. Another noted that, because Arizona's legislative session lasts only one-hundred days, legislators do not have enough time to discuss such issues in depth, and find it better and easier to leave them to medical experts to resolve.[38]

These reasons for defunding organ transplants either accept the expressed preferences of citizens and colleagues, without making any effort to inform or change them, or take the authority of experts as the final word. If legislators had argued that they were bound to follow their constituents on this issue, and that they had tried and failed to change their view, they would have been on the way toward giving a provisional justification (though still an insufficient one). So would any legislators who argued that a fiscally conservative policy would benefit the least advantaged citizens in the long run (though the empirical claim would be hard to establish by reliable methods of inquiry against an opposing claim that fiscal conservatism unnecessarily deprives the least advantaged citizens of basic opportunity goods). An appeal to authority could be justified if, for example, legislators could show that the most significant issues on which the dispute over health care funding turned were technical. In this case, however, the medical and scientific information, though important, could not determine the choices that affected basic opportunities.

All things considered, it is not clear that any of these further reasons could have justified the Arizona legislature's decision. In any case, Arizona officials did not give them. They assumed, without any argument or effort to bring about change in the total amount of funding for health care, that the constraints of scarcity and imperfect knowledge were immutable. To this extent they fell short of satisfying the principle of reciprocity. The reasons they gave represented assertions of unsubstantiated opinion and unfounded authority rather than reasons guided by reciprocity.

The forum in which Arizona officials presented, or more accurately failed to present, their reasons also fell short of what the publicity condition of deliberation requires. Although the press gave extensive coverage to the plight of Dianna Brown and several others who were denied transplants, neither the press nor any other public forum focused on the hard choices in health care policy or on the question whether the choice had to be so hard. Most of the discussion of the issue in the legislature took place informally or else in small groups. As one legislator described the process: "There is such a select group in the legislature that actually dealt with the AHCCCS issues—there were probably eight of us at the most, and then probably only three to four of us who were intimately involved with the discussion. I don't think [the others] considered [transplants one way or the other]. In the broad scheme of things, the bill looked okay."[39]

Legislators cannot take an active part in, and inform themselves and the public fully on, every issue on which they vote. They have to rely on their colleagues, and they have to delegate many decisions to committees. But the choices of priorities in health care of the significance of those raised in this case should be at the center of "the broad scheme of things." The reasons for these priorities should be brought to the public's attention, and legislators should be open to public responses to their reasons. Legislators who do not give an adequate public account of their decisions on such questions do not act deliberatively.

To whom do they owe such an account? Most of the Arizona legislators would probably have said to their electoral constituents. But deliberative accountability extends beyond electoral constituents. At one point in the Arizona episode, a legislator who represented the district where the leading heart transplant hospital was located managed to secure legislative authorization for funding heart transplants, dropping any support for liver and bone marrow transplants.[40] Perhaps he thought that his position would better serve future generations by advancing research in this important field. But his actions seemed to serve his electoral constituents rather than any more general good. Certainly his actions were more easily justified to his electoral constituents, or at least some of them, than to Dianna Brown and others who needed the transplants that his compromise precluded. Compared to this legislator, those representatives who took a broader view of their responsibilities better fulfilled the spirit of the principle of accountability.

In its most general form, deliberative accountability may appear neither practicable nor desirable, insofar as it calls on citizens and public officials to give attention to the claims of everyone who might be affected by their political actions. Many of the people who would be seriously affected by Arizona's policy were not residents of Arizona; they were not the constituents of any legislator. Dr. Schaller opposed funding heart transplants partly because he believed that the policy would encourage people to come to Arizona for treatment from states such as Idaho and California, which did not pay for transplants. He argued that it would be unfair if the citizens of Arizona had to pay for the transplants of residents of other states that had refused to fund such procedures. Schaller's argument has some moral force, but it raises more difficulties than it resolves. At the least it suggests that the problems of health care policy cannot be solved by the states alone. But it also forces us to consider to what extent and in what way the moral claims of those who are not present should be represented. These include not only nonresidents but future generations as well.

The principle of accountability does not solve this problem, but it does bring out its moral significance, and rules out some kinds of solutions to it. Accountable citizens and public officials look beyond not only their self-interest but also the interests of their own community and consider the interests of others. This is an ideal, and most democracies, perhaps inevitably, fall far short of it. Yet deliberative democracies stand a better chance of realizing it to some degree than do democracies that do not expect their public officials or citizens to justify their actions by substantive principles, but are content to rely on procedural practices and political pressures. Officials represent the legitimate claims of citizens who are not present only if officials have to justify their policies to those who do not have power over them as well as to those who do.

Perhaps Arizonans are not obligated to pay for the transplants of Californians and Idahoans. But if so, Arizonans should be able to offer good moral reasons why people suffering from heart disease in Idaho or California should not have access to the same life-saving good as residents of Arizona. This moral account may take the form of a public argument, satisfying the standard of reciprocity, which concludes that we should all contribute to some version of a national health plan. It may take other forms. But the account cannot rest, even implicitly, on the mere fact that the residents of Arizona have bargaining power in the legislature and the residents of California and Idaho do not.

We have not shown how the controversy over defunding organ transplants in Arizona should be resolved. Developing the principles of deliberative democracy, we have tried to sort out the better and worse arguments and the better and worse approaches to deal with the controversy. But given the nature of the principles as we have interpreted them, no resolution should be expected that stands outside the deliberative process. Even within it the best that can normally be expected is a provisional resolution. Citizens and officials have to interpret and apply the principles of basic liberty, basic opportunity, and fair opportunity—in a process governed by the conditions of deliberation. They must also engage in deliberation to make morally justifiable decisions on questions that lie beyond the authority of the constitutional principles of liberty and opportunity.

The greater the degree of deliberation citizens exercise in democratic decision making, the more confident they can be of the democratic decisions they make. Complete confidence may be beyond reach, but mutually acceptable justification is attainable if citizens are willing to respect all the principles of the constitution of deliberative democracy. Our analysis of the Arizona case helps show why the principles that constitute a deliberative perspective are not properly considered exclusively substantive or procedural. Each of the *conditions* of deliberation—reciprocity, publicity, and accountability—has substantive as well as procedural content and value. Each element of the *content* of deliberation—basic liberty, basic opportunity, and fair opportunity—depends on deliberative procedures to advance a common understanding of its substance. Public policies are justifiable insofar as they satisfy the principles that constitute both the content and the conditions of deliberative democracy, according to the best understanding of the meaning and implications of each that citizens can achieve at any particular time.

The principles of deliberative democracy do not guarantee morally right results, but they offer a more defensible way of reaching mutually justifiable policies than do the principles of utilitarianism, libertarianism, or egalitarianism alone. Despite their differences, utilitarianism, libertarianism, and egalitarianism all imply that democratic decisions are justifiable only if they can be shown to be morally correct on principles determined independently of democratic deliberation. For every important question of distributive justice, these perspectives as commonly interpreted imply either that there exists a single correct answer that should, at least in theory, trump democratic deliberation, or (when their own theoretical principles are indeterminate) that there is no correct answer at all as far as justice is concerned. In deliberative democracy, by contrast, the search for justifiable answers takes place through arguments constrained by constitutional principles, which are in turn themselves developed through deliberation.

_7_

The Latitude of Liberty

"OVER HIMSELF, over his own body and mind, the individual is sovereign."[1] So concludes John Stuart Mill in what has become the classic statement of the liberal principle of liberty. The Millian principle remains, explicitly in theory and implicitly in practice, the starting point for most defenses of liberty. It is also our starting point in this chapter because it captures some fundamental features of basic liberty. The idea of individual sovereignty over body and mind invokes the elements of personal integrity that we treat as central to basic liberty. Like basic liberty in a deliberative constitution, Mill's principle sets limits on what government and society can demand of citizens, and what citizens can demand of one another. It gives liberty priority over other moral values that government and society may decide to pursue.

But the basic liberty of deliberative democracy differs significantly from Mill's liberty, and in ways that make it more defensible as a constitutional principle of deliberative democracy. Millian liberalism rejects absolutely two kinds of claims that are prominent in political debate. It rejects the claims of *moralists,* who would legislate on the basis of social morality in the absence of individual harm, and it rejects the claims of *paternalists,* who would legislate on the basis of individual welfare in the absence of individual consent. By contrast, basic liberty, as protected by deliberative democracy, grants both moralists and paternalists standing in the making of public policy.

Both moralism and paternalism express important values that a deliberative perspective should respect. But both also make claims that conflict with liberty in any form, or at least deny the priority of basic liberty. Were a democratic government authorized to prohibit a practice because it is immoral even though it harms no one, or an action because it harms the individual even though she wants to do it, little room would be left for the free choice of individuals. Moralists and paternalists would prevent citizens from acting in certain ways even when they do not harm others, or more precisely for reasons that have nothing to do with harming others. The challenge for deliberative democracy is to find ways to recognize the legitimate claims of moralism and paternalism while maintaining the priority of basic liberty.

We show how a principle of basic liberty can meet this challenge by examining an area of public policy where the claims of moralists and paternalists are notably cogent: the issue of contract parenting. As adoption has become more difficult and new reproductive technologies more accessible, an increasing number of citizens are turning to nontraditional methods to fulfill the traditional desire to have a family. One of the most common is contract parenting or, as it is more popularly known, surrogate parenthood. In the typical case a married couple (the recipient parents) who cannot have a child contract with a fertile woman (the birth mother), who agrees to be artificially inseminated with the sperm of the husband. The birth mother agrees to surrender all parental rights to the husband, the biological father, who, along with his infertile wife, agrees to adopt the child at birth. The would-be parents pay the expenses of the birth mother, and promise to pay her a fee at the time of delivery.

Like conventional ways of creating a family, surrogate parenting need not involve the government. All parties to the process could be left free to create children as they wish. From the case of Baby Ishmael, chronicled in the Book of Genesis, until the more recent case of Baby M, recounted in the records of a New Jersey court, thousands of couples have arranged for surrogate births without any government intervention. The government stood ready to protect the children born of these arrangements against serious abuses, and in some states to enforce some parts of the contracts that facilitated them. But public policy usually governed making babies by means of surrogacy to no greater an extent than making babies by more conventional means.

The *Baby M* case dramatically put the issue on the public agenda, and forced officials and citizens to take a new look at the widely accepted laissez-faire attitude toward contract parenting. In 1985 William Stern and his wife, Elizabeth, contracted with Mary Beth Whitehead to bear a child.[2] After the baby was born, Whitehead found that she could not bear to give her up. The Sterns insisted that she fulfill the contract. But New Jersey, the state in which they all lived, had no policy or precedents to resolve the dispute. As a result, the child, called Baby M by the court because White-head and the Sterns could not even agree on a name, had only temporary legal parents while the birth mother and contract parents struggled to gain permanent custody of her. Finally, a state court ruled in favor of the Sterns on the grounds that granting them custody was in the best interests of the child. Even those who thought that the court's decision served the child's interests did not claim that the state's laissez-faire policy served anyone's interests well in this case.

Confronted with the unhappy consequences of the policy of doing nothing, many state legislatures decided to do something. Several appointed committees to study contract parenting and to recommend a policy for dealing with the practice. One of the first and most impressive efforts took place in New York, where the state's Senate Judiciary Committee and subsequently the New York State Task Force on Life and Law issued thoughtful reports, recommending quite different courses of action.

The reports agreed that governments should not restrict the basic liberties of citizens, but they disagreed about whether the capacity to enter into a surrogate contract constitutes a basic liberty. The Judiciary Committee staff concluded that the use of commercial surrogacy falls within the realm of basic liberty because "surrogate parenting is a logical extension of the right to procreate," though there are also "state interests and parties to be protected within the surrogate parenting arrangement, which necessitates state regulation of the surrogate parenting process."[3] In contrast, the task force concluded that government should discourage the practice by "legislation that declares the contracts void as against public policy and prohibits the payment of fees to surrogates."[4] The task force reached this conclusion after arguing that "the claims of surrogates and intended parents to reproductive freedom . . . are attenuated in several ways: by the commercial nature of the arrangements; by the potential conflicts between the rights of parties to the surrogate contract; and by the risks of harm to other individuals."[5] When the state Assembly considered a bill to ban commercial surrogacy in 1992, members drew on these reports. Proponents of both positions gave thoughtful statements and engaged in serious deliberation on the issue.[6]

The two reports and the debate they stimulated demonstrate not only the relevance of moral concerns in the making of public policy, but also the capacity of political institutions to deliberate in a principled manner about controversial matters of basic liberty. The lessons of this controversy also have implications for many other issues of public policy, such as pornography and prostitution. More directly for the purposes of this chapter, the contrasting perspectives of the reports provide a context for understanding moralist and paternalist challenges to basic liberty. The task force shows more than a little sympathy for moralism and paternalism, while the Judiciary Committee staff remains faithful to Millian liberalism. By considering their opposing claims, we show how basic liberty can inform the content of public policy and still accommodate a range of moralist and paternalist considerations.

The Scope of Basic Liberty

To what extent should a principle of liberty accommodate the claims of moralists and paternalists? We can see the shape of an answer to this question if we compare the principle of liberty in Millian liberalism with basic liberty in the constitution of deliberative democracy.

THE MILLIAN PRINCIPLE AND ITS LIMITS

According to Mill, "one very simple principle" defines the scope of liberty: "The only part of the conduct of any one, for which he is amenable to society, is that which concerns others. In the part which concerns merely himself, his independence is, of right, absolute."[7] The government is justified in intervening only when a citizen's action harms other people, never when it is merely wrong, and never when it harms only himself. Or, as the principle is often put, the self-regarding actions of citizens must be left absolutely free from interference; their other-regarding actions may be subject to legal sanction.

Critics have objected that the distinction between self-regarding and other-regarding actions is pointless: almost any citizen's actions affect other citizens and often society as a whole. If you harm yourself, you harm others who depend on you; if you act immorally, you may tempt others to act immorally. Here is one of the strongest versions of the objection:

> How (it may be asked) can any part of the conduct of a member of society be a matter of indifference to other members? No person is an entirely isolated being; it is impossible for a person to do anything seriously or permanently hurtful to himself, without mischief reaching at least to his near connections, and often far beyond them . . . If by his vices or follies a person does no direct harm to others, he is nevertheless . . . injurious by his example;

and ought to be compelled to control himself for the sake of those whom the sight or knowledge of his conduct might corrupt or mislead.[8]

This expresses the standard objection to Mill's principle—and it comes from Mill himself. Mill clearly does not want to deny that most individual actions affect other people, or even that the actions may cause significant harm or benefit to society. One reason he does not want to deny it is that it is true. Another reason is that his justification of liberty depends on its being true. An important value of securing a realm of liberty for all citizens is that liberty fosters individual creativity, which in turn encourages social progress, and therefore greatly affects other citizens and society in general.[9]

Mill attempts to preserve a self-regarding sphere by establishing two strict criteria for what is to count as a harmful other-regarding action. The first criterion specifies the type of harm, and the second the object of the harm. The first criterion holds that the action must cause definite harm or pose a definite risk of harm. "Definite" means that the harm follows directly from the action in predictable ways. Children born of surrogate mothers may suffer psychological insecurities, or women who serve as surrogates may suffer marital difficulties, but neither of these potential harms would be definite enough to justify prohibiting surrogacy contracts. "Harm" means that the action does more than violate a moral rule or manifest a moral wrong; it must inflict substantial physical or mental injury on an identifiable individual or individuals. By this criterion, in the absence a showing of definite injury, the moral claim that surrogacy is degrading or exploitative would not be sufficient to justify government interference.

The second criterion stipulates that the definite harm must be caused to other people, not to oneself only. Society may force one to fulfill "a distinct and assignable obligation" to other citizens, but it may not force one to fulfill some general obligation to do good for others.[10] By the second criterion, women cannot be forced to become mothers even if society needs more children, and women cannot be prevented from becoming mothers, surrogate or otherwise, even if motherhood poses a definite risk of harm to themselves.

These criteria give more content to the self-regarding sphere but do not completely answer the objection that no action is purely self-regarding. Although on these criteria some particular action might be shown to be self-regarding, it would be difficult to demonstrate in advance that any general type of action deserves this status, and it is in types of actions that public policy deals. Rather than trying to sort *actions* into self- and other-regarding categories, we would do better to use Mill's distinction to mark different kinds of *reasons* for government intervention. The Millian principle would then hold that the justification for intervention must always refer to some definite harm or risk of harm to others; it should never be based on other kinds of moral wrongs or harms that individuals cause to themselves.

In this form the Millian principle establishes a strong presumption in favor of individual liberty. Some such presumption, we have suggested, should be part of a deliberative perspective. But now we question whether deliberative democracy should adopt the Millian principle, so interpreted, which says that governments may never regulate or prohibit conduct unless they can show that it definitely harms (or definitely risks harm to) other citizens. We also question the further step that the Millian principle takes in restraining government. The principle holds that even some harm you cause me as a result of an agreement we voluntarily made should not be grounds for government intervention. Consent, on the Millian view, turns harm to others into self-harm.

In the case of surrogacy, the Millian principle would require the government to enforce contracts necessary for citizens to carry out their plans.[11] In the spirit of this principle one of the opponents of the ban on surrogacy argued during the debate in the New York State Assembly: "It is ironic that we [ban surrogacy] in the name of liberty and freedom. I think we close down freedom for couples who desire that freedom to do something that all of us want to do, or at least most of us want to do."[12] Similarly, the Judiciary Committee staff affirmed the right of the recipient parents and the surrogate mother to enter into an agreement to create a child in this unconventional way. If all the parties voluntarily enter into the contract, the government has no reason to intervene to protect any of the parties; all have freely assumed the risk of harm for themselves.

There is of course a risk that the child who is born as a result of the contract may be harmed, and that is an other-regarding reason for the government to regulate the terms of the contract, as the Judiciary Committee staff emphasized. But this reason does not provide as much scope for governmental intervention on Millian grounds as one might think at first. The Millian principle would not, for example, justify prohibition. Ironically, it is the task force, which favors prohibition, that most clearly brings out why harm to the child cannot be a decisive reason to intervene by pointing out that the proper evaluative standpoint for public policy "occurs prior to conception when the surrogacy arrangements are made. The issue then is not whether a particular child should be denied life, but whether children should be conceived in circumstances that would place them at risk. The notion that children have an interest in being born prior to their conception and birth is not embraced in other public policies and should not be assumed in the debate on surrogate parenting."[13]

The task force's argument supports the conclusion that children born of surrogacy contracts do not have a right to be born because they do not have interests prior to conception. But it does not show that the circumstances of conception in surrogacy arrangements create risks that require, or even warrant, prohibition on Millian grounds. Indeed, contrary to the general thrust of the task force's report, this argument removes one kind of reason for intervention. Even if the children of surrogacy face some serious psychological risks (such as developing fears of abandonment), we cannot count these risks as harms to these children unless (as seems improbable) they are so severe that the children would wish they had not been born. The children can complain that the surrogacy arrangement could have been better, but they cannot claim that they are harmed by the surrogacy arrangement itself because without it they would not exist.[14]

The Millian principle may still be able to justify something short of prohibition, such as intervention (and some restrictions on the contract) to protect those children who are born, but the most plausible grounds would be paternalism toward children, which the Millian principle permits. The state would limit the liberty of children in order to protect them from risks they themselves may not recognize, and lack the moral status to claim for themselves. But the risks of harm to children are not severe enough to justify prohibition of most surrogacy arrangements on Millian grounds. The Millian principle cannot justify overriding the liberty of citizens who wish to become contract parents with the intent of providing a loving and caring environment for children. Divorce and adoption also pose serious risks to children. They may "weaken the ties between children and parents, but very few people would be willing to give the state the right to forbid divorce or adoption on such grounds."[15]

The Millian principle, then, supports an extensive sphere of liberty, permitting contract parenting along with the government intervention necessary to make it effective. But despite its attractions, the Millian principle is not an adequate standard of basic liberty for deliberative democracy. It is not adequate because it does not meet the challenges posed by moralism and paternalism. The challenges of moralism and paternalism correspond to Mill's two criteria identifying other-regarding reasons for government intervention. The first challenge—moralism—attacks the first criterion (that definite harm must be shown); the second challenge—paternalism—attacks the second criterion (that harm to others must be established). While claiming to refute both, Mill himself clearly recognizes the difference between the two kinds of attacks on his liberty principle. The moralist would justify government intervention "because, in the opinion of others, to do so would be wise, or even right," and the paternalist would intervene "because it will be better for [one]" or "because it will make [one] happier."[16]

An adequate principle of basic liberty should accommodate these claims by recognizing that some wrongs that are not definite harms, and some definite harms to oneself, may be legitimately regulated by law. Basic liberty, based on personal integrity, may require public policies different from those required by the Millian principle, which absolutely resists all claims of moralism and paternalism toward adults. These claims deserve a place in a deliberative perspective, but if and only if (1) they are consistent with personal integrity; and (2) they express important moral values that can be mutually accepted at least as much as the alternative of Millian liberty.

PERSONAL INTEGRITY AND VOLUNTARY CONTRACTS

How can moralist and paternalist claims be consistent with personal integrity? Respecting personal integrity, like Millian liberty, requires that citizens sometimes be free to engage in practices that others consider immoral or practices that cause harm to themselves (but not to others who have not agreed to assume the risks of this harm). But the basic liberty of deliberative democracy does not raise as absolute a barrier as the Millian principle does to restrictions on individual liberty. The principle of basic liberty itself opens up the question whether entering into a surrogacy contract is essential to personal integrity. Considerations of personal integrity supply some reasons to restrict individual liberty that the Millian principle does not endorse. To clarify the point, we begin by assuming that the freedom to enter into surrogacy contracts is consistent with respect for personal integrity and therefore protected by considerations of basic liberty. We begin with this assumption in order to illustrate one significant difference between Millian liberty and basic liberty. We then relax this assumption to illustrate a second difference between them.

Basic liberty, unlike Millian liberty, provides grounds for permitting one of the parties to a surrogacy agreement, the surrogate mother, to decide not to carry out all of its terms. If her personal integrity would be violated by requiring the surrogate mother to fulfill some of the terms, public policy may legitimately decline to enforce these terms. But how could enforcing an agreement that a citizen freely made violate personal integrity, especially since the right to make the agreement in the first place is based on the value of personal integrity?

If there is an adequate answer to this question, it must lie in some morally relevant difference between the circumstances in which the agreement is made and the circumstances in which it is to be carried out. The difference cannot simply be a new preference, for part of the point of any contract is to protect against the possibility that one party will prefer not to perform when the time comes to do so. But in order to be effective, contracts need not protect against all foreseeable changes, such as those that are more profound than mere preference changes. Contract parenting would probably still take place even if surrogate mothers retained the right to keep the child when they have a profound change of heart or develop a new moral perspective on what it means to give up a child they have borne. In the past, few surrogate mothers failed to fulfill contracts, even in states where they were not enforceable under these conditions.

What could justify a surrogate mother's refusal to give up the child? If the surrogate mother in good faith and for good reason comes to see giving up the child as morally wrong or as inconsistent with her sense of self-identity, requiring her to fulfill the contract in full could be said to violate her personal integrity. (She might still be required to compensate the disappointed parents, perhaps by means of prior insurance guaranteed as part of the contract.) The change in circumstances that would justify not fulfilling the contract would on this view be a profound change in perspective on the part of the surrogate mother, not merely a momentary change of preference. Unless contracts dealing with issues that implicate the core of a person's self-understanding allow for such a change in perspective, they do not make adequate provision for free choice. With such a contract, you bind yourself to perform an action in the future, without adequate information or experience at present to appraise the fundamental meaning of the action in your life. In this sense the decision to enter into such a contract could be regarded as unfree, itself a violation of personal integrity.

Millian liberals, too, would rule out some contracts because they violate liberty, but they tend to consider only more extreme cases as candidates for prohibition. Mill argues that liberty does not extend to permitting anyone to contract to be a slave. One does not have the freedom to give up one's freedom totally.[17] But this restriction on the liberty of contracts, even if consistent with Mill's absolutist defense of liberty, is severely limited in its application.[18] It prohibits only contracts that sacrifice virtually all of one's future liberty. It would not rule out surrogate contracts that require the mother to give up the child under all circumstances. Such contracts cannot be said to restrict the future liberty of the mother in the way that a slavery contract would. Not only is the range of restricted action much less in surrogacy contracts, but also the question whether liberty is restricted at all is temporally contingent. At the time the contract is made, the contract looks to all the parties to be a means of fulfilling their plans, a way of exercising their liberty rather than restricting it. Only later does one of the parties come to believe that what seemed originally to be an exercise of basic liberty is actually a violation of it. In contrast to Millian liberty, basic liberty thus makes room for what might be called retrospective recognition, the possibility that citizens may change their views of the status of their own claims to liberty. To clarify this possibility, and the conditions under which it may justify limiting the Millian liberty of citizens in the name of basic liberty, it is necessary to look more closely at contract parenting from the perspective of the surrogate mother.

We begin by considering an analogy between surrogacy and forced labor. Suppose you earn a modest living working as a waitress, and you also are a moderately talented writer. A new publishing house, specializing in romantic novels with ribald characters and racy plots, offers you an attractive contract to write a novel in their standard style, with an advance on royalties of $10,000. Seizing what you think may be your only opportunity for publication, and hoping you can produce a work that will have some literary value, you sign the contract. The novel is due in nine months, and you begin writing immediately. The writing is not easy, but it goes reasonably well for three months. Then the process starts to become frustrating and agonizing, far more difficult than you imagined, as you try to satisfy the publisher's expectations and your own literary standards. By the eighth month you feel that you simply cannot continue, not because you literally cannot write anymore, but because you find the conflict between what the publisher wants and what you think proper is greater than you had expected. Before signing the contract, you knew that this difficulty might arise, but only through the actual process of writing the novel have you come to develop and understand your own standards, and to see the depth of the conflict between them and what now seems to you the debased standards of the publisher. To finish the manuscript and let the publisher distribute it in this form now seems to you a betrayal of your principles and your sense of self-identity, a violation of your integrity. Should the government nonetheless enforce the contract and require you to produce the book as you agreed?

Grant that the publisher should have the right to reclaim the advance and perhaps even to sue for damages. But should he also be able to enlist the law to force you to finish the novel? Should the law require what is called "specific performance"? Although current law varies somewhat and is not completely settled, most labor contracts are not enforceable by requiring "specific performance."[19] What could be the justification for allowing someone to refuse to fulfill the terms of a contract not made under duress? A mutually acceptable justification appeals to personal integrity. Forcing you to perform specific tasks against your present will comes close to forcing you to labor under the control of another's will. It constitutes a substantial intrusion on your own control of your body and mind, the essence of personal integrity. The analogy might be extended even further: forcing you to labor on a project that is such a major part of your life begins to resemble indentured servitude.[20] If so, as the aspiring novelist you might reasonably object, on grounds of basic liberty, to producing the manuscript according to the publisher's wishes, now that you have come to see the project as in conflict with your deepest convictions and sense of self-identity.

This justification is one that publishers (and the disappointed parties to other kinds of labor contracts) can themselves accept. They should accept it not merely because trying to make people work against their will is often counterproductive. Even if you would still produce the novel the publisher wanted, the publisher could appreciate that forcing you to do so would violate your basic liberty, which he along with all other citizens values more highly than enforcing contracts in this way. The publisher should know in advance that this means of enforcement is not available, and in return the law should protect him against extortion by unscrupulous authors who would withhold their product in order to gain unfair return for their labor. But with this kind of legal protection in place, a general prohibition on specific performance expresses the judgment that protecting personal integrity takes priority over enforcing a voluntary contract.

How far can this conclusion be extended? If we take enforcing specific performance as a clear case of violating personal integrity, we can consider how closely it resembles more controversial cases and better decide how they should be resolved. Specifically, we can ask whether contract parenting that, without exception, prevents the surrogate mother from keeping the child violates personal integrity in the same (or a sufficiently similar) way as does enforcing specific performance. If basic liberty excludes forced labor, might basic liberty also rule out being forced to give up a child that is born of one's labor?[21] (The analogous question with regard to your book contract is whether a publisher might be prevented from forcing you to publish the manuscript if you discover only after completing it that publication would violate your sense of self-identity.)

Most surrogacy contracts, like most labor contracts, are fulfilled. Of the thousands of recorded cases in the United States, fewer than 1 percent have been challenged in court. Yet coming to terms with these exceptional cases is critical for understanding the scope of basic liberty, for they show us the clarity of the conflict between prior commitment and personal integrity. Mary Beth Whitehead had contracted with William Stern to bear a child in exchange for her expenses and a fee of $10,000. But while in the delivery room giving birth to the child, she realized that she could no longer bring herself to fulfill the terms of the contract. She would not accept the fee, and she did not think it was right that she should give up the child. When Whitehead finally turned the child over to the Sterns, she was "stricken with unbearable sadness. She had to have her child. She could not eat, sleep, or concentrate on anything other than her need for her baby."[22] It is not a strained interpretation to see her reluctance as expressing her deepest convictions concerning her personal integrity. She now perceived what she might not have been able to know before: that her attachments and responsibilities to a child she had borne could not be attenuated even by a prior contract.

Would requiring Whitehead to give up the child under these conditions violate her personal integrity? At the time of the *Baby M* case, the laws of New Jersey and most other states were silent on the question whether surrogate parenting contracts are enforceable. Although the New York State Judiciary Committee and the task force agreed that legal silence on this issue redounded "to the detriment of children born of these arrangements," they disagreed about whether surrogacy contracts should be enforceable.[23] In recommending that contract parenting be completely prohibited, the task force implied that contracts should not be enforced against the will of the birth mother but never addressed the issue of specific performance. The Judiciary Committee staff did address the issue, concluding that "surrender of the child should be enforceable through the remedy of specific performance." But the staff did not respond to the objection that this remedy can violate the basic liberty of the birth mother.[24] The reports thus begin but do not carry through the deliberation necessary to resolve the question; they do not consider the basic liberty claims of the surrogate mother at the time of the birth of the child.

To carry their deliberations further, the Judiciary Committee and the task force could have discussed the differences between contract parenting and the standard labor contract, which most people would regard as a clear case of an enforceable agreement. Three differences stand out. First, parties on both sides of the surrogacy contract have a close personal connection to the product of the labor; the recipient father as well as the birth mother have a biological tie to the newborn child, a connection that would not have existed in the absence of the contract they both signed. Second, surrogacy contracts do not require forced labor but rather only force one party to give up the product of her labor; disputes usually arise only at or after the time of birth. Third, the product of the labor is a human being, whose well-being may arguably be the most important consideration. In this section we consider the moral relevance of the first two distinctions. The third raises issues of paternalism, which we discuss in the last section of the chapter.

Consider a case of contract parenting in which only the first distinction obtains: a birth mother wants to end her pregnancy because she now finds it morally offensive or a violation of her sense of self-identity to bear a child that she must give up to strangers. If it is wrong to require specific performance, then it is also wrong to force a woman to continue her pregnancy just because she is under contract.[25] This conclusion of course presupposes that she has a right to have an abortion (a question we examined in Chapter 2). If a man's genetic tie to a fetus does not annul a woman's right to abortion in the general case of pregnancy within marriage, then neither should it nullify a woman's right to abortion in the specific case of a contract pregnancy. The only relevant difference in this case is the existence of a specific labor contract. But at this stage of the pregnancy the analogy with forced labor is at its strongest. Requiring the woman to continue to carry the child could literally be described as forced labor. Thus, in a society where abortion is a constitutional right, a birth mother should be free to terminate a contract pregnancy.

Now, consider the more common case of a birth mother who continues her pregnancy but objects to giving up the infant she has borne after nine months. Here the second difference obtains: the birth mother is claiming the right not to be forced to give up a child rather than the right not to be forced to labor. Should a birth mother's only alternatives be either to give up the infant that she bears, or to terminate its life before birth? In such a case one may assume that the birth mother would find aborting the fetus at least as abhorrent as giving up the child at birth. Neither alternative is satisfactory because neither protects the integrity of birth mothers who, like Whitehead, object to giving up the child they have borne.

The objection in this case would not be based on the analogy with forced labor. Here force takes a different form: a forced choice between two morally objectionable alternatives. The question then is whether this kind of forced choice could be said to violate personal integrity. It is plausible to think that it does. The surrogate mother faces an almost impossible dilemma. It is true that she is partly responsible for the plight in which she finds herself. She signed the contract. But public policy also contributes to the dilemma—forcing a choice between aborting the fetus or giving up the child. In the case of ordinary adoption, current policy recognizes that women should not have to confront such a dilemma. Adoption contracts generally provide for a "grace period" of weeks or months after the birth of a baby, during which a mother can change her mind and retain custody of the child she had previously agreed to give up for adoption. If this provision is seen as a protection of the personal integrity of women, then surrogacy contracts should also contain such a provision. In both kinds of contracts one would restrict one's liberty to enter into a completely binding agreement for the sake of safeguarding a greater liberty, which is necessary to protect the integrity of women.[26]

What about the integrity of men who initiate surrogacy contracts, the recipient fathers like Stern? They care deeply about raising a genetically related child, and they not only pay for the services of a birth mother but also donate their sperm, expecting that they will have exclusive custody of the child. Is Stern's basic liberty violated if the surrogacy contract is not enforced? Because New Jersey had not created a stable and justifiable set of expectations for both parties to the surrogacy contract, Stern had some basis for making a basic liberty claim. He entered into this arrangement with the reasonable expectation that his desire to have his own child would be fulfilled. But at most his claim competes with Whitehead's (and is in any case completely contingent on the state of the law); it does not override hers. In this context the two claims constitute a reasonable moral disagreement. Under these circumstances the court might have granted him joint custody (if this solution were not contrary to the interests of the child). If the law were settled and the recipient father had no expectation of custody, his claim would be weaker, resting on the fact that he contributed his sperm. This contribution, though biologically just as necessary as that of the surrogate mother, could be regarded by most people (including men) as a less weighty reason for establishing a claim of personal integrity than is nine months of carrying a child. Nonetheless, a weaker claim is still a claim, and it might be the basis for a shared custody settlement.

So far we have assumed that individuals should be free to enter into surrogacy contracts. We have argued that as a matter of basic liberty, surrogate mothers should have the option of keeping the children they bear if giving them up would violate their sense of personal integrity. We have also suggested that a contract lacking this option is one to which citizens cannot freely agree. Many critics of contract parenting go further. Like the New York State Task Force, they argue that surrogacy contracts must be prohibited because they cannot be voluntary. We now need to consider to what extent the principle of basic liberty can guide responses to such arguments.

The task force argued: "It is not possible for women to give informed consent to the surrender of a child prior to the child's conception and birth." This is not because women are less capable than men of anticipating the consequences of their commitments. It is "not because women differ from men in making important life decisions, but because women alone can bear children. The inability to predict and project a response to profound experiences that have not yet unfolded is shared by men and women alike."[27] The task force is right to point out the difficulty of anticipating how one's views about decisions that deeply affect one's life may change with new experiences. But the most this argument shows is that surrogacy contracts should be regulated so as not to violate the integrity of individuals, even if they have given prior consent, not that they must be prohibited. To protect those women whose integrity would be violated by surrendering the child, the state does not need to restrict the liberty of those whose integrity would not be violated.

Prohibition might be warranted if it could be shown that surrogacy contracts are involuntary in a more far-reaching way. Some critics believe that they can show just that. These critics go further than the task force. "To portray surrogacy contracts as representing meaningful choice and informed consent on the part of the contracting surrogate mother, rather than to see her as driven by circumstances," one critic writes, "reveals an idealized perspective and a failure to take account of realities."[28] If all (or even most) surrogacy contracts are involuntary on the part of the birth mother, then the contracts are void, and the recipient parents have no valid claims to custody.

What further response to such an objection would be appropriate in a deliberative democracy? The objection that surrogate mothers do not genuinely choose surrogacy but are "driven by circumstances" proves either too little or too much. If the objection is taken as expressing an empirical claim about the state of mind of women who enter into surrogacy arrangements, it proves too little. Certainly, if a woman was deceived about the terms of the agreement or manipulated into signing the contract, she should not be held to its performance. It would be void from the beginning, a clear violation of basic liberty. But the evidence about the extent of coercion in the making of surrogacy contracts is scanty, and does not clearly support the critics' general claim about surrogacy contracts.

Some surrogate mothers, like Whitehead, believe in retrospect that their decision to enter into the contract was not genuinely free, that they were misled about the possible consequences. But by far the majority of those who have been interviewed afterward express satisfaction with their choice and do not claim that they were deceived, manipulated, or otherwise pressured in their role. Many birth mothers testify that they are pleased to have had the opportunity to bear a child for an otherwise childless couple and to earn some money in the process. Here is the testimony of three surrogate mothers who value their experience for reasons that even those who would criticize their decision should not completely dismiss:

> I'm not going to cure cancer or become Mother Teresa, but a baby is one thing I can sort of give back, something I can give to someone who couldn't have it any other way.[29]

> I think being a surrogate mother has made me a better person. Never a day goes by that I don't thank the Lord for my own kids.[30]

> I'm an adult, and I take responsibility for my actions. Being a surrogate mother never seemed strange or wrong to me. In fact, to not help somebody would have been wrong.[31]

The testimony of these and other women is not decisive, but it casts some doubt on the claim that all women enter into surrogacy contracts involuntarily or against their better judgment. One of the advantages of adopting a principle of basic liberty based on personal integrity is that we do not have to discredit the testimony of these surrogate mothers in order to conclude that surrogacy contracts should not be enforced in those circumstances where a birth mother objects to giving up the child.

But advocates of prohibition can argue that we should look behind what the women say and consider the circumstances in which they say it. Perhaps women are not, strictly speaking, coerced into signing surrogacy contracts, but most make their decisions under conditions in which the alternative of surrogacy seems irresistible. The typical surrogate mother has fewer job opportunities and is much poorer than the typical recipient parents. She often may have no other opportunity to improve her circumstances. She may see the $10,000 fee as a start toward a better life, and thus an offer not to be refused.

In its general form this argument proves too much. It would invalidate many labor contracts that are ordinarily considered unobjectionable. All those employees who are poorer than those for whom they are working and would be even worse off if they did not enter into the contract would be regarded as being "driven by circumstances" into a labor contract.[32] Nor does the evidence support the claim that most surrogate mothers are driven to their decision by financial need.[33] Although only 15 percent of birth mothers surveyed say that they would have acted as surrogates even without compensation, only 1 percent say that they did it for the money alone.[34] Mary Beth Whitehead and her husband earned about $28,000 in 1987, an income that certainly makes the $10,000 fee attractive but not an offer that they could not refuse. Many other women in similar circumstances are not tempted by such offers.

Another reason offered for prohibiting surrogacy contracts focuses not on the circumstances in which the woman decides to enter into the contract but on the circumstances in which she carries out the contract, specifically on its the effects on her state of mind. One critic writes: "Regardless of her initial state of mind, *she is not free,* once she enters the contract, to develop an autonomous perspective on her relationship with her child. She is contractually bound to manipulate her emotions to agree with the interests of the adoptive parents."[35] She is made to "feel guilty and irresponsible for loving her own child."[36] Contract parenting on this view constitutes a "violation of the mother's personhood." Because "few things reach deeper into the self than a parent's *evolving* relationship with her own child," the contractual constraint on a woman's freedom, this critic writes, is incompatible with her autonomy.[37]

Unlike the other objections considered so far, this one appeals directly to the value of personal integrity. It qualifies as an argument from basic liberty, which a deliberative democracy therefore must address as it attempts to find a justifiable public policy in this area. At the very least, this argument provides additional support for the suggestion that a surrogate mother should not be forced to give up her child at birth, and that the right not to do so should be known in advance and guaranteed in surrogate contracts. But the further question remains: Does the argument also support the conclusion that critics wish to reach—that surrogacy contracts must be prohibited? This is a difficult question to answer without more information and understanding than is now available. Citizens and their representatives may face a deliberative disagreement here in which neither critics nor advocates of legalization have arguments capable of establishing beyond a deliberative doubt a constitutional right grounded in basic liberty. On the one side, advocates of surrogacy contracts can argue that if a birth mother knows that the surrogacy contract cannot be enforced against her will, then she is *not* "contractually bound to manipulate her emotions to agree with the interests of the adoptive parents." On the other side, critics can argue that the psychological pressure on a birth mother not to keep the child, and the practical difficulty of releasing her from the contract, remain sufficiently great even under the no-enforcement option that the very circumstances of a surrogacy contract should be regarded as manipulative.

Short of resolving this deliberative disagreement, citizens might still strive for an economy of moral disagreement, the virtues of which we discussed in Chapter 2. Supporters of surrogate contracting, for example, might defend conditions that would make surrogacy contracts more voluntary, and less exploitative.[38] One condition would be to ensure that the surrogate mother is as fully informed as possible about the physical and psychological risks of the arrangement. If surrogacy is to be legal, surrogate mothers should at least receive information from an independent authority, and should have the opportunity to obtain further advice from an attorney or counselor of her choice. Another condition would set a minimum level of payment for the service so as to protect the surrogate mother against exploitation. Even without setting an income level or identifying a comparable service, it should be possible to defend a mutually acceptable range for the payment.

But determining an appropriate payment raises a deeper and more controversial question, one that lies at the heart of the deliberative disagreement over whether surrogacy contracts should be prohibited. What exactly is the value at stake, and what if anything is comparable to it? If the product is a baby, as those critics who call surrogacy contracts "baby selling" suggest, then the value is infinite, or at least the highest value that public policy imputes to life. On this view, the difficulty lies not in finding the fair price or setting the appropriate fee but in placing any monetary value on the product at all. Even if the issue is seen as not the value of the product but the worth of the service, the question of a fair price is no more appropriate. Bearing a child is not a service for hire, critics argue, but a human achievement that money cannot, or should not, buy.

This criticism goes further than any considered so far. It focuses neither on the pressures nor on the circumstances surrounding the contract, but on the content of the contract itself. What is wrong is what is agreed to, not the conditions under which the agreement is made. It is morally wrong to agree to bear a child in exchange for financial compensation. This is the moralist claim, and examining its validity for the purposes of making public policy takes us beyond the Millian principle of liberty into the principled but perilous world of moralism.

Moralism

Surrogate contracts are dehumanizing and degrading. This is the claim of the task force, articulating a widely shared view in our society, and it is also the argument of Elizabeth Anderson, presenting the most sustained statement of an important philosophical view.[39] Neither the task force report nor Anderson appeals to empirical evidence of harm to the surrogate mother. Both claim that the wrong is done even in those cases in which surrogate mothers testify to the contrary. These critics are not moved by the plea of a mother who says: "It wasn't my baby. There was no attachment at all. I knew from the beginning that this was their baby, not mine."[40] Surrogacy is wrong regardless of how a woman herself judges the action or whether it harms her or the child. "Contract pregnancy would be a corrupt practice," Anderson writes, "even if it did not involve commerce in children."[41]

THE FORCE OF MORALISM

Before examining the moralist argument for prohibiting contract parenting, we consider the force of moralism in less controversial cases. We focus on the implications of the most politically relevant form of moralism, sometimes called legal moralism: the view that the immorality of a practice is a reason not only for criticizing but also for regulating and prohibiting it by means of legislation.

It is a mistake to identify moralism as only, or even mainly, a doctrine of the moral majority or a monopoly of political conservatives. Both liberals and conservatives support some moralistic laws, such as those against public nudity. Contemporary movements to ban the viewing of violent pornography have been led by some feminists and opposed by many conservatives. Because it is very difficult to show that the viewing of violent pornography causes harm in the way that the Millian principle would require in order to justify its prohibition, a moralist argument may be necessary to support the case for prohibition. Whatever the strength of moralist arguments against particular practices such as public nudity and pornography, one should not think of moralism as a doctrine that enforces only views that one opposes. That would underestimate both its moral force and its popular appeal.

Among the kinds of practices that moralists would regulate or prohibit even when they do not, strictly speaking, harm any individual are adultery, sodomy, incest, fornication, prostitution, pornography, public nudity, desecration of shrines and sacred symbols, cruelty to animals, mistreatment of corpses, and commercial sale of bodily organs.[42] To this standard list contract parenting should now be added. Moralists may, and often do, argue against outlawing some of these practices, but on the grounds that legal enforcement is likely to cause even greater harm than the practice itself. Sodomy, some moralists say, is wrong; but when authorities try to prevent it, they are not likely to be successful, and in any case they may commit greater wrongs in the process.

Moralists do not assume that these practices should be free from legal interference because they do not harm anyone and therefore lie within a protected sphere of liberty. The moralists thus deny what Millian liberals grant: priority to the liberty of citizens within a self-regarding sphere. Moralists withhold this special protection on the grounds that some liberties granted by Millian liberals may be used to perform immoral actions, and citizens have no moral right to do moral wrong. The value of liberty does not extend its protection to conduct that is immoral. If incest is immoral, there is no moral reason to ensure that citizens have the right to engage in the practice even if it does not harm anyone. The mere fact that one chooses to act does not give the action value; the nature of what one chooses also determines the value of the act.

The moralist claim can be better understood by examining more closely the example of the regulation of public nudity—a policy that is widely accepted by both liberals and conservatives but is most plausibly justified on moralist grounds. In general the moralist argument has three parts. The first consists in a claim that an action or practice is wrong, independently of any harm it may cause (or, what amounts to the same thing, that immorality constitutes the harm). No one, not even the most fervent moralist, counts public nudity among the greatest sins of mankind. But many citizens who would not otherwise think of themselves as moralists believe that the display of naked bodies in public is deeply offensive even if not harmful in the strict Millian sense, and should at least be regulated so that they do not have to witness it.

The objection to public nudity cannot be based merely on the desire of others to avoid psychological distress. Many kinds of public conduct cause distress (the wearing of T-shirts advocating free love, homosexual couples kissing, punk rock bands playing in the park). Such conduct is rightly permitted so long as it does not cause other kinds of harm. Nor is it plausible to argue that public nudity may be prohibited because it would provoke disturbances or other violations of public order. That the disturbances would be serious and frequent seems unlikely, and in any case they would not be beyond the capacity of the authorities to control, which they would be obligated to do if citizens appearing in public without their clothes were within their rights.

The Millian argument here is strained. To find some other-regarding harm that would justify the prohibition of public nudity and other laws of public decency, Millian liberals appeal to these dangers of distress and disorder, but the assumptions on which the appeal depend are weak. Following the Millian principle, one cannot readily find sufficient reason to prohibit public nudity. In the absence of a showing of harm, independent of the immorality, some Millian liberals may be tempted to conclude that the practice should not be prohibited. For them, the moralist has other, more offensive examples.[43] The more straightforward response is to concede that some moralist claims may count, and to try to develop criteria for separating those that should count from those that should not.

Moralists differ over whether conduct is to be considered immoral because (1) it violates fundamental human values, as shown by invoking a principle that is independent of the values of any particular society; or (2) it violates the fundamental values of the society in question, as shown by an interpretation of principles that prevail there. The appeal in the first instance is to universal moral standards and in the second to community standards. The difference may not be as great in practice as it appears in theory, however. The two kinds of approaches usually converge in condemning the same practices. The first kind of moralist concedes that practices such as public nudity may not be wrong in other societies; the value that makes it wrong in our society (such as a respect for human intimacy) still holds in other societies, but its implications differ because the particular histories and cultures differ.

The second kind of moralist, appealing to community standards, does not deny that the standards may apply to other societies. Moreover, the standards are not simply what the majority, or even all, of the citizens of society declare them to be at any particular time. They are embedded in the history and culture of the society, and must be discovered by intersubjective methods of interpretation and justification. The values so discovered may support criticism of prevailing beliefs and practices, even those rooted in long traditions. To show that public nudity is morally offensive, it is not enough to show that most citizens in the society are offended by it. The offense must be grounded in some fundamental value shared in the society.

How could one show that public nudity violates a fundamental social value? It might be argued that, by breaking down the (admittedly conventional) barrier between the private and public display of the body, public nudity shows disrespect for the value of human intimacy.[44] It calls into question the value of preserving a sphere of life that citizens share only with their families and others with whom they are intimate. Public nudity thrusts the private into the public, deliberately and flagrantly, as if to declare that preserving a private sphere is not important to anyone. There are, of course, nudists of principle. They object to the social conventions that limit their natural inclination to go without clothes. But even they cannot reasonably reject the value of intimacy. Their objection may go not against the principle on which the prohibition of public nudity is based, but only against the conventional ways of expressing that intimacy. Until alternative ways of defining a realm of intimacy become more widely acknowledged, citizens may understandably wish to preserve the only conventions they have to serve that function. The justification for prohibiting public nudity, then, expresses important moral values that are accessible even to those who reject the prohibition itself.

This kind of justification clearly is incomplete as it now stands. No doubt there are other interpretations of why public nudity may rightly be regarded as offensive. The point is not to complete the justification but to indicate that the justification the moralist needs differs on the one side from the liberal argument based on harm, and on the other from a conservative argument grounded in tradition and public opinion. The form of the justification falls within the mutually acceptable standards of deliberative democracy, but it remains incomplete as a rationale for regulating or prohibiting immoral practices. The moralist can offer it as a legitimate argument that diverges from those of Millian liberals, but it is not yet sufficient to justify regulation or prohibition.

The second step of the moralist argument shows that the morally wrong or offensive practice may be regulated or prohibited by law. That a practice is wrong does not yet make it the legitimate subject for legal action, even in principle. The moralist must show that the wrong is of sufficient relevance to public purposes to warrant the attention of public policy. Public nudity by its nature commands public attention, but some other morally wrong actions (cheating in a local softball tournament or failing to fulfill your pledge to public television) should not.

In the third step in the argument, the legal moralist shows that legal regulation or prohibition would not itself cause greater harms or wrongs than it is seeking to prevent. Legal moralism therefore cannot be accused of licensing government to interfere with the liberty of citizens regardless of the consequences for individual and social welfare. Since the legal enforcement of morality can do more harm than good, legal moralists often agree with Millian liberals that the government should not intervene. But unlike some activities that moralists deem offensive, particularly those that take place in private, public nudity can be regulated without causing great harm. The regulations do not require, for example, government intrusion into the homes of citizens. Legal enforcement is not likely to be counterproductive, and the unintended side-effects are few if any.

The case of public nudity might give the impression that the moralist argument applies only to activities thrust on an unwilling public, that its validity depends entirely on the fact that other citizens are involuntarily subjected to the activities in question. Another example should dispel that impression. In New York State, at about the same time that the surrogacy controversy was going on, another, more curious dispute came to public attention. Promoters in several communities in the state were sponsoring two unusual sports called dwarf bowling and dwarf tossing.[45] In dwarf bowling, the bowlers roll dwarfs on skateboards instead of balls. In dwarf tossing, a dwarf is strapped in a harness and hurled against a rubber mattress. The promoters provided the dwarfs with protective clothing, established some basic safety standards, and paid attractive wages. The bowlers, tossers, and spectators evidently enjoyed the sport. The crowds (who gathered mostly in bars) were large and enthusiastic, cheering on their favorite dwarfs. The sport attracted dwarfs from other states and several foreign countries; they seemed to be not only willing but eager to take part. The events were open to the public, but no one could complain that the sponsors did not provide adequate notice of what the spectators would see. Given the mutual consent of all participants and spectators, it is difficult to argue that anyone was harmed in the strict sense. The Millian principle would not prevent the state from prohibiting this sport, and in France in 1992 the courts upheld the sport, evidently more common there, on just these grounds.[46]

Yet the governor of New York proposed, and the legislature accepted, legislation that banned dwarf bowling. The governor stated: "Any activity which dehumanizes and humiliates these people is degrading to us all. This bill recognizes that and, in effect, declares these bizarre games to be debased."[47] The force of this argument is clearly moralist. A decent society simply should not tolerate this kind of spectacle: it is degrading for both the dwarfs and the spectators. If we probed officials and citizens for the basis of their objection to this practice, we would no doubt find many different kinds of reasons, including the paternalist consideration of restricting the liberty of dwarfs for their own good. But the dominant reasoning and the most cogent justifications for the ban rely on moralist categories (without which even the paternalist arguments, which should be set aside here, would have far less force): offensiveness, degradation, dehumanization, exploitation, and the like. Despite the important differences among these rationales, they all support the conclusion that the activity is morally offensive even if it could not be prohibited by the terms of the Millian harm principle. (Some activities and practices that are prohibited for these moralist reasons may also be harmful to others, and under some circumstances the harm may be a sufficient reason for prohibiting them.)

Consistent with the second step in the moralist argument, critics of dwarf bowling could say that although it was not thrust upon an unwilling public, it took place in public, with the sanction of public authorities, and amid considerable public attention. The state could legitimately argue that its consequences significantly affected public purposes.

Taking the third step, critics could plausibly argue that prohibiting the activity would not be likely to be counterproductive, and would probably not cause more harm than good for the society. The most serious cost would be the loss of employment for the dwarfs, but the state could undertake to find other job opportunities for them. In any case, on the moralist view they do not have an absolute right (or a basic liberty) to use their bodies to earn money in any way they wish.

The ban on dwarf bowling is perhaps the closest we can come to a clear case of justified intervention on moralist grounds. And even in this case the justification is not simple, and is not beyond deliberative disagreement. Mere offensiveness is not enough; other morally defensible conditions have to be satisfied. Moreover, the prohibition may be relatively easy to accept because the activity does not play a central role in most citizens' life, and any claim that it should play such a role seems bizarre. Although the prohibition still is not consistent with the Millian harm principle, the claim that the ban violates a basic liberty is subject to more reasonable doubt than are similar claims about most other practices that moralists might ban. To some extent the same is also true of public nudity.

In both these cases the first step of the moralist argument—showing that the practice violates a moral principle grounded on fundamental values in our society—is relatively easy to take. In other cases, where the immorality of the practice is more doubtful, or where equally strong moral considerations favor the practice, the moralist argument has a less certain claim on public policy. But we cannot therefore say that the Millian principle wins out, morally speaking. So long as there is deliberative disagreement about the morality of the practice, and the other two conditions of a qualified moralism are satisfied, then the most one can say is that neither moralism nor the Millian harm principle can constitutionally constrain public policy independently of the outcome of deliberation in democratic forums. In its cautious form with all the conditions we have so far attached to it, moralism should be granted a place in a deliberative perspective. But is moralism even in this qualified form consistent with basic liberty? Whether and when moralism is consistent with protecting basic liberty opens up another important and often neglected realm for democratic deliberation. By returning to case of surrogacy, we can show how far moralists may justifiably press their claim in a contestable case.

MORALIST ARGUMENTS AGAINST CONTRACT PARENTING

To justifiably prohibit or regulate a practice that does not harm others, the moralist must satisfy two kinds of conditions. The first—call it the immorality condition—consists in completing the three steps of the moralist argument itself, which were examined in the last section. The regulated or prohibited practice must be shown (1) to violate values or principles that are not reasonable to reject; (2) to implicate important public purposes; and (3) to respond to government intervention without producing greater social harm. The second—the liberty condition—involves showing that the intervention is consistent with basic liberty: that it either violates no basic liberties or preserves basic liberties better than nonintervention would.

Unlike Millian liberalism, then, a deliberative approach guided by basic liberty grants some weight to moralist claims. Also, deliberative democracy does not assume that basic liberty is always best protected if the government does not intervene; nonintervention is no more neutral or privileged than intervention. Unlike moralism, deliberative democracy preserves a sphere of basic liberty. Moralist reasons are not sufficient to justify violations of basic liberty, and only certain kinds of moral reasons (those of a public character) count at all even as part of a justification for intervention.

In the case of surrogacy, the most difficult part of the argument is the immorality condition—not so much showing that the practice is morally wrong, but establishing that it is wrong in a way that would justify prohibition. The moralist succeeds better in showing that the practice is immoral in some circumstances, or at least that the surrogate mother is justified in so interpreting it, than in showing that the practice should be prohibited. There is a credible (but reasonably disputable) claim of basic liberty on the part of couples who want to contract to bring a child into the world whom they will love and care for as much as other parents do. Their claim does not call into question the provision for permitting the surrogate mother to share custody of the child under the circumstances discussed earlier, but it does call into question the argument for banning surrogacy contracts in the first place.

Critics may reply that contract parenting is an inherently immoral practice which should not be considered part of anyone's basic liberty. Contract parenting degrades and exploits women. The contract is degrading because it reduces "pregnant women to the status of mere housing for fetuses."[48] It exploits women because it takes advantage of their vulnerability, financial or psychological, to enlist them in a project they would not otherwise undertake. As a member of the New York State Assembly said during the debate: "Contract surrogacy also poses a grave potential for the exploitation of poor women who may be coerced by the need for money into this practice."[49] Although many critics, including the task force,[50] make both of these criticisms, they raise somewhat different issues, and each should be evaluated separately.

Consider first the argument from degradation. How might a surrogate mother be degraded? She is bearing a child for another couple, not for herself. She loses the value of an important part of the experience of pregnancy—developing an emotional bond with a child whom she would otherwise raise as her own. The value of pregnancy for surrogate mothers may be reduced—one could say degraded—compared to what other women enjoy. But there is also a reasonable response to the charge of degradation, which denies that the surrogate mother is reduced to a breeder, "a mere housing for fetuses." Many surrogate mothers find considerable satisfaction in providing a child for another couple, and this is hardly a degrading motive. Furthermore, to prohibit surrogacy on the grounds that it degrades women in this way would imply that every pregnant woman is degraded if she does not develop an emotional attachment during or immediately after pregnancy.

Neither does the mere fact that the surrogate mother is paid for her services necessarily degrade her. Commercialization of the practice may raise some potential moral problems, but by itself it is not sufficient to make the practice immoral. If it were, many other no less invaluable services that men and women perform for compensation would be morally suspect.[51] Those who provide child care are not generally seen as degraded because they are paid for their efforts. That one earns a living by caring for the sick or teaching the young is not thought to degrade either the person or the practice, let alone to constitute a reason to punish the person or to prohibit the practice.

The moralist charge of exploitation is initially more plausible. To make the charge stick, one need not show that the woman does not gain from the contract. Exploitation can occur even when both parties benefit from the arrangement, as they apparently do in most cases of contract parenting. This is "mutually advantageous exploitation."[52] The recipient parents exploit the birth mother when they offer her a substantially lower fee for her services, or impose significantly more onerous requirements, than would be possible if the parties were in more nearly equal bargaining positions. Although the birth mother benefits from the arrangement, she does not receive a fair price for her services. Specifying the background conditions for bargaining that would produce a fair price is extremely difficult.[53] But even without a precise specification, a plausible case could still be made that the relative economic deprivation of most surrogate mothers compared to recipient parents, like that of many laborers relative to their employers, creates a severely unequal bargaining situation, which is likely to lead to mutually advantageous arrangements that nevertheless exploit surrogate mothers. All parties to the contract benefit, and believe that they benefit. The contract is typically not coercive. But the surrogate mother may still suffer a serious moral wrong.

Nonetheless, even if surrogate mothers are sometimes (or even generally) exploited, the question persists: Does this wrong justify prohibiting the practice? The exploitation is a moral wrong, but is it the kind of wrong that itself necessarily warrants government intervention? Permitting such contracts violates no basic liberties, whereas prohibiting them may do so. (The uncertainty here is sufficiently great to put the dispute within the realm of deliberative disagreement.) Other agreements in which exploitation occurs are not generally prohibited. When a poor artist sells a great painting to a rich patron at a price far below its fair market value, the artist has been exploited. But governments should not prohibit, let alone criminalize, this kind of market exchange. Artists should be free to sell their paintings even at the risk of exploitation. To be sure, a painting is not a child, but this difference does not make the exploitation any less. Intervention to protect the child would be based on paternalist, not moralist, considerations.

Another line of argument against contract parenting is not explicitly moralist, but it functions like a moralist claim in determining the proper public policy on this issue. The criticism comes from egalitarians, who argue that contract parenting "reinforces a long history of unequal treatment"of women.[54] It can thus be seen "as a form of harmful discrimination" that may reinforce the social subordination of women in our society.[55] These egalitarians do not claim that surrogacy degrades or exploits women, or that if it does, that would be a reason to prohibit it.[56] Rather, they suggest that it contributes to the social and economic subordination of women in our society, which should be morally unacceptable to men as well as women.

Egalitarians worry about a group of social practices that contribute to "creating second-class citizenship for women."[57] They argue that surrogacy is one of these practices: "Pregnancy contracts reinforce stereotypes about the proper role of women in the reproductive division of labor" and "involve substantial control over women's bodies."[58] As part of the contract with the Sterns, Whitehead agreed "not to smoke cigarettes, drink alcoholic beverages, or take medications without written consent from her physician. She also agreed to undergo amniocentesis and to abort the fetus 'upon demand of William Stern, natural father, if tests found genetic or congenital defects.' "[59] The terms of the contract do not violate White-head's basic liberty if it is reasonable to assume that she consented to them (though this assumption could be questioned). But the main issue, one egalitarian critic points out, "is that in contract pregnancy the body that is controlled belongs to a woman, in a society that historically has sub-ordinated women's interests to those of men, primarily through its control over her sexuality and reproduction."[60] In deliberative democracy this crit-icism invokes the principle of basic opportunity. If the criticism is correct, contract parenting adversely affects the basic opportunities not only of surrogate mothers but also of women more generally by both reflecting and reinforcing the inequality in a society that discriminates against women.

Insofar as this argument depends on empirical evidence, it is difficult to assess. The stage is set for deliberative disagreement. No doubt discrimi-nation against women persists in our society, but whether contract par-enting makes it worse, or is made worse by it, is uncertain. One egalitarian critic acknowledges the difficulty of establishing these connections: "It is possible that the effects [of social subordination] will occur only a little or not at all . . . It is possible that a prohibition on surrogacy would . . . help erase the fact that the process of carrying a fetus to term is actually a form of work . . . Social attitudes about the appropriate roles of men and women are affected by numerous factors, of which surrogacy arrange-ments might well be a quite minor one."[61]

Partly because of these uncertainties, egalitarian critics are often reluc-tant to recommend a general ban on contract parenting. They are reluctant also, presumably, because they recognize that a basic liberty may be at stake. Instead of a ban, some propose measures "to discourage contract pregnancy and to strengthen the position of the 'surrogate,' who is the most economically and emotionally vulnerable party in any such arrange-ment."[62] This proposal can be seen as practicing the economy of moral disagreement in the face of deliberative uncertainty. Another egalitarian critic similarly reduces the remaining moral disagreement between mor-alism and the Millian principle when he concludes that "a refusal to en-force such agreements when the birth mother declines to hand over the child seems far preferable to a criminal ban." He adds that "much will depend on the details," thus leaving development of the policy to further deliberation in a democratic forum.[63]

Even if the evidence about the discriminatory effects of contract parenting were compelling, prohibition would not be justified from a deliberative perspective so long as a basic liberty was at stake. The principle of basic liberty takes priority over the principle of equal opportunity. But, having taken into account the best arguments on both sides of the prohibition debate, we seem to be left with a deliberative disagreement as to whether a basic liberty is in fact at stake in this commercial transaction. Mill himself entertained doubts whether commercial transactions, some of which are analogous to commercial surrogacy, can properly be considered part of the protected sphere of self-regarding action.[64]

The most one can say here is that there is no strong evidence of the discriminatory effects of contract parenting. Absent such evidence, the egalitarian criticism seems to rely for its defense of prohibition on a moralist argument: that the contract itself embodies or expresses a morally offensive relationship. By the terms of deliberative democracy, this is a legitimate but inconclusive basis for making public policy so long as no basic liberty is being infringed. In the context of a society that has denied equal opportunities to women, surrogate mothers might reasonably come to see the contract as a manifestation of discrimination and to see themselves as victims of subordination. Quite apart from its effects on other women, the meaning of the contract could carry a message of subordination for the surrogate mother herself. Similarly, some surrogate mothers may come to interpret the surrogacy arrangement as degrading or exploitative, and they may reasonably do so even in the absence of any evidence showing effects on other people.

In this way, both the egalitarian and the moralist criticisms of contract parenting serve a similar function. Although neither provides sure grounds for prohibiting contract parenting, both supply a strong reason for the surrogate mother to object to the contract, and therefore a strong reason for public policy to ensure that she has a way to act on her objection. Other citizens, men as well as women, might also interpret surrogate contracts as expressing an immoral relationship (whether degrading, exploitative, or subordinating), and they should be encouraged to offer their interpretations in the public forum, and to call for policies that would discourage or even prohibit surrogacy contracts. But without other evidence or other arguments, the critics of contract parenting cannot settle the case in favor of criminalizing these contracts. The balance of reasons, as best one can now judge, favors legalization with protection for the birth mother against specific performance. Based on considerations of basic liberty, birth mothers must be able to gain custody of the child if they change their mind about the consistency of the contract and their personal integrity.

So long as contract parenting remains legal, the moral issue for surrogate mothers goes beyond whether to support or oppose further legislation. They must decide whether to keep or give up a child they have borne. Their personal integrity may be at stake in the decision in a way that it is not when citizens or their accountable representatives decide what policy on surrogate parenting they should support. We have earlier argued that basic liberty requires that surrogate mothers should have the option of keeping the child. We also suggested that moralist considerations could legitimately play a role in making public policy in a deliberative democracy. Moralist critics of contract parenting do more than just offer reasons for regulating or banning contract parenting. They also help us better understand the kinds of considerations that could lead a surrogate mother to insist on keeping the child.

From a deliberative perspective, a justifiable public policy would explicitly allow a surrogate mother to break the contract and keep the child she had borne. Considerations of basic liberty speak more ambiguously to the remaining issues as to whether contract parenting should be legal and, if so, how it should be regulated. Some regulations protecting the parties to the contract, including the recipient parents, are almost certainly warranted, but any such policy is likely to be morally provisional. As one of the egalitarian critics wrote, "much depends on the details," and the details depend on our state of social knowledge.[65] New evidence (for example, about a policy's discriminatory effects on women) might favor a change in policy. Further refinements of the notion of basic liberty, as citizens continue to deliberate about surrogacy and other reproductive practices, might change what should count as the most mutually acceptable views about the importance of contract parenting and its relation to our other liberties.

For the same reasons, some states might justifiably decide to accept a different kind of policy from the one that, on balance, our arguments in this chapter favor. New York State did. Toward the end of the 1992 session, the legislature passed a law that banned commercial surrogacy, much as the task force had recommended.[66] Some legislators seem to have been moved by what we call moralist reasons, and others by concerns about harm. The leading proponent of the bill said that its main purpose was to protect children.[67] The law also embodied a kind of moral compromise.

While prohibiting commercial surrogacy, it left citizens free to enter into surrogacy arrangements that involve no financial transaction. Although this led some members to object that the policy was inconsistent, the legislature's action is better seen as acknowledging that, in the absence of commercial motives that put a price on bringing a child into the world, citizens may have a basic liberty to enter into a surrogacy contract.[68]

Paternalism

Like moralists, paternalists claim that regulation or prohibition of a citizen's conduct may be justified without showing that the conduct harms others. The paternalist claim is not that the conduct is morally wrong but that it is harmful to the citizen herself. In the case of surrogacy, public policy is concerned not only with the welfare of the surrogate mother but also with the welfare of the child she bears. Both concerns are paternalist, the first directed toward an adult who has her own ideas about what is good for her, and the second toward a child (or a potential child) who is not yet capable of forming any such idea. It is only the first that Millian liberalism opposes. Before assessing the paternalist view of contract parenting, we examine the paternalist argument in its general form.[69]

THE POWER OF PATERNALISM

Legal paternalism is the restriction by law of an individual's liberty for his or her own good.[70] The justification that the government gives, as Mill observed, is that the restriction "will be better for [one]" or "will make [one] happier."[71] Paternalism thus aims to protect the welfare of citizens, even at some sacrifice of their liberty.

It is this sacrifice of liberty to which Millian liberals object, and it is what leads Mill to insist that paternalism toward adults is never justified. As with their objection to moralism, Millian liberals need not maintain that some actions affect only the individual who performs them. They can claim simply that the harms that individuals cause to themselves should never count as a reason for government intervention. As before, the claim is based on their commitment to an expansive principle of liberty. Citizens should be free to make mistakes, even at the risk of great harms to themselves. These liberals ascribe overriding value to choice itself, subordinating the value of the end chosen.

This absolute opposition to paternalism is difficult to maintain consistently, especially in contemporary society, where citizens face so many risks they cannot adequately evaluate even when they receive information about them. Many of the regulations and prohibitions that even most liberals now accept are most plausibly interpreted as paternalist in their purpose. Among them are safety laws and regulations (mandating seat belts, ignition interlocks, and air bags, or requiring motorcyclists to wear helmets); health regulations (requiring prescriptions for drugs, and banning certain drugs such as laetrile); criminal law (criminalizing suicide, and disallowing consent as a murder defense); and general social policy (restrictions on gambling, prevention of high-risk recreational activities such as swimming in a local quarry, and licensing of professionals).[72]

Some liberals try to meet the challenge of paternalism by denying its existence. They either try to find "social harm" in every instance of alleged paternalism or try to show that the intervention does not really infringe liberty. In their effort to maintain that paternalism is never justified, they go to great lengths to prove that any policy that appears to be paternalist can actually be shown to prevent harm to others or to protect individual liberty without restricting it. In either case it would be consistent with the Millian principle. If the policy is really an instance of preventing harm to others, then it may be justified for "other-regarding" reasons. If the policy is a case of realizing individual desires, then it may be justified directly as protecting liberty; no "self-regarding" reasons need be invoked.

Just how far some Millians are prepared to go to avoid acknowledging that paternalism might sometimes be justified is illustrated by the controversy over laws requiring motorcyclists to wear helmets, which most states have enacted in recent years. Safety-minded reformers who favor these laws but who evidently fear being branded as paternalists desperately look for some social harm that would warrant restricting the riders' liberty. But their claims of social harm are weak. Helmetless riders are no more likely to injure others than riders with helmets. If helmetless motorcyclists increase other people's insurance and medical costs, then the government could raise their rates to cover their costs rather than require them to wear helmets. Trying to justify helmet laws on the nonpaternalistic grounds that government has an interest in the viability of its citizens opens the door to almost unlimited intervention. The government's interest, so understood, would extend to restricting freedoms as far-ranging as enjoyment of less than healthy foods, smoking, and mountain climbing. The moral burden of a paternalistic justification to show that such restrictions are actually in the interests of the people whose freedom is restricted disappears under the government interest rationale. This kind of rationale is therefore far more dangerous than acknowledging that paternalism may sometimes be justified. Perhaps some social harms should be considered in developing the helmet policy, but to try to force all considerations of individual self-harm into the strait-jacket of social harm is neither necessary nor desirable.

Citizens can avoid these and other similarly strained efforts if they confront the challenge of paternalism more directly. They should acknowledge that some paternalism may be justified, and seek to develop through democratic deliberation some mutually acceptable criteria to limit its scope, and to ensure that it is consistent with basic liberty. As with moralism, we begin by specifying the conditions a cautious paternalism would place on itself. We then consider a second set of conditions that would be necessary to make paternalism consistent with basic liberty. A deliberative perspective in this way can still maintain its commitment to basic liberty while to some extent recognizing the value of individual well-being that paternalists seek to protect.

The conditions that legal paternalists should set for themselves parallel the three steps of the argument of legal moralists. First, the paternalist shows that some action that individuals take is not in their own interest, and they would be better off if they were prevented from taking it. In the absence of a restriction on the action, people risk harm to themselves, or they fail to benefit themselves as much as they could. This step is usually the least difficult to take because the policy goals that paternalists choose to promote are usually not controversial. Few citizens claim that it is normally in their interest to take addictive drugs or drive in cars that have a high risk of causing death. When the goals are less obvious, or when the risks are lower or uncertain, the first step becomes more problematic.

In the second step of the argument, the paternalist seeks to show that the conduct in question may be legitimately regulated or prohibited by law. The claim is that government may in principle protect the well-being of citizens against their failure of judgment or their weakness of will. The main burden here is to show both that the government has a responsibility for promoting this kind of well-being, and that citizens do not have a right to resist government intervention that would promote it.

The responsibility is relatively easy to establish. It is a widely accepted goal of government to promote the well-being of citizens. The difficulty arises when citizens do not wish to have their well-being promoted. The paternalist may argue that citizens have no moral right to harm themselves, any more than they have a moral right to harm others. The purpose of a system of rights is to promote the well-being of citizens, and it would undermine that purpose to admit a general right to harm oneself. Or the paternalist may argue, in a more limited way, that the restriction is simply one that citizens have imposed on themselves to protect themselves against future temptations. Just as Ulysses asked his sailors to tie him to the mast so that he could not succumb to the Sirens' call, so citizens ask their government to bind them to laws that prevent them from acting on self-destructive impulses and passions in the future. This more limited argument works better for the majority who vote for the laws than for the minority who oppose them. Just as Ulysses was justifiably acting in a paternalistic way toward his (future) self, so too may the majority by agreeing to limit its future liberty for its own good. Both are instances of self-imposed paternalism.

The third step is to show that the regulation or prohibition would not cause more harm than it prevents. Even if government is a legitimate agent of paternalism, it may not be the most effective agent to carry out the paternalist aims. Families or private organizations may serve these purposes better in some cases. The paternalist therefore must show that the conduct or practice in question calls for the kind of general and uniform treatment that public policy is most likely to provide.

HOW BASIC LIBERTY LIMITS PATERNALISM

The second set of conditions that a justifiable paternalism must satisfy derives from the principle of basic liberty. These conditions specify what would warrant our claiming that restricting a citizen's action protects his or her basic liberty better than not restricting it. To see what the conditions would look like, consider an example that Mill presented with a quite different purpose in mind: "If either a public officer or anyone else saw a person attempting to cross a bridge which had been ascertained to be unsafe, and there were no time to warn him of his danger, they might seize him and turn him back, without any real infringement of his liberty; for liberty consists in doing what one desires, and he does not desire to fall into the river."[73]

Mill here falls victim to the tendency of denying that there is any "real" infringement of liberty in cases of justified paternalism. This denial is especially dangerous for liberals: by eliminating the tension between individual desire and individual well-being, it removes any limit on governments that would override desire in the name of well-being. It is preferable, even from a Millian perspective, to concede that liberty is limited in this case. The officer who intervenes is restricting the person's liberty to cross the bridge, which is what he wants to do, even though he also does not want to fall into the water and drown. The officer thwarts the person's desire for his own good, but thereby makes it possible for him to enjoy more freedom in the future. This is a clear case of justified paternalism, which can be defended on the grounds that a person's future liberty is enhanced by the paternalistic restriction on his present liberty.

By asking what features of this case seem to justify the paternalism, one can identify the conditions that would have to be met to make paternalism consistent with basic liberty.[74] Notice, first, that the would-be bridge crosser is ignorant of a critical fact about the situation in which he acts. His decision to cross the bridge is impaired, and the grounds for saying so are independent of whether or not we believe he should cross the bridge. The first condition, then, is that the decision of the person whose liberty is to be constrained must be *impaired* in some way, and the basis for establishing the impairment must be independent of the good or end that the individual chooses.

In the case of contract parenting, some surrogate mothers, like White-head, later suggest that they did not have full information about the consequences of their decision to enter into the arrangement, and that therefore their decision was impaired. Most of the proposals for legalizing contract parenting, such as that of the Judiciary Committee staff, now include elaborate provisions for ensuring that all parties will be fully informed about the risks.[75] With such protections, it would be difficult to argue that, in general, surrogacy contracts satisfy the first condition for justified paternalism (with respect to the mothers). In any case, the evidence for showing that a decision is impaired must be based on lack of information, emotional distress, or some similar deficiency, not on disapproval of commercial surrogacy itself. Those who take the task force's view that a woman is "dehumanized in the process" may be tempted to conclude that no one in her right mind would consider becoming a surrogate mother.[76] But in any analysis of paternalism, it is important to keep views of the morality of the practice separate from views about the competence of those who decide to engage in it. The views often have quite different implications for policy.

Another salient feature of Mill's case of bridge crossing is that the intervention is *limited*. The public officer may stop the person from crossing the bridge, but the action is temporary and reversible. After being warned, the person could decide to cross it anyhow. The second condition is that the constraint on the person's liberty be as limited as possible in its duration and in its effects, consistent with achieving the goal of the intervention. Alternatively, the paternalistic intervention should employ the least restrictive measure for preventing the harm or promoting the good in question.

One practical implication of this condition is that if citizens are inclined toward a paternalistic policy on surrogacy, they should favor regulation over prohibition. To protect against the risks that women face in surrogacy arrangements, the government would be more justified in preventing a surrogate mother from alienating her parental rights until some limited period after she has given birth than in preventing her from entering into a surrogacy contract in the first place. Many of those critics who object to contract parenting on grounds that it harms the surrogate mother take a valid point too far; they try to stretch a point that might support regulation to reach a conclusion for prohibition. Even if women risk harm to themselves by entering into surrogacy contracts, prohibition is probably not the least restrictive way to protect them against that risk. (We say "probably" because this judgment depends on the possibility of instituting a policy that secures unmanipulated, informed consent on the part of all the parties to the contract.)

A third feature of Mill's case of the bridge crosser suggests another condition that any paternalist intervention should satisfy. The harm that the public officer is trying to prevent—death—is one that most people wish to avoid. Even if the officer cannot be sure that the bridge crosser wishes to avoid death, he knows that stopping him excludes few other ends that he might have. Stated less restrictively and more generally, the condition holds that the goal of the intervention must be *inclusive* in this sense: the goal of the intervention must be either one that the person accepts, or (if that is not possible because the person is incompetent or incapacitated) one that excludes as few future choices as possible.

Most of the arguments for prohibition of contract parenting assume goals that are not inclusive in this sense. Both the women who seek to be surrogate mothers and the recipient parents may consider surrogacy a significant part of their life plans, and they could reasonably reject the description of the goal of the practice as dehumanizing, degrading, or harmful. Regulation of contract parenting also meets the test of this third condition better than prohibition. For example, the government may be justified in requiring that intended birth mothers and recipient parents receive independent psychological or psychiatric counseling and retain independent legal counsel. The goal of these restrictions is to help the parties to the contract understand the probable consequences of what they are doing before they enter into an agreement that is likely to affect their lives profoundly. This is a goal that birth mothers and recipient parents could accept and also one that excludes few future choices.

If a paternalistic policy satisfies these three conditions, citizens may conclude that the intervention is consistent with basic liberty. Each of the conditions identifies a respect in which the individual choice that the policy would restrict is less free than it should be. If each condition is met, the individual's basic liberty is enhanced in that respect. The assumption is not that individual's choice is not really free, or that the intervention does not really restrict freedom. It is rather that restricting basic liberty in specific ways can increase basic liberty in other specific ways.

All of these conditions call for further interpretation. Even when their meaning is clear in an individual case, it does not translate directly into public policies for all cases. The third condition is especially vulnerable to contestable interpretations when applied to public policy. Policymakers cannot be sure, for example, that every potential birth mother is sufficiently risk-averse to want to minimize chances of entering into a contract that she will later regret. There is a wide range of reasonable degrees of risk aversion. Some people, perhaps a small minority, want to live spontaneously, at the edge, taking much larger risks than others. Because many paternalistic policies turn on these disagreements about important moral values, the question of whether they are justified—whether the conditions are met—typically requires extensive and continuing deliberation. The conditions themselves set some limits, or at least provide some guidance for democratic deliberation, but they cannot determine the right outcome. The deliberation continues not only because new issues, such as surrogacy, force themselves onto the public agenda, but also because, as citizens come to terms with these issues, they may change our own views about the risks they wish to run and the goals they wish to pursue.

Through democratic deliberation, citizens decide what constraints they want to impose on themselves for their own good, and in some cases what constraints they want to impose on others for *their* own good. Citizens act not only as Ulysses acted when he asked his shipmates to bind him to the mast, but also as his mates would have acted if they had bound him before he asked. In their public capacity citizens bind themselves by laws and policies so that, when in their private capacity they later desire to use dangerous drugs, or take foolish risks in cars, or neglect their health and future well-being, or enter into binding surrogacy contracts, the law will restrain them. Some of these laws also restrain other citizens who may have opposed them, and some of these laws restrain *only* other citizens (as when men vote to ban surrogacy for the good of women). When citizens and officials limit the liberty of other citizens, they should of course be more cautious, more inclined to give the benefit of the doubt to the opposition. But the form of the justification is not fundamentally different: it should still track the three conditions we have presented.

The form of the justification remains the same even when the paternalistic policy is directed toward children. But here the justification goes through more easily. Millian liberals agree that paternalism toward children is warranted. Mill writes:

> It is in the case of children that misapplied notions of liberty are a real obstacle to the fulfillment by the State of its duties. One would almost think that a man's children were supposed to be literally, and not metaphorically, a part of himself, so jealous is opinion of the smallest interference of law with his absolute and exclusive control over them; more jealous than of almost any interference with his own freedom of action: so much less do the generality of mankind value liberty than power.[77]

In the case of children, the first condition (impaired decision) is in effect satisfied because the capacity of children to make reasonable or rational decisions has yet to develop, and will not develop adequately without the aid of adults. For infants and very young children, paternalism provides the essential conditions for basic liberty. Any paternalistic policy toward children would still have to meet the other two conditions. It should be the least restrictive measure for achieving the goal, and the goal should be consistent with, or conducive to, the child's enjoyment of basic liberty in the future.

Just because citizens agree that paternalism toward children is justified, they should not expect to reach consensus on how that paternalism should be exercised. Indeed, for three reasons they should expect *more* moral conflict in applying the conditions to children than to adults. First, when the goal is to prepare children to exercise liberty in the distant future, it is more difficult to determine what constitutes the least restrictive alternative. Second, paternalism toward children cannot usually be guided by specific goals that children themselves accept or will accept in the future; it can only be guided by general goals in which all children are assumed to have an interest, such as the capacity to be free and equal citizens. These general goals are less determinate and more contestable than some of the specific goals of adult paternalism. Third, the question who should be the agent of paternalism, often an administrative matter in the case of adults, becomes a highly charged moral issue in the case of children.[78]

Citizens cannot look to paternalistic claims about children to resolve the controversy over contract parenting. Controversy over one issue alone—the question who should be the paternalistic agents—should be enough to dash any hopes that the appeal to the well-being of children will solve the problem. One might be tempted by the seemingly simple principle, favored by some Millian liberals, that paternalistic agents should be those who, according to one's best information, are most likely to act in the best interests of the children. But this kind of principle conceals two misunderstandings of what is at stake in authorizing paternalistic agents.

First, to decide who will best serve the interests of children one has to know how well various possible agents would satisfy the conditions of justifiable paternalism. But, as we have seen, these conditions are open to competing interpretations; they are indeterminate in ways that call for further democratic deliberation. Moreover, even when the paternalistic criteria are determinate, the evidence available for deciding which agents will best satisfy the conditions is often insufficient.

Suppose citizens assume that paternalism should help further a child's capacity to enjoy basic liberty, and that this capacity requires a child to develop a sense of personal integrity. In the case of a contested surrogacy contract, citizens then must ask what custody arrangement would best help develop this sense of integrity. This question admits of conflicting reasonable answers. But one of the most common answers is also seriously deficient: authorizing a court or government agency to decide on a case-by-case basis which adults will serve "the best interests of the child." This practice usually results in the child's spending an extensive period under foster care, which is likely to be considerably worse for the child than either permanent alternative the court is considering. Such methods of decision making also give rise to class and racial biases, and impose on contract parents a far higher standard than society requires for parents in general. It would be better, one writer suggests, simply to flip a coin in the many hard cases that would otherwise result in prolonged custody disputes.[79] It would be better still for a democratic society collectively to decide on a determinate rule of custody, publicize and enforce it, and periodically review it in light of experience with its implementation.

The second reason why a principle based on the best interests of the child is not adequate is that nonpaternalistic claims also play a role in determining who should be the paternalistic agent. On many issues, ranging from formally educating children to awarding custody rights, many different people, representing both private and public interests, assert claims to serve as paternalistic agents, and on grounds that are at least partly independent of whether they will best serve the interests of children. Public policy must take into account the recipient parents' claim based on contract and expectation of becoming parents at the time of conception, the recipient father's claim based on genetic connection, the birth mother's claim based on gestational labor and emotional bonding during and immediately after pregnancy, and (in some cases) the birth mother's genetic connection.

Even if (as we have argued) the birth mother has a basic liberty claim to custody of the child, so may the recipient parents have a claim based on the contract coupled with the father's genetic link to the child. It therefore remains an open question whether the recipient parents should share custody of the child with the birth mother. On the one hand, a policy of awarding joint custody in case of conflict respects the moral claims of both parties to the contract. On the other hand, the policy may be worse for the child than granting exclusive custody to either the birth mother or the recipient parents. In any case, such a policy might further discourage contract parenting. It would put both birth mother and recipient parents on warning that neither can expect exclusive custody of the child if the contract does not go as originally intended. But whether the consequences of this policy would be desirable depends on whether contract parenting is morally desirable.

Neither advocates nor critics of contract parenting, then, can rely on paternalism to clinch their case. Paternalistic considerations are relevant to contract parenting (and many other issues of public policy), but the gap between agreement on the conditions of paternalism and paternalistic policies is great. It leaves plenty of room for democratic deliberation. Nevertheless, the principles we have presented provide guidance for that deliberation, and they rule out certain policies, and certain reasons for policies. The basic liberty principle, for example, rules out a policy that would allow adults to buy and sell children even at the children's request. In addition, the conditions for justifiable paternalism can remind citizens that the immorality of the conduct alone is not a sufficient reason for paternalistic intervention.

We have used the case of contract parenting to illustrate how much—

and how little—work a principle of basic liberty can do in a deliberative democracy. What it can do is significant. The principle casts doubt on what many advocates of contract parenting assume: that citizens have a right to enter into surrogacy arrangements without any interference by the government. It also gives good reason to doubt what many critics claim: that government must prohibit surrogacy arrangements because they are immoral or harmful to the parties. The basic liberty principle leaves citizens with much deliberative disagreement and ample room to practice the economy of moral disagreement. They can recognize that even if some kind of contract parenting is permissible, surrogate mothers should retain a right to at least joint custody, and surrogate contracts should be as voluntary and free of exploitation as possible.

The kinds of policies consistent with the principle of basic liberty and the virtues of deliberative democracy lie in a region between the territory claimed by the New York Judiciary Committee staff and that declared by the Task Force on Life and Law. Such policies are likely to be more complex than the recommendations of either of these bodies because they seek to accommodate more competing moral claims—not only that of basic liberty but also to some extent those of moralism and paternalism. The principle of basic liberty constrains public policy but does not settle many important issues, such as the content and extent of government regulation or the desirability of joint custody. Further experience with contract parenting and further deliberation about it can improve public understanding of the value of contract parenting itself in relation to personal integrity.

No abstract statement of a principle of basic liberty can adequately express its role in deliberation about moral conflicts of these kinds. There is no substitute for exploring its implications for particular policies in the political process, identifying paradigm cases, and comparing them with other more controversial cases in public discourse. The discussion in this chapter has explored cases mostly involving one issue, but the implications go well beyond contract parenting. The conclusions about the claims of basic liberty and its relation to moralism and paternalism bear on many other moral disagreements, such as the legalization of pornography and prostitution. Some of the specific claims in these disputes take the same form as those in the surrogacy controversy—invoking, for example, claims based on comparable considerations of harm, degradation, exploitation, and social subordination. More generally, the structures of the arguments are often remarkably similar.

The principle of basic liberty, suitably formulated and deliberatively reformulated over time, can meet the challenges of moralism and paternalism. To do so, it must depart in critical respects from Millian liberalism. The principle most appropriate for a deliberative perspective does not presume that liberty is protected only when the government does not intervene. Nor does the principle absolutely reject the claims of moralism and paternalism. Deliberating under its influence, citizens begin by asking what policy best enhances personal integrity. They might well conclude that some practices should be regulated or prohibited "because in the opinion of others it would be right," or "because it will be better for [one]" But if in this way moralism and paternalism are admitted into the public forum, they are also kept under the firm control of basic liberty.

—8—

The Obligations of Welfare

IN THE THEORY of deliberative democracy, liberty takes priority over opportunity, but in actual deliberation about public policy opportunity often comes first. One reason is that since so many disputes about policy assume that the basic liberties of citizens have been guaranteed, the main challenge is to secure their opportunities. But another reason concerns the nature of opportunity itself. It is so prominent on the public agenda because it embraces such a wide range of goods. They include both what we have called basic and fair opportunities, and their distribution is governed by two different principles. The focus of this chapter is the basic opportunity principle, which provides standards for distributing health care, education, security, and—the subjects of the main case in this chapter—income and work. All these goods are basic because citizens needed them to live a decent life and to enjoy other non-basic opportunities. (Goods that are not basic in this sense, such as highly skilled jobs and other socially valued goods to which only some citizens may have legitimate claims, are the province of the fair opportunity principle, and the subject of the next chapter.)

In deliberative democracy the basic opportunity principle would secure citizens an *adequate* level of basic opportunity goods. In the case of basic income, an adequate level is that which is necessary to live a decent life according to the current standards of the society in question.[1] What policies this principle requires must be left partly to democratic deliberation, but the range of acceptable policies is not unlimited. As we indicated in Chapter 6, basic opportunities should not be distributed simply on the basis of need. The main problem with such a standard is that needs are omnivorous.[2] More positively, basic opportunities should be distributed by standards that fulfill the fundamental purpose of the opportunity principle. Distributive policies for such goods should mitigate the effects that the morally arbitrary distribution of natural talents and abilities have on basic opportunities. The essential point is that citizens should not be denied basic opportunities on the basis of factors for which they are not responsible.

Although the question of what should count as an adequate level of a basic opportunity good is an important one, the more controversial issue in contemporary debates is what should count as an adequate reason to deny citizens such a good, at whatever level it is provided. Specifically, it is justifiable to deny citizens a basic opportunity good on the grounds that they are responsible for providing it themselves. When we considered the distribution of health care, we assumed that lack of access to basic opportunity goods is beyond the control of needy citizens. We took for granted that Dianna Brown was not responsible for her illness. Even in the case of health care, however, this assumption is questionable (especially for diseases related to smoking or diet). In the case of many other opportunity goods, it becomes a central issue. We therefore need to consider what obligations the basic opportunity principle may impose on citizens as a condition of their receiving basic opportunity goods.[3]

This question lies at the heart of contemporary controversies over the reform of welfare policy in the United States.[4] The debate is complex, but for our purposes the dispute popularly described as "welfare versus workfare" raises the critical issues. In this dispute "welfare" typically refers to a policy of providing income support to citizens regardless of their willingness to work. "Workfare" is a policy of providing support to able-bodied citizens on the condition that they agree to accept a job or training for a job.

The idea of a work requirement has long figured in discussions of welfare. Alexis de Tocqueville, the social theorist who first explicitly anticipated the contemporary objections to public welfare, asked, "Why could work not be imposed as a condition on the able-bodied indigent who asks for public pity?" He implied that making work "the price of relief" would address one of his major concerns about public welfare—that it encourages the "natural passion for idleness." But he firmly rejected any work requirement because he doubted that there would be enough work to be done, and thought that even if there were, no government could effectively match unemployed citizens to productive jobs.[5] Some contemporary opponents of welfare seem prepared to follow Tocqueville in advocating its complete abolition. But others, no more favorable toward public charity than he, believe that modern governments can successfully implement a work requirement.

In this chapter we explore the issues that workfare raises by examining the controversy over welfare reform in the state of Wisconsin in the mid-1990s. The focus is the debate over the "Work-Not-Welfare" Act, sponsored by Republican Governor Tommy Thompson and enacted into law in December 1993 with overwhelming bipartisan support. The act established a pilot program of workfare, with the aim of eventually eliminating the major federal welfare program, Aid to Families with Dependent Children (AFDC).

Under the terms of the Wisconsin act, no citizen in certain designated counties can receive AFDC benefits for themselves or their dependents unless they satisfy work requirements set by the state. With the exception of those unable to work because of illness, advanced age, or responsibility for the care of an infant, all citizens over sixteen must hold a full-time job. If they cannot find work in the private sector on their own, they must accept an assigned private- or public-sector job, or enroll in a job training program. In return, the state issues supplementary cash allowances to any participant whose wages fall short of what AFDC would ordinarily provide. The state also pays for full-time child care, transportation to work, and job placement assistance. Although the state provides public service work if no private sector job is available, this guarantee disappears at the end of two years, with no resumption of AFDC payments. This provision—referred to as "two years and you're out"—is intended to lead to the abolition of the entire AFDC program in Wisconsin by January 1, 1999.

After the passage of Work-Not-Welfare, the governor and many legislators also pressed for a "family cap," which (following the lead of New Jersey) would deny AFDC recipients who have a child while on welfare the additional payments they would previously have received. Although Wisconsin did not immediately enact a statewide family cap, the Department of Health and Human Services granted a waiver from federal requirements so that the state could do so. As part of the pilot program, the state put the cap into effect in two counties in 1995. The state also began the so-called Bridefare program in four counties, which cut in half the normal benefit for a child born to an unmarried teenager.[6]

The Work-Not-Welfare Act together with the family cap plan made basic income conditional on two obligations of citizens—an obligation to work and an obligation not to bear additional children while receiving welfare. Are these obligations of welfare morally justifiable in a democracy? Many egalitarians argue that they are not. When government denies some parents adequate income, it also deprives their children of basic opportunity goods. This appears to be a clear violation of the opportunity principle: these children suffer through no fault of their own. They are hardly responsible for either their need or their inability to meet it. Yet proponents of the Wisconsin plan argue that the obligations are justified. Some base their argument on a libertarian view that no citizen should depend on the government for income support.[7] The basic opportunity principle, on this view, does not require, and may even forbid, the government to provide for citizens who are capable of providing for themselves. By offering welfare without conditions, the government also is likely to perpetuate the cycle of dependence that undermines the liberty of citizens now and in the future.

The basic opportunity principle seems to be caught in a moral bind: on one interpretation it appears to justify, and on another to condemn, welfare policies like that adopted by Wisconsin. Is there an interpretation of the principle that could escape this bind, and prescribe a policy that can be justified from a reciprocal perspective? To answer this question, we look more closely at the two common interpretations and their implications for welfare reform in the United States.

We first examine the egalitarian view that citizens are entitled to adequate income support regardless of their willingness to work. We then turn to the libertarian interpretation of opportunity, which ties income support to work. In the third section we defend what we call *fair workfare,* a policy of income entitlement that builds on and extends the common ground between the egalitarian and libertarian positions. Fair workfare responds both to the egalitarian worry that unconditional workfare will inflict injustice on some individuals, especially children, and the libertarian concern that welfare will make citizens dependent on government and thereby less free. Fair workfare takes individual responsibility seriously as a requirement in welfare reform. But it is grounded on a value of mutual dependence, which is implied by reciprocity, rather than the value of independence or self-sufficiency, which libertarians stress. The obligations of welfare should be mutual: citizens who need income support are obligated to work, but only if their fellow citizens fulfill their obligation to enact public policies that provide adequate employment and child support.

In the last section we consider whether fair workfare is consistent with the conditions of citizenship in a deliberative democracy. Some basic income support is necessary to enable citizens to participate in politics, and more generally to make effective use of their political liberties. Yet welfare reforms such as fair workfare are usually the creation of political leaders and policymakers who initiate and implement them without the participation of the beneficiaries. The basic opportunity of welfare is provided at the expense of a basic opportunity of citizenship. We challenge this top-down model of welfare reform, and argue for the participation of poor citizens in the reforms that are aimed at empowering them.

Welfare without Obligation

Gwendolyn Moore grew up on welfare, and went on to become a state legislator. In 1994 she stood almost alone on the Wisconsin Senate floor urging her colleagues to oppose the Work-Not-Welfare bill. One of only four members who voted against the bill, she argued that the state should not end welfare without ensuring that the basic needs of poor citizens would be met. Work-Not-Welfare, she said, would merely create "low-wage workfare treadmills."[8] Before government is justified in ending welfare, it should put into effect universal health care, universal child care, job placement services, public transit, a higher minimum wage, better unemployment insurance, and more sex education. The primary aim of welfare policy, Moore believed, should be not to put citizens to work but to end poverty. Work is only a means to this end. This egalitarian end of providing basic opportunities for all citizens should take priority, she suggested, over imposing any obligations on citizens to contribute to their own welfare. She also opposed the family cap, which she argued would only punish children and reflect the public's "prurient interest in the sex lives of poor people."[9]

In a time of fiscal austerity, egalitarian politicians like Moore who urge that government spend more on the poor may be "practically pariahs among lawmakers."[10] But some egalitarian philosophers continue to press for expanding welfare even beyond what Moore proposed. They argue for universal income support at a high level, with no obligation to work.[11] Each citizen has a claim to a level of support that would ensure equal basic opportunities (in order to make what these philosophers call "equal liberty" effective). Without the income and other goods that enable citizens to choose their own life plans, they would be denied the basic opportunities that other citizens enjoy.

Given this strong version of the principle, the level of support should be higher than that at which Wisconsin or any other state now aims. The problem with "welfare as we know it" is not that the government gives handouts to undeserving citizens, as some critics claim, but quite the reverse. Current welfare policy, on this egalitarian view, provides too little to citizens who have legitimate claims for greater support.[12] Under the present system, neither a single-parent nor a two-parent family with two young children can make ends meet with a full-time minimum-wage job.

Not only does this strong interpretation of the opportunity principle imply a high level of income support, but also it gives little or no weight to an obligation to work. Indeed, on this view a work requirement actually violates basic opportunity in two ways. First, in the less than full employment economies of modern democracies, more citizens want to work than can find jobs. Imposing a work requirement under these conditions would deny citizens basic opportunities as a result of factors that are beyond their control.

A second argument that some egalitarians use against the work requirement goes further.[13] It rejects the idea that citizens have any obligation at all to provide for their own welfare. Citizens have a claim to basic income to pursue their life plans, and to enjoy equal effective liberty, so long as they do not harm others. Denying those who do not wish to work the support they need forces them to follow a different way of life than they would otherwise choose. As Philippe Van Parijs vividly concludes, even citizens who would rather surf all day off Malibu are entitled to welfare.[14]

But in refusing to work, are the surfers not harming others by failing to fulfill their obligations to their fellow citizens? No, say these egalitarians. So long as there is any unemployment at all, citizens who do not work benefit citizens who want to work; those who choose leisure in effect leave more jobs—a scarce and valuable social resource—for those who would choose work. Holding a decent job gives citizens the chance to gain more rewarding employment, social standing, and self-esteem. Citizens therefore should not be required to work, but they should be offered good jobs if they want them. Some reformers suggest that the government could encourage the private sector to create more good jobs by enabling people to resist taking jobs that are poorly paid.[15] Whether or not such a strategy would succeed, egalitarians still insist that the government must provide, without strings or stigma, the income necessary to ensure basic opportunities.

Egalitarians especially object to requiring parents to take a job outside the home as a condition of adequate income support. Poor women who stay home to take care of their children are already working, though no one pays them any wages. The government should not prevent women— or men—from choosing a career as parent and homemaker. The implication for welfare policy is that parents should receive child support allowances sufficient to permit them to choose either to be a full-time parent or to take another full-time job and pay someone else to provide child care.[16]

A welfare policy that provides unconditional income support in these ways is benevolent, but it may not be just. In a deliberative democracy citizens need to ask: Is income support without any obligation to work outside the home required by reciprocity? Senator Moore herself did not defend such an unconditional form of welfare. She objected not to the work requirement itself but to giving it priority over other egalitarian goals. She would presumably disagree with those who assume that citizens cannot secure basic opportunities without holding a job outside the home. But most of her disagreement with her fellow senators turned on whether poor citizens could in fact find decent jobs if they tried, and whether the work requirement created a positive incentive for them to look for such jobs. This dispute could continue even among those who accept an interpretation of the opportunity principle that would impose obligations on citizens to provide for their own welfare if they are able to do so.

The stronger interpretation of the opportunity principle, however, is not so easy to reconcile with reciprocity. To demand income but to refuse to work is to make a claim on one's fellow citizens that they may reasonably reject. First of all, the premise underlying the opportunity principle—that citizens should not be denied basic needs because of factors over which they have no control—readily suggests a corollary: that citizens may be denied public provision of basic needs if they could secure them for themselves. The corollary is just a way of saying that the opportunity principle, if it takes individual responsibility seriously, offers no reason to justify providing for citizens who do not provide for themselves.

This corollary turns into an even stronger claim—citizens who are able but refuse to work not only may but *should* be denied welfare—in light of a further reason for objecting to unconditional income support from a reciprocal perspective. Citizens who decline to work are in effect refusing to participate in a scheme of fair social cooperation that is necessary to sustain any adequate policy of income support. Society's capacity to secure a basic income for needy citizens depends on economic productivity, and economic productivity depends in turn on citizens' willingness to work. Even if some citizens get better jobs because the Malibu surfers do not take them, other citizens are likely to receive less support than they would under a policy with a work requirement, and probably less than they need to secure basic opportunities. Democratic government therefore cannot be neutral between ways of life that contribute to economic productivity and those that do not.

This preference for the productive life does not mean that citizens are obligated to choose the life that produces the most economic value for a society. But if they choose to spend their life surfing at Malibu, they cannot reasonably expect their fellow citizens to support them. Nor can they expect to receive the respect that citizens owe one another as social and political equals. Egalitarians should be the first to recognize the importance of expecting all citizens to accept at least this minimal obligation to contribute to society. Indeed, some egalitarians insist on such an obligation, basing it on values of equal concern and respect.[17]

Notice that this obligation applies not only to those citizens at the bottom of the economic ladder but also to those at the top. Those who choose to live off inherited wealth without contributing their own labor to society may deserve no more respect from their fellow citizens than the Malibu surfers. The idle rich, it is true, do not ask for welfare (though they often claim benefits that they did nothing to earn). If they choose to exempt themselves from a scheme of social cooperation, they may rightly be denied the equal respect of citizens who are motivated to support social cooperation. Considerations of this kind could even form the basis of a case for imposing steeper inheritance taxes. If egalitarians recognized the egalitarian turn that the obligation to work may take, they might be less inclined to deny its legitimacy.

Some egalitarians offer yet another argument for unconditional welfare that might seem to be acceptable from a reciprocal perspective. It begins with an assumption shared by many traditional liberal philosophers, including John Locke and John Stuart Mill, that a society's external, unearned common inheritance (such as its natural resources) are not created by anyone's labor.[18] From this premise Van Parijs argues that this common inheritance should be divided equally among all equally endowed citizens, whether they work or not. Were natural resources the only external unearned assets, the total economic value to be divided would not generate a significant universal income for any citizen. But natural resources are not the only, or even the most valuable, unearned external asset. There are also the far more substantial unearned economic "rents" that accrue to most citizens who work in an economy with involuntary unemployment and imperfect competition. Under these conditions, both employers and employees are rewarded with sizable economic rents—income that derives not from the willingness to labor but from the unequal bargaining power of equally endowed workers under conditions of economic interdependence. "Even in the absence of collective organization," Van Parijs points out, "workers can durably claim a wage that significantly exceeds the market-clearing level because of the bargaining power they derive from the existence of hiring, training, and firing costs."[19] (Markets clear whenever there remain no qualified job seekers who would be willing to do someone else's job at or below the going wage rate.) Involuntary unemployment swells the level of economic rents, leaving a surplus to be distributed among the unemployed.

But why should unearned economic rents be distributed unconditionally to all citizens who do not have adequate income rather than only to those who are willing but unable to work? Van Parijs himself acknowledges the difficulty: "Should one not instead restrict the benefits of rent sharing to the involuntarily unemployed?" His direct answer appeals to an assumption we have already shown cannot be sustained. Rejecting the claims of the Malibu surfers would violate "the liberal ban on discrimination between conceptions of the good life."[20] But neither the liberal state nor any plausible reciprocal perspective can remain neutral between those conceptions of the good life that include productive work and those do not.

Van Parijs's other line of reply is no more successful. In a variation on his general claim that holding a job is to appropriate a scarce resource, he argues that "those who . . . give up their share of that resource and thereby leave more of it for others should not therefore be deprived of a fair share of the value of the resource. What holds for scarce land holds just as much for scarce jobs."[21] The analogy between scarce land and scarce jobs is misleading. An individual's labor contributes to a social product that can provide income support in a way that mere ownership of land does not. Even in an economy suffering from massive unemployment, productive labor is an expandable resource in a way that land is not, and its expansion is desirable for reasons other than satisfying people's "expensive taste" for work. Expanding productive labor helps democratic governments provide better health care, education, and other needs and thus better satisfy the demands of the opportunity principle. A deliberative democracy can reasonably reject the claims of those who have a "taste" for surfing while accepting the claims of those who have a "taste" for work.

So far we have argued that the strong interpretation of basic opportunity, which would provide unconditional income support without any obligation to work, is not consistent with reciprocity. The somewhat weaker interpretation suggested by Senator Moore, which would impose some work requirements, is in principle consistent, but it makes formidable demands on the government. The conditions that she insists must be satisfied before a work requirement would be justified are so stringent that they are not likely to be met in the foreseeable future. In practice, her position thus leads to unconditional income support—welfare as we know it—and at an even higher level.

Yet, despite her political defeat in the Wisconsin legislature, she stands on firm moral ground unless there are other moral reasons we have not yet considered for imposing an unconditional obligation to work, or that there are other less stringent conditions that would justify imposing the obligation to work in return for income support. In the next section we consider and reject the claims of those who argue for the unconditional obligation to work. Then we propose some conditions that are as justifiable as Moore's but focus more specifically on providing employment.

Work without Welfare

Like Senator Moore, Wisconsin state representative Antonio Riley, Jr., was once on welfare. Also like Moore, Riley is a Democrat who represents one of the poorest urban districts of the state. But unlike Moore, Riley voted in favor of the Work-Not-Welfare bill. He even went beyond Governor Thompson's original plan by proposing the amendment that terminates all AFDC payments at midnight, December 31, 1998. The welfare system has failed, Riley argued, because it tells poor people that it is "a smarter economic decision . . . to choose welfare over work." Defending Work-Not-Welfare, Riley asked: "Isn't it better to pay people to work and give them the chance to pass on the example and dignity of work to their children than it is to pay them to stay home? There're no two ways about it."[22]

There are, however, at least two ways to defend work without welfare, one more radical and one more moderate. Riley takes the moderate way. Both ways treat work as an essential aspect of self-sufficiency or independence; it is a good that provides citizens with the capacity to exercise liberty, to live their lives free from interference by, and dependence on, the state and their fellow citizens. In this respect both ways are consistent with a libertarian perspective. But Riley's moderate version would end welfare only if work is available, while the more radical version would end welfare regardless of the availability of work. "If the state is going to emphasize the value of work," Riley insisted, "it better make sure work is available." He argued that the "two-years and you're out" rule is justified only if there are jobs to be had, in either the private or the public sector. He therefore urged that the government provide "community service jobs as part of the equation if all else fails."[23]

The more radical view was implicitly endorsed by some representatives members of the legislature who favored unconditional workfare. They opposed the creation of community service jobs because they believed that such a policy would encourage permanent dependency on government. Workfare, rightly understood, should make citizens independent of government. These representatives were prepared to impose the "two-years and you're out" rule, without any safety net (except for the disabled), in order to send the message that citizens cannot depend on government for their support. None of the legislators presented a sustained argument for this view, but the policy theorist Charles Murray offers one that serves their aims.

Murray bases his defense of unconditional workfare on a meritocratic interpretation of equal opportunity. Social policy, he says, should "make it possible to get as far as one can go on one's merit, hardly a new ideal in American thought." Murray thinks that "some people are better than others," and that "they deserve more of society's rewards." He argues that "a principal function of social policy is to make sure" that these "better" people "have the opportunity to reap those rewards. Government cannot identify the worthy, but it can protect a society in which the worthy can identify themselves." The "worthy" can identify themselves, in this view, only if the government does not guarantee a job to every citizen who is willing to work. Merit in the domain of income is measured by what citizens earn on the market, without any guarantees from the government. This encourages genuine self-sufficiency and promotes basic liberty, enabling the most deserving citizens to make the most effective use of their opportunities.[24]

His view, Murray believes, shows "no lack of compassion" and actually expresses "a presumption of respect." He explains: "People—all people, black or white, rich or poor—may be unequally responsible for what has happened to them in the past, but all are equally responsible for what they do next."[25] Welfare and guaranteed jobs reduce the chances that citizens will make use of opportunities to show that they can take responsibility for what they do next. Unconditional workfare tells citizens that they themselves have the capacity to control their own lives.

It might at first seem curious that libertarians would defend a policy that requires citizens to work. After all, it is libertarians who object most strenuously to anything that comes close to "forced labor," which, as we noted in Chapter 6, some think includes even taxation. Is not a work requirement equivalent to forced labor? The libertarian position is not vulnerable to this objection. The freedom not to work does not carry an entitlement to an adequate income. Just as the freedom not to be friendly does not entitle one to friendship, so the freedom not to work does not guarantee one a regular paycheck. Although income support (unlike friendship) is a basic opportunity, citizens who willingly forgo employment are not denied a basic opportunity by anyone other than themselves. Their inadequate income is a consequence of their own choices, not a violation of their liberty.

The libertarian argument fails, however, because it does not offer an adequate interpretation of individual responsibility. Contrary to Murray's claim, his meritocratic version of equal opportunity does not take individual responsibility seriously in any form that can be consistent with reciprocity among citizens. Suppose that one citizen can find work that pays, but another, who tries equally hard, cannot. If we treat each as equally responsible, then we should conclude that the second is no more blameworthy and no less meritorious than the first. Taking responsibility seriously implies just the opposite conclusion from that which libertarians assert. Any acceptable opportunity principle should acknowledge that the difference between the successes and failures of equally responsible citizens may be due to luck, misfortune, or injustice.

Following Tocqueville, some contemporary critics may be inclined to deny that we can "separate unmerited misfortune from an adversity produced by vice."[26] But the principle of responsibility does not have to be applied so precisely and so individually. It is not so applied in the case of government relief for the harms of natural disasters such as earthquakes, floods, and hurricanes, even though some citizens take more precautions and have more insurance than others. Some of the major factors affecting the likelihood of finding a job—notably, the general condition of the economy—are like natural disasters. They and their consequences are beyond the control of any individual and respond if at all only to collective actions of citizens and governments. What Murray calls "triage by self-selection" may have some basis in nature, but has none in a just society.[27]

To recognize that those who succeed may be no more responsible or more meritorious than those who fail is consistent with the idea that some merit what they receive while others do not. But it is not consistent with the libertarian claim that by letting citizens make their own choices, no matter what their options, and bear the consequences, no matter what the harms, a democratic government demonstrates respect for individual responsibility. Genuine respect for individual responsibility calls for public policy that seeks to provide the conditions in which citizens can take control of their lives, and it acknowledges a social or governmental responsibility for sustaining those conditions. When government fails in its responsibility, citizens with the least control over the forces that shape their lives should not suffer the consequences.

This is why defenders of unconditional workfare are mistaken when they say that "employment must become a duty, enforced by public authority . . . regardless of how we interpret the mysterious phenomenon of non-work, or irregular work, among many low-income people."[28] From the perspective of the opportunity principle, whether the duty is justified at all depends critically on how we understand this "mysterious phenomenon." If citizens do not work because decent jobs are not available, they are scarcely to blame for failing to fulfill the duty.[29] Healthy adults who expect an adequate income (or need an adequate income to support their families) have a duty to work only on the condition that work that pays is available.

Some libertarians accept that government may in principle have such a responsibility but argue that in practice the public policies it requires—community service jobs, income supplements, universal health care, child care—are likely to be counterproductive. Instead of encouraging self-sufficiency, these policies create a culture of poverty. Children raised in such a culture tend to follow the example of their parents: they learn the habit of depending on the government for their support. Although government subsidies are intended to enable more citizens to secure jobs, they create incentives that encourage many citizens to malinger, to get divorced, and to have illegitimate children. Subsidies reinforce the culture of poverty, as the habits of dependency pass from one generation to another. The only way to break this cycle is to force the poor to become more self-sufficient. Although some may fail through no fault of their own, the injustice that they suffer is less serious than the injustice that flows from subsidizing generations of citizens who do not work, and from promoting illegitimate childbirth at the state's expense.

It would be necessary to accept a trade-off between injustices of this kind if libertarians were right about the effects of welfare. But there are at least two reasons to doubt that they are. First, only a small fraction of welfare recipients and an even smaller fraction of poor citizens—the inner-city poor or the so-called "underclass"—live in conditions that could be accurately described as a culture of poverty.[30] There is no evidence that most welfare recipients fit the profile attributed to the members of that culture. Second, even if libertarians limit their claim to only the inner-city poor, they do not offer credible evidence that public subsidies are a major cause of this culture of poverty.[31] The most careful empirical studies acknowledge that it is not possible to separate the causal contributions of culture from the other circumstances of poverty—unemployment, drug addiction, crime, broken families, and illegitimate births. Most researchers, whatever their ideological inclinations, agree that these factors interact in complicated ways over time.[32]

Even with respect to the trend that libertarians most vigorously condemn—the rise of single-parent families—there is reason to doubt that welfare has the effects they allege. Libertarians argue that the availability of AFDC benefits significantly contributed to the dramatic increase in the number of families headed by women in the period from 1972 to 1984. The problem with this claim is that during the same period the number of children receiving AFDC benefits declined, and so did the value of the benefits. As one analyst asks rhetorically: "How on earth can AFDC be the cause of the growth in children in single-parent families when fewer and fewer children are getting benefits?"[33] Neither is the libertarian argument valid for black families. During the same period the number of black children living in female-headed families increased by 25 percent, but the number of black children on AFDC fell by 15 percent.[34] Declining government subsidies for children can scarcely be the place to look for the cause of the increasing numbers of single-parent families.

Unconditional workfare may also have a detrimental effect that libertarians such as Murray ignore. As Riley pointed out in the legislative debate, the policy is likely to be racially discriminatory in practice because jobs are scarcest in inner cities where, as in Milwaukee, the poor are disproportionately black. If the government is not committed to creating jobs, then cutting off welfare benefits after two years will disproportionately hurt blacks and other disadvantaged minorities.[35] Yet it was Riley himself who introduced the amendment that would terminate all AFDC benefits in 1999. His intention may have been to embarrass his Republican colleagues into supporting policies that would create more jobs in the state. But his 1999 cutoff of AFDC passed without the appropriation of a single dollar for planning for a future without welfare.[36] In the absence of further action, Riley's own constituents would be among those citizens who will suffer the most serious consequences of ending welfare as we know it.

Riley and the moderate libertarians certainly did not intend these consequences. They wanted to make their support for ending welfare conditional on the government's providing more jobs. But the dynamics of legislative politics drove them into the camp of those who favor unconditional workfare. Once they agreed that work should replace welfare, they found it difficult to oppose the elimination of welfare as a first step. This dynamic was only partly political. It was also driven by the underlying rationale for workfare that both the moderates and the radicals accepted. Both identified the idea of individual responsibility with self-sufficiency. Individuals should be as independent as possible, and rely as little as possible on the government and their fellow citizens. This interpretation of responsibility leaves little room for imposing obligations on citizens to provide for one another's welfare, and therefore little basis for requiring the government to provide any backup income support when some citizens are not able to find a job to support themselves. The reciprocal idea of mutual dependence, as we suggest in the next section, offers a more promising basis for workfare, and also for establishing the conditions that could justify ending "welfare as we know it."

On almost any interpretation of individual responsibility, young children can not be expected to provide for their own support. Here at least it would seem that there should be some common ground between the egalitarians, who would provide welfare without any obligations, and libertarians, who would insist on work without any welfare. As even Murray acknowledges, "There is no such thing as an undeserving five-year-old."[37] Both egalitarians and libertarians should agree that children are entitled to basic opportunity goods no matter what their parents deserve. On this ground citizens could then challenge Wisconsin's family cap plan, which denies to mothers who have children while on welfare any additional cash payments to meet their increased household expenses. If there is no such creature as an undeserving five-year-old, how can family caps be justified?

Democratic state senator Chuck Chvala of Wisconsin defended the family cap as "a step toward having fewer people in our dependency."[38] This is a variation on the argument that the libertarians use to urge the end to welfare more generally. If a family cap actually discouraged poor women from having more children whom they are not able to support, it would be worth considering as part of a policy to promote more individual responsibility. But there is little evidence that lowering AFDC benefits deters childbearing among poor women.[39] Given the low levels of benefits that women in Wisconsin received before the family cap ($77 a month for a second child and $100 per month for a third child), it would be surprising if eliminating the benefits would deter women from having more children.

Public officials who support family caps also appeal to the value of fairness. They argue that it is not fair for poor families to get extra income for having children while middle-class families do not. But the fairness argument actually cuts in the opposite direction. When Republican state representative Bonnie Ladwig complained that no one gets a raise for having more children, Senator Moore replied, "I did. I got more tax cuts."[40] The senator was referring to the fact that federal tax policy gives a break for each additional child to all parents who pay income taxes. The family cap plan, under current tax law, in effect discriminates against poor women because it denies them a subsidy that other women receive for having additional children. "I take exception to the [implication] that only rich women should have children," Moore argued, "None of us would be able to afford children if we did not receive federal subsidies."[41]

Nor is it the case, as some legislators evidently believed, that poor women tend to have more children than better-off citizens. As the Wisconsin Catholic Conference "wryly noted" in opposing the family cap plan, "The average welfare family has fewer children (1.9) than does the average state senator (2.6)."[42] Senator David Helbach pointed out yet another aspect of the family cap that is unfair to poor women: the cap puts a further burden on welfare mothers who care for their children while letting the biological fathers "get off scot free."[43]

Proponents of the family cap offer a further plea on its behalf. Wayne Bryant, a legislator who sponsored the family cap plan in New Jersey, argued that "you can't use kids to shield these parents, or we won't have welfare reform at all."[44] Murray makes the same general point against liberal critics of welfare reform, accusing them of a "reflexive response" that has the effect of blocking every "attempt to make public assistance less attractive than employment at low wages." Murray calls this response, "INFTC"—"It's Not Fair To The Children."[45] But Murray's point is more of a lament than an argument. Since, as we have noted, the family cap is in fact not fair to children, the appeal to fairness expresses a legitimate objection to the policy, one that should be acceptable even from the perspective of Murray and other libertarians. Driving home the point that children should not suffer for the sins of their parents, U.S. Senator Daniel Patrick Moynihan suggests: "What you're really saying with that [family cap] approach is: 'Look you . . . little 8-month-old, I don't like the way your mother is behaving, and I'm going to show you! No more bottles, no more Pampers, no more nothing!' "[46] The family cap policy, Moynihan thinks, in effect tells babies "to shape up or starve."[47]

In one last desperate move to escape this implication of the family cap, some libertarians offer what one might suppose to be a modest proposal in the spirit of Swift but evidently is meant to be taken seriously. If poor parents are unable to work to support their children, Murray suggests, then the government should put their children in state orphanages. The proposal has attracted some support even among public officials. The Democratic mayor of Milwaukee, John Norquist, has declared that "if a mother, a parent, is so irresponsible as to not work to support her children and has no money, then we will have to review custodial laws. You don't solve this problem by giving more money to the mothers, you solve it, if necessary, by building more orphanages."[48]

To take children from their parents under these conditions would violate the basic liberty of the parents. It is not likely that building more orphanages would save the government more money or give children a better life than providing more income support for them, more community service employment, or the higher quality of schooling that would be made possible by a similarly large investment of social resources. Orphanages are justifiable, if at all, for children from homes where their parents have abused them, and therefore at least temporarily relinquished their basic liberty to raise children. This rationale, which applies to any parents who continually abuse their children, is distinct from the idea of designing orphanages specifically for the welfare system. Furthermore, any proposal along these lines, however equitably implemented, will give the state vast control over the lives of large numbers of children, a consequence that libertarians such as Murray, who worry about the totalitarian tendencies of an activist government, should be among the first to decry.[49]

Libertarians are on firmer ground if they hold fast to their initial presumption—that children are not responsible for the failures of their parents—and acknowledge that any welfare reform should include protections for children. Trying to put in perspective "the temptation to 'get tough' on welfare recipients," state representative Barbara Notestein reminded her colleagues: "Most of the recipients are children."[50] This part of the common ground seems firm from almost any perspective. It is here that the bedrock of any plausible interpretation of individual responsibility is to be found. But taking a stand on this ground creates a serious problem for welfare reform. The presumption that children must be protected not only casts doubt on family caps and unconditional workfare but also threatens to undermine the case for imposing any obligation to work, and thereby calls into question all workfare policies. This problem can be brought out more clearly by recalling how the argument has gone so far.

We first argued against egalitarians who hold that adequate income support should be unconditional. At least in principle, we suggested that an entitlement to adequate income support should be tied to a willingness to work. We then argued against libertarians who claim that the obligation to work should be unconditional. An obligation to work should be contingent on the availability of work. Furthermore, even when employment is available, children should not be penalized for their parents' unwillingness to work, and therefore family caps are not justifiable. But the most powerful moral objection to family caps—that they may make innocent children suffer—seems to apply to any policy that results in some parents' receiving less than an adequate income for themselves and their children. Any policy that enforces an obligation to work with the threat of ending welfare payments could have just this consequence. There appears to be no way to deny parents income to which they are not entitled without depriving their children of basic opportunity.

The basic opportunity principle thus seems to be caught between two conflicting moral imperatives for welfare reform—one imposing and the other rejecting the obligation to work as a condition for receiving income support. For the sake of fairness to adults, public policy must make income conditional on the willingness to work. But for the sake of fairness to children, it must not make income conditional on any actions of parents over which children have no control. Any welfare reform that is justifiable from a reciprocal perspective has to satisfy both of these imperatives. In the next section we explore what the elements of such a reform might look like.

Fair Workfare

Asked what lessons other states might learn from Wisconsin's Work-Not-Welfare and family cap plans, Governor Thompson responded: "My advice is, don't be timid. Be as radical as you possibly can. No matter what you do, it's bound to be an improvement over the existing system."[51] In a political climate in which nearly all public officials and most citizens—even those on welfare—have nothing but contempt for the current policy, the governor's advice finds a receptive audience. But not every radical change is bound to be an improvement over the existing system. Some of the proposed changes we have criticized would eliminate even the minimal support necessary to ensure basic opportunities. "The Work-Not-Welfare concept is great," says Fannie Mims, one of many mothers on welfare who have joined the Welfare Rights Organizing Committee. "It's a lot of welfare recipients' dream to work and be self-sufficient. But the way [Thompson's] got it structured, he's just putting people on the street."[52]

The Work-Not-Welfare plan and similar reforms in other states are designed not to put poor people on the street but to help them find work and become more self-sufficient. If these reforms fall short, it is not because they fail to be radical. In one respect Work-Not-Welfare is too radical. "Two years and you're out" breaks with the tradition, followed even by the Reagan administration, that maintains some social insurance for basic opportunities for those citizens who are willing to work but cannot find a job. Even libertarians who reject welfare rights still accept the need for a "safety net."[53]

In another respect Work-Not-Welfare is not radical enough, but not in the way the governor implied. The reform does nothing to guarantee that decent work is available to all citizens who are willing to work. From a reciprocal perspective the focus should be not on how radical the policy is but on how well citizens can justify it to one another. That justification entails determining whether it fulfills the demands of the principle of basic opportunity. Instead of "welfare reform, done harshly," as critics characterized the Wisconsin plan,[54] the basic opportunity principle calls for workfare, done fairly. The aim was well stated by John Stuart Mill: "Give the greatest amount of needful help with the smallest encouragement to undue reliance on it."[55]

A government guided by the opportunity principle should seek to mitigate the effects of the social lottery so that citizens are not denied adequate life chances because of factors beyond their control. Welfare policy can violate that principle in many different ways: it can directly or indirectly discriminate against citizens on grounds of race, gender, age, and class. In this chapter we focus primarily on effects on the opportunities of children and poor citizens. Under current social conditions the poor who are most vulnerable to changes in welfare policy are disproportionately female and black, a fact that any adequate application of the opportunity principle cannot afford to ignore. But the distinctive place of race and gender in that principle is better brought out in the context of employment policy, which we consider in the next chapter.

Properly interpreted, the opportunity principle is consistent with imposing an obligation to work on able-bodied citizens. But that obligation must have a basis other than self-sufficiency or independence, which denies the relevance of our social interdependence. A more appropriate foundation adopts a concept of individual responsibility that regards citizens as mutually dependent, each obligated to contribute his or her share in a fair scheme of social cooperation.[56] The obligation to work is matched by an obligation to provide for others when they cannot provide for themselves. The aim is not to seek independence for its own sake. It is rather to secure a limited dependence—enough to avoid dependence that interferes with basic opportunities. On this approach, the challenge for policy is not only to define the conditions under which more needy citizens should have to take jobs, but also to specify the measures that government should adopt to fulfill the obligations of less needy citizens. From a reciprocal perspective this approach has several advantages.

First, unlike the view that equates responsibility with self-sufficiency, our approach supplies a positive reason for supporting citizens who, through no fault of their own, fail to be self-sufficient. It is therefore more likely to avoid many of the problems we identified in the policies of unconditional workfare—in particular, the implication that citizens who do not provide for themselves not only may but must be denied support.

Second, the aim of limited dependence that our approach seeks is probably more attainable and plainly more desirable than that of complete independence. For most citizens living in or close to poverty, the alternative to dependence on government is not independence but other forms of dependence, usually reliance on relatives and friends.[57] Again anticipating many contemporary critics of welfare, Tocqueville believed that "the right of the poor to obtain society's help . . . lowers" and "degrades" those who exercise it.[58] But neither he nor his followers convincingly show why dependence on other individuals is better than dependence on government. Relying on family, friends, or private charity is less predictable and may be more open to exploitation than relying on government.[59] It can often be even more degrading, and more detrimental to basic opportunities. That fervent critic of dependence Jean-Jacques Rousseau, in his search for ways to recapture the natural virtues of self-sufficiency in modern society, concluded that dependence on the state rather than on other individuals offers the closest approximation.[60] In any case, since some kind of dependence seems inevitable in modern society, citizens in a deliberative democracy should focus less on its source than on its consequences, specifically on its effects on basic liberty and opportunity.

Third, basing the obligation to work on mutual dependence better reveals its connection with citizenship. In our society having a job is a necessary condition of what has been called social dignity—maintaining the respect of one's fellow citizens.[61] (Having a job of course includes being a homemaker in a family where others have a job outside the home.) The point is not merely that having a job shows that you can take care of yourself; more important, it shows that you are carrying your share of the social burden. What your fellow citizens think of you in this sense should matter. An obligation to work founded on mutual dependence acknowledges the legitimate effect of their opinion on your standing. More generally, as we show further in the last section of this chapter, work should be seen as an essential part of citizenship.

A fourth advantage of this approach is its consonance with the conditions of deliberative democracy. In deliberating about welfare reform, citizens are asked to consider what obligations they could mutually accept, what it is reasonable for them to require of one another, in order to guarantee basic opportunities for all. This kind of question sets an agenda quite different from one that begins with asking citizens how they can become more independent of one another. Similarly, the idea of responsibility as mutual dependence reinforces, and in turn is reinforced by, the principles of publicity and accountability, both of which encourage citizens to acknowledge their mutual responsibilities rather than to seek self-sufficiency.

What then are the obligations of welfare that all citizens should accept? The most promising answer is fair workfare. It asks citizens, and through them their government, to accept three obligations, each of which is intended to mitigate conditions that are beyond the control of needy citizens, and thereby better satisfy the basic opportunity principle. If the government fulfils these obligations, then citizens who expect to receive public support must accept an obligation to work or to contribute in other ways that their fellow citizens deem appropriate. The obligations on government can be simply stated: (1) guarantee child support; (2) make work pay; and (3) make work available.[62] What specific reforms each of these implies is ultimately a question to be pursued in a process of democratic deliberation, but we can suggest the general shape that the answers might take.

GUARANTEEING CHILD SUPPORT

Any view of individual responsibility that is acceptable from a reciprocal perspective must ensure that children are not punished for their parents' irresponsibility. All citizens, acting collectively through government, therefore have an obligation to provide support for children whose parents fail to do so. Public support, however, is the last resort. Parents should be held responsible for supporting their own children, and the first task of government in fulfilling its obligation is to try to make sure that parents fulfill theirs.

More than half of all children in the United States now spend some time in single-parent families, most of which are headed by women. Over a fourth of all children under the age of eighteen now live with a single parent who has never married.[63] When government does not force absentee parents to pay child support, it throws the whole burden on the custodial parents, who find themselves driven deeper into poverty. Collecting child support from absentee parents therefore is an essential feature of fair workfare.[64] Collecting child support is also necessary to avoid gender discrimination in workfare.

Wisconsin acknowledged the importance of this feature by passing its "Children First" policy in 1988, which automatically withholds child support from the paycheck of the absentee parent. An effective system of child support requires more than Wisconsin or any state by itself can provide. Experts on child support policy recommend, for example, a national registration system that would identify by social security number the mother and father of every newborn child.[65]

Since absentee parents are equally responsible for bringing children into the world, they should also be held equally responsible for supporting them. They should be expected to work in order to support their children, provided decent work is available. If, however, government fails to collect child support from an absentee parent, it should provide backup support for the custodial parent.[66]

Custodial parents have obligations, too. They may be required to seek employment outside the home to supplement the child support guaranteed by the government. This obligation should be contingent not only on the availability of employment but also on the provision of child support at a level sufficient to make child care affordable. Child support could be supplemented by granting low-income parents a tax credit (usually a refund) for child care. Middle-income and high-income parents already enjoy such a benefit. Generous child support and child care allowances would make it possible for custodial parents to work, even at minimum wage jobs, without sacrificing the well-being of their children. Without child support and child care allowances, workfare would not only punish innocent children but also saddle custodial parents with a burden that neither absentee nor affluent parents are expected to bear.

Some critics of welfare may be tempted argue that public policy would not have this discriminatory effect if child care allowances of all kinds were abolished. They might argue further that abolishing the allowances would deter the poor from having more children. We have already noted the paucity of evidence for such a deterrent effect. But even if abolishing all child support did discourage poor parents from having more children, the policy would still be questionable. This is clear if we take the logic of this approach to its conclusion. If deterrence is a sufficient justification, then in principle there would be a strong case for making it a crime for the poor to have more children. (The crime would of course apply to biological fathers as well as mothers.) No one who opposes child allowances is willing to follow the logic of the argument this far, and for good reason. Prohibiting the poor from having children would violate almost any adequate version of both the liberty and opportunity principles. No liberty principle should permit government to forbid people to have children. No opportunity principle should justify preventing citizens who are poor through no fault of their own from becoming parents while not placing any similar restrictions on relatively affluent citizens, who are no more (or less) responsible for their ability to support children.

Providing child support allowances for all citizens, regardless of their income, would avoid this form of discrimination, but it would not alone resolve the aspect of the moral dilemma of welfare reform that concerns children. If, on the one hand, child support is substantial, it would seem to relieve parents of the responsibility to work, a responsibility that is accepted by most other parents. If, on the other hand, child support is not substantial, it threatens to be unfair to children whose parents do not work. The second obligation of fair workfare addresses this dilemma.

MAKING WORK PAY

Providing substantial child support makes sense only if the wages of full-time work supplement rather than substitute for such support. Otherwise, the child support policy would discriminate against most working parents, leaving them with little more for their labor than they would receive for staying at home. For full-time work to supplement child support, it must pay enough to enable adults to lift their families out of poverty. What that level should be of course varies with the standard of living of the society and region, and within limits is a matter for determination by democratic deliberation. But considerations flowing from the opportunity principle suggest what some of those limits should be.

It is not only politically unrealistic but also morally unjustifiable to expect that governments should provide child support at levels sufficient to guarantee an adequate income to healthy parents who do not work. If child support were so generous that parents did not need to work, it would be expressing the mistaken idea that children are primarily the responsibility of government instead of parents. If government should not selectively deter people from having children, neither should it selectively invite people to have them. To maintain an equitable stance toward these important life-shaping decisions, public policy should ensure that full-time employment pays enough so that, combined with child support, work is a reasonable alternative for parents who have the dual responsibility of caring for their children and financially supporting them.

It follows that making work pay means ensuring that people who work full-time are not still poor, as measured by the conventional standards of our society at any particular time. Full-time work that keeps parents in poverty is unfair to both parents and children, depriving them of the possibility of adequate income support and adequate child care. A policy to make work pay would require a number of new programs, only some of which can be mentioned here. We have already given (in Chapter 6) some reasons why government should provide adequate health care to all citizens, but the imperative of making work pay adds yet another reason. Universal health care coverage is essential to basic opportunity because many Americans could not otherwise afford to work. Many low-income citizens who work do not receive the basic medical coverage to which they would be entitled if they did not work and were poor enough to be eligible for Medicaid. Just as any morally defensible interpretation of individual responsibility obligates healthy citizens to work, so fair workfare requires government to make sure that citizens do not lose their health care coverage simply because they are willing to work. It is unreasonable to expect people who work at the minimum wage to pay for their own health care coverage unless the minimum wage is raised to cover all basic living expenses plus the cost of health care.

To make work pay, the minimum wage could be raised, and perhaps even more effectively, the level of the earned income tax credit could be increased so that it yields an adequate income. A great advantage of tax credits that can be converted into refunds is that they subsidize low incomes without stigmatizing citizens, invading their privacy, or limiting their freedom, as the present welfare system tends to do.[67] The aim of an earned income tax credit is straightforward: to ensure that citizens who work full-time can earn enough to support themselves and their families.

Making work pay in these ways is also necessary to prevent single parents with young children from having to make a choice between outside work and child care. When citizens have both obligations, on any reasonable interpretation of the basic opportunity principle, public policy should not force them to choose to fulfill only one. Parents of young children should not be expected to work when the jobs they can get pay less than welfare, especially when welfare itself does not provide enough to cover child care and the other expenses of work. Many parents on welfare supplement their payments with unreported wages in order to make ends meet.[68] Both welfare in its traditional form and low-paid workfare on the Wisconsin model in effect force poor parents to jeopardize their own well-being and that of their children for the sake of a moral obligation that should have no force unless work provides an adequate income.

The dilemma of outside work versus child care could be avoided, it might seem, if child support payments were set high enough that single parents of young children did not have to work. Then it might not matter so much whether work paid adequately. But, as we have emphasized, the opportunity principle places an independent value on work; it gives independent reasons for obligating citizens to work and thus for obligating the government to try to make sure that work pays.

But then, it might be argued, parenting should be regarded as a form of work that should be compensated. It is certainly no less demanding and no less socially valuable than many other kinds of labor. The fact that most parents voluntarily undertake it, and receive satisfaction from doing it, does not distinguish it from other work for which people are paid. Part of the reason to resist the idea of paid parenting is that taking care of one's own children is rightly regarded as part of an intimate and loving relationship in which financial compensation is inappropriate. It is as if we were to demand wages for caring for our spouse, or for our senile parents. The compensation seems to deny the intrinsic value of the relationship.

Yet, as we acknowledged in the discussion of contract parenting in the previous chapter, receiving pay for a service or talent does not necessarily undermine its intrinsic value. That great artists are paid for their work does not make the product of their work, or even the work itself, any less worthy. But in the case of parenting there is a further, more mundane reason that tells against compensation. There is no adequate way for government to assess the quality or quantity of the work that a parent does in caring for a child. The problem is less the difficulty of formulating adequate standards of care than the undesirability of the procedures necessary to ensure that the standards are being met. The procedures would almost certainly be highly intrusive, thereby violating the value of privacy.

Whether the income takes the form of compensation or child support, it has a further disadvantage if it substitutes for adequately paid work. Parents who drop out of the job market for many years to care for children have a difficult time finding decent work when they try to reenter. They are likely to join the ranks of the persistently unemployed, and endure the indignities and suffer the lack of self-respect that such status brings. Moreover, their own status is bound to affect the psychological attitudes, social standing, and future opportunities of their children. Children who grow up with unemployed parents are therefore likely to be disadvantaged relative to children who grow up in low-income households where at least one parent works outside the home.

Thus, an acceptable policy of income support should try to ensure that when citizens go to work instead of the welfare office, they bring home a paycheck that (together with child support, tax credits, and other benefits) enables them to support themselves and their family at least up to the poverty line. The opportunity principle establishes this lower limit on wages so that work pays, while acknowledging an upper limit on benefits so that leisure does not pay more than work.[69]

MAKING WORK AVAILABLE

It is not enough to make work pay if the work that pays is not available for some citizens who need it. Under such circumstances, these citizens should not be obligated to work as a condition of receiving adequate income support. The availability of jobs that pay a decent wage is necessary not only to justify a work requirement but also more broadly to mitigate various forms of discrimination that would violate the opportunity principle. Because of child-rearing patterns in this country, women are disproportionately hurt when job opportunities are limited. Because of residential patterns, poor blacks (who live where unemployment rates are typically highest) also disproportionately suffer the effects of inadequate employment opportunities. It would seem, then, that the opportunity principle should require a backup welfare system for those who are involuntarily unemployed and for the children who depend on them. But such a system itself creates problems for the opportunity principle that may be worse than the one that it is intended to solve.

A permanent welfare policy for the involuntarily unemployed may be unfair to citizens who manage to find full-time work but would prefer to stay home rather than work for wages just slightly above what they could receive on welfare. It would not be unfair so long as the welfare recipients were genuinely trying and failing to get work, but eventually many would be likely to lose the confidence and motivation to continue to do so. In these circumstances it would be hard in practice to distinguish the voluntarily from the involuntarily unemployed, and low-paid workers could reasonably complain that the welfare policy was unfair to them.

If unfairness toward working citizens who earn only a minimal income were the only problem of a permanent welfare policy, then perhaps the policy could be justified as the lesser unfairness. All citizens, and especially children, would be guaranteed basic opportunity, though at the cost of some inequity toward some hard-working lower-income citizens.

But there are three other problems with a backup system. Each reproduces a familiar defect of the policies in Wisconsin and many other states. First, such a system creates incentives not to work. The incentives are even more troublesome than in traditional welfare policy because they have to be set at a higher level. Second, to prevent some citizens from taking advantage of the system, the government must continually collect information from all recipients to confirm that they are trying to find jobs. The resulting bureaucratic activities are likely to be not only costly but also intrusive and demeaning. Third, even if the system provides adequate income support for the involuntarily unemployed, it offers no help in regaining the social standing necessary for the exercise of democratic citizenship. (We discuss this connection between fair workfare and equal citizenship the final section of this chapter.)

These problems can be avoided, or at least mitigated, if welfare reform includes an extensive program of job creation. The lack of such a program is the most conspicuous deficiency of Wisconsin's Work-Not-Welfare plan.[70] To the extent that public policy succeeds in encouraging the growth of employment opportunities, the need for a backup welfare system is reduced.[71] Under these conditions, maintaining the work requirement as a condition of receiving income support is less likely to cause unfairness to the involuntarily unemployed and their dependents. The job creation program would have to be combined with some transitional support in the form of continuing education, job training, and unemployment insurance. But, unlike the backup support in a permanent welfare system, these forms of assistance could be designed to help the unemployed return as quickly as possible to the work force and at the same time develop their capacity to exercise the rights and fulfill the duties of political citizenship.

THE RESIDUAL OBLIGATION TO WORK

Suppose that all three of these conditions of workfare were satisfied. It would then be fair to expect all healthy adults to work in order to receive adequate income support, and it would then be fair for all who were willing to work to expect such support. A policy of workfare would thus almost resolve the dilemma of the obligations of welfare with which we began. The "almost" alludes to an aspect of the dilemma that still persists. Assume that some parents refuse to accept employment, thereby depriving their dependent children of adequate income support as well as the social standing that comes with having a parent who has a job. How should the government treat them? If the government gives these parents enough income so that their children will not suffer, it in effect licenses some citizens to ignore their obligation to contribute their fair share. But if the government declines to support these parents, it fails to carry out the obligation that all citizens have to protect the basic opportunities of children.

The most straightforward way to resolve this dilemma is to force these parents to work in order to support their children.[72] This requirement is even more stringent than the unconditional obligation to work favored by libertarians. Since it is imposed for the sake of the children, not as a condition of receiving income support, it justifies making parents work even if they would be willing to forgo welfare for themselves. This comes close to a policy of forced labor, to which libertarians rightly object, but it may be justified if it is the only feasible way to get parents to support their children. The alternatives are morally worse. Maintaining the parents on welfare is unfair to those who work, and denying them welfare is unfair to their children. Worse still would be prohibiting welfare recipients from having children or putting their children in orphanages. If a policy of fair workfare were in place, parents would have no good reason to refuse to work, and the government would probably have to enforce the obligation to work only rarely. But the residual power to enforce that obligation on behalf of all citizens should be acknowledged by any adequate opportunity principle.

From Work to Empowerment

Defending the family cap plan in the New Jersey legislature, Representative Bryant declared: "I want to empower people. I'm not telling people they can't have more children. I'm saying, I see [welfare] as a transitional system, not a permanent one . . . So if it's transitional I can set some rules: Get educated, get job trained . . . If you decide to enlarge your family, you must be willing to go out and work for it."[73] Bryant introduces into the debate an important and neglected value—empowerment—one that should have a central place in any income support policy in a democracy. But his use of it is doubly inappropriate. First, as we have already noted, there is good reason to believe that family cap plans limit rather than expand the basic opportunity of welfare recipients, and do so in a discriminatory manner. Denying welfare recipients basic opportunities available to more affluent citizens can hardly count as empowerment. Second, Bryant's use of the first person ("*I* can set some rules") unwittingly reveals an authoritarian approach that runs counter to efforts to give welfare recipients a voice in the making of the rules and policies that affect them. It expresses a top-down approach to empowerment in which the means of reform may frustrate its end.

Empowerment is a critical aim in deliberative democracy. If citizens are to participate effectively in deliberation, they must enjoy basic opportunities that include adequate income and decent jobs. They would not otherwise have the social and economic resources to exercise their obligations as democratic citizens. The demands of deliberation are not modest. But simply giving these citizens the resources they need in a manner and in a form that the government or other citizens think appropriate is not likely to empower them. The resources may fail to achieve their purpose because those who provide the resources may not understand the needs of those who are supposed to benefit. And even if their needs are met, the beneficiaries lose an opportunity to develop the political skills that would enable them to participate more effectively in other political decisions. They remain passive recipients of, rather than active participants in, the politics that shape their lives.

Welfare reform thus seems to face a bootstrap dilemma. To exercise their political liberty, citizens need basic opportunities. But unless they take part in securing those opportunities themselves, they are not likely to develop the capacity to exercise this political liberty. Can the process of reforming welfare policy be consistent with the aim of empowering citizens? To answer this question, we first consider how fair workfare could empower citizens who are economically disadvantaged, and then turn to the question whether the process of designing fair workfare can itself contribute to empowering citizens who do not yet enjoy their fair share of political liberty.[74]

EARNING AS EMPOWERMENT

Workfare can contribute to empowerment if the policy recognizes, as Judith Shklar emphasizes, that "earning is like voting."[75] Although most citizens take for granted the right to vote and the opportunity to get a job, both are essential to social dignity. Because earning is not only a means of making a living but also a mark of equal citizenship, democratic governments empower citizens by making a "comprehensive commitment to providing opportunities for work to earn a living wage for all who need and demand it," Shklar writes. The effective opportunity to earn a living wage "may not be a constitutional right or one that the courts should enforce, but it should be a presumption guiding our policies. Instead of being regarded as just one interest among others, it ought to enjoy the primacy that a right may claim in any conflict of political priorities."[76] Shklar's explication of this political dimension of work provides a further justification for the obligation to work, and also points to the need for a more comprehensive workfare policy to ensure that available work makes a positive contribution to political empowerment, or at least does not make a negative one.

Fair workfare can help secure the equal standing of citizens in any society such as ours, in which social respect depends on being an " 'earner,' a free remunerated worker, one who is rewarded for the actual work he has done . . . He cannot be a slave or an aristocrat."[77] Neither, we should add, can "he" be a woman who has no chance to earn her own living if she needs to do so. On this understanding, women who are not by choice but by necessity economically dependent on their spouses also lack the equal standing of citizens. Each of the conditions we have suggested for fair workfare should be understood as implying policies that would discourage gender discrimination in welfare policy. To that end, they are likely to require substantial changes in the workplace as well as in welfare policy.[78] The social importance of earning is thus one feature of fair workfare that empowers citizens while at the same time securing an adequate income for them. Unlike the family cap or unconditional workfare, it does not deprive any citizen of basic opportunities or discriminate against those who are economically disadvantaged.

Some may think that the connection between work and citizenship rests on a set of beliefs—a "Jacksonian web of ideas"—that is "irrational and unfair." Public policy must take these beliefs into account because they are "enduring and deeply entrenched," but they have no other moral justification.[79] But we showed earlier that accepting the work requirement for income support is based on an obligation to contribute one's fair share to a cooperative scheme from which one expects to benefit. That moral justification may be extended to political citizenship. Those who benefit or wish to benefit from the political process have an obligation to participate in that process, and therefore to develop their capacities to do so. One of those capacities is the acquisition of the social respect that work brings.

By the same token, other citizens and the government that acts in their name have a corresponding obligation to create and maintain the conditions that would make effective participation possible. In this way work becomes part of the process that enables citizens to face one another more nearly as equals in the political forum, and thereby to engage in the kind of politics that would more nearly satisfy the principles of deliberative democracy.

PARTICIPATING AS EMPOWERMENT

The process of designing and implementing a policy of fair workfare cannot presuppose that welfare recipients are politically empowered. That has to be one of the major aims of workfare itself because, in the United States today, the poor are politically weak. Citizens who are poor participate in politics far less frequently than more affluent citizens.[80] They also have fewer informal means of influencing public officials. Although the poor themselves may not yet be in a position to create their own workfare program, legislators could still try to design a program that grants the poor more power in its administration and revision in the future. Legislators could also make greater efforts to solicit the views of the poor in the design of the program itself.

If the aim of creating institutions that guarantee the fair value of political liberty is justified, then—other things being equal—so is the choice of a more empowering process of design and implementation for fair workfare. The "other things being equal" proviso implies that if legislators have good reason to believe that involving welfare recipients and the working poor in the process would produce a significantly less beneficial outcome, then choosing a less empowering process could be justified as a transitional measure.

But legislators have good reason to believe just the opposite. Most legislators know more about, and tend to identify more readily with, their more affluent constituents. Legislators therefore stand to learn from a process that involves welfare recipients and the working poor. One welfare mother who was a member of the Welfare Rights Organizing Committee put her complaint about Work-Not-Welfare this way: "We're the ones living in the system, and even though they're the ones implementing the system, they need to come out and talk with us about what could get people off of welfare, like providing child care and better wages."[81] Even if legislators already know that a fair workfare plan must provide higher wages and effective access to child care, they may find a better way of providing these basic opportunity goods if they seek the views of welfare recipients. In the same way, both legislators and administrators may also discover means to improve the system if in their continuing evaluation of workfare programs they actively involve the citizens who are most affected by the programs.

Unless public officials encourage the participation of economically and educationally disadvantaged citizens on a regular basis, they are also likely to develop a morally skewed view of the priorities of workfare. Recent efforts toward welfare reform in the United States have favored achieving short-term savings to taxpayers over making work available and making it pay. Welfare recipients and the working poor are more likely than middle-class citizens to call these to the attention of both officials and the public. From a reciprocal perspective, the short-term tax savings on workfare are often short-sighted, but this perspective is not likely to be sustained in democratic politics unless welfare recipients and the working poor have an effective voice in the democratic process.

Drawing more disadvantaged citizens into the process of welfare reform and workfare policy-making could be both a short-term and a long-term antidote to what Wisconsin representative Riley called "this poor-bashing thing." More extensive participation should also moderate what Riley rightly identifies as one of the causes of poor-bashing—the fact that the poor "don't vote and they don't fight back" as much as more advantaged citizens. "That makes them easy targets."[82] The point is not that the poor should seek more power so that they can take their rightful place among the other interest groups jostling for influence in democratic politics. It is rather that an increase in power—an enhanced opportunity for political participation—is necessary to ensure that their views receive a fully informed and vigorous presentation in democratic deliberation.

Although participation is important not only to keep workfare fair but also to help empower citizens, it may not always have these effects. Poor citizens are especially vulnerable to the familiar dangers of participatory politics—in particular, the risk that they will be coopted to lend legitimacy to unjust policies, and the risk that they will become further disillusioned with politics when their voice is disregarded. But to the extent that poor citizens come to see that they are having an effect on welfare reform, and to the extent that they can develop habits of political deliberation, participation should contribute to empowerment. Poor citizens will come to secure the benefits of deliberation that we suggested in Chapter 1 all citizens should expect to enjoy in this kind of democratic process. Furthermore, by making more vivid a view that should be part of the reciprocal perspective, poor citizens help their fellow citizens to learn better "to weigh interests not [their] own," one of the important advantages that Mill ascribed to deliberation.[83] Ensuring the fair value of political liberty for the poorest citizens thus becomes a morally effective means of its own realization for all citizens. Empowerment through participation is a basic opportunity that from a reciprocal perspective all citizens could accept in deliberative democracy.[84]

The longer it takes to empower the least advantaged citizens, the harder it is likely to be. Perceptions of political impotence tend to intensify over time, as the prospects for influencing the course of welfare reform appear to diminish. This downward spiral further erodes the social respect and political liberties of those very citizens whose deliberative voices are most needed to press public policy in the direction of greater social justice. These consequences should be especially troubling to deliberative democrats, and provide further reason to give high priority to finding a justifiable policy of income support.

We have suggested that the best hope for reconciling the conflicting obligations of welfare is to be found in a policy of fair workfare. In a deliberative democracy, not only are the benefits and burdens that the policy distributes important, but so too are the ways in which the policy is created and sustained. The policy of fair workfare favored by the principle of basic opportunity includes not only an obligation to work and an obligation to provide conditions that make work acceptable, but also an obligation to respect and enhance the political capacities of citizenship. The fairness of workfare turns on its content as well as on the conditions of its creation and reformation. In Wisconsin those conditions fell short of what deliberative democracy demands. Although Senator Moore spoke forcefully for the poor, she did not claim that her presence in the legislature could substitute for the empowerment of poor people themselves. The policy that the legislature adopted neither advanced that aim nor fulfilled the obligations of welfare. The legislature did not guarantee child support, make work pay, or make work available.

—9—

The Ambiguity of Fair Opportunity

THE twenty-five-year-old white male employee whose criticism of affirmative action at AT&T we quoted at the beginning of Chapter 1 was concerned about his chances for "moving up in the company."[1] He believed that to promote women and blacks with less experience in the company ahead of him was simply not fair. He was not demanding some minimum level of an opportunity good such as health care or income; he was asking for a fair chance at a better job. To assess his complaint, we move beyond the principle that governs basic opportunity goods such as those discussed in the previous chapter, and consider the principle that regulates the distribution of opportunity goods to which citizens do not necessarily have a right.

Prominent among these goods are skilled jobs. Although having a job may be necessary for living a decent life, having the job that best suits one's talents or satisfies one's highest aspirations is not.[2] But because having a job that suits one's talents or aspirations is an important part of what citizens reasonably seek in their quest for a good life, they should be able to compete for these jobs on fair terms. Determining whether the way in which jobs are distributed is fair is thus an important task of public policy in a deliberative democracy. It is the purpose of the fair opportunity principle to provide some guidance in this task. The principle holds that government should ensure that each citizen has a fair chance to secure opportunity goods such as advanced education and skilled employment. What the principle requires in practice depends on what fair opportunity means in the context of any particular opportunity good. When considering a policy on skilled jobs, citizens encounter a conflict within the principle itself, or more precisely between two interpretations of it. Clarifying that conflict is the principal challenge that this chapter addresses.

On what we call the liberal interpretation (or the liberal principle), fair opportunity requires that jobs should go to those who are most qualified. This is simply a process of fair competition. According to the liberal principle, what counts as fair for the purpose of distributing jobs does not vary with the distribution of basic opportunity goods such as education and income. On what we call the egalitarian interpretation, fair opportunity permits or requires that some jobs go to those who are most disadvantaged, or at least to those who are relatively disadvantaged among those who are basically qualified. The failure of a society to distribute basic opportunity goods justly, according to the egalitarian interpretation, makes a difference in how skilled jobs should be distributed. When background conditions make it much harder for some people to compete for skilled jobs than others, then public policy should give an advantage to disadvantaged citizens in the competition. This amounts to a process of preferential hiring, which favors a basically qualified person of a relatively disadvantaged race or sex over a more qualified person of a relatively advantaged race or sex.

The contrast between the two interpretations of fair opportunity is not well described by saying that the first requires only equality of chances while the second demands equality of outcomes.[3] Both refer to processes of distribution, and both propose criteria, not quotas, for filling jobs. The most practical way of implementing preferential hiring may be to require that the composition of the work force contain certain proportions of women or minorities. But the principle underlying the policy refers only to the qualities of applicants which a fair process should consider in distributing jobs.

In order to determine what makes opportunities equal, the egalitarian interpretation looks deeper into the social and historical background conditions than does the liberal interpretation. But defenders of the liberal principle need not simply ignore these conditions. They may call for government to live up to its basic opportunity principle—to provide adequate education, income, health care, and housing for currently disadvantaged citizens—instead of altering the terms of fair opportunity. Although the egalitarian interpretation offers a challenge to this response in the name of fairness, the liberal interpretation, when tied to other redistributive policies, has a strong claim to be included in a deliberative perspective. This chapter narrows the conflict between liberal and egalitarian interpretations of fair opportunity, but also recognizes the reasonable disagreement that remains for democratic deliberation to resolve.

The conflict between liberal and egalitarian interpretations of fair opportunity can be seen in the contrast between the complaint of the young AT&T employee and the statement by the management of the company defending their policy of preferential hiring (also quoted at the beginning of Chapter 1). Under pressure from the Equal Employment Opportunity Commission and other agencies of government in the early 1970s, AT&T agreed to a plan that would give women and minorities preference in hiring and promotion. The management did not admit that the company had discriminated against women and minorities, but agreed that the only way to end the effects of social discrimination was to hire more women and minorities "at a pace beyond that which would occur normally." The plan included a provision that required the company to hire and promote blacks and women over better qualified white men for as long as blacks and women were not represented in the company in proportion to their numbers in the labor force. This provision meant that some white males who would have been promoted lost out to less qualified blacks or women, some of whom had just been hired. This is what led the employee who cried "not fair" to complain that "I work for the company but my chances are less than someone on the street."[4] The plan thus enhanced the opportunities of some (such as those on the street), but diminished the opportunities of others (some of those in the company). Whose opportunities should take priority?

We use the case of the AT&T settlement to examine the responses that may reasonably be offered by liberal and egalitarian interpretations of fair opportunity.[5] We choose this case partly because it was the "largest and most impressive civil rights settlement in the history of this nation."[6] The settlement with Ma Bell was the mother of them all. It set the pattern for many other major settlements, including those with General Motors and Sears, hundreds of administrative actions by the EEOC and state agencies, and influenced several lines of judicial decisions that are still shaping ongoing law in the area of employment. Because it was the first major case, it also presents the issues in particularly sharp relief. The disputants had not yet learned how to obscure their moral differences by pretending that they agreed on values but disagreed only on facts.

We pursue the meaning and implications of fair opportunity in three stages. In the first section of the chapter we argue that fair opportunity generally implies a policy of nondiscrimination in the distribution of jobs.

In the second section we assess the strongest claims of those who argue that nondiscrimination is not enough, and call for a policy of preferential hiring. Some of these claims go further than a deliberative perspective should accept, and others do not go far enough. In the third section we show how a defense of preferential hiring that appeals to the value of nondiscrimination itself can satisfy deliberative standards. Preferential hiring is not without its moral costs, however. Neither is the alternative of simply giving equal consideration to all qualified candidates. Striking the balance between these alternatives is a task for further deliberation focused on particular policies that may combine elements of each under specific social conditions.

Fair Opportunity as Nondiscrimination

When a company advertises that it is an "equal opportunity employer," it is not claiming that it will make sure that all job applicants have the same chance to be hired or, once hired, the same chance to rise in the company. "Equal" in any defensible principle of opportunity does not imply that the life chances of each citizen must be equalized with respect to any good that is not basic. Equal implies only that opportunities should be fair, in some as yet unspecified sense.

Why should a deliberative perspective reject an interpretation of fair opportunity as a demand for equalizing life chances? One reason is implicit in the basic liberty principle. The freedom to raise children is a basic liberty, and even though it is far from unlimited, this freedom precludes the kind of government intervention that would be necessary to equalize life chances. So long as some parents devote more attention and resources to their children than other parents do, children will not have equal life chances.

A second reason to resist this interpretation of fair opportunity is that it sacrifices too many other values in the pursuit of an ideal of equality. Imagine a society that succeeds in satisfying a more modest principle of fair opportunity. In this society each citizen enjoys an adequate level of all basic opportunity goods and competes on fair terms for other opportunity goods, such as skilled jobs, which are not basic. No one lacks adequate health care, education, and security, and no one is discriminated against in the competition for jobs and other similar goods. Under these conditions, how should citizens regard a demand from one member of society that the government make his life chances equal to those of the most advantaged members? Even if he were willing to claim the same on behalf of other citizens in his position, and even if he acknowledged the limits set by basic liberty, his fellow citizens might still reasonably regard his claim as carrying equality further than justice requires.[7] To be sure, much of what others have may not be deserved, but that in itself is not a sufficient basis for requiring a general equalization of life chances without regard to specific opportunities.

If fair opportunity does not mean equal life chances, or even equal chances for jobs and other similar goods, it does imply fairness in the sense of providing the same chance to receive a social good to all those who satisfy the appropriate criterion for its distribution. In the case of jobs, the most obvious relevant criterion is the applicant's ability to do the work. Fair opportunity then requires that each qualified applicant receive equal consideration for the job. This in simple terms is the liberal principle of fair opportunity, the main aim of which is to prohibit discrimination.

RELEVANT QUALIFICATIONS

Two distinct parts of the principle should be recognized—one referring to *relevant qualifications* and the other to *equal consideration*. First, the principle requires that the qualifications for an office be relevant to the social functions of the job. Jobs are privileges or powers that should benefit society, and job qualifications should try to ensure that those who hold them will effectively serve that social function.

In the years before AT&T instituted its new employment policy, no one could be hired as a switchman in some divisions without first passing a weight-lifting test. Only men became switchmen. At Southern Bell a female employee, Lorena Weeks, who presumably could not lift weights or did not care to try, wanted the job. She challenged this requirement, arguing that weight lifting was not a relevant requirement for the job of switchman. There was no evidence that switchmen needed to do heavy lifting in order to do the job effectively. Southern Bell was forced to abandon the requirement, and Lorena Weeks became a switchman.

Discriminatory tests like these are only the most dramatic instances of the ways in which qualifications can block the opportunities of women and minorities. Such practices lead some critics to be skeptical about any use of "qualification" in applying a principle of opportunity. They argue that most criteria are not neutral or technical, and most have built-in normative and cultural biases, often favoring already advantaged groups in society.[8]

No doubt many jobs call for several different kinds of skills, talents, and attributes, including some (such as an ability to get along with co-workers) that cannot be described in technical or completely objective terms. Because qualifications have normative and cultural dimensions, citizens cannot rely entirely on experts or officials to set them. Determining qualifications raises issues that require democratic deliberation, and call for wider participation by citizens and workers.[9] But from the fact that qualifications are not always obvious or objective, it does not follow that they are entirely arbitrary, that any qualifications will do for any job, or that if they are set by workers themselves, they will necessarily be consistent with fair opportunity. The primary qualifications, those that should receive the greatest weight, are often clear enough; minimum standards can be specified, and plainly irrelevant standards rejected. In choosing doctors, medical competence should certainly count a great deal, and good looks should not count at all. Similarly, telephone repair workers should be hired and promoted primarily on the basis of their ability to maintain telephone equipment, not on the basis of their race or gender.

The liberal principle does not completely preclude considering race or gender as relevant qualifications. Just because these are ascriptive rather than earned characteristics does not mean that they should be regarded as irrelevant. People do not earn their height either, but being tall is certainly a relevant qualification for being drafted to play in the NBA (though not of course a sufficient or primary one). Race or gender is rarely a primary qualification for a job, but sometimes these may be among the many considerations relevant to assessing how well a person is likely to serve the social function of the particular job. In choosing doctors for a battered women's shelter, gender may be relevant, and in choosing doctors for inner-city clinics, race may be relevant, if these characteristics are correlated with effective performance of the job. Because these characteristics are not the most relevant qualifications, however, this broadening of the criterion of relevance does not necessarily open the door to a practice of hiring primarily or generally on the basis of race or gender. The liberal defender of nondiscrimination refuses to go that far. The egalitarian advocate of preferential hiring is not so averse to such a practice.

EQUAL CONSIDERATION

For most jobs, like that of Southern Bell switchman, there are more qualified applicants than openings to be filled. No applicant has a right to a job simply because he or she is qualified for it. Whenever there are more qualified candidates than positions, a further requirement is needed to govern the process of deciding among qualified applicants. Not only must the qualifications be relevant to the social function of the job, but all qualified candidates must also be given equal consideration.

We say equal *consideration* in order to avoid a common misunderstanding. Sometimes applicants may claim that they deserve a job, and that they have been denied fair opportunity if they fail to get it. Such a claim ignores a simple distinction between the right to a job and the right to an opportunity for the job. The distinction is important because, although each qualified applicant deserves to be considered fairly for the job, no one deserves the job itself (in the absence of any special promises, contracts, or the like). This distinction has been supported from many different philosophical positions.[10] It is therefore well suited for a deliberative perspective, which welcomes the convergence of different arguments on the same moral claim.

What does equal consideration require? The answer depends in part on the nature of the job in question, and whether the employee is seeking to be hired, promoted, retained, or compensated. In general, all qualified candidates should have roughly the same chance to present their credentials with regard only to the qualifications of the job.[11] This is inevitably vague, but it is definite enough to rule out certain practices and to require others. After Southern Bell removed its long-standing weight-lifting requirement for switchmen, it could not then decide to fill the position by inviting only men to apply. It could not favor the sons and daughters of retired switchmen, or those who belonged to the local Democratic party.

But neither would it have been sufficient for Southern Bell simply to announce that anyone could apply, even if it then gave all applicants equal consideration. The legacy of past discrimination—the fact that women had not been allowed to apply in the past—continued to influence who would apply now. Women might still not apply because they assumed that the managers and even fellow workers did not think that this was the kind of job a woman should have. Equal consideration therefore requires that employers, especially those with a history of discriminatory hiring practices, take steps to inform their potential applicant pool of the new, nondiscriminatory qualifications for positions, and make further efforts to encourage those who have been excluded in the past to apply in the future.

Measures such as these constitute a policy of affirmative action, which includes virtually all efforts short of preferential hiring that are intended to ensure equal consideration for women and minorities. The distinction between goals (or targets) and quotas tracks the difference between affirmative action and preferential hiring. Goals are predictive estimates used to measure progress in an employer's effort to implement a nondiscriminatory hiring policy. Quotas are fixed numbers of positions that are reserved for members of certain groups. Although critics and even some defenders of preferential hiring claim that this distinction collapses in practice, it need not do so if the government and employers work to maintain it.[12] Employers who use goals and those who use quotas follow quite different policies, standing on different sides of an important moral divide.

AT&T used quotas in hiring women and minorities, although its Model Plan misleadingly called them "goals" or "targets." During each of the six years in which the plan was in effect, AT&T held a specific number of places in each designated job category for minorities and women, regardless of whether better qualified white males applied. If AT&T had really used goals, the company would have followed quite a different course. It would first have calculated the number of women and minorities that it would be likely to hire if its employment practices were actively nondiscriminatory. To carry out this calculation, the company would have estimated the percentage of women and minorities in the available pool of qualified candidates for management positions, and then multiplied these estimates by the number of open positions in each of the next six years. The product of this calculation would have been the yearly goals of affirmative action employment over the following six years, which the company would have met only if it could have done so without hiring less qualified over more qualified candidates.

Some critics of affirmative action believe that the distinction between goals and quotas cannot in any event be maintained in practice. They would argue that if AT&T had tried to implement a policy of affirmative action, the company would have experienced pressure, both internal and external, to turn goals into quotas. It would then have found itself hiring less qualified women and minorities just to meet its goals, thereby turning them into quotas. To show that it was making enough progress toward nondiscrimination, the company would have been driven to a policy of preferential hiring like that which the plan imposed. This is mere speculation in the case of AT&T, and it turns out to be no more than that in the case of other companies as well.[13]

The critics typically do not present any systematic evidence to support the claim that goals tend to become quotas.[14] One argues that although "there has not yet been a case where good faith efforts [to meet goals by nondiscriminatory means] have not been accepted [by the government], . . . this ignores the cases in which they have been exceeded."[15] But few institutions exceed their goals for hiring women and minorities; many fall short. There are no systematic studies showing that the pressure on most employers is overwhelmingly in the direction of preferential hiring. Given the culture of most corporations and the exigencies of the market, employers such as AT&T are at least as likely to feel internal and external pressure against preferential hiring as in its favor. They also face strong incentives to hire and promote the most qualified applicants.

THE SIGNS OF DISCRIMINATION

With the requirements of relevant qualifications and equal consideration in place, the liberal principle makes a strong statement against discrimination. It provides a potentially powerful tool for criticizing employment practices and prescribing a broad affirmative action policy. But its actual power in deliberation depends on finding an acceptable criterion for identifying discrimination. In theory it should be clear enough what counts as discrimination, but it is not so clear in practice. To justify a charge of discrimination, does one have to find a discriminatory intent on the part of the employer, or is disproportional effect enough? And can one establish discriminatory intent by pointing to disproportional results—such as fewer women hired for a position than men, or a smaller number of blacks than whites hired relative to their proportion in the general population?

The broad claim that disproportional results can prove discrimination is relatively easy to dismiss. Even in a society that did not discriminate against anyone, statistical differences in job preferences and qualifications might be found between women and men, blacks and whites, and many other social groups. Women may simply want certain jobs on average more than men, and vice versa. The same may be true for blacks and whites, and members of various religious and other ethnic groups. Even in the absence of discrimination, these differences in preferences could produce significant statistical differences in the distribution of some offices by gender, race, religion, or ethnicity. Individuals may legitimately make career choices on the basis of a wide variety of factors, some of which may be associated with their gender, racial, religious, or ethnic identity.

If statistical differences in hiring women or blacks do not prove discrimination, might they still provide some evidence of discrimination? This question is harder to answer. In defending itself against charges of gender discrimination before the settlement, AT&T pointed to the fact that more than half its total work force was female. This use of statistical evidence was misleading because it obscured the great gender differences that existed between job categories. Telephone operators, secretaries, and clerical staff, which made up a large percentage of AT&T's work force, were overwhelmingly female, whereas women held only 1 percent of the career management positions in the company. In general, women, along with disadvantaged minorities, held a far smaller proportion of high-level positions at AT&T than their representation in the population at large. Sex segregation by job at AT&T was also greater than throughout the country as a whole.

The disproportionately large concentration of men in high-level positions and women in low-level positions is a suspicious sign, but by itself does not establish that the company discriminated against women. It is possible, as AT&T pointed out in its own defense, that women's career preferences just differed from those of men. Fewer women wanted careers in the high-level positions, AT&T argued, and it was not up to AT&T to try to change those preferences; failing to do so does not make the company guilty of discrimination.

In their defense against a charge of discrimination several years later, Sears made a similar argument, attributing the disproportionate number of men in certain positions to the fact that men prefer to take more risks than women. The argument seemed to draw support from those feminists who argue that women should not demand equal treatment in the sense of the same treatment, but instead should respect the differences between men and women. But as other feminist critics have pointed out, even the feminists who emphasize difference do not have to accept the dichotomy between equality and difference that the Sears argument seems to pose.[16] Different women have different preferences, and denying a woman a fair opportunity either to take a "male" job or to follow a "female" career is discriminatory.

But most women did seem to follow traditional "female" careers at AT&T and Sears. To sustain their argument, neither AT&T nor Sears needed to claim that women freely chose these career preferences. They could argue (with some feminists) that the career patterns are the result of a socialization process in a discriminatory society that implicitly sends women the message that they are subordinate to men and should choose their careers accordingly. These sources of discrimination lie deep within the society, in institutions such as the family and the schools, over which even large companies such as AT&T may have relatively little influence.

This argument is sound as far as it goes, but it does not go very far. Suppose we grant that other institutions in society are the deeper or more important cause of discrimination. AT&T still may be contributing to the discrimination—even directly contributing to it. The statistical patterns that do not provide sufficient evidence of discrimination may nonetheless be grounds for a further investigation that would turn up sufficient evidence, or would at least leave the controversy open to reasonable claims on both sides of this question. Citing the patterns becomes the first step in a process of seeking the information that would determine whether discrimination took place.

Such an inquiry would closely examine the personnel practices of the company. It would not be necessary to find actual instances of deliberate discrimination—evidence that a manager intentionally denied someone a job or a promotion on grounds of sex or race. The aim would be to identify some widespread and persistent practices in the company that had serious discriminatory effects and were not necessary for the conduct of the business of the company. What should count as a business necessity is of course a matter of judgment, and therefore is itself an appropriate subject for deliberation. Statistical disparities can point to discriminatory personnel practices which in turn can prompt a rexamination of assumptions about what is necessary for the company to succeed in its business. In the case of AT&T, the underrepresentation of women and minorities in high-level positions became a clue that led to the discovery of a wide range of practices that together constituted evidence for a compelling case that, whatever its intention, AT&T discriminated against women and minorities. Some examples will illustrate the kinds of evidence that should count toward a charge of discrimination in such cases.

· *Unequal pay for equal work.* A craft position called "frameman" was open only to men. In one of its divisions, Michigan Bell, a position with exactly the same job description was open only to women. It was called, significantly, "switchroom helper." Framemen were paid more than switchroom helpers.

· *Exclusionary testing and promotion procedures.* By offering different entry tests to men seeking craft positions and women seeking operator and clerical positions, AT&T made it all but impossible to compare the qualifications of male and female applicants. The testing procedures prevented women from demonstrating that they were as qualified as men, or better qualified, for the craft positions. Furthermore, nearly all management positions were filled by promotions from the craft positions, almost all of which were held by men.

- *Differential response to similar complaints.* When women operators complained about low pay and few promotion opportunities, a company report viewed the complaints as originating with "problem girls." The report recommended changes in hiring procedures to discourage applications from women who were looking for "glamorous careers." When the same kind of complaints came from male workers, another report recommended that their promotional opportunities be improved, their wages increased, and their jobs better tailored to their skills.

The first part of AT&T's agreement with the government was designed to compensate those employees who, the government charged, had been victims of discrimination. The agreement constituted about as clear a case as one can expect to find for compensation based on the liberal principle of fair opportunity. No doubt some women and blacks were never hired and therefore not compensated. Some AT&T staff were probably owed promotions, not just back pay. But many of the victims of discrimination in this case were identifiable: women and minorities who had been passed over for promotions or paid less than white men for the same work. AT&T gave more than fifty-thousand individuals compensation amounting to a total of over $75 million.

AT&T also agreed to change many of its policies on recruitment, transfer, and promotion, which the government had branded as discriminatory. The company abolished separate hiring offices, separate tests, and different job descriptions for women and men, blacks and whites. The company also revised job qualifications to reflect the actual functions of the positions. It instituted equal pay for equal work, and instructed its managers to make working conditions equally hospitable to all employees regardless of their gender or race. (It went so far as to instruct managers not to say "Thanks, sweetie" to female employes—unless they also said the same to male employees.)

Although some aspects of this part of the settlement were contested (and still might be), most now seem fully justified under the liberal interpretation of fair opportunity. Indeed, this part of the settlement is a paradigm case of implementation of the liberal interpretation. Faced with this kind of evidence of discrimination, a fair opportunity principle could do no less than call for what AT&T agreed to do in this part of the settlement of this case.

But should a principle of fair opportunity demand more? Specifically, should it require, or at least permit, the policy of preferential hiring that constituted the second part of the settlement with AT&T? The government and others who favored preferential hiring argued that compensating victims of past discrimination and ending discriminatory practices for the future did not go far enough. Because the effects of past discrimination in the company and in the broader society persist, they suggested, any effective policy must take additional measures to ensure that women and minorities have fair opportunities at AT&T. The most important such measure was to hire and promote women and minorities faster than they would have been hired and promoted under a policy that merely prohibited discrimination.

But preferential hiring is not simply an additional, stronger measure. On its face it conflicts with the liberal interpretation of fair opportunity, which supports the first part of the settlement but does not permit giving preference to less qualified individuals. To determine how serious this conflict is, we need to explore more fully the second part of the settlement and the egalitarian interpretation of fair opportunity that makes sense of it. Then we can better show how a deliberative perspective can accommodate both parts of the settlement and both liberal and egalitarian interpretations of fair opportunity, suitably qualified.

Fair Opportunity as Preferential Treatment

Because preferential hiring creates this potential conflict, citizens should be reluctant to adopt it if they can find other policies that are less problematic but would still adequately fulfill the goals of fair opportunity. The most promising candidates are all those policies that together would satisfy the basic opportunity principle. These include policies that would provide adequate educational opportunities for all children, and basic health care coverage, employment opportunities, and income to the extent necessary to give everyone—regardless of their race, gender, or relative place in the income distribution—the effective opportunity to compete on fair terms for skilled jobs. The strongest case against preferential hiring makes the claim that public policies should concentrate on creating these basic opportunities for all members of society. Both liberals and egalitarians can favor some version of each of these policies, which together would relieve the pressure on preferential hiring.

Fulfilling the demands of the basic opportunity principle establishes background conditions that are necessary for a fully fair competition for skilled jobs. Liberals and egalitarians can agree on this, but the liberal argument against preferential hiring goes further. It rejects preferential hiring policies on the grounds that there is generally a decisively better alternative: fulfilling the demands of the basic opportunity principle and practicing nondiscrimination in hiring (according to the liberal interpretation of the fair opportunity principle). The liberal criticism of preferential hiring raises two questions that do not have obvious answers. First, would fulfilling the basic opportunity principle make preferential hiring unnecessary even in the short run? Second, would preferential hiring be justified by showing that the basic opportunity principle is not fulfilled? Appreciating the difficulties in answering these questions will show that, even if the liberal criticism of preferential hiring has much truth, deliberative disagreement about preferential hiring persists.

THE LIMITS OF EDUCATION AND INCOME

If educational opportunities were more nearly equal and income more nearly adequate for the least advantaged members of our society, then citizens could compete for jobs on fairer terms. There would be much less need to intervene at the later stages of the opportunity chain to compensate for unfairness in the earlier stages, and therefore there would be fewer of the moral conflicts that later interventions inevitability create (for example, between legitimate expectations and compensatory demands). If government works diligently for the "educational and economic development of disadvantaged people, regardless of race," it will not need to turn to preferential hiring, which attacks "one form of discrimination with another."[17] Public policies should concentrate on creating equal opportunity in education, along with income redistribution, job training, and health care.

There is much value in this approach, as our discussion of the basic opportunity principle suggests. A high level of elementary and secondary education is certainly a basic opportunity good for almost all citizens. Without it, access to a decent job is difficult and fair competition for a good job impossible. Employment opportunity therefore cannot be equalized until all children are far better educated than they are now. Basic opportunity in education is thus certainly necessary for fair opportunity in employment.[18] An equally powerful case can be made for fair workfare being necessary for fair opportunity in employment. Without fair workfare, which guarantees work that pays and child support to every adult who is willing and able to work (and a basic income to those individuals unable to work), some children will be unfairly disadvantaged in competition for jobs. Similarly, adequate health care and physical security are also necessary conditions for fair opportunity in employment.

Yet all these conditions may not be sufficient, at least in the short run, to make preferential hiring unnecessary. Even if these reforms improve the opportunities for citizens in the future, they may not do enough for citizens in the present, particularly those who have already experienced substantial discrimination on the basis of race and class. Given this problem plus the difficulty of instituting these reforms and their uncertain effects, the present lack of fair opportunity will probably persist for a long time. In the meantime, so long as the basic opportunity principle remains unfulfilled or only partially fulfilled, fair opportunity will be a hollow promise for millions of citizens. Advocates of preferential hiring can reasonably claim that it tries harder to make good on that promise right now, at least for some disadvantaged citizens.

Meanwhile, the continuing denial of fair opportunity has secondary effects on the children of the current generation. These effects point to a second reason why improving basic opportunities is not likely to be enough. The lack of fair employment opportunities for some adults makes it extremely difficult to provide adequate education for their children. Children of parents disadvantaged in employment are likely to be disadvantaged in education. The effects of past discrimination can persist in this cyclical way indefinitely. Preferential hiring intervenes directly—more directly than even massive income redistribution—to break this cycle, and thereby increases the likelihood that education will be more effective in the next generation.

A third reason why we may not be able to rely on basic opportunity to the exclusion of preferential hiring is related to the problems of limited resources and limited generosity. To achieve the background conditions of education, income, health care, and physical security that would make the competition for skilled jobs fair, and therefore consistent with the liberal interpretation of fair opportunity, government would have to invest more public resources than it is likely to be able to command with the consent of citizens. A democracy should do as much as it can to secure basic opportunities, but no society has yet achieved a level of abundance, let alone generosity, that would enable it to supply every basic opportunity good to the extent necessary to make the competition for skilled jobs fully fair. This provides no excuse for citizens to rest content with what they are now doing to secure basic opportunities for those who are less advantaged than they are. But it does suggest why basic opportunity alone cannot resolve the controversy over preferential hiring.

By itself, preferential hiring certainly does not satisfy the demands of fair opportunity. It cannot substitute for securing the basic opportunities that are background conditions for fair opportunity. But preferential hiring may be a morally necessary, or at least a defensible, supplement to these essential efforts. From a deliberative perspective, the less adequately a society fulfills the demands of basic opportunity, the more defensible the policies of preferential hiring become.

Even if the demands of basic opportunity were fulfilled, there would be yet another reason to defend preferential hiring. We have been focusing on basic opportunity goods, such as elementary and secondary schooling. But a relevant qualification for many high-status, highly paid, and highly valued jobs in society is success in higher education. As long as this is so, providing an adequate level of basic education for all black Americans, for example, will fall significantly short of realizing fair opportunity in employment on the liberal interpretation. If the government tries to equalize the opportunities of blacks in higher education, it runs into the same problem that the liberal critics of preferential hiring are trying to avoid. Just as elementary and secondary education is a basic opportunity good like health care, so higher education is a (non-basic) opportunity good like discretionary employment. The principle of fair opportunity as nondiscrimination governs the distribution of places in higher education just as it should govern the distribution of jobs. If citizens adopt preferential admissions in higher education in order to overcome discrimination in employment, they merely move the problem of preferential treatment from the sphere of employment to that of higher education. They still must face the problem of whether preferential treatment is justified. Basic opportunity goods, including education and income, are essential background conditions for fair opportunity, but they offer no escape from dealing directly with fair opportunity in employment.

PREFERENCES AT AT&T

We therefore return to the most controversial part of the AT&T Model Plan—the scheme of preferential hiring. The plan set hiring and promotion quotas (misnamed "targets" or "goals"), which corresponded to the proportions of women, blacks, and Hispanics in the relevant labor force. The explicit purpose was to achieve proportional representation of women, blacks, and Hispanics in fifteen job categories over a six-year period. To meet its "goals," the plan reserved places for women and minorities: " To the extent that any Bell System operating company is unable to meet its intermediate targets . . ., the Decree requires that . . . selections be made from any at least basically qualified candidates for promotion and hiring of the group or groups for which the target is not being met."[19]

The plan required the company to pass over the most qualified applicants in order to achieve proportional representation of women and blacks in most job classifications; in the case of equally qualified candidates, the company would have to pass over those with longer company service. This was called an "affirmative action override," but it clearly went beyond affirmative action, understood as measures designed to increase the pool of qualified women and minorities and ensure that they receive fair consideration in hiring and promotion. The override constituted a policy of preferential hiring.

The override was the core of the most extensive government-sanctioned program of preferential hiring ever carried out by an American company.[20] During the six-year period of its operation, the program applied to some 800,000 workers, and led to an estimated 50,000 cases of preferential hiring. When AT&T eliminated the override in 1979, the company had achieved roughly proportional representation of women and blacks in its top job classifications. It had also increased the representation of men in clerical and operator positions by a parallel policy of reverse preferential hiring, which passed over more qualified women in order to hire men for these lower-level positions. As a result of this policy, a female records clerk, Bertha Biel, applied for a promotion to the position of operations clerk but lost out to a man hired from outside because the company had not met the targets for male representation in these positions. Bertha Biel could also say, "This is not fair."[21]

Can this kind of policy be accepted from a deliberative perspective? We have already suggested that this perspective requires at least a policy of nondiscrimination. The strongest justification for preferential hiring would then try to show that it is compatible with nondiscrimination.[22] We now consider whether such a justification can succeed by examining the two distinct elements of preferential hiring, which correspond to—and potentially conflict with—the two elements of the nondiscrimination policy.

The first element of preferential hiring addresses the criterion of *relevant qualification*. Making race or gender the basis for hiring and promoting employees seems to violate the nondiscrimination principle by setting qualifications that are not relevant to the social function of the job. But most proponents of preferential hiring define social function so broadly that race and gender come to be treated as almost always relevant qualifications. Furthermore, they adopt a threshold rather than a comparative standard for satisfying the other qualifications, such as technical competence, that the nondiscrimination standard emphasizes. Instead of appointing the most qualified, a preferential hiring policy would appoint those who are basically qualified. In combination, the broad understanding of social function and a threshold standard for qualifications have the effect of making race or gender the decisive (and in this sense a primary) consideration in employment policy for applicants above the threshold.

The second element of preferential hiring deals with the status of the persons who are to be hired or promoted. Applicants or employees are considered on the basis of their membership in a group, rather than as individuals. This element therefore seems to go against the requirement of *equal consideration.* Proponents of preferential hiring, however, try to show that equal consideration of individuals requires taking into account the effects of past discrimination, which in turn requires taking into account the group identities of applicants and employees.

GENDER AND RACE AS RELEVANT QUALIFICATIONS

Some critics might object to using gender or race as qualifications at all on the grounds that all racial qualifications, even those that favor members of disadvantaged races, are inherently invidious. But in moral terms this would be a mistake. As Ronald Dworkin argues, there is no standard of merit, no set of skills or talents, independent of the social function of the job: "If quick hands count as 'merit' in the case of a prospective surgeon, this is because quick hands will enable him to serve the public better, and for no other reason. If a black skin will, as a matter of regrettable fact, enable another doctor to do a different medical job better, then that black skin is by the same token 'merit' as well."[23] Dworkin admits that this argument may strike some as "dangerous," but this is "only because they confuse its conclusion—that black skin may be a socially useful trait in particular circumstances—with the very different and despicable idea that one race may be inherently more worthy than another."[24]

Nonetheless, this general defense of using race and gender as qualifications does not confront the question of the extent to which its use is justified in particular cases. In what ways could gender and race count as relevant qualifications? Two different arguments need to be distinguished. One is an argument from the social function of the job, which we already discussed briefly when we introduced the liberal principle of nondiscrimination. The other is an argument from the need for role models.

Because of the nature of some jobs, setting race or gender as a qualification may help serve the social function of the job. Some jobs may be better performed by blacks and women. Black teachers, for example, may be more effective than white teachers with black students, or black police officers may be more effective than white officers in the black community. Whether this argument is valid in any particular case depends on empirical evidence. Sometimes the argument seems to be correct, although the evidence is often scant. In the early 1970s many school boards in large cities began appointing black principals who would not have qualified under the standard examination. The boards bypassed the normal appointment procedures because they believed that the largely black student body would learn better if some blacks were in positions of authority. The available evidence is uncertain but consistent with the claim that the discipline and respect which are necessary for effective teaching were in fact strengthened in some of these schools.[25]

In other instances the functional argument is less certain. In the famous *Bakke* case it was used to defend the admissions policy of the University of California at Davis Medical School, which gave preference to black and Hispanic Americans over otherwise more qualified white students.[26] Defenders of the University of California Regents argued that being black or Hispanic is a relevant qualification for being a doctor, and therefore for being admitted to medical school, because the black and Hispanic communities need to have more doctors. But the Regents' defenders offered no evidence that black and Hispanic graduates of medical schools actually do go on to serve the black and Hispanic communities more than do doctors of other races. This may be the case, but the functional argument depends for its strength on evidence, not speculation.

The functional argument, consistently applied, is double-edged. It may support hiring women, blacks, and members of other disadvantaged groups in preference to white males, but in a society still marked by discrimination it may also support just the opposite. Its sexist-racist edge tends to show itself more often. In a sexist or racist environment, evidence may very well show that being white and male will help one do a job more effectively. A white male supervisor at AT&T, for example, may command more respect from racist and sexist co-workers who do not want to work for blacks or women, or who believe that only white males should be in positions of authority.[27]

One way to avoid this implication is to argue, as Dworkin does, that these factors should not count at all because they are based on "external preferences," which refer to "the assignment of goods and opportunities to others."[28] If external preferences are counted, some citizens will enjoy greater standing than others; those who have preferences about what others should be assigned as well as what they themselves should receive will have twice as much weight as those who express preferences only about what they should receive. To preserve the value of political equality, Dworkin argues, external preferences must be discounted. If they are, then the racist and sexist edge of the functional argument is blunted. AT&T customers or workers who want to deal with white men because they have contempt for women, blacks, and Hispanics are expressing external preferences. Their preferences, which in effect imply that white males should have greater liberties and opportunities in employment than other people, should not count at all.

These examples are misleading, however, since they suggest that Dworkin's argument excludes only those external preferences that are distasteful to proponents of preferential hiring, when it actually excludes all external preferences, including the external preferences of black men and women who want to work for black men and women, and women who want to work for women. These preferences must also be discounted, according to this argument, just like the preferences of white men who want to work only for white men. Every preference that is parasitic on any moral judgment—right or wrong—about the relative social value of associations among individuals of different groups, whether they be whites, blacks, or women, must be excluded (on this argument) because it entails double-counting.

A black woman may choose a black woman for her physician simply because she finds that relationship more comfortable, or more appropriate for her needs. Such choices express personal preferences. But many other reasons she may have for choosing a woman physician would not count. That she admires women for their success in a largely male profession, or that she wants to encourage more women to become doctors, or that she thinks society would be better if more men and women chose women doctors—these are all external preferences, and would have no weight in determining public policy. Neither would analogous reasons that some people might have for preferring persons of a different race or sex. A white man's preference for a black doctor could also be external, based on considerations of social justice that also entail double-counting.

Because an external preference is any preference for assigning goods and opportunities to others, the functional argument remains double-edged even if one adds a proviso that excludes external preferences. A more defensible distinction might be to permit morally benign but not morally pernicious external preferences. But then the question arises, what is the basis of the distinction between morally benign and pernicious preferences? The strongest answer takes into account their consequences. Morally benign preferences are those that move society closer to a condition in which nondiscrimination in hiring would no longer be unfair to members of disadvantaged groups. Morally pernicious preferences move society away from such a condition. The defense of this distinction is parasitic on the argument for preferential hiring that we pursue in the next section: preferential hiring at its strongest is a means of moving toward a society in which nondiscrimination would work the way the liberal principle mistakenly assumes that it already works. The functional argument is now subordinated to another, quite different consideration: the use of hiring policy to move toward a just society.

In its strict form, the functional argument for favoring women and minorities is quite limited in its application. It does not apply to the vast majority of jobs in society for which women and minorities compete at a disadvantage. It is doubtful that it applied to many if any of AT&T's 800,000 jobs. No one who defended the AT&T Model Plan claimed that the job of AT&T manager or craft worker would be better performed by women or blacks because of their sex or race.

Perhaps because it is so limited in its strict form, some of its defenders try to stretch the idea of function much more broadly so that it includes every consideration of social justice that could be used in favor of hiring members of disadvantaged groups. Doing a good job might be taken to mean doing as much as possible to bring about a society of fair opportunity. But stretching the notion of function this far threatens to eliminate the very problem that puts preferential hiring on the political agenda in the first place. The excessively broad idea of social function obscures the distinction—and potential moral conflict—between two quite different personnel policies: one that fills positions with people who can best carry out the specific social functions of a job, and another that overrides job qualifications for reasons of social justice largely unrelated to carrying out those functions. In an ideal society the distinction would not be important because the conflict would not exist. In our society it is a problem that cannot be eliminated by stretching a concept in the hope that it will somehow span both sides of the moral disagreement.

The second argument for treating race or sex as a primary qualification emphasizes the importance of role models. To be a role model is to serve as a positive social symbol of success, communicating by one's visibility and the importance of one's position that younger people who share the same characteristics can aspire to hold similar positions. If young blacks and women see adults of their race or sex in skilled positions, the argument suggests, they will be more likely to strive to succeed and eventually to hold such positions themselves.

Some critics of this argument grant that women and blacks need role models, but insist that private institutions such as corporations and universities do not have an obligation to provide them. Judith Jarvis Thomson (herself a defender of preferential hiring) argues that providing role models is an incidental service rather than a central function of these institutions. She draws an analogy with athletics in universities. No doubt it is good for university students to be offered opportunities for physical exercise, but there is no reason to think that universities should be required to provide facilities for athletics, or taxpayers required to pay for those facilities. Thomson does not deny that universities may legitimately support athletics, much as they provide health services or career counseling for students. But she insists that students have no right to such services in the way that they have a right to an adequate education.[29]

The analogy with athletics in universities is too weak to carry the argument, however. Unlike the athletic prowess of the faculty or teaching staff, its sexual and racial composition is not simply an optional service, an add-on to the educational mission. The racial and sexual composition may convey a message relevant to educational opportunity. An all-white or all-male teaching staff may tell students that blacks and women cannot become teachers, and this runs contrary to one of the explicit messages that teaching is supposed to convey in a society committed to fair opportunity. Teaching should convey to all students that they have a chance, by studying hard and gaining the relevant qualifications, to achieve positions of respect in society. Their hopes must start where they are, and where they are is in school.

This message is urgent in a society like that of the United States, which has historically subjected women and minorities to systematic discrimination in the educational system itself. A public school staff or a university faculty without athletic role models does not express an anti-athletic message by its very composition. The faculty may look like wimps, and actually be wimps, but students have no trouble finding their athletic role models elsewhere. Role models in the educational system are more credibly and closely connected to later success and are therefore more directly related to fair opportunity.

To the extent that role models have a positive effect on educational and occupational opportunities, the role model argument for making gender and race relevant qualifications for some positions is powerful. In some circumstances it can convert what would otherwise be a case of preferential hiring into a case of nondiscrimination. When role models are sufficiently important, gender and race become relevant qualifications, and giving preference to women and minorities over white men is not discriminatory. Nevertheless, the role model argument is still deficient in ways that parallel the limitations of the functional argument.

First, the role model argument may support what is commonly known as tokenism in personnel policy. AT&T needed to hire only a relatively few women and minorities in various management and other high-level positions to accomplish the purpose of encouraging other women and minorities to believe that they too could aspire to high-level positions. Even if the need for women and minority role models is important in American society, it can be satisfied by hiring and promoting far fewer women and minorities than the number who would be hired and promoted under a preferential hiring plan like the one that AT&T carried out. The tokenism could even be counterproductive if the appointed candidates are perceived as less qualified than others and therefore as negative rather than positive role models. Whether and when tokenism backfires is an unresolved empirical issue. But in any case, once role models exist in each important job in an institution or a profession, the force of the role model argument for considering gender and race as relevant qualifications is exhausted.

Another aspect of the tokenism of the role model argument is its tendency toward elitism. Even if it could be shown that many more minorities and women are needed as role models in some positions, the argument would be most applicable to the upper-status levels of society, such as executive positions and the professions. The role model argument loses much of its force when applied to the recruitment of women and minorities into less prestigious positions. Critics of AT&T did not argue that the company should hire more minorities as telephone operators because they would be role models for young people who would otherwise fail to aspire to be telephone operators. Opening up access to such positions for minorities is no less an important social goal than opening up higher-status positions.

A second limitation of the role model argument arises from the same double-edged tendency that plagues the functional argument. To hire role models for telephone operators, secretaries, and clerical staff, AT&T had to give preference to men, not women. This form of reverse preferential hiring faithfully follows the logic of the role model argument, and from a reciprocal perspective should be seen as a strength of the argument. Men were needed in these traditionally female occupations in order to show other men that the occupations are worth pursuing. In general, on this argument, being male could be regarded as a relevant qualification for any kind of job that is by tradition exclusively or predominantly female, such as elementary school teacher, nurse, telephone operator, or secretary.

This reverse effect—the preference for men over women—is not a reason to reject the role model argument, but it does reveal its limits as a means of benefiting those social groups that are generally disadvantaged or discriminated against. In the AT&T case the net result was a plan that gave preference to more men than women. There were simply more lower-level positions without male role models than there were upper-level positions without female role models. Consequently, not only did many women fail to benefit from the plan, but also many, like Bertha Biel, believed that they were wronged by it. Their claims have merit in a deliberative perspective.

REMEDYING PAST DISCRIMINATION

Because both the functional and role model arguments are double-edged, they do not provide a stable defense for hiring only—or even primarily—members of disadvantaged groups. This may be why in practice these arguments often turn into quite a different argument, one based on remedying the effects of past discrimination. An exchange during a congressional hearing illustrates how those who try to argue that race and sex are relevant qualifications tend to be driven to appeal instead to the effects of past discrimination. Mary Gray, representing the American Association of University Professors, is making a case for giving special consideration to women and blacks in educational institutions:

Dr. Gray: The argument to the special relevance of race and gender as *qualifying* characteristics draws its strength from a recognition of the richness which a variety of intellectual perspectives and life experiences can bring to the educational program. Therefore I think you can consider what serves the needs of the institution and, in this case, that might require that you give special consideration to hiring more women.[30]

This is a version of the functional argument, but notice what happens in the course of questioning:

Rep. John Dellenback: And it would also be possible and proper in the reverse situation, if the decision-makers felt that the institution was better served by having a male president, to insist that it be a male even though there is an equally well qualified, or even academically superior, female?

Dr. Gray: What we are talking about is *remedying the effects of past discrimination* and we are not talking about general policies as to what people think is best and what people think is not best.[31]

Gray begins with the claim that gender is a relevant qualification because appointing more women and minorities "serves the needs of the institution." But when pressed to consider one of the double-edged implications of that standard of relevance—that it might justify hiring more men than women—she shifts ground. She then argues that sexual preferences are necessary to "remedy the effects of past discrimination." A deliberative perspective seeking the strongest defense of an egalitarian version of fair opportunity skips the first step in Gray's testimony and goes straight to the second. It turns from the double-edged functional argument to a single-edged argument based on remedying the effects of past discrimination.

There are two different ways in which public policy might remedy the effects of past discrimination, each of which corresponds to a different justification for preferential hiring. The first is an argument from *fair competition*. Public policy takes into account the effects of past discrimination in order to try make the present competition fair. AT&T's Model Plan, on this rationale, is trying to correct the competitive disequilibrium between men and women, and between blacks and whites, caused by the discriminatory practices of the company and the broader society in the past.

The second argument sees preferential hiring as repaying a *historical debt*. It looks to past discrimination for the purpose of compensating for injustice that has already occurred. AT&T's preferential hiring plan would then be viewed as offering compensation or reparations for the discriminatory wrongs that were committed in the past. The compensation is given without regard to its effects in the present or future (except as necessary to calculate its present value).

Both of these arguments are reasonable attempts to satisfy the equal consideration requirement of nondiscrimination. In effect, both say that equal consideration requires taking into account the past because its lingering effects unfairly disadvantage women and minorities in the present. Both arguments also recognize that our social history is one of injustice in employment. Neither necessarily rests on the claim that active discrimination continues today, but both assume that women and minorities still suffer from the effects of past discrimination. This is a plausible assumption in our society. AT&T's history of discrimination against women and minorities may differ in significant ways from that of other companies, but the general patterns of discrimination reviewed earlier are not unique to AT&T. The patterns of unequal pay for equal work, discrimination by irrelevant qualification, exclusionary testing and promotion practices, and differential response to similar complaints were common among American businesses.[32] Moreover, the effects of those patterns of discrimination on employment opportunities for women and minorities were widespread, not limited to those citizens who were directly involved with the practices of discriminatory companies.

FAIR COMPETITION

The first argument for remedying past discrimination would compensate for the effects of past discrimination on the present competition for jobs. President Lyndon Johnson invoked this argument most dramatically in a major speech on civil rights. He used an analogy—life as a race—which bears a surprising resemblance to one used by Thomas Hobbes three centuries earlier.[33] Johnson asked his audience to

> imagine a hundred yard dash in which one of the two runners has his legs shackled together. He has progressed 10 yards, while the unshackled runner has gone 50 yards. How do they rectify the situation? Do they merely remove the shackles and allow the race to proceed? Then they could say that "equal opportunity" now prevailed. But one of the runners would still be forty yards ahead of the other. Would it not be the better part of justice to allow the previously shackled runner to make up the forty yard gap; or to start the race all over again? That would be affirmative action towards equality.[34]

A virtue of Johnson's analogy is that it provides the basis for a powerful reply to the white male who is denied a job as a result of preferential hiring. To the young AT&T worker who complains that "this is not fair," AT&T does not have to say that he was more responsible than any other citizen for the past injustice that its preferential hiring policy is trying to correct. AT&T only has to remind him that, as a white male, he stands to benefit from the past policy of gender and racial discrimination. In the absence of preferential hiring, he gains a competitive edge.[35]

To this extent the analogy of the race is helpful. But in other respects it is misleading. In a fair race all the runners start at the same time from the same line. Anyone who jumps the gun is disqualified, or the race must begin again. If competition for jobs is a race, it is a race that cannot be started over again. The race in which women and minorities have been shackled is life, and neither AT&T nor the U.S. government can restart that race. The best either could do would be to let the shackled runners catch up to where they would have been had they not been shackled.

But where would they have been? If the analogy is taken seriously, this question must be asked in all its complex particularity. Where would individual women and blacks have been in the race for positions at AT&T had they not been shackled? It is difficult to imagine how one might carry out the analysis necessary to answer this question. This task would run up against one of the fundamental sources of moral disagreement: incomplete understanding.

Along with the formidable practical challenge of answering any such complex counterfactual question, consider the counterintuitive moral implications of some of the answers that might be found. Suppose you are a white woman from an affluent family. You were valedictorian of your high school class. You attended Princeton, went on to Harvard Law School, and now you are a candidate for the position of legal counsel for AT&T. In deciding between you and a white male candidate, is AT&T supposed to determine how much more you would have accomplished by now had you not been handicapped by your sex? (They company cannot even rule out the possibility that you might have accomplished *less* had you grown up as a privileged white male.) Or suppose you are a black man with similar background and credentials. Should AT&T give you preference over a more qualified white candidate because you would have been even more qualified had you not been disadvantaged by your race? What if the white male candidate against whom you are competing in either case grew up in poverty, with indifferent parents who did not contribute to his education or self-confidence, while you grew up in affluence with attentive parents who supported you financially and psychologically?

The competitive argument has curious moral implications that few people would wish to defend. It justifies passing over not only the most qualified candidates of the advantaged sex or race, but also the most qualified candidates of the disadvantaged sex or race, if those candidates have not been the most shackled in the competition for jobs. On the competitive rationale, instead of giving preference to the most qualified women and minorities, AT&T would have had to offer jobs to less qualified women and minorities who happened to be the most heavily shackled in the competition for jobs. No one should want to follow the logic of the competitive argument this far. Jobs are not only or even primarily rewards for a winning a race. They are at least partly means of performing services for society. Trying to use jobs to correct a competitive disequilibrium tends to subordinate completely this social function of jobs. This is a moral as well as a practical mistake.

These difficulties reflect a more general problem with the competitive rationale. It calls for judgments about individuals, but preferential hiring applies to members of groups. AT&T and other companies that would follow this rationale would have to go beyond assessing how past discrimination has disadvantaged women or blacks as a whole, for it is not women or blacks as a group but individual women and blacks who are to be granted the competitive gains. If employers such as AT&T were committed to restoring a competitive equilibrium, they would need to look closely at the background of each individual candidate, rather than make generalizations based on sex and race. But this individual attention is exactly what preferential hiring policies do not encourage because they are based on group preferences.

Nor would preferential treatment based on economic class overcome this problem. It is no more individualized than preferential treatment based on race or gender. Whatever the merits of giving preference to people based on their family income or economic class, such a policy does not respect individual differences within groups or classes. A deliberative perspective could in principle consider measures that would give preference to individuals on the basis of the specific competitive disadvantages that are beyond their control. But preferential treatment of this individualized kind is extremely difficult to put into practice in general policies.

HISTORICAL DEBT

The second interpretation of remedying the effects of past discrimination—the argument from historical debt—avoids the difficulties of trying to rectify the terms of present competition for jobs. On this argument, preferential hiring helps restore the moral rather than the competitive equilibrium in our society. It compensates citizens who have suffered injustices by giving them a highly valued opportunity good—a job. A position of responsibility provides the victims of discrimination not only with income, prestige, and perhaps even some power, but also with self-respect, perhaps the most important good of all for victims of long-lasting discrimination.[36]

Some critics of preferential hiring have questioned whether jobs gained in this way are such a benefit after all, and specifically whether they enhance self-respect. Preferential hiring may have exactly the opposite effect, they argue, undermining self-respect by raising doubts about whether women and disadvantaged minorities are good enough for the jobs they receive. According to one critic, preferential policies, especially at higher levels, "can have a decidedly negative impact on the esteem of the [minority and female] groups, because it can lead to the general presumption that members of the beneficiary groups would not be able to qualify for such positions without the help of specific preference."[37]

Such an effect is no doubt possible, perhaps even likely, but what weight it should have against preferential hiring is a question worth more democratic deliberation than it has yet received. The effects on the attitudes of white males in the wider society are sometimes taken to be a decisive reason to reject preferential hiring, but a public policy that has some chance to ameliorate discrimination should not be abandoned simply because it is opposed by prejudicial attitudes. A more defensible, though also far from decisive, reason to reject preferential hiring would be evidence that the prejudicial reaction to the policy impedes the general aim of overcoming racial and gender discrimination more than the policy itself promotes it. But such evidence is now lacking.

If the concern is to nurture the self-respect of women and minorities, the intended beneficiaries of preferential hiring, then a less paternalistic response would show them more respect. An employer should permit them to choose whether they wish to accept the job and suffer the (alleged) loss of self-respect, or refuse the job and keep their self-respect. Of course, it would be better if these were not the only alternatives. It would be better if women and minorities were chosen, and perceived to be chosen, only on the basis of their qualifications, and if they then attained high-level jobs and promotions in significant numbers. But then the problems that preferential hiring are intended to address would have been solved.

This is not to say that the critic's argument from self-respect should be dismissed. Even if the individual women and minorities who are offered the advantages of preferential hiring accept the disadvantages that attend them, the advantages may not be worth the damage done to the self-respect of women and minorities, taken as a whole. Preferential hiring programs may have a detrimental effect on all those women and minorities who hold skilled jobs but are not themselves the beneficiaries of preferences. They may suffer a loss of self-respect because of a widespread misperception that they are in fact the beneficiaries of preferential hiring.

Equally troublesome is a related effect: the "self-reinforcing cycle of negative expectations."[38] The belief that minorities and women are not qualified for their jobs may cause managers to demand less of them, and co-workers and subordinates to expect less from them. Workers of whom less is expected may simply do less, and managers in whom their subordinates have less confidence may be less likely to succeed. The belief that blacks may be less competent, even if initially without any basis in fact, could eventually come to be true as result of this cycle. If preferential hiring causes these kinds of effects, it would not have much appeal from any perspective, liberal or egalitarian.

No one has convincingly established whether the cycle of negative expectations actually occurs, and if it does occur on what scale and at what employment levels, and whether once begun it persists, stops on its own, or can be easily arrested. Considerations like these call for democratic deliberation because the evidence is likely to remain ambiguous. In the absence of evidence, the more the intended beneficiaries of preferential hiring reject it on the basis of these considerations, the more reason we have to doubt the soundness of the policy.

A more definite critique of the historical debt argument for preferential hiring focuses directly on its moral justification for compensating victims of past injustices. The critique points to a difficulty in determining what kinds of discrimination should count and how much is necessary to qualify for compensation by means of job preferences. This critique points to a recurring problem with the underlying idea of preferential hiring—a tension between the individual and group claims that preferential hiring seeks to satisfy.

One important version of the egalitarian interpretation of fair opportunity would discount individual claims for compensation and therefore obviate the need to make complex determinations of compensation based on the nature and degree of past discrimination. This egalitarian argument for compensating groups has three parts.[39] First, some kinds of group membership constitute the identity of all individuals. Identification is a matter of degree, but it is likely to be stronger for racial, ethnic, and gender groups than in, say, avocational or alumni associations. In our society "blacks are viewed as a group: they view themselves as a group; their identity is in large part determined by membership in the group."[40]

Second, some of the kinds of groups that define individual identity in this way deserve special consideration in public policy. Black Americans are the paradigm. Their relatively low status and the long history of discrimination contributing to that status are characteristics that distinguish blacks from many other groups.[41] Furthermore, unlike the group called "the poor," blacks do not cease to be blacks when they rise in social status.

Third, the benefits of preferential treatment go primarily to the group, only incidentally to the individuals in it. This means that no individual within the group can complain when some members of the group receive more of these benefits than he does, even if he is more deserving according to the very criterion by which the group is entitled to receive the benefits in the first place. Preferential treatment for "rich blacks may be justified in terms of improving the position of the group . . . Members of that group have obtained these positions of power, prestige, and influence that they otherwise might not have and to that extent the status of that group is improved."[42]

Although each step of the argument may be questioned, the first two, suitably qualified, are less problematic than the third. It cannot simply be assumed that all members of a group benefit when the high-status members succeed. Even when this is true (for example, when role models help everyone in the group), it would not meet the objection of unfairness within the group (the fact that the most advantaged benefit the most). Even granting that a group as a whole can benefit (its status can be improved, its moral standing raised, its moral claim on society respected), citizens should still ask why benefiting the group in this way should matter morally more than compensating those members of the group who are most entitled to compensation based on the injustices done to them. How benefits are distributed within a disadvantaged group cannot be morally irrelevant, as this version of the egalitarian argument requires us to believe. Individual members of disadvantaged groups typically expect equal consideration, as both the liberal and the egalitarian principles, taken at their strongest, demand they receive.

REPARATIONS

Another approach, still egalitarian in spirit, seeks to respect the claims of individuals. This approach is favored by those who disapprove of preferential hiring but are sympathetic to its underlying aims. They propose instead a policy of monetary reparations. They believe that this policy avoids the problem of group-based claims in preferential hiring but still serves the egalitarian purpose of compensating citizens, particularly blacks, for the injustices they have suffered as members of the group. They offer two reasons why monetary reparations are a better form of compensation than jobs.

First, reparations are likely to benefit those who have suffered the most from discrimination. They go to the most disadvantaged citizens rather than to the most qualified, who benefit more under preferential hiring but who have generally suffered less from the effects of discrimination. A policy of reparations does not require that employers disregard the relevant reasons for distributing jobs or deny equal consideration to all qualified candidates.[43]

The second reason to favor monetary reparations over preferential hiring relates to the distribution of costs. In preferential hiring the costs fall on "the weakest or the next-weakest group. Unless one is prepared to give up the very idea of qualification, the costs cannot be distributed any further."[44] With a reparations program based on taxation, the costs could be far more fairly distributed. They would fall on the whole society, not as an expression of collective guilt, but simply as the fairest way to cover the costs of compensating individuals for an injustice when its agents can no longer be identified and moral responsibility no longer assigned.

Why then should citizens not choose a policy of reparations instead of a policy of preferential hiring? The former satisfies the essentials of the egalitarian principle without violating the liberal principle of fair opportunity. It would therefore seem to be just the kind of policy that a deliberative perspective seeks. This assessment of the moral merits of a reparations policy is sound, as far as it goes. But it does not go far enough to warrant rejecting preferential hiring unless a democratic government is actually prepared to institute a substantial reparations policy. Critics of preferential hiring have yet to offer any compelling reasons to reject preferential hiring when they lack a politically viable alternative to put in its place.

A deliberative perspective is committed to taking into account the actual conditions of moral disagreement in non-ideal societies. This commitment should not be confused with settling for a second-best policy if a morally better policy is achievable. Because the morally best policy is sometimes not achievable, a deliberative perspective must not reject a second-best alternative. To do so would privilege the status quo, which may be morally worse.

Even if a reparations policy were feasible, citizens still should not assume that it would make preferential hiring unnecessary, at least in the short run. Preferential hiring may still be required in the short run as a means of providing role models and making the competition for jobs fair for many citizens who have suffered from past injustices because of their group identity. A reparations policy would certainly be a morally important supplement to preferential hiring, and perhaps even preferable to it if the choice were between the two. Reparations would provide compensatory justice in its own right and also greatly increase the prospects of overcoming the historical injustices of racism in the United States. But even the best reparations policy might not be a sufficient substitute for preferential hiring. The two policies address different dimensions of the shared aim of overcoming racial injustice.

Although preferential hiring is more politically acceptable than reparations, the motives of many of those who prefer it are not entirely admirable. Preferential hiring is far less threatening than massive reparations to the political and economic power of more advantaged citizens. At AT&T the negative impact of preferential hiring did not fall on the top executives or the most affluent citizens.

The political appeal of preferential hiring leads some of its critics to take a cynical view of the motives of its advocates. Preferential hiring is not "displeasing to politically elected officials, to whom it provides the means of quickly accommodating the demands of organized groups. Nor will it displease the world of corporate and governmental employers . . . for whom the cost of hiring less qualified workers is often substantially less . . . than the cost of litigating."[45] However unattractive such motives may be, they actually serve, contrary to the critics who cite them, to strengthen the moral case for preferential hiring. The self-interested motives of some supporters make it easier to adopt a policy that may also be justified by the public-spirited reasons of a deliberative perspective. We have not found a conclusive justification for preferential hiring, but neither have we found an adequate alternative that addresses the entire problem and resolves the deliberative disagreement between advocates and critics. Proposals to pay reparations go far beyond what our society has ever come close to undertaking. But as long as efforts to secure basic opportunities for all citizens fall far short of satisfying the defensible aims of nondiscrimination in hiring, proponents of preferential hiring retain a strong moral advantage.

Preferential hiring has serious moral shortcomings, but it may be the best available means for advancing toward a more just society. The argument that supports this suggestion, to which we now turn, faces up to the present-day conflict between the liberal and egalitarian interpretations of fair opportunity but seeks to remove the conflict in the future by creating the conditions under which preferential hiring will no longer be necessary. The point of the argument is to try to sustain an economy of moral disagreement between liberal and egalitarian interpretations of fair opportunity.

Preferential Treatment as Nondiscrimination

"In order to get beyond racism," Justice Harry Blackmun once wrote, "we must first take account of race. There is no other way."[46] In order to get beyond racism and sexism, proponents of the Model Plan would say that AT&T must first take account of sex and race in their personnel policies. The general claim is that, among politically feasible policies, preferential hiring is necessary to overcome the effects of past discrimination and to achieve a society in which there exists fair opportunity for women and minorities. This kind of argument for overriding the liberal principle of fair opportunity is more promising than the others we have considered because it rests precisely on the value—nondiscrimination—that justifies the principle itself. On this view, a policy that violates the requirements of relevant qualification or equal consideration is now justified in order to create later a society in which those requirements can be satisfied without wronging any (or as many) citizens. In a deliberative perspective for distributing job opportunities, citizens should therefore consider whether and to what extent preferential hiring can be justified as a means of reducing discrimination in employment in the future.

Begin with the case of blacks, who have the strongest claim for preferential treatment of large groups in this country. If preferential hiring for black Americans is not justified, then it is not likely to be justified for women or any other large group. If it is justified for black Americans, then it may also be justified for other groups if their situation is similar enough in morally relevant respects. To build a case for preferential hiring for blacks, citizens should seek an economy of moral disagreement with critics of preferential hiring, and therefore should begin on some common ground on which both critics and advocates stand.

If this country did not have a history of racial discrimination, there would be no compelling reason to go beyond the liberal interpretation of fair opportunity. Many critics and advocates can agree on this point, which has an important moral implication. If black Americans did not suffer today from the effects of past (or present) discrimination, then they would have no claim to special treatment, or at least no claim sufficiently strong to override the liberal interpretation of fair opportunity. (Like any other group in society, they might ask for subsidies or privileges to protect or enhance their cultural identity, and these may be justified, but only if they did not violate principles of basic liberty and opportunity.) Even in the absence of a history of discrimination, a democratic society might still find it necessary to institute employment practices to prevent discrimination, and to ensure that jobs have relevant qualifications and that black Americans receive equal consideration. In a multiracial society it might be unreasonable to reject a policy of affirmative action as a means to guard against the future possibility of discrimination. But the step from affirmative action to preferential hiring requires at minimum a showing of past discrimination of a substantial and systematic kind. (Critics may claim that the step requires more, but they can agree that it requires at least this much.)

Critics and advocates should also agree that preferential hiring cannot be justified as a permanent replacement for a policy that gives equal consideration to all qualified candidates for jobs. Preferential hiring is at best justified as a temporary measure to advance toward a society in which it will no longer be necessary. Agreement on this point is significant, first, because some defenders of preferential hiring seem to deny that preferential hiring does any wrong at all.[47] Recognizing the temporary status of any justification acknowledges that preferential hiring involves a moral wrong, which is justified if at all only because it prevents a more enduring moral wrong.

Agreeing that preferential hiring can be justified only temporarily is also important for a second reason. It helps identify what any justification from a deliberative perspective needs to establish. It must show that equal consideration is not sufficient to create fair opportunity in society now. This might be because alternative policies are (like reparations) not fully feasible or (like affirmative action) not fully effective in making job opportunity fair. But it might also be because a policy of equal consideration actually undermines itself. Giving equal consideration to all qualified candidates amounts to discriminating against black Americans if the jobs are traditionally white, and if most blacks have never had much reason to think that they could effectively compete for them on fair terms. Any successful justification must also show that preferential hiring itself is more likely to achieve the aims of equal consideration in the future than alternative (feasible) policies. Here the advocates affirm and the critics deny that special treatment will break the cycle of deprivation and encourage young blacks to strive for better jobs in the next generation.

To agree that if preferential hiring is justified, it is only as a temporary measure, does not prevent one from arguing, as some critics would, that it is not justified even in this form. The agreement that at best the policy should be only temporary is nevertheless important in exposing the nature of the remaining disagreement, which turns out to be less moral than empirical.

Some critics of preferential hiring are skeptical of the advocates' claim that a policy of preferential hiring would be only temporary. They suspect that once begun, it would never end. But the success of the AT&T settlement shows that preferential hiring can be a temporary policy, and can help bring about a hiring policy that is nondiscriminatory. When preferential hiring ended after six years at AT&T, the work force probably looked more like it would have looked had racial and gender injustice not characterized our country's past. Just as important, after six years of preferential hiring, equal consideration reigned again in personnel decisions at AT&T.

Set aside for the moment the larger question whether AT&T's preferential hiring plan as a whole was justified and focus on the preferential treatment for blacks under the Model Plan. One of the advocates' strongest claims is that preferential hiring was necessary to break down the racial stereotyping of management and craft positions at AT&T. The advocates credibly claim that affirmative action alone—open search and selection procedures, extensive recruitment, and the like—would take a lot longer to erase the effects of discrimination, particularly the effects of stereotyping of positions. Giving equal consideration rather than preference to basically qualified black candidates would perpetuate stereotypes for an indefinitely long time.

So long as very few managers are black, the composition of the work force itself sends the message that black Americans do not "fit" into management positions as well as whites do. Blacks therefore are less likely to aspire to these positions, less likely to prepare themselves to serve in them, and less likely to be qualified for them. As the stereotyping persists, the few blacks who do win promotions to higher levels are seen as exceptions that prove the rule, role models only for the remarkable. Preferential hiring breaks down this stereotyping, directly and immediately, provided that the blacks hired and promoted perform reasonably well. At AT&T they did. (The company was also very profitable during the period when the Model Plan was in effect.)[48]

Does this kind of argument for preferential hiring of blacks extend to women as well? If one of the strongest cases for preferential hiring rests on its capacity to eradicate the stereotyping of positions, then the case for preferential hiring of women for many jobs parallels the case for black Americans, and is in principle just as strong. The discrimination that generates the stereotypes may be less severe and extensive in the case of women, but for those positions that are affected, it is no less an obstacle to fair opportunity. Management and craft positions at AT&T were stereotyped by gender as well as by race, and for similar reasons. Like many other employers, AT&T had systematically discriminated against women as well as minorities in recruitment and promotion to high-level positions. Had AT&T simply stopped discriminating, the sexist stereotyping of these positions would have lasted indefintely. The Model Plan radically increased the proportion of women and minorities in craft and management positions in a period of six years, thereby ending the tendency created by past discriminatory practices that marked some positions as exclusively male and others as exclusively female.

From a reciprocal perspective, this argument for preferential hiring has the additional advantage of not being biased toward the claims of women and minorities over men. It supports preferential treatment of men when necessary to break down the gender stereotypes created by past discrimination. AT&T's Model Plan gave preference to men for those positions, such as telephone operator, clerk, and secretary, from which they had been traditionally excluded. Although these paid less than many of the traditionally male positions, many men were eager to fill them. In an economy of less than full employment, men welcomed the opening of a vast number of new positions for which they could compete. The strongest defense of preferential treatment therefore is double-edged—but with an important twist. The purpose of giving preference to men in lower-level positions traditionally occupied by women is not only, or even primarily, to help men. Giving preference to men in these positions served to raise the status of the positions and to make a policy of equal pay for equal work more likely for both men and women.

In these ways the AT&T policy successfully mounts both steps of the strongest argument in favor of preferential hiring. At the time when AT&T instituted its Model Plan, equal consideration would not have been sufficient to provide fair opportunities to blacks and women. AT&T's preferential hiring policy was also far more likely to achieve (and in fact did achieve) the aims of equal consideration in the near future than the alternative of no preferential hiring. Had AT&T instituted a policy of only equal consideration in the early 1970s, it probably would not be in a position even today to provide fair opportunities for blacks and women. Under any reasonable assumptions of job turnover, the time it takes to break racial and gender stereotyping of jobs is significantly longer without preferential hiring than with it.

Whether other companies in other times could meet this test is an empirical question, though it is of course one informed by moral considerations. And moral considerations, we have indicated, can lead critics reasonably to reject even the strongest argument for preferential hiring, at least in the abstract. Because the case for or against preferential hiring is often a morally close one, the justification of specific policies should not be decided in advance of actual deliberation. In such a process citizens can consider the particular context of the policy, letting moral considerations of fair opportunity shape the inquiry into the facts of the case, and letting the facts help shape the policy. Although the facts are critical, they alone do not determine the question whether preferential hiring is on balance the best available policy.

We have offered a two-step argument for preferential hiring of the kind that AT&T instituted in its Model Plan. We have also recognized that, given the enduring uncertainty about the effects of preferential hiring, some critics might reasonably reject even the best preferential hiring plan. What critics cannot reasonably claim, however, is that the choice is between a morally pure policy of nondiscrimination and a morally tainted policy of preferential treatment. The choice before our society is instead between two morally imperfect means of attempting to end discrimination. This was the dilemma that AT&T faced, and the one that many companies still face in the non-ideal society in which they operate. In these circumstances the choice of a policy that best satisfies the demands of fair opportunity is much more difficult than it would be in a more nearly ideal society.

It is therefore not reasonable to reject preferential hiring simply on the grounds that it wrongs some citizens. On the most defensible alternatives to preferential hiring, some (other) individuals are also subjected to a moral wrong, and these citizens are among the least advantaged in our society. Because of the continuing effects of past discrimination, no employment policy, even the most justifiable, can avoid wronging someone. Given the multiple dimensions of the moral balance sheet, citizens should not rule out in advance the possibility that preferential hiring is the morally preferable policy. Whether it is and if so what form it should take are questions that, within the limits of the constitution of deliberative democracy, must be left to actual deliberation.

Preferential hiring is a morally questionable means to the morally obligatory end of fair opportunity in employment. Both liberals and egalitarians can agree that the means are questionable, and that the end is obligatory. Some liberals may find the means so objectionable that they should never be used, and some egalitarians may find the means so valuable that they should be used indefinitely. (On a radical egalitarian view, preferential treatment of disadvantaged citizens may be justified regardless of whether it is necessary to prevent discrimination in employment in the future. It is justified to correct for all inequalities, even differences in talent and temperament.) But if liberals and egalitarians are to deliberate within the constraints of reciprocity, they need to acknowledge both the moral wrong that preferential hiring imposes on some citizens and the moral obligation that fair opportunity imposes on society.

The strongest criticism and the strongest defense of preferential hiring both fall within the range of deliberative disagreement. Under non-ideal conditions, advocates and opponents may disagree about whether public policy should protect the claims of the most qualified or promote the claims of the least advantaged. They may also disagree about how long is too long to wait for achieving the kind of society in which these claims could be reconciled. Yet they can agree that they should seek at least this kind of society, whatever else they may also desire.

A deliberative perspective leaves more scope for reasonable disagreement than either the conventional liberal or egalitarian interpretations of preferential hiring admit, and therefore more scope for wider differences in employment policies than the conventional views suppose. But this perspective also imposes on citizens a greater obligation to account for their choice of policy than they usually assume. Justifying a policy of preferential hiring or a policy of nondiscrimination requires giving reasons to those citizens most disadvantaged by the policy—reasons that they can respect even if they deliberatively disagree with them. In the process of considering these reasons, all citizens can come to understand better the moral meaning and policy implications of fair opportunity.

Conclusion

WHEN democratic citizens morally disagree about public policy, what should they do? They should deliberate with one another, seeking moral agreement when they can, and maintaining mutual respect when they cannot. That in the simplest terms is the answer we have defended in this book. To justify this answer, we developed a complex conception of democratic politics—deliberative democracy—that gives moral argument a prominent place in the political process.

Moral argument already pervades democratic politics, and although it often fails to produce moral agreement, citizens evidently hope that it will, or they would not engage in it. Demanding justifications from public officials and giving justifications to fellow citizens is part of the American tradition. Officials and citizens in many different political forums continue to employ moral arguments to defend and to criticize public policies.

Although the ideal of deliberative democracy has long been recognized, it has been imperfectly realized both in practice and in theory. The fragments of dialogue with which this book began signal not only the prevalence of moral argument in politics but also its inadequacy. Neither of the parties in the several disputes seemed to be looking for any common moral ground. The president was mistaken in implying that government has no moral responsibility to women who cannot afford abortions, but his critics failed to see the moral force of his point that having a right does not necessarily mean that the government should fund the exercise of it. The white male employee at AT&T who feared losing out to a less qualified woman or black with no experience in the company did not appreciate that he may owe his position to a system that has been unfair in the past.

But neither did AT&T or the government give sufficient weight to the moral objection that he and other employees, including some women, were unfairly denied promotions. Dianna Brown's advocate overstated her case by equating capital punishment with the state's failure to fund her transplant, but the doctor who denied her claim by appealing mainly to overall costs and benefits did not recognize the state's responsibility to respect her basic opportunities. Throughout this book we have encountered citizens and officials similarly engaged in serious moral argument, sometimes reaching agreement, sometimes maintaining mutual respect, but often falling short of both.

Conventional theories of democracy have not been friendly to the ideal of deliberative democracy. Some have simply neglected it, implying by their silence that it does not matter. Others have put obstacles in its path, creating frameworks that leave little or no room for deliberation in everyday politics. One obstacle is a proceduralism that tells citizens to agree on some neutral rules of fair play and keep their moral disagreements to themselves, safely confined to their private lives, categorically removed from the public agenda. Another obstacle is a constitutionalism in which the tasks of moral deliberation and the defense of rights are assigned to an institution that is supposed to be above politics—the Supreme Court. Constitutionalism of this kind neglects the way in which other institutions can contribute to a more deliberative public policy as well as a better understanding of rights. Since both of these obstacles find counterparts in the thinking of many public officials and citizens, conventional theory and practice combine to make moral deliberation in politics less than it could be. One of our aims has been to show how these obstacles might be overcome, and democracy might be made safe for deliberation.

Moral argument in politics can be socially divisive, politically extremist, and morally inconclusive, but avoiding it for these reasons would be self-defeating. The divisions, the extremism, and the inconclusiveness would persist, while the prospects of finding better terms of social cooperation would deteriorate. The need for deliberation originates in the human condition, in circumstances that are not likely to disappear: scarcity, limited generosity, incompatible values, and incomplete understanding. Moral argument will almost certainly intrude into politics no matter what our theories say or what our practices imply. The important question is what kind of moral argument our democracy should foster—what its content should be, and under what conditions it should be conducted.

The answer we have given is a conception of deliberative democracy constituted by six principles. The first three—reciprocity, publicity, and accountability—are the chief conditions that regulate deliberation. The other three—basic liberty, basic opportunity, and fair opportunity—are the key components of the content of deliberation. This content includes claims that could be offered by a wide variety of moral theories, including libertarianism and egalitarianism. Even if what goes into the process of deliberation can be derived from these theories, what comes out is quite different. The claims lose their distinctive identity when they are required to reach some accommodation with one another and with the claims that express other fundamental values.

We distinguish the set of principles that refer to conditions from that which relates to the content because each set plays a different role in deliberation. One difference is that citizens and officials are more likely to make the content than the conditions of deliberation the subject of their actual deliberations. When Dianna Brown challenged Arizona's health care policy that denied her a liver transplant, she implicitly appealed to the principle of opportunity: "I would like a *chance for a chance.*" Neither she nor the officials to whom she appealed referred to a principle of publicity, but the policy of defunding organ transplants to which she objected could be criticized for having violated that principle. The two kinds of principles in this way typically operate on different levels: the conditions as a guide to how deliberation should be conducted, the content as part of the deliberation itself.

This difference between the two kinds of principles should not be identified with the distinction between process and substance in any of its conventional forms—such as procedure and outcome, rights and utility, or policy and principle. Neither the conditions of deliberative democracy nor its content are privileged in the way that one or the other of the terms in the standard dichotomies is. In deliberative democracy both the conditions and the content can be challenged in the political process. Citizens do not assume or seek agreement on a principle of publicity any more or less than they assume or seek agreement on a principle of opportunity. Furthermore, the moral standing of one kind of principle is not superior or prior to that of the other kind. Publicity is no more the means to the end of opportunity than opportunity is the means to the end of publicity. We can clarify the equal standing of the two kinds of principles—and more generally the place of each kind in the overall conception of deliberative democracy—by considering how the conditions and content interact.

How the Conditions of Deliberation Depend on Its Content

The principles of reciprocity, accountability, and publicity depend on the content of deliberation in several ways. First, the deliberative process and its results are more likely to be morally justified if deliberation takes place in a social context that respects the principles of liberty and opportunity. The conditions presuppose that the social and economic circumstances in which citizens deliberate meet at least some minimal demands of liberty and opportunity. No matter how earnestly citizens carry on deliberation in the spirit of reciprocity, publicity, and accountability, they can realize these ideals only to the extent that each citizen has sufficient social and economic standing to meet his or her fellows on terms of equal respect. The principle of liberty refers directly to the circumstances that make equal respect possible. As our discussion of welfare also indicated, a principle of opportunity that obligates government to make decent work or basic income available helps create the background circumstances that are necessary for adequate deliberation itself.

We do not presume that these background circumstances are easily created or maintained. But citizens and officials should not use the injustice of inequalities in liberty and opportunity as an excuse for neglecting to deliberate or failing to develop a more deliberative form of democracy. On the contrary, because deliberative democracy relies on reciprocity, publicity, and accountability, it stands a better chance of identifying and meliorating social and economic injustices than a politics that relies only on power, which is more likely to reproduce or exacerbate existing inequalities.

The most important way in which the conditions depend on the content of deliberation concerns the meanings of reciprocity, publicity, and accountability themselves. What these principles prescribe is partly determined by the values of liberty and opportunity. The conditions of deliberation themselves are not morally neutral: reciprocity, publicity, and accountability presuppose and express substantive moral values. It should not be surprising, therefore, that how citizens understand liberty and opportunity influences how they interpret and apply reciprocity, publicity, and accountability. We can show this dependence at work from two standpoints—at any particular time, and through time.

Citizens and officials bargained more than they deliberated over NAFTA. That they favored bargaining is perfectly consistent with the principle of reciprocity, if we are correct in assuming that the disagreement was not primarily moral. But the validity of this assumption depends on other substantive moral arguments—for example, establishing that none of the policy options violates fundamental liberties. If Senator Phil Gramm had been correct in suggesting that free trade is an inalienable right, then bargaining would not have been the right way to settle NAFTA. Reciprocity guides both bargaining and deliberation, but it relies on substantive moral argument to determine whether bargaining or deliberation is appropriate for any particular issue at any given time.

Reciprocity over time is similarly dependent on basic values such as liberty. The school superintendent in Hawkins County was right to insist, against the fundamentalist parents, that the schools should teach the skills of citizenship. Whatever respect might be due the parents in the name of reciprocity, it should not stand in the way of preparing their children for citizenship in the future. The curriculum that the school system adopted was justified in part as a means of fostering reciprocal deliberation in the future. But it was also a way of protecting the future liberty and opportunity of today's children. In this way, applications of reciprocity now are informed by the implications of liberty and opportunity later.

We have shown how publicity can make room for some kinds of secrecy, provided the secrecy can be justified publicly. Some of the most important justifications rest on the values of liberty and opportunity. Dianna Brown could reasonably decline, on the grounds of basic liberty, to publicize details of her personal life as a condition of public support for her liver transplant. She had a powerful claim that such a publicity requirement would threaten her personal integrity. While releasing information about employees in a general form, AT&T can justify refusing to publicize the test scores of individual black and female employees; the secrecy protects their opportunity to perform their jobs successfully in the face of enduring prejudices based on race and gender. For similar reasons, the press should be less inclined to probe secrets about an official's personal life (such as President Reagan's family relations) than secrets about official life (such as the cover-up in the Iran-Contra affair).

The meaning of publicity can also change over time as citizens develop new understandings of personal integrity and the value of the information and activities it protects. Sometimes the scope of publicity expands. Publicizing medical and psychiatric histories of candidates for high public office is no longer regarded as a violation of personal integrity because it is reasonably viewed as relevant to judging their qualifications. Sometimes a realm of privacy expands, as citizens come to see the value of protecting information that was previously ignored. The Senate Judiciary Committee, for example, respected a realm of privacy when it did not try to obtain records of the videos that Clarence Thomas had rented.

To respect the principle of accountability, representatives must give reasons to their constituents and respond to criticisms from them. But the nature of this relationship—the extent to which representatives defer to the reasons their constituents give—depends critically on what substantive values are at stake in any particular case. If South Dakota Senator Heidepriem reasonably believed that a bill restricting abortion would violate the basic liberty of women, he was not obligated to accept the reasons of his pro-life constituents, even if they reasonably believed that their opposing view was at least as compelling. The members of the city council in the "neon war" in Tacoma had far less reason to reject the objections that most of the public raised against the proposed sculpture. Basic liberties were not at stake in Tacoma, as they were in Pierre.

The scope of accountability broadens over time as citizens learn more about the circumstances of people in other countries or the claims of future generations. The logic of accountability—its universalist aspirations—encourages this kind of expansion. But without the content supplied by principles of liberty or opportunity, the logic alone cannot take citizens very far. They have to know what kind of liberty or opportunity is at stake in the moral concern they should show toward foreign countries or future generations before they can know to what extent they and their own representatives are accountable to foreigners or future citizens.

Not only do the conditions depend on the content of deliberation, but they also interact with one another and with themselves. Citizens learn more about the nature of reciprocity, as they reason according to its requirements. Because they regard the requirements of reciprocal reasoning, like its results, as provisional, their understanding of reciprocity has the capacity to correct itself over time.

The kind of reasoning required by reciprocity depends itself on what goes on in the process of deliberation. Citizens should use reciprocity in their reasoning not only to judge other principles but also to judge its own adequacy. It can therefore assume different forms and admit of different interpretations at various times. What should count as evidence of the motivation it requires, what should qualify as fair terms, what the scope of cooperation should be—all of these aspects of reciprocity may be contested, and could alter the understanding of the conditions of deliberation.

This capacity of deliberative democracy to encourage changes in its own meaning over time illustrates one of its most important qualities. Deliberative democracy expresses a bootstrap conception of the political process: the conditions of reciprocity, publicity, and accountability that define the process pull themselves up by means of the process itself. This self-defining property is paradoxical only if one mistakenly assumes that all the conditions of deliberation may legitimately be challenged at the same time or in the same way. Instead, the process should be seen as sequential. Citizens revise one condition in a process in which the other two conditions are held constant, or they alter their understanding of all the conditions by applying them in a different context or at a different time.

This bootstrap operation might have been put into practice in Arizona had its citizens been informed about the way in which their state legislature had decided to defund organ transplants. We suggested that citizens would have been justified in objecting to the closed character of the debate that set the terms of the state's health policy. In making this objection, they would have been using the very kind of public forum that they were criticizing the legislators for failing to use in debates about health care policy. During the Asarco debates, some citizens in Tacoma did in fact use a process to criticize certain features of the same process: by questioning whether all reasonable points of view could receive a fair hearing, they pointed to the failure of the process to respect reciprocity. But presumably they believed that the process was already fair enough in other respects that this objection could itself receive a fair hearing. Or at least they believed that making the objection would contribute to creating a fairer process in the future.

Is there any limit to how far this self-defining process can go? Deliberative democracy cannot accommodate the general rejection of the idea of moral reasoning in politics. To reject the idea *tout court* is to abandon not only deliberative democracy, but also any form of democracy in which public policies are justified in moral terms to the citizens who are bound by them. Some conceptions of political bargaining try to provide an indirect justification for mutually beneficial terms of cooperation. Motivated by self-interest, citizens are assumed to agree on rules for social cooperation that may coincidentally have some of the same effects as principles based directly on justice. The result of this assumption is an impoverished conception of democracy in which the range of criticism, the potential for progress, and the terms of social cooperation are all unduly circumscribed.

Such conceptions of political bargaining themselves depend on moral reasoning to defend the claim that self-seeking bargaining is the best way to find fair terms of social cooperation and desirable forms of public policy. Yet these conceptions fail to offer good reasons—either moral or empirical—for their assumption that citizens and public officials are rationally self-interested, and that moral reasoning in politics is therefore merely a rationalization of the quest for power.

Why assume that a power-based conception of democracy is the default position? In the absence of a foundational justification for moral reason, there is no compelling reason to accept a presumption of self-interested motivation. At the foundational level, no one has yet provided a justification of a power-based conception that is any more adequate than a justification of a conception based on moral reason. In any case, the most compelling defense of either kind of conception would show that it fits with considered judgments about particular cases, and that it provides a coherent and workable way of thinking about and practicing democratic politics over a wide range of decisions and policies of government. That is the kind of justification we have begun to develop here for deliberative democracy. If critics of deliberative democracy are to establish their case, they must offer a similar kind of justification for the alternative conceptions they favor. There exists no default position on which citizens can fall back when their moral reasoning leaves them divided or uncertain.

It is of course possible to reject all forms of justification—to abandon moral reason altogether and embrace political power as the sole currency in public life. There will always be some citizens and some officials who choose this way of politics. Some will no doubt enjoy successful careers, perhaps fortuitously even serving the public good. But anyone who aspires to chart a mutually justifiable course for our unavoidably common life— the leaders, activists, critics, and theorists of our time—cannot consistently renounce the quest for reasonable terms of social cooperation. Neither can responsible citizens. If they decline to search for principles that can be justified to their fellow citizens, who should listen to them? Certainly no citizen who is still motivated to find reciprocal terms of cooperation. Their audience can be only citizens who have themselves already given up on reasoned argument. Those who would renounce moral reason are trying either to persuade the converted or to reach the unreasonable. In the first case their audience has no need, and in the second no reason, to listen.

How the Content of Deliberation Depends on Its Conditions

EPA Administrator William Ruckelshaus recognized that utilitarianism in the form of policy analysis could not tell him whether to close the Asarco copper smelting plant. By asking the citizens of Tacoma to help him make the decision, he invited a challenge not only to the principle of utility but also to other principles that purport to determine policies prior to democratic deliberation. If libertarians had argued that the property rights of Asarco decided the question against closing the plant, their claim would have had no special standing to override what Ruckelshaus decided after due deliberation. If egalitarians had argued that the plant must stay open because the most disadvantaged citizens needed the jobs, their claim would have been another voice in the democratic debate, but again with no special priority over a deliberative decision.

Proponents of principles of this kind often speak as though their claims were decisive independently of a process of deliberation, evidently assuming that the principles are the only reasonable and sufficient standards for resolving the dispute. Acting on this assumption in the face of moral disagreement in politics makes further deliberation appear unnecessary. Deliberative democracy rejects the assumption because its citizens remain open to the possibility of respecting reasonable positions with which they disagree.

The principles that constitute the content of deliberative democracy leave substantial room for deliberation about what policies should bind citizens. Basic liberty, basic opportunity, and fair opportunity submit themselves to the conditions of deliberative democracy over a greater range than the more comprehensive and single-valued principles of utility, liberty, and equality admit. The deliberative process can again be viewed from two different standpoints. At any particular time, the scope of deliberative principles is more limited; and through time, their status is more provisional.

Basic liberty constrains what democracies can justifiably legislate, but it does not claim sovereign authority over the whole range of public policy as does liberty on a libertarian understanding. Basic liberty would clearly prevent policies that compel citizens to donate organs, to labor against their will, or to abandon their religious beliefs. By analogy its scope can be extended from these clear cases to initially more difficult ones, such as surrogacy, where basic liberty protects the freedom of a mother such as Mary Beth Whitehead to keep her child (for example, in a joint custody arrangement with the contracting parents). But the basic liberty principle does not reject taxation as if it were on a par with forced labor. Nor does it accept the demand to meet all health care needs as an unqualified right. In deliberative democracy, reciprocity constrains the claims of liberty so that other important values receive the hearing that they deserve.

Like basic liberty, the principle of basic opportunity constrains democratic decision making in a limited domain. Arizona's health care policy did not infringe upon Dianna Brown's basic liberty by denying her a transplant, but it may have violated her claims to basic opportunity. Yet even basic opportunity stops short of supplying all the goods that some egalitarians say must be provided in the name of equal opportunity. It does not support the expansive requirement of equalizing everyone's life chances, for example, by providing all the medical care that anyone needs, or all the kinds of high-level jobs that might be necessary to compensate for past discrimination. In any society in which scarcity persists, supplying all the medical care and other opportunity good that everyone needs (assuming that such a policy were economically feasible) would mandate a drastic reduction in the range of valuable ways of life that citizens could freely pursue. Such policies can be reasonably rejected by citizens who nonetheless respect every person's basic liberty and opportunity. To consider these policies to be mandatory constraints on democratic decision making therefore fails to respect the principle of reciprocity.

The principle of publicity similarly limits the claims of liberty and opportunity. The value of publicity blocks any unqualified attempt to avoid controversial political discussions even of the kind that threaten to diminish liberty or opportunity. It is an inadequate argument against holding public hearings on Anita Hill's charges against Clarence Thomas to claim, for example, that the hearings might reinforce racist attitudes in this country. Open discussion has value as a democratic means by which citizens can deal responsibly with difficult moral disagreements over basic values of liberty and opportunity. So too should liberty and opportunity sometimes make room for the needs of democratic accountability. Schemes of representation of the kind we considered in Chapter 4, which advance the opportunities of some disadvantaged groups in society, are more acceptable to the extent that they are also consistent with deliberative accountability.

Not only do the conditions of reciprocity, publicity, and accountability restrain the more expansive claims of liberty and opportunity, but also they encourage a more conciliatory response to the legitimate claims of competing values. This was the spirit in which the chapters on liberty and opportunity proceeded. We developed a principle of basic liberty that can embrace the legitimate claims of both moralists and paternalists. We presented a principle of fair opportunity that merges the legitimate claims of liberals and egalitarians, and helps reconcile their respective policies of nondiscrimination and preferential hiring. The theoretical aim was to develop the content of a deliberative perspective that can stand the test of its conditions. This is also the practical aim of the actual democratic process that a deliberative perspective recommends.

Reciprocity, publicity, and accountability also inform the content of the deliberative perspective over time. When citizens and officials engage the dynamic of deliberative democracy, they use the principles of liberty and opportunity to bring about changes in the sources of moral disagreement—especially in the degree of scarcity of resources and the nature of the diversity of reasonable moral points of view. The principles of deliberative democracy (and any agreement they create) are thus provisional. They not only are subject to revision in light of new information and better arguments, but also are a cause of such revision. Responsible citizens should thus regard many of their own moral claims as provisional.

The results of collective deliberation are provisional in a further way. Even when citizens have good reason to be confident about their own moral views, and even when those views legitimately prevail in the democratic process, citizens should act so as to ensure that the results remain open to correction. This capacity for change is one of the important virtues of deliberative democracy. Its self-correcting capacity cultivates the possibility of moral progress in democratic politics. It contains the means of its own alteration. Deliberation proceeds through stages, as citizens and officials propose, respond, revise, and react. To a remarkable extent, this is how citizens and officials in Oregon conducted the discussions that developed the priorities for the state's publicly funded health care. The moral promise of deliberative democracy depends on the political learning that reiterated deliberation makes possible.

The Arizona legislators who decided to defund transplants might have done better if they had tried to engage in this kind of deliberation. Given the resources available to the state at the time, they may have been warranted in refusing to fund liver transplants. But they still could not have justified their decision without at least trying, through continuing democratic deliberation about the needs of citizens like Dianna Brown, to make more resources available. Arizona officials were obligated to make clear that the reason for denying funding was based partly on alterable circumstances of scarcity, not mainly on an immutable interpretation of basic opportunity. In this way, the opportunity principle and its practical implications are subject to the discipline of the deliberative conditions of reciprocity, publicity, and accountability.

The conditions also influence how citizens understand and apply principles of liberty and opportunity through time even in the face of continuing conflict over their meaning. That is part of the point of seeking an economy of moral disagreement. Citizens should try to minimize the range of their disagreement not only so that they can cooperate now on other policies on which they might agree, but also so that they might discover policies in the future that diminish their disagreement. Pro-choice advocates in the abortion controversy should avoid making claims about liberty and opportunity that completely deny the fetus any moral standing. Pro-life advocates should avoid making claims about the fetus that imply that anyone who is uncertain about its moral standing is unreasonable.

Seeking an economy of moral disagreement has similar implications for employment policy. Egalitarians can justify preferential hiring under current circumstances, but they should not rely on an understanding of opportunity that dismisses the claims of better qualified workers who fail to win jobs or promotions because of a policy of preferring less qualified workers. Any adequate opportunity principle, whatever it may require now, should encourage government to find ways in the future to avoid denying promotion to workers like Bertha Biel, the records clerk at AT&T, who lost out to a man simply because the company had to meet the targets for male representation in certain positions. A deliberative perspective should enable all citizens to appreciate the moral force of Biel's plea, "This is not fair."

The Practice of Deliberative Democracy

The gap between the theory and practice of deliberative democracy is narrower than in most other conceptions of democracy. To be sure, its highest ideals make demands that actual politics may never fulfill. But its principles modulate their demands in response to the limits of political necessity: they speak in the idiom of "insofar as" or "to the degree that."

Even more important, the theory of deliberative democracy partly constitutes its own practice: the arguments with which democratic theorists justify the theory are of the same kind that democratic citizens use to justify decisions and policies in practice. In contrast to some forms of utilitarianism, deliberative democracy does not create a division between reasons that are appropriate in theory and those that are appropriate in practice. In contrast to some other conceptions of democracy, deliberative democracy does not divide institutions into those in which deliberation is important and those in which it is not. This continuity of theory and practice has implications for the design of institutions in modern democracies.

In the course of analyzing the principles in the context of cases, we mentioned a number of institutions that could make democracy more deliberative. We did not undertake to provide an inventory of institutional changes because the design of the institutions of deliberative democracy depends critically on developing principles to assess them. That is the prior task on which this book has concentrated. Once the principles of deliberative democracy are better understood, the search for their most suitable institutional expression can become more productive. The best forum for considering the design of deliberative institutions is likely to be one in which deliberation, however nascent, has a prominent place.

Without trying to propose specific institutional reforms, we can set out some implications of the continuity of theory and practice that should influence institutional design in a deliberative democracy. Each implication may be understood as expressing a caution against dividing deliberative labor in ways that check that continuity. The essential idea is that all institutions of government have a responsibility for deliberation. Institutions should be arranged so as to provide opportunities and incentives for officials and citizens to engage in moral reasoning. Institutions should also be transparent in the sense that their actual purposes should coincide with their publicly acknowledged purposes.

The first implication tells against the tendency to designate some institutions as forums for reason and others as arenas of power. It challenges those constitutional democrats who see courts as the agents of deliberation and legislatures as the brokers of interests. In a democracy in which citizens are governed on the basis of values adopted and refined through collective deliberations, all the makers of public policy—legislators as well as judges—should give reasons based on principles that reflect these values. Legislatures as well as courts, then, should be designed to encourage these reason-giving practices.

Second, deliberative labor should not be divided so that representatives give reasons while citizens merely receive them. Representation is necessary in modern democracies, but exclusive specialization in moral reasoning about their policies is neither necessary nor desirable. Some citizens already make remarkably good use of the limited opportunities for deliberation that exist. Deliberation may not have produced the best possible solution to health care priorities in Oregon or environmental risks in Tacoma, but its results were probably no worse than less deliberative means would have achieved, and they surely advanced public understanding further. Forums like these could be designed to consider a far wider range of issues; they could also play a role in the consideration of national issues, perhaps even in political campaigns.

Third, the practice of deliberation should not be confined to the institutions of government. Unless citizens have the experience of reasoning together in other institutions in which they spend more of their time they are not likely to develop either the interest or the skill that would enable them to deliberate effectively in politics. That is why it is so important that the processes of decision making that citizens encounter at work and at leisure should seek to cultivate the virtues of deliberation. The discussion that takes place in these settings not only is a rehearsal for political action, but also is itself a part of citizenship in deliberative democracy. Deliberative democracy does not demand that all social institutions primarily serve its ends, but its success does depend on the support of the whole range of intermediary institutions—those that act on citizens (such as the media, health care organizations, professional sports), those in which they act (interest groups, private clubs, trade unions, professional associations), as well as those in which they work (corporations, small businesses, government agencies, military services).

In any effort to make democracy more deliberative, the single most important institution outside government is the educational system. To prepare their students for citizenship, schools must go beyond teaching literacy and numeracy, though both are of course prerequisites for deliberating about public problems. Schools should aim to develop their students' capacities to understand different perspectives, communicate their understandings to other people, and engage in the give-and-take of moral argument with a view to making mutually acceptable decisions. These goals, which entail cultivating moral character and intellectual skills at the same time, are likely to require some significant changes in traditional civics education, which has neglected teaching this kind of moral reasoning about politics.

Finally, deliberative democracy should avoid any rigid division between the structure and the culture of institutions. Political reformers tend to pay more attention to structure than to culture. Certainly it is important to consider changes in the formal rules and the informal incentives that could influence how officials and citizens act. But the attitudes that institutions cultivate are also critical. In tracing the ways that deliberation can help resolve various controversies, we have repeatedly noted how dispositions can promote deliberative practices in political institutions. Among the most notable dispositions of this kind are the virtues of civic integrity and civic magnanimity, which express the essential value of mutual respect. To flourish—sometimes even to survive—in the face of fundamental moral disagreement, institutions need to cultivate these virtues in citizens.

A deliberative culture in an institution not only helps citizens develop the virtues of civic integrity and magnanimity but also enables those who already have these virtues to act in accordance with them. Practicing civic virtues, moreover, can in turn improve the practices of democratic institutions. Even without changing the structure of legislative debate, members of Congress who concentrate on the substance of issues contribute to developing a culture more favorable to deliberation. By contrast, when a culture encourages the practice of impugning the motives of one's opponents instead of assessing the merits of their positions, deliberation withers. When the "imputation of bad motive" dominates an institutional culture, citizens do not reason together so much as they reason against one another. They reflexively attack persons instead of policies, looking for what is behind policies rather than what is in them. In a culture where moral disagreement turns so readily into general distrust, citizens are not disposed to think and act in a reciprocal frame of mind.

A reciprocal perspective is important not only to enable citizens to resolve disagreement but also to enable them to learn to live with it. Certainly citizens should welcome agreement when they can agree that what they can agree on is morally right. But given the intractable sources of disagreement, citizens cannot expect to reach mutually justifiable agreement over the whole range of significant issues in politics.

Many theorists of democracy refuse to face up to this moral fact of political life. They assume that it is simply the result of misunderstanding, which could be overcome if citizens would only adopt the correct philosophical view or cultivate the proper moral character. Among secular views, utilitarianism is the most prominent example, but many other comprehensive moralities also fail to take disagreement seriously. Other theorists accept the persistence of disagreement but try to defuse it by redrawing the boundaries of political communities so that more public policy is made by like-minded citizens. This is the strategy of some communitarians. Still other theorists suggest that disagreement could be overcome if communities cultivated the right virtues of character in their citizens. But important as cultivating good character is, it cannot promise to dissolve the moral disagreements at the heart of the kind of controversies we have been considering. Bad character certainly exacerbates many political disagreements, but good character is hardly sufficient to resolve controversies over subsidizing abortion, giving preference to blacks and women, or funding organ transplants.

Proceduralism and constitutionalism recognize that moral disagreement is here to stay, but in different ways try to keep it in check. Many proceduralists hope that if citizens agree on some basic rules of the game, they will be able to domesticate the remaining disagreement by leaving it to political bargaining or by moving it off the political agenda into private life. Many constitutionalists hope that after carving out a sphere of agreement on fundamental values and protecting it from the pressures of ordinary politics, they can safely let the remaining disagreement simmer. Again, the important moral questions are to be settled at the borders of democratic politics.

The conception of deliberative democracy defended here puts moral reasoning and moral disagreement back at the center of everyday politics. It reinforces and refines the practices of moral argument that prevail in ordinary political life—the ways in which citizens deal with moral disagreement in middle democracy. Its principles show citizens and their representatives how to live with moral disagreement in a morally constructive way. Deliberative democracy is more idealistic than other conceptions because it demands more than democratic politics normally delivers. It is more realistic because it expects less than moral agreement would promise. While acknowledging that we are destined to disagree, deliberative democracy also affirms that we are capable of deciding our common destiny on mutually acceptable terms.

Notes

Introduction

1. The best-known version of the method of "reflective equilibrium" is John Rawls, *A Theory of Justice* (Cambridge, Mass.: Harvard University Press, 1971), pp. 48–51. A more recent systematic account of a closely related method is in Henry S. Richardson, "Specifying Norms as a Way to Resolve Concrete Ethical Problems," *Philosophy & Public Affairs*, 19 (Fall 1990): 279–310. See also Norman Daniels, "Wide Reflective Equilibrium and Theory Acceptance in Ethics," *Journal of Philosophy*, 76 (May 1979): 256–282.
2. We have generally chosen cases for which a fuller description is available elsewhere so that readers can develop their own interpretation of the events we discuss. Many of the cases are available in the reader that we originally prepared for our courses; see Amy Gutmann and Dennis Thompson, eds., *Ethics and Politics*, 2d ed. (Chicago: Nelson-Hall, 1990).

1. The Persistence of Moral Disagreement

1. President Jimmy Carter responding to reporter Judy Woodruff's question at a press conference (July 12, 1977) following a Supreme Court decision upholding denial of state funding for elective abortions. Cited in Joseph A. Califano, *Governing America* (New York: Simon and Schuster, 1981), p. 70.
2. Excerpt from AT&T's Model Affirmative Action Plan, adopted in 1973 as part of a consent decree after the government charged the company with employment discrimination; and the comments of a company employee. Cited in Robert K. Fullinwider, "Affirmative Action at AT&T," in *Ethics and Politics*, ed. Amy Gutmann and Dennis Thompson, 2d ed. (Chicago: Nelson-Hall, 1990), pp. 213, 217.
3. Dr. Leonard Kirschner, director of Arizona's health care program for the indigent, defending the need to deny funding for some organ transplants; and a writer in the *Arizona Republic* criticizing the law that denied forty-three-year-old Dianna

Brown a liver transplant. Cited in Pamela Varley, "Defunding Organ Transplants in Arizona," in Gutmann and Thompson, *Ethics and Politics,* pp. 187, 178.

4. For other discussions of the basis of deliberative democracy, see Seyla Benhabib, "Deliberative Rationality and Models of Democratic Legitimacy," *Constellations,* 1 (April 1994): 26–52; Joseph Bessette, *The Mild Voice of Reason: Deliberative Democracy and American National Government* (Chicago: University of Chicago Press, 1994), pp. 1–66; Joshua Cohen, "Deliberation and Democratic Legitimacy," in *The Good Polity: Normative Analysis of the State,* ed. Alan Hamlin and Philip Pettit (Oxford: Basil Blackwell, 1989), pp. 17–34; John S. Dryzek, *Discursive Democracy* (Cambridge: Cambridge University Press, 1990); David M. Estlund, "Who's Afraid of Deliberative Democracy? On the Strategic/Deliberative Dichotomy in Recent Constitutional Jurisprudence," *Texas Law Review,* 71 (June 1993): 1437–77; James Fishkin, *Democracy and Deliberation* (New Haven: Yale University Press, 1971); Charles Larmore, *Patterns of Moral Complexity* (Cambridge: Cambridge University Press, 1987), esp. pp. 59–66; Bernard Manin, "On Legitimacy and Political Deliberation," *Political Theory,* 15 (August 1987): 338–368; Jane Mansbridge, "Motivating Deliberation in Congress," in *Constitutionalism in America,* ed. Sarah Baumgartner Thurow, 3 vols. (Lanham, Md.: University Press of America, 1988), 2:59–86; Jane Mansbridge, "A Deliberative Theory of Interest Representation," in *The Politics of Interests: Interest Groups Transformed,* ed. Mark P. Petracca (Boulder, Colo.: Westview Press, 1992), pp. 32–57; and Cass Sunstein, *The Partial Constitution* (Cambridge, Mass.: Harvard University Press, 1993), pp. 133–145.

5. Madison favored political discussion, in which "minds [are] changing," in which "much [is] gained by a yielding and accommodating spirit," and in which no citizen is "obliged to retain his opinions any longer than he [is] satisfied of their propriety and truth." See "Jared Sparks: Journal," summarizing James Madison's views on the secret discussion in the Constitutional Convention and Congress, in *Records of the Federal Convention of 1787,* rev. ed., ed. Max Farrand, 4 vols. (New Haven: Yal University Press, 1966), 3: 479. The passage is quoted in a somewhat different form in Sunstein, *The Partial Constitution,* p. 164.

6. In the same spirit, Jürgen Habermas identifies deliberative democracy with the idea of a "decentered society" in "Three Normative Models of Democracy," *Constellations,* 1 (April 1994): 1–10. For discussions of neglected deliberative forums, see David Mathews, *Politics for People* (Urbana: University of Illinois Press, 1994); and Fishkin, *Democracy and Deliberation.*

7. Our view of deliberation should be distinguished from that presented by Bessette, who also looks at actual arguments in political debate, in particular those in the U.S. Congress. Although he also sees deliberative democracy as "reasoning on the merits of public policy" (*Mild Voice of Reason,* p. 46), one of his main arguments is that there is already more deliberation in Congress than most political scientists assume. Whether or not he is correct, we do not presume that the present state of deliberation in Congress and American politics generally is adequate, and in any case we do not focus, as he does, only on the need for deliberation among political elites and their role in preventing spontaneous or passionate judgments by the masses. Perhaps because he is content with deliberation among political

elites, Bessette is skeptical about publicity and argues in favor of secrecy (pp. 208–209). In another respect, Bessette demands more of deliberation than we do. For him the "singular mark" of a deliberative process is that it must have "a real persuasive effect" and involve "some kind of change or development in the policymaker's understanding" (pp. 52–53). We do not insist that deliberation must change people's minds to be valuable.

8. See Kurt Baier, *The Moral Point of View* (Ithaca, N.Y.: Cornell University Press, 1958), pp. 187–213; and John Rawls, *A Theory of Justice* (Cambridge, Mass.: Harvard University Press, 1971), pp. 130–136.

9. Once the classic example of a people with an amoral if not immoral culture, the Ik, anthropologists now think, were unfairly maligned; they seem to be morally no worse in attitude and behavior than most cultures. See Robert Edgerton, *Sick Societies: Challenging the Myth of Primitive Harmony* (New York: Free Press, 1992), pp. 6–8.

10. An evaluation of various forms of moral relativism is in Amy Gutmann, "The Challenge of Multiculturalism in Political Ethics," *Philosophy & Public Affairs,* 22 (Summer 1993): 171–206.

11. The most prominent contemporary example is Rawls, *A Theory of Justice.* See also Bruce Ackerman, *Social Justice in the Liberal State* (New Haven: Yale University Press, 1980).

12. In this respect the hypothetical approach may have a role in assessing deliberation, but only in combination with an empirical approach that examines the actual conditions under which deliberation takes place. Brian Barry shows how these approaches, when combined to evaluate a theory of justice, "provide a check on one another," in *Justice as Impartiality* (Oxford: Oxford University Press, 1995), pp. 195–199.

13. This critic, Frederick Schauer, concludes that deliberation is no "more likely to ameliorate than to exacerbate the existing inequalities in a society." The only alternative suggested by Schauer is a "more controlled communicative environment." Would the people who controlled communication do so without obtaining deliberative assent from citizens or their accountable representatives? If so, why should we think that they would be more egalitarian in their policies than people who are willing to subject their exercise of political power to the deliberative assent of citizens? See Frederick Schauer, "Discourse and Its Discontents," Working Paper no. 94–2, Joan Shorenstein Barone Center on the Press, Politics, and Public Policy, Cambridge, Mass., September 1994, p. 9.

14. Jürgen Habermas, "Discourse Ethics," in *Moral Consciousness and Communicative Action,* trans. Christian Lenhardt and Shierry Weber Nicholsen (Cambridge, Mass.: MIT Press, 1993), p. 94.

15. Thomas McCarthy, "Introduction" to Habermas, *Moral Consciousness and Communicative Action,* p. xi. McCarthy writes that this is why Habermas is critical of Rawls's two principles of justice. But one may criticize the two principles for going beyond what moral reasonableness demands while still recognizing the need for some principles of liberty and opportunity that give content to a common perspective and are not solely conditions of deliberation.

16. Another important deliberative democrat, Seyla Benhabib, argues that delibera-

tion can ensure the legitimacy but not the rationality of outcomes: "We accept the will of the majority at the end of an electoral process that has been fairly and correctly carried out, but even when we accept the legitimacy of the process we may have grave doubts about the rationality of the outcome." If deliberation aims only at legitimacy, and legitimacy is defined as whatever "result[s] from the free and unconstrained public deliberation of all about matters of common concern," then deliberation may succeed (by definition) at ensuring legitimacy. Benhabib, "Deliberative Rationality," p. 26. But this concept of legitimacy has too little moral content to provide a robust defense of deliberative democracy. Why should we defend deliberation, so understood, over a conception of deliberative democracy that is dedicated both to respecting basic liberty and opportunity and to subjecting these principles to ongoing deliberation?

17. Habermas, "Discourse Ethics," p. 100. See also Jürgen Habermas, "Reconciliation through the Use of Public Reason: Remarks on John Rawls's Political Liberalism," *Journal of Philosophy,* 92 (March 1995): 109–131.

18. Benhabib, "Deliberative Rationality," p. 27. Habermas writes that participants in deliberation must be "free and equal" and the discourse "inclusive and noncoercive" ("Reconciliation," pp. 109ff.). This description calls into question his earlier characterization of discourse ethics as offering "a rule of argumentation only" which "does not prejudge substantive regulations" ("Discourse Ethics," p. 94). Discourse ethics is "not compatible with all substantive legal and moral principles," as Habermas recognizes, partly because it is committed to a substantive view of what counts as ideal deliberation. The deliberative ideal lends itself to a stronger defense when it acknowledges the (partly) independent values of basic liberty and opportunity.

19. Benhabib, "Deliberative Rationality," pp. 30–35. Once content is given to reasoned discourse, a common perspective becomes far less purely procedural than Benhabib suggests: "Agreements in societies living with value-pluralism are to be sought for not at the level of substantive beliefs but at the level of procedures, processes, and practices for attaining and revising beliefs" (p. 34).

20. Habermas, "Discourse Ethics," p. 67.

21. Thomas Hobbes, *Leviathan,* ed. Michael Oakeshott (New York: Macmillan, 1962), chap. 4, pp. 39–40.

22. For a sample of contemporary challenges to the self-interest paradigm in politics and political science, see Jane J. Mansbridge, ed., *Beyond Self-Interest* (Chicago: University of Chicago Press, 1990); and Robert Goodin, *Motivating Political Morality* (Oxford: Basil Blackwell, 1992).

23. Brian Barry, *Theories of Justice* (Berkeley: University of California Press, 1989), p. 285. It should be noted that Barry's use of "impartiality," at least insofar as this point is concerned, does not differ significantly from our use of "reciprocity."

24. David Hume, *A Treatise of Human Nature,* 2d ed., ed. L. A. Selby-Bigge (Oxford: Clarendon Press, 1978), bk. 3, pt. 2, sec. 2, pp. 484–501.

25. David Hume, *An Enquiry Concerning the Principles of Morals* (1777), sec. 3, pt. 1 ("Of Justice"), in Hume's *Enquiries Concerning the Human Understanding and Concerning the Principles of Morals,* 2d ed., ed. L. A. Selby-Bigge (Oxford: Clarendon Press, 1963), pp. 183–192 (quote at p. 183).

26. Ibid., p. 184: "Let us suppose that nature has bestowed on the human race such profuse abundance of all *external* conveniences that, without any uncertainty in the event, without any care or industry on our part, every individual finds himself fully provided with whatever his most voracious appetites can want, or luxurious imagination wish or desire."

27. Ibid., pp. 184–185.

28. See D. Clayton Hubin's discussion of this example in "The Scope of Justice," *Philosophy & Public Affairs*, 9 (Fall 1979): 3–24, esp. 18. We are also indebted more generally to Hubin's analysis of Hume on the scope of justice.

29. Some courts have decided such cases, distinguishing between intentional killing where the choice of a victim is based on fair principles such as drawing straws, and intentional killing where no fair principles of selection are employed. The former killing is excused, whereas the latter is fully punished. See A. W. B. Simpson, *Cannibalism and the Common Law: The Story of the Last Voyage of the "Mignonette" and the Strange Legal Proceedings to Which It Gave Rise* (Chicago: University of Chicago Press, 1984).

30. Hubin, "Scope of Justice," p. 10.

31. Philosophers who have developed versions of this view in recent years include Isaiah Berlin, "Two Concepts of Liberty," in *Four Essays on Liberty* (Oxford: Oxford University Press, 1969), pp. 118–172; Thomas Nagel, *Mortal Questions* (Cambridge: Cambridge University Press, 1979), pp. 128–141; Bernard Williams, "Ethical Consistency," in *Problems of the Self* (Cambridge: Cambridge University Press, 1973), pp. 166–186; and Michael Walzer, "Political Action: The Problem of Dirty Hands," *Philosophy & Public Affairs*, 2 (Winter 1973): 160–180. For a sample of views on both sides, see Christopher Gowans, ed., *Moral Dilemmas* (Oxford: Oxford University Press, 1987).

32. This recognition is compatible with most forms of moral realism, according to which some moral beliefs are objectively true or false, though moral realists may overestimate the extent to which we are able to discern moral truths about controversial political issues. For a useful introduction to the debate surrounding moral realism, see Geoffrey Sayre McCord, *Essays on Moral Realism* (Ithaca, N.Y.: Cornell University Press, 1988). For a realist who emphasizes the compatibility between deliberation and realism, see David Brink, *Moral Realism and the Foundations of Ethics* (Cambridge: Cambridge University Press, 1990), esp. pp. 29–31.

33. We do not offer an extensive argument for any general moral foundations for democracy here since our focus is on the comparative moral merits of different conceptions of democracy for addressing moral conflict. We take it for granted that at least one of the moral justifications for democracy that political theorists have presented establishes its superiority over non-democracy. For a defense of a plurality of democratic foundations, see Amy Gutmann, "Democracy and Philosophy: Does Democracy Need Foundations?," *Politisches Denken Jahrbuch, 1993* (Stuttgart: J. B. Metzler, 1994), pp. 39–45. Some discussions of the general justification of democracy that we have found helpful include Robert A. Dahl, *Democracy and Its Critics* (New Haven: Yale University Press, 1989); David Held, *Models of Democracy* (Stanford: Stanford University Press, 1987); Jack Lively,

Democracy (New York: St. Martin's Press, 1975); William Nelson, *Justifying Democracy* (London: Routledge and Kegan Paul, 1980); and J. Roland Pennock, *Democratic Political Theory* (Princeton: Princeton University Press, 1979). We also rely on our own earlier discussion of this topic in Amy Gutmann, *Liberal Equality* (Cambridge: Cambridge University Press, 1980); Dennis Thompson, *The Democratic Citizen* (Cambridge: Cambridge University Press, 1970); and Dennis Thompson, *John Stuart Mill and Representative Government* (Princeton: Princeton University Press, 1976).

34. Compare Jürgen Habermas, who makes a similar point about the capacity of deliberative democracy to integrate what he calls the "liberal" and "republican" views of democracy ("Three Normative Models of Democracy," esp. p. 6). See also his "Remarks on Discourse Ethics," in *Justification and Application,* trans. Ciaran P. Cronin (Cambridge, Mass.: MIT Press, 1993), pp. 19–111. Nonetheless, our conception of deliberative democracy should not be identified with the "discourse theory" as criticized by Frederick Schauer for assuming that deliberation is "self-evidently desirable" or an "unqualified human good" ("Discourse and Its Discontents," p. 1). Deliberative democracy, in our view, is not purely procedural, and deliberation is an imperfect procedure. Unlike some discourse theories, deliberative democracy, as we develop it, has the capacity to criticize deliberative outcomes even in a "procedurally perfect" society.

35. We take Robert Dahl as a paradigmatic procedural democrat, in part because his subtle form of proceduralism recognizes that "the democratic process is . . . itself a rich bundle of substantive goods" (*Democracy and its Critics,* p. 175). Other proceduralists who specifically defend majority rule include Elaine Spitz, *Majority Rule* (Chatham, N.J.: Chatham House, 1984); and Douglas Rae, "Decision Rules and Individual Values in Constitutional Choice," *American Political Science Review,* 63 (March 1969): 40–56. More generally, the pluralist tradition in American political science, beginning most notably with the work of David Truman, provides numerous examples of proceduralism. Our criticism is not directed against those understandings of procedural democracy that reject the claim that popular rule is the fairest way to resolve moral conflicts.

36. In a famous footnote to his opinion for the Supreme Court in *United States v. Carolene Products Co.,* Justice Harlan Stone wrote that "prejudice against discrete and insular minorities may be a special condition, which tends seriously to curtail the operation of those political processes ordinarily to be relied upon to protect minorities, and . . . may call for a correspondingly more searching judicial inquiry." 304 U.S. 144, 152–153n.4 (1938). Precisely who constitutes a "discrete and insular" minority is a complex matter, especially for constitutional law, but we need not enter into these complexities here to recognize that disadvantaged minorities who are the targets of prejudice are not treated fairly by a simple majoritarian procedure.

37. A prominent example is John Hart Ely, *Democracy and Distrust* (Cambridge, Mass.: Harvard University Press, 1981).

38. For critiques of procedural democrats such as Ely, see Ronald Dworkin, *A Matter of Principle* (Cambridge, Mass.: Harvard University Press, 1985), pp. 57–65; Frederick Schauer, *Free Speech: A Philosophical Inquiry* (Cambridge: Cambridge

University Press, 1982), pp. 15–34; Sunstein, *The Partial Constitution*, esp. pp. 143–145; and Jeremy Waldron, "A Rights-Based Critique of Constitutional Rights," *Oxford Journal of Legal Studies*, 13 (Spring 1993): 18–51.

39. Brian Barry, "Is Democracy Special?," in *Democracy, Power and Justice: Essays in Political Theory* (Oxford: Clarendon Press, 1989), pp. 29–30, citing his early discussion in Brian Barry, *Political Argument* (London: Routledge and Kegan Paul, 1965), p. 312. The example in the text is similar in structure to the example that Barry uses—five passengers trying to decide whether to permit smoking in a railway car.

40. Barry, "Is Democracy Special?," p. 30.

41. In addition to the protection of "discrete and insular minorities" for which proceduralists explicitly provide, two other background conditions of cases in which majority rule seems an appropriate solution are worth noting: first, when only one question is the subject of decision; and second, when the question offers only two, dichotomous alternatives (such as "funding organ transplants" or "not funding"). When there are multiple decisions to be made, or more than two alternatives, as there almost always are in political life, then there are also likely to be procedures other than simple majority rule that are reasonable ways of resolving the controversies. Plurality rule, for example, may be a reasonable way of resolving disagreements with more than two alternatives. See Barry, "Is Democracy Special?".

42. Cf. ibid., p. 37.

43. Ibid., p. 38.

44. Deliberative democracy also rejects the claim, which is sometimes associated with constitutional democracy, that decisions can be fully just without being legitimately arrived at. For an important discussion of democratic legitimacy, see Arthur Isak Applbaum, "Democratic Legitimacy and Official Discretion," *Philosophy & Public Affairs*, 21 (1992): 240–274.

45. Dahl, *Democracy and Its Critics*, p. 167; and Michael Walzer, "Philosophy and Democracy," *Political Theory*, 9 (1981): 379–399, esp. 397. Stuart Hampshire, who in his later writings is a thoroughgoing proceduralist, may disagree, but he also may not think that democracy is necessary to justice. See Stuart Hampshire, *Innocence and Experience* (Cambridge, Mass.: Harvard University Press, 1989). He argues for the need for procedural justice, but never claims that the procedures must be democratic to be just. See also Stephen Holmes, "Precommitment and the Paradox of Democracy," in *Constitutionalism and Democracy*, ed. Jon Elster and Rune Slagstad (Cambridge: Cambridge University Press, 1990), pp. 195–240.

46. As Robert Dahl reminds us, "all the [procedural] alternatives to majority rule are also seriously flawed" (*Democracy and Its Critics*, p. 162).

47. See William Riker, *Liberalism against Populism* (San Francisco: W. H. Freeman and Co., 1982); and Kenneth Arrow, *Social Choice and Individual Values*, 2d ed. (New York: Wiley, 1963).

48. In "Social Choice and Deliberative Democracy," *Political Studies*, 40 (1992): 60–63, David Miller discusses how deliberation can overcome the potential arbitrariness in democratic decision making which is revealed by social choice theorists.

49. Dahl, *Democracy and Its Critics*, p. 167. For a more extensive discussion of how

procedural democrats can recognize rights, see Amy Gutmann, "How Liberal Is Democracy?," in *Liberalism Reconsidered,* ed. Douglas MacLean and Claudia Mills (Totowa, N.J.: Rowman and Allanheld, 1983), pp. 25–50. For a valuable discussion of why these internal and preconditional constraints on popular rule are inadequate to an understanding of democracy, see Ronald Dworkin, "Equality, Democracy, and Constitution: We the People in Court," *Alberta Law Review,* 28 (Winter 1990): 324–346.

50. Dahl, *Democracy and Its Critics,* p. 167. In "Equality, Democracy, and Constitution," Dworkin makes a similar distinction between his own view and that of John Hart Ely (pp. 328, 343).

51. John Rawls is widely taken to be the paradigmatic constitutional democrat because he provides the most comprehensive theoretical rationale for constitutionalism. His theory is also compelling in so many ways that it is important for us to distinguish our own view from his. Other important views of constitutional democracy that we do not discuss in detail include Laurence Tribe, *American Constitutional Law* (Mineola, N.Y.: Foundation Press, 1978); and Ronald Dworkin, *Taking Rights Seriously* (Cambridge, Mass.: Harvard University Press, 1977), *Law's Empire* (Cambridge, Mass.: Harvard University Press, 1986), and *A Matter of Principle.*

52. For a related argument on the scope of constitutional law, see Lawrence G. Sager, "Justice in Plain Clothes: Reflections on the Thinness of Constitutional Law," *Northwestern Law Review,* 88 (Fall 1993): 410–435 (quote at 435). Compare Dworkin, "Equality, Democracy, and Constitution," pp. 343–346.

53. Rawls, *A Theory of Justice,* p. 356.

54. Ibid., p. 83.

55. Ronald Dworkin is a constitutional democrat who directly confronts the challenge of finding principled resolutions to moral conflicts over politically relevant issues such as legalizing abortion, pornography, and preferential hiring. Our conception of deliberative democracy, however, seeks to avoid Dworkin's overwhelming concentration on the judicial interpretation and enforcement of constitutional values, as we explain in the final section of this chapter.

56. In some respects our notion of a deliberative perspective resembles Rawls's "overlapping consensus" (*Political Liberalism* [New York: Columbia University Press, 1993], pp. 132–172). Both are intended to provide a standpoint from which to judge competing moral claims as far as possible independently of any popular comprehensive moral views. But we argue that a deliberative perspective can be fully established at any given time and place only through actual deliberation, and we also admit more competing claims that may be part of a comprehensive moral view into the public forum as legitimate grounds for legislation. See Amy Gutmann and Dennis Thompson, "Moral Conflict and Political Consensus," *Ethics,* 101 (October 1990): 64–88.

57. Rawls, *Political Liberalism,* p. 229.

58. Ibid., p. 230.

59. Ibid.

60. Rawls, *A Theory of Justice,* p. 234.

61. The process we describe is a simplified version of the constitutional and legislative

stages of the "four-stage sequence" in Rawls, *A Theory of Justice,* pp. 195–201. The scheme Rawls outlines is intricate and somewhat elusive. We are less concerned with its details than with the general strategy it represents for resolving specific moral conflicts.

62. Rawls, *A Theory of Justice,* p. 201.

63. In Chapter 6 we discuss an important exception to this tendency among constitutional democrats: Ronald Dworkin's development of a justifiable health care policy in "Will Clinton's Plan Be Fair?," *New York Review of Books,* January 13, 1994, pp. 20–25.

64. Rawls, *A Theory of Justice,* p. 359.

65. Rawls's move toward deliberative democracy is evident throughout Lecture 6 ("The Idea of Public Reason") in *Political Liberalism,* but he still permits comprehensive moral reasons to be introduced in public deliberation only in an unjust society (as when slavery exists), and only if there is reason to believe that appealing to such reasons would help make society more just. In Section 5 of the new introduction to the paperback edition of the book (New York: Columbia University Press, 1996), he explicitly revises this view: reasonable comprehensive doctrines may be introduced in public reason at any time to support a law or policy, provided that in due course reasons consistent with reciprocity are presented to support the same law or policy.

66. In this respect, Rawls's comment about deliberation in *A Theory of Justice,* p. 359, still stands: "Thus we arrive at the problem of trying to formulate an ideal constitution of public deliberation in matters of justice, a set of rules well-designed to bring to bear the greater knowledge and reasoning powers of the group so as best to approximate if not to reach the correct judgment. I shall not, however, pursue this question."

67. See Dahl, *Democracy and Its Critics;* Barry, "Is Democracy Special?"; Michael Walzer, *Spheres of Justice* (New York: Basic Books, 1983); and George Kateb, *The Inner Ocean: Individualism and Democratic Culture* (Ithaca, N.Y.: Cornell University Press, 1992), for four different interpretations of democratic government that could be seen as converging on the fundamental importance of equal respect for individual citizens.

68. An interesting exception is the constitutional theorist Bruce Ackerman, who explicitly argues for taking "the moral ideals that divide us off the conversational agenda of the liberal state." He calls this "the path of conversational restraint" and admits that "doubtless the exercise of conversational restraint will prove extremely frustrating—for it will prevent each of us from justifying our political actions by appealing to many of the things we hold to be among the deepest and most revealing truths known to humanity." Yet he claims that this mutual restraint brings a "priceless advantage" of not obliging any of us "to say something in liberal conversation that seems affirmatively false." Bruce Ackerman, "Why Dialogue?," *Journal of Philosophy,* 86 (January 1989): 16–17. The path of deliberation that we defend here does not require citizens to affirm anything that they know to be false, but neither does it require them to be silent in politics about their moral ideals or the most revealing truths.

69. John Stuart Mill, *Considerations on Representative Government,* in *Collected*

Writings, vol. 19, ed. J. M. Robson (Toronto: University of Toronto Press, 1977), chap. 3, p. 68. For discussion of empirical evidence that supports Mill, see Thompson, *John Stuart Mill and Representative Government,* pp. 38–43, 49–53.

70. See, e.g., Dworkin, *A Matter of Principle,* pp. 9–71, and *Law's Empire,* pp. 355–399. Although the court system is the focus of his writing, Dworkin also expects legislatures and other public forums to consider matters of principle: "Political debate . . . include[s] argument over principle not only when a case comes to the Court but also long before and long after." Yet public officials "would not be so sensitive to principle without the legal and political culture of which judicial review is the heart." Judicial review provides "the national argument of principle." Dworkin views it as the leading institution that "calls some issues from the battleground of power politics to the forum of principle" (*A Matter of Principle,* pp. 70–71). Even if this were descriptively accurate of existing democracies, it would still be important for democratic theory to emphasize that democracies work best when courts are not the primary forum of principle against a "battleground of power politics." In "Equality, Democracy, and Constitution," Dworkin defends a more extensive realm of deliberation when he writes that "an attractive political community wishes its citizens to engage in politics out of a shared and intense concern for the justice and rightness of the results" (p. 334); see also *Law's Empire,* pp. 217–219. But Dworkin does not take it to be his project to pursue the implications of this insight for extending the deliberative forums of society beyond the judiciary.

71. Owen Fiss, "Foreword: The Forms of Justice," *Harvard Law Review,* 93 (November 1979): 10.

72. See, e.g., Herbert Wechsler, "Toward Neutral Principles in Constitutional Law," *Harvard Law Review,* 73 (November 1959): 22–23; Ely, *Democracy and Distrust,* pp. 103; Robert Bork, "Neutral Principles and Some First Amendment Problems," *Indiana Law Journal,* 47 (Fall 1971): 10; and Alexander Bickel, *The Least Dangerous Branch* (Indianapolis: Bobbs-Merrill, 1962), pp. 24–28. Although Ronald Dworkin is often associated with this contrast, his writings provide grounds for making legislatures as well as courts more deliberative. See *Taking Rights Seriously,* pp. 82–90; *A Matter of Principle,* pp. 31–32, 69–71; and especially *Law's Empire,* pp. 217–219. In *Political Liberalism,* Rawls also notes that while the U.S. Supreme Court serves as an exemplar of public reason, "the other branches of government can certainly, if they would but do so, be forums of principle along with it in debating constitutional questions" (p. 240). Those who explicitly dispute the contrast include Paul Brest, "The Fundamental Rights Controversy," *Yale Law Journal,* 90 (April 1981): 1106–7; and Sunstein, *The Partial Constitution.*

73. Deliberation also has an important place in the executive branch in the inner councils of government when advisers present their views to agency heads, cabinet officers, and even the president. The process of "multiple advocacy," in which advisers present diverse views in a structured setting designed to give each view its due, promotes deliberation insofar as it includes relevant moral as well as empirical arguments, and insofar as it encourages a similar debate in a wider public. See Alexander L. George, "The Case for Multiple Advocacy in Making Foreign Policy," *American Political Science Review,* 66 (September 1972): 751–

785; and John P. Burke and Fred I. Greenstein, *How Presidents Test Reality* (New York: Russell Sage Foundation, 1989), pp. 286–289.

74. Fiss, "Foreword," pp. 12–13. See also Bruce Ackerman, *Reconstructing American Law* (Cambridge, Mass.: Harvard University Press, 1984), pp. 96–101; Bickel, *Least Dangerous Branch,* pp. 26, 156; Paul Brest, "A Conscientious Legislator's Guide to Constitutional Interpretation," *Stanford Law Review,* 27 (February 1975): 585–601; Stephen Carter, "The Morgan 'Power' and the Forced Reconsideration of Constitutional Decisions," *University of Chicago Law Review,* 53 (Summer 1986): 819–863; Abram Chayes, "The Role of the Judge in Public Law Litigation," *Harvard Law Review,* 89 (May 1976): 1315–16; Dworkin, *A Matter of Principle,* pp. 70–71; Michael Perry, *The Constitution, The Courts, and Human Rights* (New Haven: Yale University Press, 1982), p. 25; Lawrence Sager, "Fair Measure: The Status of Underenforced Constitutional Norms," *Harvard Law Review,* 91 (April 1978): 1212–64; and Harry H. Wellington, "Common Law Rules and Constitutional Double Standards: Some Notes on Adjudication," *Yale Law Journal,* 83 (December 1973): pp. 246–249.

75. *Harris v. Macrae,* 448 U.S. 297 (1980).

76. For a strong argument that any adequate theory of justice must be both substantive and procedural in a fundamental sense, see John Rawls, "Reply to Habermas," *Journal of Philosophy,* 92 (March 1995): 170–180.

77. Walzer, *Spheres of Justice,* p. 310.

2. The Sense of Reciprocity

1. See John Rawls, *Political Liberalism* (New York: Columbia University Press, 1993), pp. 48–54; and T. M. Scanlon, "Contractualism and Utilitarianism," in *Utilitarianism and Beyond,* ed. Amartya Sen and Bernard Williams (Cambridge: Cambridge University Press, 1982), pp. 103–128. Our interpretation of reciprocity owes much to the conceptions developed by Rawls and Scanlon, especially the fundamental idea of the fair terms of social cooperation. As will become clear, however, we give greater emphasis than they do to actual political deliberation and draw different implications with respect to the content of the principles of justice. Our understanding of reciprocity also converges in many respects with the theory of justice that Brian Barry develops in *Justice as Impartiality* (Oxford: Oxford University Press, 1995), which appeared after our manuscript went to press; but the substantive convergence is obscured by terminological contrariety. Barry uses the term "reciprocity" to refer to a hybrid theory that is closer to mutual advantage, or what we call prudence, (pp. 46–51, 271); and he uses "impartiality" to refer to what we along with Rawls and Scanlon call reciprocity (pp. 7–8, 52, 60n, 193–194).

2. See Barry's astute discussion of the political conditions that promote "the willingness to accept reasonable objections to a proposal regardless of the quarter from which they come" (*Justice as Impartiality,* pp. 99–111).

3. Impartiality could also be regarded as an alternative interpretation of reciprocity—a perspective that is mutually acceptable because it abstracts from most of the usual sources of disagreement. This is clearest in a familiar form of impar-

tiality (sometimes called neutrality), which would bracket all particular conceptions of the good in moral reasoning about politics. We criticize that interpretation in the context of the dispute about the legalization of abortion. The "impartiality" that Barry defends, however, should not be confused with the impartiality we criticize here. Barry's concept—"principles and rules that are capable of forming the basis of free agreement among people seeking agreement on reasonable terms"—is closer to what we call reciprocity (*Justice as Impartiality*, p. 11). Barry does claim that his conception of justice is neutral in two respects: it does not rest on any particular conception of the good, and it treats all conceptions of the good equally (p. 123). But he rejects the notion of neutrality that critics often ascribe to liberal conceptions, which would require a law or policy to be justified without invoking any conception of the good (p. 143).

4. Lawrence C. Becker, *Reciprocity* (London: Routledge and Kegan Paul, 1986), pp. 73–144.

5. The most sophisticated contemporary version of this type of theory is David Gauthier, *Morals by Agreement* (Oxford: Oxford University Press, 1986). We believe that the critical objections we make in the text apply to his theory, but we do not claim to do justice to the complexities of his analysis. For a careful criticism of Gauthier and more generally of the deficiencies of bargaining as a basis for justice, see Brian Barry, *Theories of Justice* (Berkeley: University of California Press, 1989), pp. 3–142; and Barry, *Justice as Impartiality*, pp. 28–51.

6. See Barry, *Theories of Justice*, pp. 160–163, 241–254. To the extent that the proponents of bargaining adjust the outcomes to compensate for the initial inequalities, they escape this kind of objection, but at the price of introducing standards that are not subject to bargaining.

7. Roger Wertheimer, "Understanding the Abortion Argument," in *The Rights and Wrongs of Abortion*, ed. Marshall Cohen et al. (Princeton: Princeton University Press, 1974), pp. 50–51.

8. For a criticism of this argument for religious toleration, and a defense of the stronger, Lockean argument for religious toleration, see Amy Gutmann and Dennis Thompson, "Moral Conflict and Political Consensus," *Ethics,* 101 (October 1990): 65–69.

9. Greg Stankiewicz, "The Controversial Curriculum," case study, Woodrow Wilson School, Princeton University, 1991.

10. Nomi Maya Stolzenberg shows that standard judicial approaches and political theories (not only liberalism but also civic republicanism and communitarianism) fail to escape the paradox of toleration for the intolerant. Teaching toleration and critical thinking, she argues, creates an environment that threatens the fundamentalists' way of life, and therefore does not represent a tolerant stance toward the fundamentalists ("'He Drew a Circle That Shut Me Out': Assimilation, Indoctrination, and the Paradox of a Liberal Education," *Harvard Law Review,* 105 [January 1993]: 581–667). In this respect her argument is consistent with the criticism we make in the text. We depart from her analysis, however, to the extent that she assumes that a satisfactory resolution of the paradox must accept the fundamentalists' objection on its own terms—for example, by showing that tol-

eration and critical thinking can be justified in a democracy only if they do not threaten the fundamentalists' beliefs or way of life.

11. Stankiewicz, "The Controversial Curriculum," p. 6; emphasis added.
12. *Mozert v. Hawkins Cty. Bd. of Educ.*, 827 F. 2d 1058 (6th Cir. 1987), *cert. denied*, 484 U.S. 1066 (1988) at 1065.
13. *Congressional Record*, November 18, 1993, p. S16058.
14. Ibid.
15. *Congressional Record*, November 20, 1993, p. S16631.
16. *Congressional Record*, November 19, 1993, p. S16381.
17. Ibid.
18. Habermas's model of deliberative democracy also appears to make room for bargaining. See Jürgen Habermas, "Three Normative Models of Democracy," *Constellations*, 1 (April 1994): 5–6.
19. Wertheimer, "Understanding the Abortion Argument," pp. 23–51.
20. Ibid., pp. 31, 37.
21. Ibid., p. 41. Some legal theorists have sought to avoid the issue of the status of the fetus by basing the case for legalization on principles of equal protection. The most cogent argument is presented by Cass Sunstein, who sees legal prohibition of abortion as "an impermissibly selective co-optation of women's bodies" (*The Partial Constitution* [Cambridge, Mass.: Harvard University Press, 1993], pp. 273–285). The government may not impose on women an obligation that it does not impose on men—in this case the duty to protect fetuses by co-opting one's own body. Although many abortion restrictions no doubt perpetuate gender discrimination in various ways, Sunstein's conclusion is too broad, at least from a perspective that respects the morally serious claims of pro-life advocates. Since the only way to prevent the destruction of a fetus is to require a woman to carry it to term, the fact that the law imposes a selective obligation on women would not be a sufficient basis for a claim of discrimination so long as one thinks that another life is at stake. If there are analogous cases in which the law does not restrict men's liberty with regard to their bodies for the sake of preventing them from actively destroying a human life, then the discrimination claim would be persuasive. As far as we know, there are no cases that are this closely analogous to restricting the liberty of women with regard to abortion. The analogy that Sunstein suggests—a father is not compelled to undergo a risk-free kidney transplant to save the life of his child (p. 274)—is not sufficiently close. Neither men nor women are required to donate organs. The permanent sacrifice of a part of the body is in some respects more, and in some respects less, intrusive than enduring an unwanted pregnancy, but the differences between preventing the destruction of a fetus and not requiring organ donations to save the life of one's child are great enough to require different moral arguments for each kind of case. The unique relation of the mother to a fetus makes it difficult to sustain the analogy with forced organ donations.
22. This is often the reaction of thoughtful students who carefully read and reflect on the articles in *The Rights and Wrongs of Abortion*. See also Laurence H. Tribe, *Abortion: The Clash of Absolutes* (New York: Norton, 1990).

23. Ronald Dworkin, *Life's Dominion: An Argument about Abortion, Euthanasia, and Individual Freedom* (New York: Alfred A. Knopf, 1993), chaps. 2–6.
24. This is only a rough summary of a more nuanced argument that Dworkin presents in *Life's Dominion*.
25. Elizabeth Mensch and Alan Freeman, *The Politics of Virtue: Is Abortion Debatable?* (Durham, N.C.: Duke University Press, 1993), pp. 130–133.
26. Ibid., p. 131.
27. Ronald Dworkin, "You'd Better Believe It," in *Incommensurability*, ed. Ruth Chany (Cambridge, Mass.: Harvard University Press, forthcoming).
28. Ibid.
29. For a discussion of moral accommodation that is generally consonant with our approach, see David Wong, "Coping with Moral Conflict and Ambiguity," *Ethics*, 102 (July 1992): 763–784.
30. In contrast to what has been called *recognition respect* (what one owes to all persons simply by virtue of their personhood), mutual respect is a form of *appraisal respect*; it expresses a positive evaluation of a person for manifesting some excellence of character. This "enables us to see that there is no puzzle at all in thinking both that all persons are entitled to respect just by virtue of their being persons and that persons are deserving of more or less respect by virtue of their personal characteristics." Stephen L. Darwall, "Two Kinds of Respect," *Ethics*, 88 (October 1977): 46; also 38–39, 45.
31. On the significance of some of these qualities for democratic character, see Albert Hirschman, "Having Opinions—One of the Elements of Well-Being?," *American Economic Association Papers and Proceedings*, 79 (1989): 75–79.
32. Quoted in Joseph A. Califano, Jr., *Governing America* (New York: Simon and Schuster, 1981), p. 84.
33. For other theorists who in different ways emphasize the importance of similar virtues for democratic citizens, see the valuable discussions in Stephen Macedo, *Liberal Virtues* (Oxford: Clarendon Press, 1990), pp. 254–285; and William Galston, *Liberal Purposes: Goods, Virtues, and Diversity in the Liberal State* (Cambridge: Cambridge University Press, 1991), pp. 213–237.
34. Remarks of Representative Bill Green, *Congressional Record*, September 9, 1988, p. H7351; emphasis added.
35. Nonetheless, Representative Green's opponents did not draw the conclusion that he wished from the existence of moral controversy: that "the decision as to what should happen to the product of that rape . . . is best left to the woman's own conscience" (ibid.). In effect, he was invoking a version of the neutrality argument to try to remove the issue from the political agenda.
36. Remarks of Representative William Dannemeyer, *Congressional Record*, September 22, 1983, p. H7319. Although Dannemeyer also said that the "economic consequences of the moral issue should not be permitted to resolve the matter," his entire speech was devoted to the "fiscal consequences."
37. Representative Barbara Mikulski, ibid.
38. We discuss in Chapter 5 Bentham's criticism of the use of arguments from motive (*Handbook of Political Fallacies* [New York: Harper, 1962], pp. 86–87).

39. For discussion of the significance of openness for democratic character, see Hirschman, "Having Opinions."

40. Califano, *Governing America*, p. 68; emphasis added. Califano also comments that he was obliged to do all he could to avoid "unnecessary provocation" (ibid.).

41. Mario Cuomo, "Religious Belief and Public Morality: A Catholic Governor's Perspective," speech delivered at the University of Notre Dame, September 13, 1984. Ken Winston called our attention to the significance of this passage. For a sustained analysis of Cuomo's position in relation to the role of religion in public life, see John H. Garvey, "The Pope's Submarine," *San Diego Law Review*, 30 (Fall 1993): 849–876.

42. Dworkin, *Life's Dominion,* chap. 3.

43. The requirement of an economy of moral disagreement bears some resemblance to Charles Larmore's "universal norm of rational dialogue," which he explains as follows: "When two people disagree about some specific point, but wish to continue talking about the more general problem they wish to solve, each should prescind from the beliefs that the other rejects, (1) in order to construct an argument on the basis of his other beliefs that will convince the other of the truth of the disputed belief, or (2) in order to shift to another aspect of the problem, where the possibilities of agreement seem greater" (*Patterns of Moral Complexity* [Cambridge: Cambridge University Press, 1987], p. 53). There are, however, important differences between Larmore's understanding and ours. On our understanding of mutual respect, people who disagree (but wish to continue talking) need not prescind from publicly professing beliefs that others reject. Nor should they "retreat to neutral grounds." Instead they should search for common grounds (seeking to satisfy the principles of accommodation). An economy of moral disagreement aspires to a mutual commitment to substantive moral principles that are not necessarily neutral with respect either to prevailing conceptions of the good life or even to the specific controversy. It should also be clear from the place of an economy of moral disagreement within deliberative democracy that the recommendation to prescind from invoking values at odds with some citizens' beliefs is contingent on those beliefs' meeting the requirements of reciprocity.

44. In two respects the kind of agreement sought by an economy of moral disagreement goes beyond Rawls's "overlapping consensus" (*Political Liberalism,* Lectures 4 and 6, and sec. 5 of introduction). First, the economy of moral disagreement guides deliberation not only, or even primarily, about constitutional essentials and matters of basic justice, but about all matters of justice and public morality. In many cases, citizens and officials cannot even determine what counts as a matter of basic justice without engaging in deliberation that respects the value of an economy of moral disagreement. Second, the economy of moral disagreement supports mutual respect of conflicting moral perspectives as an end in itself, not just as a means for achieving agreement on political questions or promoting public reason.

45. Judith Jarvis Thomson, "A Defense of Abortion," in Cohen, *The Rights and Wrongs of Abortion*, pp. 3–22.

46. Ibid., pp. 4–5.

47. *Roe v. Wade,* 410 U.S. 113 (1973), pp. 162–164.

48. Ibid., pp. 163–164.
49. *William L. Webster et al. v. Reproductive Health Services et al.*, 492 U.S. 490 (1989). See especially Justice O'Connor's concurring opinion at 522–34, and compare Justice Blackmun's partial dissent at 537.
50. See *Akron v. Akron Center for Reproductive Health, Inc.*, 462 U.S. 416 (1983).
51. 109 S. Ct. (1989), 2820.
52. For an astute discussion of *Casey*, viewing the decision as a reasonable but somewhat misguided way of affirming the sanctity of human life, see Dworkin, *Life's Dominion*, pp. 151–154, 171–175.
53. George Sher, "Subsidized Abortion: Moral Rights and Moral Compromise," *Philosophy & Public Affairs*, 10 (Fall 1981): 361–372.
54. Ibid., p. 369. Frances M. Kamm presents a concept of "moralized compromise," which is closer to the form of compromise that reciprocity would permit ("The Philosopher as Insider and Outsider," *Journal of Medicine and Philosophy*, 15 [August 1990]: 361–367). More generally on moral compromise, see Arthur Kuflick, "Morality and Compromise," in *Compromise in Ethics, Law, and Politics*, ed. J. Roland Pennock and John Chapman (New York: New York University Press, 1979), pp. 38–65; and Martin Benjamin, *Splitting the Difference: Compromise and Integrity in Ethics and Politics* (Lawrence: University Press of Kansas, 1990).
55. Sher, "Subsidized Abortion," p. 370.
56. Ibid., p. 371.
57. Ibid.
58. Justice Brennan in *Harris* v. *McRae* (1980) 448 U.S. 297 at 334. The government of course could try to avoid this objection simply by not making the offer (i.e., by not funding childbirth either). Perhaps that is what Justice Stewart had in mind when he argued, "The fact remains that the Hyde Amendment leaves an indigent woman with at least the same range of choice in deciding whether to obtain . . . an abortion as she would have had if Congress had chosen to subsidize no health care costs at all" (ibid. at 316–317) But the fact remains that Congress did decide to subsidize childbirth, and would have violated the principle of basic opportunity with respect to health care if it had not done so, as the argument in Chapter 6 will indicate.
59. A similar proposal was actually introduced in the House of Representatives as the National Indigent Women's Abortion Trust Fund Checkoff Act of 1985, which would "allow every individual to designate that $1 of his income tax payment shall be paid into such a trust fund" (H.R. 608, 99th Cong., 1st sess., January 22, 1985).
60. For some examples of characteristics of legislative institutions that encourage and discourage deliberation, see Jane Mansbridge, "Motivating Deliberation in Congress," in *Constitutionalism in America*, ed. Sarah Baumgartner Thurow, vol. 2 (Lanham, Md.: 1988), pp. 59–86. See also Barry, *Justice as Impartiality*, pp. 99–111.
61. Cf. Rawls, *Political Liberalism*, p. 54.
62. See Alasdair MacIntyre, *After Virtue* (Notre Dame, Ind.: University of Notre Dame Press, 1981), esp. pp. 6, 20–21, 189; and Michael Sandel, *Liberalism and*

the Limits of Justice (New York: Cambridge University Press, 1982), esp. p. 183. In later writings Sandel gives less emphasis to a pursuit of a common good and more to the process of deliberation itself: "On a . . . deliberative conception . . . we respect our fellow citizen's moral and religious convictions by engaging, or attending to them—sometimes by challenging and contesting them, sometimes by listening and learning from them . . . There is no guarantee that a deliberative mode of respect will lead in any given case to agreement" ("Political Liberalism," *Harvard Law Review,* 107 [May 1994]: 1794).

3. The Value of Publicity

1. Immanuel Kant, *Eternal Peace,* in *The Philosophy of Kant,* ed. Carl J. Friedrich (New York: Random House, 1949), p. 470. In the theory of John Rawls, "the point of the publicity condition is to have the parties [to the original position] evaluate conceptions of justice as publicly acknowledged and fully effective moral constitutions of social life" (*A Theory of Justice,* [Cambridge, Mass.: Harvard University Press, 1971], p. 133).
2. Jeremy Bentham, "Of Publicity," chap. 2 of *Essay on Political Tactics,* in *The Works of Jeremy Bentham,* ed. John Bowring (Edinburgh: William Tait, 1839), pt. 8, p. 310.
3. Woodrow Wilson, Address to a Joint Session of Congress, January 8, 1918, in *The Papers of Woodrow Wilson,* ed. Arthur S. Link, Vol. 45 (Princeton: Princeton University Press, 1984), 536. This passage comes from the first of Wilson's famous "Fourteen Points."
4. Woodrow Wilson, Gubernatorial Campaign Address in Trenton, N.J., October 3, 1910, in *The Papers of Woodrow Wilson,* ed. Arthur S. Link, vol. 21 (Princeton: Princeton University Press, 1976), p. 232. William Safire, *Safire's Political Dictionary* (New York: Ballantine Books, 1978), p. 536, cites a 1912 presidential campaign speech by Wilson that also mentions this issue.
5. Kant, *Eternal Peace,* p. 470.
6. See Shirley Letwin, *The Pursuit of Certainty* (Cambridge: Cambridge University Press, 1965), p. 173. Letwin refers to portfolio 96, fol. 10, in the Bentham manuscript collection at University College, London, p. 190.
7. See *The Papers of Woodrow Wilson,* ed. Arthur S. Link, vol. 51 (Princeton: Princeton University Press, 1985), p. 495. The words were written not by Wilson himself but by Frank Cobb and Walter Lippmann working in Paris under the auspices of Wilson's emissary, Colonel Edward House.
8. Information Security Oversight Office, *1993 Report to the President* (Washington, D.C., March 1994), p. 22.
9. Elaine Sciolino, "CIA Director Announces Plan for More Access to Agency Files," *New York Times,* February 22, 1992, p. A9.
10. Stanley I. Kutler, *The Wars of Watergate: The Last Crisis of Richard Nixon* (New York, Norton, 1992); and Theodore Draper, *A Very Thin Line: The Iran-Contra Affairs* (New York: Hill and Wang, 1991).
11. Jessica Mathews, "Secrecy's Radioactive Legacy," *Washington Post,* January 5, 1994, p. A19.

12. Other theorists, often identified as republicans, also converge in defending publicity from the perspective of democratic values. See, e.g., Jean Jacques Rousseau, "Dedication to the Republic of Geneva," in *Discourse on the Origin of Inequality,* in *The Social Contract and Discourses,* trans. G. D. H. Cole (London: Dent, 1988), pp. 32–33. For a less apparently democratic defense of publicity, see G. W. F. Hegel, *Hegel's Philosophy of Right,* trans. T. M. Knox (Oxford: Oxford University Press, 1967), pp. 203–204.

13. Bentham, "Of Publicity," pp. 310–312.

14. Ibid., p. 313.

15. Ibid., p. 314.

16. Ibid.

17. Serge Taylor, *Making Bureaucracies Think: The Environmental Impact Statement Strategy of Administrative Reform* (Stanford: Stanford University Press, 1984), pp. 292–295. Robert Goodin comments: "The evidence suggests that U.S. government agencies are much more sensitive to environmental considerations—both much more conscious of and much more solicitous toward those interests—simply by reason of having to make that public declaration" (*Motivating Political Morality* [Oxford: Blackwell, 1992], p. 136).

18. Taylor, *Making Bureaucracies Think,* pp. 295–297.

19. Immanuel Kant, "Perpetual Peace: A Philosophical Sketch," in *Kant's Political Writings,* ed. Hans Reiss (Cambridge: Cambridge University Press, 1970), p. 125.

20. John Stuart Mill, *Considerations on Representative Government* (1861), chap. 10, in *Collected Works of John Stuart Mill,* ed. J. M. Robson, vol. 19 (Toronto: University of Toronto Press, 1977), p. 494. Mill was criticizing the secret ballot, which he had earlier thought necessary to protect voters from intimidation and coercion. The greater danger, he now believed, was that voters under the cloak of secrecy would forget that voting is a public trust. Modern democracies remain committed to Mill's earlier position, making an exception to the requirement of publicity in order to protect the basic liberty of voters and the integrity of the electoral process. For a more recent discussion sympathetic to public voting, see Geoffrey Brennan and Philip Pettit, "Unveiling the Vote," *British Journal of Political Science,* 20 (July 1990): 311–334.

21. For a far-ranging and insightful account of the value of secrecy in private and public life, see Sissela Bok, *Secrets* (New York: Pantheon, 1982).

22. Alan Greenspan, Chairman of the Federal Reserve Board, testimony before the House Banking Committee, in Federal Information Systems Corporation, *Federal News Service,* October 19, 1993, p. 2.

23. Henry Gonzalez, Chair of House Banking Committee, quoted in *New York Times,* October 20, 1993, p. D13. See also Alan Greenblatt, "Look Who's Talking Too: Taping of the Federal Reserve System Meetings," *Washington Monthly,* 25 (December 1993): 42.

24. Greenspan, testimony, p. 2.

25. John M. Berry, "The Fed, Under the Glare of the Spotlight," *Washington Post National Weekly Edition,* December 20–26, 1993, p. 17.

26. Greenspan, testimony, p. 2; emphasis added.

27. There are conflicting accounts of what the President approved: see Theodore Draper, *A Very Thin Line*, pp. 156–160.

28. For further discussion of forms of accountability, see Dennis F. Thompson, *Political Ethics and Public Office* (Cambridge, Mass.: Harvard University Press, 1987), pp. 22–31.

29. *Freedom of Information Act*, in *United States Statutes at Large*, vol. 81, 90th Cong., 1st sess. (1967). Clause b(8) states that the act does not apply to matters that are "contained in or related to examination, operating, or conditions reports prepared by, or on behalf of, or for the use of an agency responsible for the regulation or supervision of financial institutions."

30. Philip J. Hilts, "Surgeon General–Designate Weathers Senate Hearing," *New York Times*, July 24, 1993, p. A6; and "Word on Faulty Condoms Hushed Up," *Chicago Tribune*, July 22, 1993, p. 3.

31. We discuss the relation of personal integrity to basic liberty in Chapter 7, and the content of the principle of basic opportunity in Chapter 8.

32. Several paragraphs in this section are drawn from Thompson, *Political Ethics and Public Office*, pp. 120–121.

33. See Richard A. Rettig, "The Policy Debate on End-Stage Renal Disease," in *Ethics and Politics*, 1st ed., ed. Amy Gutmann and Dennis Thompson (Chicago: Nelson-Hall, 1984), pp. 144–162.

34. Steven E. Rhoads, "How Much Should We Spend to Save a Life?," in *Valuing Life*, ed. Steven E. Rhoads (Boulder, Colo.: Westview Press, 1980), p. 304. Robert Goodin also seems to suggest that policymakers may pretend that they are not putting a price on life even though they are in fact doing so: "The polite fiction might just be enough to protect people's self-respect" (*Political Theory and Public Policy* [Chicago: University of Chicago Press, 1982], p. 121).

35. Kristen Luker, *Abortion and the Politics of Motherhood* (Berkeley: University of California Press, 1984), p. 77.

36. Goodin, *Motivating Political Morality*, p. 142.

37. Goodin in a footnote concedes as much: "It may well be the case that the illusion that abortions were carried out only in special circumstances could not have been sustained for much longer, anyhow, in the face of mounting demands for them from a new 'liberated' generation of women" (*Motivating Political Morality*, p. 142).

38. See Archon Fung, "Making Rights Real: *Roe*'s Impact on Abortion Access," *Politics and Society*, 21 (December 1993): 465–504.

39. Goodin, *Motivating Political Morality*, p. 140. The assumption is explicit: "Let us simply take it as given, for purposes of this example: (a) that the moral truth lies with those who think that a woman should legally have the right to choose what happens to her own body; and (b) that implies a right to abort an unwanted fetus, at least right up to the point at which that fetus is capable of sustaining an independent existence" (pp. 140–141).

40. Morris Fiorina, "The Decline of Collective Responsibility," *Daedalus*, 109 (Summer 1980): 41.

41. See Donald R. Kinder and David O. Sears, "Prejudice and Politics: Symbolic Racism versus Racial Threats to the Good Life," *Journal of Personality and Social*

Psychology, 40 (March 1981): 414–431; and D. O. Sears, "Symbolic Racism," in *Eliminating Racism: Profiles in Controversy,* ed. Phyllis A. Katz and Dalmas A. Taylor (New York: Plenum Press, 1988), pp. 53–84.

42. Tali Mendelberg,"The Politics of Racial Ambiguity: Origin and Consequences of Implicitly Racial Appeals" (Ph.D. diss., University of Michigan, 1994), esp. pp. 152–247.

43. Bentham, "Of Publicity," p. 315.

44. The phrase "private life" should not be taken as referring to conduct or actions that are in some way essentially or intrinsically private, and therefore by their very nature insulated from public scrutiny. On the contrary, we argue that conduct that would sometimes be private (in the sense of protected from public scrutiny) ceases to be so protected when it is relevant to assessing a person's public responsibility. "Private life" in these discussions is therefore better understood as referring to conduct that would be private in the absence of a showing of substantial relevance to public duties. For further discussion of these issues, see Thompson, *Political Ethics and Public Office,* pp. 126–129.

45. See Kim Sheppele's distinction between "strategic" and "private" secrets, in *Legal Secrets* (Chicago: University of Chicago Press, 1988), pp. 11–12.

46. U.S. Senate Select Committee on Ethics, *Report to Accompany S. Res 168* [expulsion of Sen. Robert Packwood], 104th cong., 1st sess., September 5, 1995.

47. The account relies on an original case study prepared under our supervision by Jillian P. Dickert, "Privacy and Publicity: The Senate Confirmation of Justice Clarence Thomas," Harvard University, Kennedy School of Government Case Program, 1992. See also Jane Mayer and Jill Abramson, *Strange Justice: The Selling of Clarence Thomas* (Boston: Houghton Mifflin, 1994).

48. See Dickert, "Privacy and Publicity," p. 10.

49. Throughout the time that Hill was confiding her allegations to staffers, she requested confidentiality. On September 10, 1991, for example, Hill had a telephone conversation with James Brudney, chief counsel to Senator Howard Metzenbaum's Labor Subcommittee, to whom she "detailed her allegations . . . and expressed reservations about making allegations if no other woman made similar charges." When she spoke two days later to Harriet Grant, the chief counsel for the Judiciary Committee's nominations unit, Hill "repeated her concern that a single complainant would not be believed and again expressed her desire for confidentiality—according to Grant, Hill did not want the nominee to know her name or that she had stated her concerns to the committee." Grant told Hill that "her charges would be kept confidential, but 'little could be done' unless Thomas was informed and given an opportunity to respond [to the allegations]." Ibid., p. 12.

50. Mayer and Abramson, *Strange Justice,* pp. 244–279.

51. Yet another way in which the committee might have inclined toward liberty is by limiting the *modes* of publicity to those that would have been least threatening to the integrity of Hill and Thomas. Had the hearings not been televised but had otherwise been open to the press, would the values of publicity and integrity both have been better served?

52. Max Farrand, ed., *The Records of the Federal Convention of 1787,* rev. ed., 4 vols. (New Haven: Yale University Press, 1966), 2: 33n; 3: 73, 368.

53. Ibid., 3: 76.
54. George Will, "Smoking Out the Barons," *Washington Post,* September 19, 1993, p. C7; emphasis added.
55. David S. Broder, "Less Deliberative Democracy," *Washington Post,* October 3, 1993), p. C7; emphasis added.
56. The first federal court ruling was *American Association of Physicians and Surgeons, Inc., v. Clinton,* Civil Action no. 93–0399, March 11, 1993, 813 F. Supp. 82, 1993 U.S. Dist. Subsequent rulings from the U.S. District Court include Civil Action no. 93–0399 (RCL), November 9, 1993, 837 F. Supp. 454, 1993 U.S. Dist.; and Civil Action no. 93–0399 (RCL), December 1, 1994, 1994 U.S. Dist.
57. For a contemporaneous defense of the secret deliberations, see "Health Team Needs Breathing Room," *St. Louis Dispatch,* March 31, 1993, p. C2. For a critique, see "Let's All Be Health Care Insiders," *New York Times,* March 13, 1993, p. A20.
58. Joseph Bessette cites, as an example in favor of secrecy, the first 1986 Tax Reform Bill, which was quietly drafted by Treasury Department officials in private, and was generally regarded as much better than the bill later produced in the glare of publicity (*The Mild Voice of Reason: Deliberative Democracy and American National Government* [Chicago: University of Chicago Press, 1994], pp. 206–209.) The "better" bill, like Clinton's health care plan, was never passed.
59. Graham Allison and Lance Liebman, "Lying in Office," in *Ethics and Politics,* ed. Amy Gutmann and Dennis Thompson, 2d ed. (Chicago: Nelson-Hall, 1990), p. 44. According to Helms, the CIA never tried to overthrow the government, but attempted only to dissuade the Chilean congress from confirming Allende's electoral victory; and the CIA did not give any money directly to the candidates, only to groups that supported or opposed candidates.
60. David Nacht, "The Iran-Contra Affair," in Gutmann and Thompson, *Ethics and Politics,* pp. 56, 57.
61. Thomas Powers, *The Man Who Kept Secrets: Richard Helms and the CIA* (New York: Simon and Schuster, 1979), p. 391.
62. Peter W. Morgan, "The Undefined Crime of Lying to Congress: Ethics Reform and the Rule of Law," *Northwestern University Law Review,* 86 (Winter 1992): 177–258.
63. Morgan "takes as a given that the use of deliberate lies by executive officials in communications with Congress distorts and degrades the process of democratic government," but argues that the applicable statute is overly broad (ibid., p. 189).
64. "Any man who tries to be good all the time is bound to come to ruin among the great number who are not good. Hence a prince who wants to keep his post must learn how not to be good, and use that knowledge, or refrain from using it, as necessity requires." Niccolo Machiavelli, *The Prince,* trans. and ed. Robert M. Adams (New York: Norton, 1977), chap. 15, p. 44. See also Hannah Arendt, "Truth and Politics," in *Philosophy, Politics, and Society,* 3rd ser., ed. Peter Laslett and W. G. Runciman (New York: Barnes and Noble, 1967), pp. 104–133.
65. Sissela Bok presents a more general argument, which underscores the importance of deliberation as a deterrent to unwarranted compromising of moral principles:

"Just as unreflective appeals to morality too often turn, in practice, into moralizing, so unreflecting appeals to the 'dirty hands' rationale too often turn, in practice, into needless and unjustified exceptions to moral principles" (*A Strategy for Peace: Human Values and the Threat of War* [New York: Pantheon, 1989], p. 127; more generally, see pp. 125–131).

66. For the distinction between deep and shallow secrets, see Sheppele, *Legal Secrets*, pp. 3–23.

67. Jeff Gerth, "Quiet Handling of a Nominee's S&L Tenure," *New York Times*, July 21, 1994, p. 1.

68. Andrew Rosenthal, "Bush's In-Flight Show: Pique, and a Bumpy Ride for the Press," *New York Times*, February 16, 1990, p. A12.

69. John R. MacArthur, "Remember Nayirah, Witness for Kuwait?," *New York Times*, January 6, 1992, p. A17.

70. Charles R. Babcock and Bob Woodward, "Tower: The Consultant as Advocate," *Washington Post*, February 13, 1989, p. A1.

71. Anthony Lewis calls for such self-constraint in "Freedom of the Press," *New York Times*, December 24, 1993, p. A27.

72. Jon Elster, "The Market and the Forum: Three Varieties of Political Theory," in *Foundations of Social Theory*, ed. Jon Elster and Aanund Hylland (Cambridge: Cambridge University Press, 1986), pp. 112–113. Similarly, Jürgen Habermas suggests that unconstrained discourse will produce a common interest: "The interest is common because the constraint-free consensus permits only what *all* can want" (*Legitimation Crisis*, trans. Thomas McCarthy [Boston: Beacon Press, 1975], p. 108). Cf. John Stuart Mill's comment on the secret ballot, cited in note 20.

73. Donald R. Matthews, *U.S. Senators and Their World* (Chapel Hill: University of North Carolina Press, 1960), pp. 99–100 (cited in Goodin, *Motivating Political Morality*, p. 133).

74. Compare Goodin's discussion of this exchange in *Motivating Political Morality*, p. 133.

4. The Scope of Accountability

1. The bill would have banned all abortions except when the mother's health was endangered by pregnancy, when the child would be born with "profound and irremediable physical or mental disabilities," or in cases of rape or incest. We rely on the account by Jillian P. Dickert, "Senator Scott Heidepriem and the South Dakota Anti-Abortion Bill," Case Program, Kennedy School of Government, C16-93-1213.0, 1993.

2. On the inadequacy of the trustee-delegate dichotomy, see Dennis F. Thompson, *Political Ethics and Public Office* (Cambridge, Mass.: Harvard University Press, 1987), pp. 99–102, and the citations there. The absence of significant correlations between citizens' preferences and legislators' roll call votes does not show that legislators are not accountable to citizens, because legislators can anticipate the reactions of citizens (and presumably therefore can sometimes have some influence on the reactions). For a theory of congressional accountability that emphasizes

this anticipatory behavior and thereby transcends the trustee-delegate dichotomy, see R. Douglas Arnold, *The Logic of Congressional Action* (New Haven: Yale University Press, 1990), esp. pp. 8–12, 267–274.

3. See Amy Gutmann, *Liberal Equality* (Cambridge: Cambridge University Press, 1980); and Dennis F. Thompson, *The Democratic Citizen* (Cambridge: Cambridge University Press, 1970), and *John Stuart Mill and Representative Government* (Princeton: Princeton University Press, 1976).

4. On the desirability of representative government (though more from the perspective of constitutional than deliberative democracy), see George Kateb, "The Moral Distinctiveness of Representative Democracy," in *The Inner Ocean: Individualism and Democratic Culture* (Ithaca, N.Y.: Cornell University Press, 1992), pp. 36–56.

5. Bertrand de Jouvenal, "The Chairman's Problem," *American Political Science Review,* 55 (June 1961): 368–372; and Robert Dahl and Edward Tufte, *Size and Democracy* (Stanford: Stanford University Press, 1973), esp. pp. 66–88.

6. Aristotle, *Politics,* trans. Harris Rackham (New York: Putnam's Sons, 1932), 1281a42–b10, pp. 221–223, and 1286a22–b22, pp. 257–259.

7. Lynn M. Sanders, "Against Deliberation," December 1993, p. 27, forthcoming in *Political Theory.*

8. See Valerie P. Hans and Neil Vidmar, *Judging the Jury* (New York: Plenum Press, 1986), esp. p. 108; but see Reid Hastie, Steven D. Penrod, and Nancy Pennington, *Inside the Jury* (Cambridge, Mass.: Harvard University Press, 1983), p. 162.

9. Hastie, Penrod, and Pennington, *Inside the Jury,* pp. 163–165; and Phoebe Ellsworth, "Are Twelve Heads Better Than One?," *Law and Contemporary Problems,* 52 (Autumn 1989): 215. More generally on jury studies, see Reid Hastie, ed., *Inside the Juror: The Psychology of Juror Decision Making* (Cambridge: Cambridge University Press, 1993).

10. "Ms. Moseley Braun's Majestic Moment," *New York Times,* July 24, 1993, p. 18.

11. Adam Clymer, "Daughter of Slavery Hushes Senate," *New York Times,* July 23, 1993, p. B6. Perhaps in some forums (e.g., a university faculty meeting or certain progressive city councils), Moseley Braun's appeal might be seen as inhibiting debate by exploiting the force of political correctness, but the danger of that in the Senate on this issue was slight, as shown by the many years of silence on the issue.

12. Ibid.

13. "Ms. Moseley Braun's Majestic Moment," p. 18.

14. Ibid.

15. See bell hooks, *Yearning: Race, Gender, and Cultural Politics* (Boston: South End Press, 1990), p. 27, cited in Sanders, "Against Deliberation," pp. 28–30.

16. C. A. J. Coady, *Testimony: A Philosophical Study* (Oxford: Clarendon Press, 1992), esp. pp. 42–53.

17. For a thoughtful study that explicitly contrasts deliberative and bargaining approaches to the role of the jury, see Jeffrey Abramson, *The Jury System and the Ideal of Democracy* (New York: Basic Books, 1994).

18. Dickert, "Senator Heidepriem," pp. 8–9.

19. Quoted ibid., p. 2.

20. Ibid., p. 3.
21. Nancy D. Kates, "Tacoma Neon Wars: Procuring Public Art," Case Program, Kennedy School of Government, C15–87–764.0, 765.0, 766.0, 1987.
22. Ibid., C15–87–766.0, pp. 2–5. See also United Press International wire press reports, October 31, December 7, and December 12, 1984.
23. Kates, "Tacoma Neon Wars," C15–87–766.0, p. 6.
24. This process of reiterated deliberation is consistent with a central feature of the models of legislative accountability developed by political scientists in recent years, in particular those of John Kingdon and R. Douglas Arnold. The relevant feature is that legislators anticipate the *potential* preferences of constituents. "Rather than assuming that policy preferences are fixed and asking what impact established preferences have on legislators' decisions," Arnold argues that we should ask "how legislators adjust their decisions in anticipation of them" (Arnold, *The Logic of Congressional Action,* p. 10). See also John Kingdon, *Congressmen's Voting Decisions,* 2d ed. (New York: Harper and Row, 1981), p. 60. This anticipatory behavior gives rise to a dynamic process, with possibilities for the multistage interaction between legislators and citizens that deliberative accountability requires. Arnold, however, does not emphasize the reason-giving aspect of accountability, presumably because he is more concerned with explaining congressional behavior than with criticizing it. Also, he is more interested in electoral than in other more deliberative interactions between citizens and legislators.
25. A useful collection of articles on the Oregon plan is Martin A. Strosberg et al., *Rationing America's Medical Care: The Oregon Plan and Beyond* (Washington, D.C.: Brookings Institution, 1992). For contrasting views of the plan and the process by which it was adopted, see Howard M. Leichter, "Political Accountability in Health Care Rationing: In Search of a New Jerusalem," *University of Pennsylvania Law Review,* 140 (May 1992): 1939–63; Leonard M. Fleck, "Models of Rationing: Just Health Care Rationing: A Democratic Decisionmaking Approach," 140 *University of Pennsylvania Law Review,* 140 (May 1992): 1597–1636; and W. John Thomas, "The Oregon Medicaid Proposal: Theoretical Paralyis, Tragic Democracy, and the Fate of a Utilitarian Health Care Program," *Oregon Law Review,* 72 (Spring 1993): 47–156.
26. Michael J. Garland, "Rationing in Public: Oregon's Priority-Setting Methodology," in Strosberg et al., *Rationing America's Medical Care,* p. 45.
27. The most cogent criticisms based on justice are presented by Norman Daniels, "Justice and Health Care Rationing: Lessons from Oregon," in Strosberg et al., *Rationing America's Medical Care,* pp. 185–195. See also David Hadorn, "Setting Health Care Priorities in Oregon: Cost-Effectiveness Meets the Rule of Rescue," *Journal of the American Medical Association* May 1, 1991, pp. 2218–25.
28. Garland, "Rationing in Public," p. 39.
29. Pamela Varley, "Defunding Organ Transplants in Arizona," in *Ethics and Politics,* ed. Amy Gutmann and Dennis Thompson, 2d ed. (Chicago: Nelson-Hall, 1990), p. 189. We discuss this case in more detail in Chapter 6.
30. John H. Cushman, "Clinton Seeks Ban on Export of Most Hazardous Waste," *New York Times,* March 1, 1994, p. A18.

31. For a thoughtful and illuminating moral analysis of the general problem, see Henry Shue, "Exporting Hazards," *Ethics,* 91 (July 1981): 579–606.

32. David E. Whiteside, "Note on the Export of Pesticides from the United States to Developing Countries," Harvard Business School, Case Study 384–097, 1983. See also "Velsicol Chemical Corporation," Harvard Business School, Case Study, 9–385–021,1984. See also Paul A. Stehr-Green, James C. Wohlleb, Wendy Royce, and Susan L. Head, "An Evaluation of Serum Pesticide Residue Levels and Liver Function in Persons Exposed to Dairy Products Contaminated with Heptaclor," *Journal of the American Medical Association,* January 15, 1988, pp. 374–377; Kenneth Cohen and Philip Felig, "Occupational and Other Environmental Diseases of the Endocrine System," *Archives of International Medicine,* 144 (March 1984): 469–471; and Ellen K. Silbergeld, "Carcinogenicity of Dioxins," *Journal of the National Cancer Institute,* September 4, 1991, pp. 1198–99.

33. "Transcript of President Clinton's Announcement," *New York Times,* June 4, 1993, p. A19. For Guinier's account of the events, see her "Who's Afraid of Lani Guinier?," *New York Times Magazine,* February 27, 1994, pp. 40–44, 54–55, 66.

34. It is a further question whether, given her views (valid or not), President Clinton should have nominated her for the position, and still another question whether her nomination should have been withdrawn under these circumstances.

35. Lani Guinier, "The Triumph of Tokenism: The Voting Rights Act and the Theory of Black Electoral Success," *Michigan Law Review,* 89 (March 1991): 1134–54. See also Lani Guinier, *The Tyranny of the Majority: Fundamental Fairness in Representative Democracy* (New York: Free Press, 1994), pp. 41–70.

36. Guinier, "Who's Afraid?," p. 55. See also Guinier, *Tyranny of the Majority,* pp. 14–16, 94–95, 149.

37. Guinier, "Who's Afraid?," p. 55. One commentator in fact argues that the "tendency of her thought is, so far, strategic" or "pluralist," which he contrasts with "deliberative." See David Estlund, "Who's Afraid of Deliberative Democracy?," *Texas Law Review,* 71 (June 1993): 1474–75.

38. Iris Marion Young, *Justice and the Politics of Difference* (Princeton: Princeton University Press, 1990), p. 184. See also Guinier, "Triumph of Tokenism," pp. 1134–54; and Lani Guinier, "No Two Seats: The Elusive Quest for Political Equality," *Virginia Law Review,* 77 (November 1991): 1461–1513 (also in *Tyranny of the Majority,* pp. 41–70 and 71–118).

39. Will Kymlicka, "Three Forms of Group-Differentiated Citizenship in Canada," in *Democracy and Difference: Changing Boundaries of the Political,* ed. Seyla Benhabib (Princeton: Princeton University Press, 1996), pp. 153–170. There is also the further problem of ensuring that the representatives of the group are genuine representatives, that they are in fact accountable to the group.

40. Ibid.

41. See Thompson, *John Stuart Mill and Representative Government,* pp. 102–111.

42. Derek Parfit, "The Further Future: The Identity Problem," in *Energy and the Future,* ed. Douglas MacLean and Peter G. Brown (Totowa, N.J.: Rowman and Littlefield, 1983), pp. 166–179. For a more extensive argument to this effect, see Derek Parfit, *Reasons and Persons* (New York: Oxford University Press, 1984),

pp. 351–438, 487–490. See also David Heyd, *Genethics: Moral Issues in the Creation of People* (Berkeley: University of California Press, 1992). More generally on future generations, see also R. I. Sikora and Brian Barry, *Obligations to Future Generations* (Philadelphia: Temple University Press, 1978); Brian Barry, "Justice between Generations," in *Democracy, Power, Justice: Essays in Political Theory,* (Oxford: Clarendon Press, 1989), pp. 494–510; and Brian Barry, *Theories of Justice,* (Berkeley: University of California Press, 1989), pp. 189–201.

43. Michael Kinsley, "Post-Boomer Bellyaching: The Dubious Lament of Generation X," *Washington Post,* March 4, 1994, p. A23.

44. Edith Stokey and Richard Zeckhauser, *A Primer for Policy Analysis* (New York: Norton, 1978), p. 173 (summarizing the "social time preference" approach, which they also criticize at p. 174).

45. Uncertainty is generally treated as part of the problem of risk valuation, analytically distinct from the idea of (risk-free) opportunity costs. See ibid., p. 173.

46. Robert Goodin, *Political Theory and Public Policy* (Chicago: University of Chicago Press, 1982), pp. 162–183.

47. Ronald Dworkin, *Life's Dominion: An Argument about Abortion, Euthanasia, and Individual Freedom* (New York: Alfred A. Knopf, 1993), p. 78.

48. Ibid., p. 155.

49. Ibid., pp. 157, 175.

50. Ibid., p. 175.

51. Cf. Dworkin: "A state may not curtail liberty, in order to protect an intrinsic value, when the effect on one group of citizens would be special and grave, when the community is seriously divided about what respect for that value requires, and when people's opinions about the nature of that value reflect essentially religious convictions that are fundamental to moral personality" (ibid., p. 157).

52. John Rawls, *A Theory of Justice* (Cambridge, Mass.: Harvard University Press, 1971), pp. 284–293,

53. Barry, *Theories of Justice,* p. 200.

54. John Rawls, *Political Liberalism* (New York: Columbia University Press, 1993), p. 274. This argument for a just savings principle was already present in certain passages in the statement of Rawls's initial theory: the principle is partly based on "an estimate that seems fair from both sides, with due allowance made for the improvement in their circumstances" (*A Theory of Justice,* p. 289).

55. William K. Stevens, "Gore Promises U.S. Leadership on Sustainable Development Path," *New York Times,* June 15, 1993, p. C4.

56. Since current generations in other countries stand to lose even more from environmental degradation, the debate also raises the other kind of challenge of constituency: To what extent should U.S. officials represent the interests of nonresidents?

57. Albert Gore, Jr., *Earth in the Balance: Ecology and the Human Spirit* (Boston: Houghton Mifflin, 1992), pp. 238–265.

58. Thomas Hobbes, *Leviathan* (1651), ed. C. B. Macpherson (Harmondsworth: Penguin, 1985), chap. 11, p. 162.

59. Nor do they arise only in the legislative branch or only for elected officials. Although this chapter focuses on legislators, the problems, with appropriate mod-

ifications, pose similar challenges for elected and appointed officials in the executive branch, as well as for any career administrators who have substantial policy discretion. On the latter, see Dennis F. Thompson, "Democracy and Bureaucracy," in *Democratic Theory and Practice,* ed. Graeme Duncan (Cambridge: Cambridge University Press, 1983), pp. 235–250.

5. The Promise of Utilitarianism

1. An excellent short exposition and critique of utilitarianism as a political morality is Will Kymlicka, *Contemporary Political Philosophy* (Oxford: Clarendon Press, 1990), pp. 9–49.
2. For a lucid account of policy analysis, see Edith Stokey and Richard Zeckhauser, *A Primer for Policy Analysis* (New York: Norton, 1978).
3. Two of the most subtle contemporary versions of utilitarian moral theories are James Griffin, *Well-Being: Its Meaning, Measurement, and Moral Importance* (Oxford: Oxford University Press, 1986); and Derek Parfit, *Reasons and Persons* (Oxford: Oxford University Press, 1984). For other important discussions of foundational utilitarianism, see Russell Hardin, *Morality within the Limits of Reason* (Chicago: University of Chicago Press, 1988); Samuel Scheffler, *Consequentialism and Its Critics* (Oxford: Oxford University Press, 1988); and Amartya Sen and Bernard Williams, eds., *Utilitarianism and Beyond* (Cambridge: Cambridge University Press, 1982). Among contemporary utilitarians who apply their theories to practical problems are Jonathan Glover, *Causing Death and Saving Lives* (New York: Penguin, 1977); Robert Goodin, *Political Theory and Public Policy* (Chicago: University of Chicago Press, 1982), and *Reasons for Welfare* (Princeton: Princeton University Press, 1988); R. M. Hare, *Freedom and Reason* (Oxford: Oxford University Press, 1971), *Moral Thinking* (Oxford: Clarendon Press, 1981), and *Essays on Political Morality* (Oxford: Clarendon Press, 1989); and Peter Singer, ed., *Practical Ethics* (Cambridge: Cambridge University Press, 1993). For the game-theoretical wing of utilitarianism, see Brian Barry's exposition and critique, *Theories of Justice* (Berkeley: University of California Press, 1989), pp. 3–142.
4. Keith Schneider, "New View Calls Environmental Policy Misguided," *New York Times,* March 21, 1993, p. 30.
5. Robert B. Reich, "Policy Making in a Democracy," in *The Power of Public Ideas,* ed. Robert B. Reich (Cambridge, Mass.: Ballinger Publishing Co., 1988), p. 147.
6. Esther Scott, "The Risks of Asarco," in *Ethics and Politics,* ed. Amy Gutmann and Dennis Thompson, 2d ed. (Chicago: Nelson-Hall, 1990), pp. 163–174, esp. p. 164. This episode took place about a year before the "neon war" in Tacoma described in Chapter 4.
7. Ibid., p. 165.
8. Ibid.
9. Ibid., p. 164.
10. Ibid., p. 165.
11. Although Bentham identified utility with pleasure, his use of "pleasure" was much broader than the ordinary sense of the term, and as he applied it the principle of

utility included nearly any end that humans might pursue. See Jeremy Bentham, *Introduction to the Principles of Morals and Legislation* (1789), in vol. 1 of *The Works of Jeremy Bentham*, ed. John Bowring (Edinburgh: William Tait, 1843).

12. John Stuart Mill, "Utilitarianism," in *Utilitarianism and Other Essays*, ed. Mary Warnock (New York: Meridian, 1974), p. 319: "That principle is a mere form of words without signification, unless one person's happiness, supposed equal in degree . . . [,] is counted for exactly as much as another's. Those conditions being supplied, Bentham's dictum, 'everybody to count for one, nobody for more than one,' might be written under the principle of utility as an explanatory commentary." It appears that Bentham never wrote this dictum in its widely (mis)quoted form. What he actually wrote expresses the sense of the dictum but less parsimoniously: "The happiness and unhappiness of any one member of the community—high or low, rich or poor—what greater or less part is it of the universal happiness and unhappiness, than that of any other?" Jeremy Bentham, *Plan of Parliamentary Reform*, in *Works*, 3: 452. For a discussion of other passages in which Bentham's writings support the commonly (mis)quoted dictum, see David J. Crossley, "Utilitarianism, Rights, and Equality," *Utilitas*, 2 (May 1990): 46.

13. Bernard Williams, *Ethics and the Limits of Philosophy* (Cambridge, Mass.: Harvard University Press, 1985), pp. 108–110.

14. Scott, "The Risks of Asarco," p. 163

15. On the problem of "illegitimate preferences" in utilitarianism, see Kymlicka, *Contemporary Political Philosophy*, pp. 25–30.

16. Quoted in Scott, "The Risks of Asarco," p. 167.

17. Ibid., p. 168.

18. Kymlicka, *Contemporary Political Philosophy*, p. 10.

19. Jeremy Bentham, *Handbook of Political Fallacies* (New York: Harper, 1962), pp. 86–87.

20. Ibid.

21. Ibid., p. 100.

22. Scott, "The Risks of Asarco," pp. 164, 167.

23. As Kymlicka points out, the status of the maximization principle in utilitarianism is ambiguous. On a "teleological" interpretation, maximization is "primary, not derivative, and we count individuals equally only because that is the way to maximize value" (*Contemporary Political Philosophy*, p. 32). On the other "egalitarian" interpretation, maximization is a "by-product of a standard that is intended to aggregate people's preferences fairly" by giving each person's interests equal weight as far as possible (p. 31). Even on the second interpretation, which is more nearly consistent with reciprocity, utilitarianism, as we explain in the text, cannot serve as the single dominant principle in deliberative democracy.

24. For a incisive argument that "social outcomes should not be based on existing preferences," see Cass Sunstein, *The Partial Constitution* (Cambridge, Mass.: Harvard University Press, 1993), pp. 162–194.

25. See Samuel Popkin, *The Reasoning Voter* (Chicago: University of Chicago Press, 1991), pp. 11–12.

26. This objection applies even more strongly against the practice of "contingent valuation," in which citizens are asked to state how much they are willing to pay for

certain "non-use" or "existence" values, such as protection of the environment. A review of this practice concludes: "We doubt that these results measure some preexisting preference that in some sense is already present in people's heads. Why should people possess preferences about choices they have never had to make. . .? Instead, the responses are simply opportunities for individuals to comment, without very much opportunity for thought, on a hard issue of public policy. In short, they most likely are exhibiting offhand opinions on the same policy issue to which the cost-benefit analyst purports to give his own answer, not private preferences that might be reflected in their own market transactions." Daniel A. Farber and Paul A. Hemmersbaugh, "The Shadow of the Future: Discount Rates, Later Generations, and the Environment," *Vanderbilt Law Review,* 46 (March 1993): 301.

27. Scott, "The Risks of Asarco," p. 173.

28. Ibid.

29. For evidence and commentary on the problem of "sound bite democracy," see Kiku Adatto, *Picture Perfect: The Art and Artifice of Public Image Making* (New York: Basic Books, 1993), esp. pp. 2, 41–42, 61–75.

30. Herman B. Leonard and Richard J. Zeckhauser, "Cost-Benefit Analysis Applied to Risks: Its Philosophy and Legitimacy," in *Values at Risk,* ed., Douglas MacLean (Totowa, N.J.: Rowman and Allanheld, 1986), p. 42.

31. Following President Reagan's Executive Order 12291 in 1981, which mandated cost-benefit analysis for all major projects conducted by federal regulatory agencies, valuation of life became widespread in the executive branch. The Department of Health and Human Services, the National Highway Traffic Safety Administration, the Consumer Product Safety Commission, the Environmental Protection Agency, and the Occupational Safety and Health Administration are among the agencies that value life as a regular part of their policy analyses. The valuations that these agencies place on life are strikingly divergent. See John D. Graham and James W. Vaupel, "The Value of a Life: What Difference Does It Make?," in *What Role for Government?,* ed. Richard J. Zeckhauser and Derek Leebaert (Durham, N.C.: Duke University Press, 1983), pp. 176–186. See also Miley W. Merkhofer, *Decision Science and Social Risk Management: A Comparative Evaluation of Cost-Benefit Analysis, Decision Analysis, and Other Formal Decision-Aiding Approaches* (Dordrecht: D. Reidel, 1987), pp. 42–47.

32. Again some utilitarian policy analysts make a more modest claim: "We fully accept the role of 'untouchable' values as overriding considerations in public decision-making" (Leonard and Zeckhauser, "Cost-Benefit Analysis," p. 42), and again the concession has the effect of limiting the domain of utilitarian reasoning and subjecting it to demands of publicity and accountability.

33. Michael Walzer, *Spheres of Justice* (New York: Basic Books, 1983), pp. 95–128.

34. Derek Parfit, "The Further Future: The Identity Problem," in *Energy and the Future,* ed. Douglas MacLean and Peter G. Brown (Totowa, N.J.: Rowman and Littlefield, 1983), pp. 175–176. For the moral and metaphysical theory on which this argument is based, see Parfit, *Reasons and Persons,* pp. 351–438 and 487–490.

35. Two philosophers who pursue the second strategy are David A. J. Richards, "Con-

tractarian Theory, Intergenerational Justice, and Energy Policy," pp. 139–42; and Douglas MacLean, "A Moral Requirement of Energy Policies," pp. 181–84; both in MacLean and Brown, *Energy and the Future.*

36. Parfit, "The Further Future," p. 175.

37. Ibid., pp. 175–176.

38. Ibid., p. 175.

39. David Brink, "Utilitarian Morality and the Personal Point of View," *Journal of Philosophy,* 83 (1986): 421–427; and Peter Railton, "Alienation, Consequentialism, and the Demands of Morality," *Philosophy & Public Affairs,* 13 (Spring 1984): 140–146.

40. For further discussion of the distinction between utilitarianism as a decision-making procedure and a standard of right action, see Kymlicka, *Contemporary Political Philosophy,* pp. 25–30.

41. Some theorists accept this possibility that utilitarianism may require nonutilitarian beliefs, but suggest that it is possible for citizens to hold both kinds of beliefs, if not at the same time, then at different times in different roles. See Frederick Schauer, "Commensurability," *Hastings Law Journal,* 45 (April 1994): 785–812. The idea (which is applicable not only to utilitarianism) seems to be that in our legislative capacity we would decide what "kinds of attitudes, ideas, ideals, and dispositions . . . all of us should have" in our ordinary roles as citizens (ibid, p. 812). But the conceptual as well as practical difficulties of such two-level views can be seen in Schauer's own insightful statement of the issue that is unresolved by these views: "We are left with difficult moral questions about the circumstances under which 'we' would try to foster certain beliefs that we did not believe because we believed that those beliefs, in the hands of 'them,' would produce the morally best world" (p. 812).

42. For criticism of "willingness to pay" and cost-benefit analysis more generally, see MacLean, *Values at Risk;* Dorothy Nelkin and Michael S. Brown, *Workers at Risk* (Chicago: University of Chicago Press, 1984); and Elizabeth Anderson, "Values, Risks, and Market Norms," *Philosophy & Public Affairs,* 17 (Winter 1988): 54–65.

43. Amartya Sen, *Collective Choice and Social Welfare* (San Francisco: Holden-Day, 1970), pp. 94–98; John Rawls, *A Theory of Justice* (Cambridge, Mass.: Harvard University Press, 1971), p. 323.

44. For a utilitarian defense of the criterion, see John C. Harsanyi, "Morality and the Theory of Rational Behavior," in Sen and Williams, *Utilitarianism and Beyond,* pp. 39–62. For a critique of Pareto optimality, see Brian Barry, "Lady Chatterley's Lover and Doctor Fischer's Bomb Party: Liberalism, Pareto Optimality, and the Problem of Objectionable Preferences," in *Democracy, Power, and Justice: Essays in Political Theory,* (Oxford: Clarendon Press, 1989), pp. 360–391. See also the essays in Jon Elster and Aanund Hylland, eds., *Foundations of Social Choice Theory* (Cambridge: Cambridge University Press, 1989).

45. Stokey and Zeckhauser, *Primer for Policy Analysis,* p. 280.

46. Hare, *Moral Thinking,* p. 118.

47. Goodin, *Political Theory and Public Policy,* p. 246.

48. Ibid., p. 17.

49. These figures are taken from a 1991 analysis by the Office of Management and Budget, reproduced in Keith Schneider, "How a Rebellion over Environmental Rules Grew from a Patch of Weeds," *New York Times,* March 24, 1993, p. A16.

50. Strict utilitarians argue, with some plausibility, that many of these departures from impartiality are not justified—for example, in the prevention of famine. See Singer, *Practical Ethics.*

51. For different views about moral considerations that might be raised against a policy of saving the maximum number of lives, see Charles Fried, *Anatomy of Values* (Cambridge, Mass.: Harvard University Press, 1970), pp. 207–238; and John M. Taurek, "Should the Numbers Count?," *Philosophy & Public Affairs,* 6 (Summer 1977): 293–316.

52. For a utilitarian attempt to take such factors into account, see Glover, *Causing Death and Saving Lives,* pp. 203–227.

53. John Harris, *Violence and Responsibility* (London: Routledge and Kegan Paul, 1980), pp. 66–84.

54. Goodin, *Political Theory and Public Policy,* p. 246.

55. Reich, "Policy Making in a Democracy," p. 149.

56. Charles Wolf, "Ethics and Policy Analysis," in *Public Duties,* ed. Joel Fleishman et al. (Cambridge, Mass.: Harvard University Press, 1981), pp. 131–132.

6. *The Constitution of Deliberative Democracy*

1. John Rawls, *A Theory of Justice* (Cambridge, Mass.: Harvard University Press, 1971), pp. 65–107. In Chapter 1 Rawls appeared as a constitutional democrat, whose principles of liberty and equal opportunity would constrain democratic majorities; in this chapter his opportunity principle serves as an exemplar of the implications of a liberal egalitarian perspective on moral disagreement.

2. Our account of this case relies primarily on Pamela Varley, "Defunding Organ Transplants in Arizona," in *Ethics and Politics: Cases and Comments,* ed. Amy Gutmann and Dennis Thompson, 2d ed. (Chicago: Nelson-Hall, 1990), pp. 178–195.

3. Ibid., p. 191.

4. Robert Nozick, *Anarchy, State, and Utopia* (New York: Basic Books, 1974), p. 33.

5. Ibid., p. 160.

6. Rawls, *A Theory of Justice,* pp. 204–205.

7. Nozick, *Anarchy, State, and Utopia,* p. 169. See also John Hospers, "What Libertarianism Is," in *The Libertarian Alternative,* ed. Tibor R. Machan (Chicago: Nelson-Hall 1974), p. 3.

8. Nozick writes that we cannot rely on the libertarian principle (which accords absolute priority to individual liberty) "to condemn any particular scheme of transfer payments, unless it is clear that no considerations of rectification of injustice could apply to justify it." In practice, this concession is fatal to the capacity of libertarianism to judge redistributive policies. Nozick, *Anarchy, State, and Utopia,* p. 231.

9. See Hillel Steiner, "Three Just Taxes," in *Arguing for Basic Income,* ed. Philippe Van Parijs (London: Verso, 1992), pp. 81–92.

10. Ibid., p. 231.
11. Varley, "Defunding Organ Transplants," p. 194.
12. Hospers, "What Libertarianism Is," p. 3.
13. Varley, "Defunding Organ Transplants," p. 191; emphasis added.
14. Cf. Rawls: "Within the limits allowed by the background arrangements, distributive shares are decided by the outcome of the natural lottery; and this outcome is *arbitrary from a moral perspective.* There is no more reason to permit the distribution of income and wealth to be settled by the distribution of natural assets than by historical and social fortune" (*A Theory of Justice,* p. 74, emphasis added).
15. Ibid., p. 73.
16. John Rawls, *Political Liberalism* (New York: Columbia University Press, 1993), pp. 291–293.
17. Ibid., p. 19. The two powers of moral personality in turn require certain powers of reason—judgment, thought, and inference—without which people cannot be free citizens.
18. The basic liberties, for Rawls, include "freedom of thought and liberty of conscience; the political liberties and freedom of association, as well as the freedoms specified by the liberty and integrity of the person; and finally, the rights and liberties covered by the rule of law." All these liberties can be understood as either constitutive or a condition of personal integrity. Ibid., p. 291.
19. Ibid., p. 291.
20. In the original position we are asked to assume that we are "normal, active, and fully cooperating members of society over the course of a complete life" [John Rawls, "Social Unity and the Primary Goods," in *Utilitarianism and Beyond,* ed. Amartya K. Sen and Bernard Williams (Cambridge: Cambridge University Press, 1982), p. 168]. For a more detailed criticism of the applicability of the difference principle to health care, see Normal Daniels, *Just Health Care* (Cambridge: Cambridge University Press, 1985), pp. 42–45.
21. As Rawls himself recognizes by denying that the difference principle is a constitutional essential (*Political Liberalism,* p. 230).
22. See, for example, Robert M. Veatch, *A Theory of Medical Ethics* (New York: Basic Books, 1981), pp. 261–264.
23. For a critique of liberal egalitarianism that emphasizes the problem of the "bottomless pit," see Charles Fried, *Right and Wrong* (Cambridge, Mass.: Harvard University Press, 1978), chap. 5.
24. The incurred reimbursement cost in 1992 was $2.013 billion. The projected cost for the year 2000 is $4.280 billion. *Annual Report of the Board of Trustees of the Federal Supplementary Medical Insurance Trust Fund* (1993), tables 2.D.9 and 2.D.10, pp. 53–54.
25. Varley, "Defunding Organ Transplants," p. 187.
26. His view seems to express a mixture of utilitarianism, egalitarianism, and perhaps a trace of paternalism, as he also said, "When I have limited resources, it's women and children first. The *Titanic* concept of medicine" (ibid., p. 187). We criticize this conception later.
27. For a critique of using either part of Rawls's second principle (the difference prin-

ciple or fair equality of opportunity) to distribute health care, see Ezekiel Emanuel, *The Ends of Human Life: Medical Ethics in a Liberal Polity* (Cambridge, Mass.: Harvard University Press, 1991), chap. 4.

28. Daniels, *Just Health Care*, p. 42. For an important critique of Daniels and liberal theories of health care more generally, see Emanuel, *The Ends of Human Life*, pp. 120–154.

29. Daniels, *Just Health Care*, p. 54.

30. In his later writings Rawls takes a step in this direction: "While some principle of opportunity is surely [a constitutional] essential, . . . fair equality of opportunity (as I have specified it) goes beyond that and is not an essential. Similarly, though a social minimum providing for the basic needs of all citizens is also an essential, what I have called the 'difference principle' is more demanding and is not" *(Political Liberalism*, pp. 228–229). Although the idea of a social minimum covering basic needs may turn out to be less expansive than the difference principle, its demands are still expansive and indeterminate without the guidance of the democratic deliberation for which we argue. Our discussion in this section applies to Rawls's later defense of egalitarian opportunity along with other constitutional theories that require government to satisfy all the basic needs of citizens.

31. Having an "adequate" job is in our terms a basic opportunity good. For an insightful discussion of why having some kind of job is an essential part of citizenship, at least in American democracy, see Judith Shklar, *American Citizenship: The Quest for Inclusion* (Cambridge, Mass.: Harvard University Press, 1991), pp. 63–101.

32. Ronald Dworkin, "Will Clinton's Plan Be Fair?," *New York Review of Books,* January 13, 1994, pp. 20–25.

33. Varley, "Defunding Organ Transplants," p. 191.

34. Ibid., p. 187.

35. Ezekiel Emanuel pointed out this problem, which is evident when one looks at the few existing scientific studies to date and tries to reinterpret them without adopting a utilitarian framework. See, e.g., Theodore Joyce, Hope Corman, and Michael Grossman, "A Cost-Effectiveness Analysis of Strategies to Reduce Infant Mortality," *Medical Care*, 26 (April 1988): 348–360; Robin D. Gorsky and John P. Colby, Jr., "The Cost-Effectiveness of Prenatal Care in Reducing Low Birth Weight in New Hampshire," *Health Services Research*, 24 (December 1989): 584–598; Michael H. Boyle et al., "Economic Evaluation of Neonatal Intensive Care of Very-Low-Birth-Weight Infants," *New England Journal of Medicine*, June 2, 1983, pp. 1330–37; and Jane Huntington and Frederick A. Connell, "For Every Dollar Spent—The Cost-Savings Argument for Prenatal Care," *New England Journal of Medicine*, November 10, 1994, pp. 1303–7. The problem with determining the effects of postnatal care, unlike prenatal care, is that the benefits (or "endpoints" for scientific analysis) are much more diffuse and difficult to measure.

36. For a theory of health care that recognizes the dependence of liberal principles on democratic deliberation, see Emanuel, *The Ends of Human Life*, pp. 155–170, 179–183. Although Emanuel comes closer to the view we defend here than do most of the liberals he criticizes, we do not assume that health care should be determined by communities in the way that he proposes.

37. Varley, "Defunding Organ Transplants," p. 191.
38. Ibid.
39. Ibid., p. 190.
40. Ibid., p. 187.

7. The Latitude of Liberty

1. John Stuart Mill, *On Liberty,* in *Collected Works of John Stuart Mill,* ed. J. M. Robson, vol. 18 (Toronto: University of Toronto Press, 1977), chap. 1, p. 224.
2. On the *Baby M* case, see Martha Field, *Surrogate Motherhood: The Legal and Human Issues* (Cambridge, Mass.: Harvard University Press, 1988), pp. 131– 150; Carmel Shalev, *Birth Power: The Case for Surrogacy* (New Haven: Yale University Press, 1989), pp. 1–9; and *In re Baby M,* 109 N.J. 396, 537 A.2d 1227 (1988).
3. New York State Senate Judiciary Committee, "Surrogate Parenting in New York— I," in *Ethics and Politics,* ed. Amy Gutmann and Dennis Thompson, 2d ed. (Chicago: Nelson-Hall, 1990), p. 307.
4. New York State Task Force on Life and Law, "Surrogate Parenting in New York— II," in Gutmann and Thompson, *Ethics and Politics,* p. 320.
5. Ibid., p. 314.
6. New York State Assembly, transcript of floor debate on Bill 1906, June 26, 1992, provided by Records Access Officer, Public Information Office, Albany. There was no debate in the Senate on the bill.
7. Mill, *On Liberty,* chap. 1, pp. 223–224.
8. Ibid., chap. 4, p. 280.
9. Ibid., chap. 3, pp. 267–269.
10. Ibid., chap. 4, p. 281.
11. As we note later, Mill expresses ambivalence about the legalization of commercial transactions in which some people are paid to counsel others to engage in activities that society deems "evil," such as prostitution and gambling. To the extent that Mill would permit brothels and gambling houses to be prohibited, he would in effect be qualifying his absolutist defense of liberty, and moving closer to accepting the basic liberty principle. See note 64.
12. New York State Assembly, floor debate, p. 308.
13. New York State Task Force, p. 317. See Ronald Dworkin's similar argument regarding the incoherence of claiming that fetuses have interests: *Life's Dominion* (New York: Knopf, 1993), pp. 15–19.
14. See the discussion of the claims of future generations in Chapter 4.
15. Debra Satz, "Markets in Women's Reproductive Labor," *Philosophy & Public Affairs,* 21 (Spring 1992): 122.
16. Mill, *On Liberty,* chap. 1. p. 224.
17. Ibid., chap. 5, pp. 299–301. Mill writes that "by selling himself for a slave, [the individual] abdicates his liberty; he foregoes any future use of it beyond that single act. He therefore defeats, in his own case, the very purpose which is the justification of allowing him to dispose of himself . . . The principle of freedom cannot

require that he should be free not to be free. It is not freedom to be allowed to alienate his freedom" (pp. 229–300).

18. Although Mill presents an absolutist defense of liberty and admits only slavery contracts as an exception, his subsequent discussion leaves open the possibility that there are other exceptions to nonenforceable contracts. He writes that only contracts "that relate to money or money's worth" should be absolutely nonre-tractable (ibid., chap. 5, p. 300). He is also uncertain about whether and when marriage contracts, for example, should be enforced against the will of one con-tracting party. This and every other exception that Mill inconclusively considers, however, would require a significant shift from his absolutist defense of liberty in the direction of the basic liberty principle.

19. See Satz, "Markets in Women's Reproductive Labor," p. 126.

20. Ibid.

21. See Margaret Jane Radin, "Market-Inalienability," *Harvard Law Review,* 100 (1987): 1849–1937.

22. *In re Baby M,* at 1236.

23. New York State Senate Judiciary Committee, p. 306. See also New York State Task Force, p. 312.

24. New York State Senate Judiciary Committee, p. 309.

25. In *Birth Power* Carmel Shalev defends the opposite conclusion. She argues that parental rights should be determined by the intentions of the parties prior to conception (p. 103). She claims that only this contractual standard recognizes women as "autonomous responsible persons" and also furthers their well-being by increasing their market power (p. 166). These claims cannot be sustained. The basic liberty principle, which makes specific performance unenforceable if per-sonal integrity is at stake, also recognizes women as autonomous and responsible beings. (The understanding of the demands of autonomy and responsibility differ.) The contractual standard mistakenly equates the well-being of a woman with her market power even when the "cost" of the equation is complete alienation of maternal rights. It is also unlikely that enforcement of surrogacy contracts will greatly enhance the market power of women.

26. Richard Posner offers two consequentialist arguments against making the contract unenforceable (*Sex and Reason* [Cambridge, Mass.: Harvard University Press, 1992], pp. 405–434]. The first is that if the birth mother reneges, the recipient parents "have lost a year or more in their quest for a baby . . . [and] they have no assurance that the next surrogate mother, and the next, will not renege also" (p. 422). This is a strange argument for a thoroughgoing consequentialist to make, and in any case a weak one. The fact is that the vast majority of birth mothers do not renege even though surrogacy contracts are widely viewed as unenforce-able. The odds are good that recipient parents will not have to keep trying. In any case, Posner offers no argument as to why a "lost year" or more in the quest for a baby on the part of recipient parents is a greater cost than the birth mother's being forced to give up all parental rights to a baby to whom she has become deeply attached. Posner also argues that adoption contracts should be legal and enforceable, and that "there are no convincing arguments for forbidding the sale of parental rights over infants" (p. 416). Yet in no case does he demonstrate that

the benefits outweigh the costs of the policy he favors. He neither offers a qualitative comparison of the different values involved in alternative policies nor tries to quantify the competing values at stake. Without any systematic argument, he suggests that lost time for recipient parents, plus a lower price for the birth mother, plus some other unquantified costs, make it wrong not to enforce surrogacy contracts. What moral or empirical standards justify this conclusion?

Posner's second argument against enforcing surrogacy contracts invokes a principle of nonextortion, which might be entailed by basic liberty (depending on what nonextortion is taken to mean). "If the law refuses to enforce contracts of surrogate motherhood," Posner writes, "it empowers surrogate mothers to commit extortion" (p. 422). The problem with this argument is that there are ways of minimizing the likelihood of successful extortion, only some of which Posner considers. Moreover, if the price of not enforcing surrogacy contracts is that a birth mother "will receive a lower price because her performance is uncertain" (p. 423), then we still need an argument to show why the chance of retaining an inalienable right to raise the child that one has borne is not worth the reduced fee. Posner does not provide the argument.

27. New York State Task Force, p. 320.

28. Field, *Surrogate Motherhood,* p. 27. Field wisely does not rest her analysis of contract parenting primarily on this argument from involuntariness. A critic who implies that the contract is involuntary writes: "To say that a woman 'chooses' to do this . . . is simply to say that when a woman is forced to choose between poverty and exploitation, she sometimes chooses exploitation as the lesser of two evils." Rosemarie Tong, "The Overdue Death of a Feminist Chameleon: Taking a Stand on Surrogacy Arrangement," *Journal of Social Philosophy,* 21 (1990): 45.

29. Field, p. 20.

30. Ibid., p. 21.

31. Ibid., p. 70.

32. There may, however, be conditions of surrogate contracting where the language of force and coercion would be appropriate. Following G. A. Cohen, we would say that surrogate mothers are forced into a contract when they have no acceptable alternative. Their alternatives are unacceptable if they are not only worse than accepting the contract but also "thoroughly bad." See G. A. Cohen, "Are Disadvantaged Workers Who Take Hazardous Jobs Forced to Take Hazardous Jobs?," in *History, Labour, and Freedom: Themes from Marx* (Oxford: Oxford University Press, 1988), pp. 239–254.

33. Were some women forced into surrogacy contracts out of financial need, the appropriate response might still not be to prohibit the contracts. Prohibition would probably compound their lack of freedom. A more justifiable response, as Stuart White suggested to us, would be to increase their job opportunities.

34. J. Parker, "Motivation of Surrogate Mothers: Initial Findings," *American Journal of Psychiatry,* 140 (January 1983): 117–118.

35. Elizabeth Anderson, *Value in Ethics and Economics* (Cambridge, Mass.: Harvard University Press, 1993), p. 178.

36. Elizabeth Anderson, "Is Women's Labor a Commodity? The Case against Surro-

gate Motherhood," *Philosophy & Public Affairs,* 19 (Winter 1990): 89; emphasis added. See also Anderson, *Value in Ethics and Economics,* p. 187.

37. Anderson, "Is Women's Labor a Commodity?," p. 90.

38. For a thoroughgoing defense of the view that surrogacy contracts are not ipso facto coercive, see Alan Wertheimer, "Two Questions about Surrogacy and Exploitation," *Philosophy & Public Affairs,* 21 (Summer 1992): 224–227. More generally on criteria for coercion, see Alan Wertheimer, *Coercion* (Princeton: Princeton University Press, 1986).

39. New York State Task Force, p. 318; and Elizabeth Anderson, "Is Women's Labor a Commodity?," pp. 71–72, 77, and 81. As Anderson writes: "Degradation occurs when something is treated in accordance with a lower mode of valuation than is proper to it . . . Children are properly loved by parents and respected by others. Since children are valued as mere use-objects by the mother and the surrogate agency when they are sold to others, and by the adoptive parents when they seek to conform the child's genetic makeup to their own wishes, commercial surrogacy degrades children insofar as it treats them as commodities" (p. 77). See also Anderson, *Value in Ethics and Economics,* p. 89.

40. Report of Phyllis R. Silverman to Harold Cassidy (one of Mary Beth Whitehead's lawyers), October 23, 1986, p. 5, quoted in Field, *Surrogate Motherhood,* p. 72.

41. Anderson, *Value in Ethics and Economics,* p. 175. Both the New York State Task Force and Anderson also suggest that the integrity of children is violated when they are reduced to the status of commodities. But the force of this claim rests on a reasonably debatable description. Whereas critics claim that contract parenting permits children to be bought and sold on a free market, like commodities, advocates claim that surrogate mothers accept payment for conceiving a child who they have good reason to believe will be loved and cared for by eager parents-to-be.

42. This list, with a few additions, comes from Joel Feinberg, " 'Harmless Immoralities' and Offensive Nuisances," in *Rights, Justice, and the Bounds of Liberty* (Princeton: Princeton University Press, 1980), p. 74. See also idem, *Offense to Others,* vol. 2 of *The Moral Limits of the Criminal Law* (New York: Oxford University Press, 1985), pp. 46, 71. For other examples and analyses of moralism, see Richard A. Wasserstrom, ed., *Morality and the Law* (Belmost, Calif.: Wadsworth Publishing, 1971). Some items on this list may, under certain circumstances, be regulated because of the harm they cause individuals, but such harm is not typically the primary basis for regulation.

43. Feinberg offers the example of defecation in public (*Offense to Others,* pp. 29, 47).

44. See the similar claim about pornography in Bernard Williams, *Obscenity and Film Censorship: An Abridgement of the Williams Report* (Cambridge: Cambridge University Press, 1981), pp. 96–97.

45. Jeannie H. Cross, "New York . . . Ban on Dwarf Tossing," United Press International, wire press report, July 24, 1990.

46. "Dwarf Tossing Cannot Be Banned, French Court Rules," Agence France Presse, wire press report, February 25, 1992. The court wrote that although the practice constituted "an attack on human dignity" and was "degrading," it was unlikely to "disrupt public order."

47. Cross, "Ban on Dwarf Tossing."
48. Anderson, *Value in Ethics and Economics,* p. 175.
49. New York State Assembly, floor debate, p. 81. See also Field, *Surrogate Motherhood,* p. 25: "One of the most serious charges against surrogate motherhood contracts is that they exploit women."
50. New York State Task Force, pp. 317–318.
51. See Satz, "Markets in Women's Reproductive Labor," p. 115.
52. Wertheimer, "Two Questions," pp. 222–223.
53. Ibid., p. 223.
54. Satz, "Markets in Women's Reproductive Labor," p. 125.
55. Cass Sunstein, *The Partial Constitution* (Cambridge, Mass.: Harvard University Press, 1993), p. 287.
56. Satz, "Markets in Women's Reproductive Labor," pp. 120–121, 128; Sunstein, *The Partial Constitution,* p. 287.
57. Sunstein, *The Partial Constitution,* p. 287.
58. Satz, "Markets in Women's Reproductive Labor," p. 127, 125.
59. Ibid., p. 125. The terms of the Whitehead-Stern contract are taken from "Appendix: Baby M Contract," in *Beyond Baby M,* ed. Dianne Bartels (Clifton, N.J.: Humana Press, 1990).
60. Satz, "Markets in Women's Reproductive Labor," p. 125.
61. Sunstein, *The Partial Constitution,* pp. 288–289.
62. Satz, "Markets in Women's Reproductive Labor," p. 129.
63. Sunstein, *The Partial Constitution,* p. 289. One the leading proponents of legalization, Richard Posner, denies the reasonableness of any opposition to surrogacy, attributing it to "hostility to markets that is a staple of the thinking of modern liberal intellectuals" and "the jurisprudence of envy" (referring to the reasoning of the New Jersey Supreme Court in the *Baby M* case) (*Sex and Reason,* p. 428; see also pp. 420–429).
64. "Fornication, for example, must be tolerated, and so must gambling; but should a person be free to be a pimp, or to keep a gambling-house? The case is one of those which lie on the exact boundary line betwen two principles, and it is not at once apparent to which of the two it properly belongs." Mill, *On Liberty,* chap. 5, p. 296.
65. Sunstein, *The Partial Constitution,* p. 289
66. Domestic Relations Law, art. 8, Surrogate Parenting Contracts, N.Y.C.L.S. Dom. Rel. at 121 (1993).
67. New York State Assembly, floor debate, pp. 79–80, 209.
68. One member who opposed the bill asked why "the practice of surrogate parenting is okay as long as there is no money involved . . . [Even if the bill is passed], you still have surrogate parenting[.] Isn't it fair to say that a lot of those same issues and dilemmas could still happen?" New York State Assembly, floor debate, June 26, 1992, p. 88.
69. As John Locke long ago pointed out, the more appropriate term is "parentalism": there is "reason to ask, Whether [power over children] might not be more properly called *Parental Power.* For whatever obligation Nature and the right of Generation lays on Children, it must certainly bind them equal to both the concurrent

Causes of it." John Locke, *Second Treatise,* secs. 52–53, in *Two Treatises of Government,* ed. Peter Laslett (New York: Cambridge University Press, 1963), p. 345.

70. Our discussion of paternalism draws on Dennis Thompson, "Paternalistic Power," in *Political Ethics and Public Office* (Cambridge, Mass.: Harvard University Press, 1987), pp. 148–177. See also Gerald Dworkin, "Paternalism," *Monist,* 56 (1972): 64–68; Joel Feinberg, *Harm to Self,* vol. 3 of *The Moral Limits of the Criminal Law* (New York: Oxford University Press, 1986); Donald VanDeVeer, *Paternalistic Intervention* (Princeton: Princeton University Press, 1986); and John Kleinig, *Paternalism* (Totowa, N.J.: Rowman and Allanheld, 1984).

71. Mill, *On Liberty,* chap. 1, p. 224.

72. Compare the similar list and discussion in Dworkin, "Paternalism," pp. 64–68.

73. Mill, *On Liberty,* chap. 5, p. 294.

74. For further discussion of these conditions, see Thompson, *Political Ethics and Public Office,* pp. 154–161.

75. New York State Judiciary Committee, p. 308.

76. New York State Task Force, p. 318.

77. Mill, *On Liberty,* Chap. 5, p. 301.

78. For a discussion of this issue with regard to education, see Amy Gutmann, "Children, Paternalism, and Education," *Philosophy & Public Affairs,* 9 (Summer 1980): 338–358; Francis Shrag, "The Child in the Moral Order," *Philosophy,* 2 (April 1977): 167–177; and Amy Gutmann, *Democratic Education* (Princeton: Princeton University Press, 1987), pp. 19–47.

79. Jon Elster, "Solomonic Judgment," in *Solomonic Judgment* (Cambridge: Cambridge University Press, 1989), pp. 163–172.

8. The Obligations of Welfare

1. The definition leaves open the possibility that some basic opportunity goods such as health care or housing should be provided in kind. The more that basic opportunity goods are so provided, the lower the level of income support that can qualify as adequate. Even if all other basic opportunity goods were provided in kind, however, some substantial level of income support or its equivalent in remunerative labor would be necessary to satisfy the standard of adequate income. People cannot live decent lives without discretionary income, which in advanced societies is rightly regarded as a need.

2. For other criticism of using "needs as such" as a basis for welfare, see Robert Goodin, *Reasons for Welfare: The Political Theory of the Welfare State* (Princeton: Princeton University Press, 1988), pp. 25–50. Goodin's own justification for welfare—to protect citizens against the risk of exploitation of their dependency (p. 21)—is consistent with the basic opportunity principle as we develop it here, but is only one of several possible goals of welfare that this principle could approve.

3. Although we do not take up the larger issue of whether welfare is justified at all, the general question of the moral foundations of the welfare state is obviously relevant to the more specific issue of the justifiability of work requirements and other obligations. For a useful collection that offers a variety of perspectives on

this question, see J. Donald Moon, ed., *Responsibility, Rights, and Welfare* (Boulder, Colo.: Westview Press, 1988). See also Goodin, *Reasons for Welfare.* More generally, in writing this chapter, we have benefited substantially from reading an unpublished manuscript on welfare by Stuart White.

4. For an insightful historical perspective on the tensions in the current debate and some suggestions about why they persist, see Theda Skocpol, "The Limits of the New Deal System and the Roots of Contemporary Welfare Dilemmas," in *The Politics of Social Policy in the United States,* ed. Margaret Weir et al. (Princeton: Princeton University Press, 1988), pp. 293–311.

5. Alexis de Tocqueville, "Memoir on Pauperism," in *Tocqueville and Beaumont on Social Reform,* ed. and trans. Seymour Drescher (New York: Harper and Row, 1968), p. 15.

6. David Newbart, "Feds Allow Statewide Welfare Cap," *Capital Times* (Madison), June 25, 1994, p. 1A; Richard Whitmire "A Look at Wisconsin's Multiple Attack on Welfare," Gannett News Service, wire press report, June 24, 1993; and telephone interview with David Ward, committee clerk, Special Committee on Welfare Reform, Wisconsin State Assembly, July 13, 1994. The statewide family cap bill passed the Senate in 1994 but died in the Assembly.

7. Libertarians also object more generally to welfare on the grounds that it violates individual liberty by forcing some citizens to labor for the benefit of others. We have already criticized that general objection (taxation is equivalent to forced labor) in its application to health care in Chapter 6. The same criticism applies here. For a further criticism specific to welfare, see Jeremy Waldron, "Welfare and the Images of Charity," *Philosophical Quarterly,* 36 (October 1986): 463–482. See also Goodin, *Reasons for Welfare,* pp. 306–331.

8. Marc Cooper, "Overthrowing the Welfare State," *Village Voice,* May 31, 1994, p. 37.

9. Ibid.

10. Jennifer A. Galloway, "The Politics of Welfare Reform," *Capital Times* (Madison), May 7, 1994, p. 1A.

11. Philippe Van Parijs supplies the boldest philosophical argument for this view ("Why Surfers Should Be Fed: The Liberal Case for an Unconditional Basic income," *Philosophy & Public Affairs,* 20 [Spring 1991]: 103–105). For other approaches and criticisms of the idea of a basic income, see the essays in Philippe Van Parijs, ed., *Arguing for Basic Income: Ethical Foundations for a Radical Reform* (London: Verso, 1992).

12. Frances Fox Piven and Richard A. Cloward defend the policy implications of a modified egalitarianism in *Regulating the Poor: The Functions of Public Welfare* (New York: Vintage, 1993), esp. pp. 343–399. See also Barbara Ehrenreich and Frances Fox Piven, "The Alarm Clock Syndrome," in *Points of Light: New Approaches to Ending Welfare Dependency,* ed. Tamar Ann Mehuron (Washington, D.C.: Ethics and Public Policy Center, 1991), pp. 38–39.

13. Van Parijs, "Why Surfers Should Be Fed," pp. 101–131.

14. Ibid.

15. Ehrenreich and Piven write: "The real problem is not welfare but the fact that any increasing number of jobs do not pay enough to subsist on. If the public sector

gave the poor and dislocated enough to live on . . ., the private sector would no longer be able to get away with coolie wages. Wages would rise, and pretty soon the work ethic would begin to make sense as something other than a bludgeon with which to beat up on the down-and-out" ("The Alarm Clock Syndrome," pp. 38–39).

16. See Piven and Cloward, *Regulating the Poor,* esp. pp. 343–399; and Ehrenreich and Piven, "The Alarm Clock Syndrome," pp. 38–39.

17. See, for example, the English socialist R. H. Tawney: "Property is moral and healthy only when it is used as a condition not of idleness, but of activity, and when it involves the discharge of definite personal obligations" (*The Acquisitive Society* [London: Bell, 1933], p. 95). In a more recent egalitarian discussion of a work requirement, Richard Arneson cogently argues that although an across-the-board requirement may not be justified at the level of principle, it may be necessary in practice because unconditional cash assistance would unfairly benefit individuals whose welfare prospects are generally good but who have a strong preference for leisure over work ("non-needy bohemians"). See Richard Arneson, "Is Work Special? Justice and the Distribution of Employment," *American Political Science Review,* 84 (December 1990): 1127–47.

18. Van Parijs, "Why Surfers Should Be Fed," pp. 101–131.

19. Ibid., p. 123.

20. Ibid., p. 126.

21. Ibid.

22. Matt Pommer, "Lawmakers Eye Jobs and Welfare," *Capital Times* (Madison), June 21, 1994, p. 3A.

23. Ibid., p. 3A.

24. Charles Murray, *Losing Ground: American Social Policy, 1950–1980* (New York: Basic Books, 1984), pp. 233, 234. Murray does not object to locally mandated transfers, including AFDC, but he never adequately explains why they are consistent with rewarding merit, as he defines it (pp. 231–232).

25. Ibid., pp. 231–232.

26. Tocqueville, "Memoir on Pauperism," p. 15.

27. Murray, *Losing Ground,* p. 234.

28. Lawrence Mead, *Beyond Entitlement: The Social Obligations of Citizenship* (New York: Free Press, 1986), p. 13.

29. For an argument that connects the unavailability of jobs in inner cities to unemployment among inner-city black males and the rise in black female-headed households, see William Julius Wilson, *The Truly Disadvantaged: The Inner City, the Underclass, and Public Policy* (Chicago: University of Chicago Press, 1987), esp. pt. 1. Wilson grants that some nonwork may be due to antiwork attitudes among the inner-city poor, but he notes that empirical support is generally lacking for Mead's thesis that such attitudes largely account for joblessness in the inner city. Emphasizing only "the social obligation of citizenship," Wilson points out, therefore sidesteps the critical problem, which is job creation (p. 162). Wilson convincingly argues that all workfare programs are problematic so long as they focus "exclusively on individual characteristics," such as lack of motivation or job training among the poor. Fair workfare, as we outline it in this chapter, seeks to

break out of this mold and constitutes a policy that should fulfill Wilson's demand for "a more comprehensive program of economic and social reform that recognizes the dynamic interplay between societal reorganization and the behavior and life chances of individuals and groups" (p. 163).

30. David Ellwood, *Poor Support: Poverty in the American Family* (New York: Basic Books, 1988), p. 193. Even if the proportion of the poor who live in urban ghettos turned out to be three times Ellwood's estimate, it would still amount to only 21 percent. See Mickey Kaus, "The Author Replies," in Mehuron, *Points of Light,* pp. 50–52.

31. As Wilson shows, "the greatest rise in black joblessness and female-headed families occurred during the very period (1972–80) when the real value of AFDC plus food stamps plummeted because states did not peg benefit levels to inflation" (*The Truly Disadvantaged,* p. 160).

32. See Ellwood, *Poor Support,* pp. 189–215. For a philosophical critique of views that hold that the culture of poverty cannot be eliminated by providing more and better opportunities, see Bernard Boxill, "The Culture of Poverty," in *Cultural Pluralism and Moral Knowledge,* ed. Ellen Frankel Paul, Fred D. Miller, Jr., and Jeffrey Paul (Cambridge: Cambridge University Press, 1994), pp. 249–280.

33. Ellwood, *Poor Support,* p. 60.

34. Ibid., pp. 60, 68.

35. That the failures of welfare policy disproportionately harm blacks does not necessarily imply that reform should be targeted toward blacks. For the argument that "universal programs" are the best way to attack welfare problems in the black community, see Kathryn M. Neckerman, Robert Aponte, and William Julius Wilson, "Family Structure, Black Unemployment and American Social Policy," in Weir, Orloff, and Skocpol, *The Politics of Social Policy in the United States,* pp. 397–419.

36. Galloway, "Politics of Welfare Reform," p. 1A.

37. Murray, *Losing Ground,* p. 223.

38. Newbart, "Feds Allow Statewide Welfare Cap," p. 1A. See also Mead, who argues explicitly in favor of a paternalistic policy toward the poor (*Beyond Entitlement,* pp. 246–249 and passim).

39. The evidence most favorable to this claim is that the birthrate among welfare recipients in New Jersey declined about 10 percent in the first year after the state's family cap went into effect. But no analyst has determined whether the drop was due to the family cap or to a declining birthrate in the state more generally. Many defenders of the family cap admit that it is not likely to serve as an effective disincentive to childbearing among poor women. Not only do poor women on welfare already bear fewer children than other women, but also the typical AFDC subsidy for each additional child is so small as to cast doubt on the assumption of any strong incentive effect on childbearing. Under the New Jersey plan, a mother already on welfare who has another child loses about $64 per month, apart from food stamps and medical care, which are still available because they are (as yet) uncapped federal programs. See Kelly Richmond, "Reshaping the Welfare State," *New Jersey Record,* June 19, 1994, p. A25.

40. Pommer, "Lawmakers Eye Jobs and Welfare," p. 3A.

41. Jeff Mayers, "Family Cap Gets OK in Senate," *Wisconsin State Journal,* March 17, 1994, p. 3B.
42. Ibid.
43. Ibid.
44. Thomas Moran, "N.J. Ready to Get Tough with Welfare Mothers, Purse-Tightening Bills Bound for Florio's Desk," *New Jersey Record,* January 12, 1992, p. A1.
45. Charles Murray, "INFTC," in Mehuron, *Points of Light,* p. 49.
46. Moran, "N.J. Ready to Get Tough," p. A1.
47. David Whitman, "War on Welfare Dependency," *U.S. News & World Report,* April 20, 1992, p. 35.
48. Cooper, "Overthrowing the Welfare State," p. 36.
49. See Murray, "INFTC," p. 50.
50. Pommer, "Lawmakers Eye Jobs and Welfare," p. 3A.
51. Anthony Flint, "A Case in Point: Wisconsin," *Boston Globe,* May 17, 1994, p. 6.
52. "Welfare Mothers Fight Back: Wisconsin," *The Progressive,* 57 (December 1993): 13.
53. See John Gray, *Liberalism* (Milton Keynes: Open University Press, 1986), pp. 79–80.
54. "Welfare Reform, Done Harshly," *New York Times,* November 8, 1993, p. A18.
55. John Stuart Mill, *Principles of Political Economy,* in *Collected Works of John Stuart Mill,* ed. John M. Robson, vol. 3 (Toronto: University of Toronto Press, 1965), bk. 13, p. 961.
56. For an argument that derives a general obligation to work from this mutual dependence (which he calls "reciprocity"), see Lawrence C. Becker, "The Obligation to Work," *Ethics,* 91 (October 1980): 39–43. Becker also argues that this general obligation should not be enforced by law, but that a "special" obligation to work in exchange for benefits provided by the state may be justifiably enforced (pp. 43–49).
57. Goodin, *Reasons for Welfare,* pp. 342–343.
58. Tocqueville, "Memoir on Pauperism," pp. 17–18.
59. Goodin, *Reasons for Welfare,* pp. 350–351.
60. Jean-Jacques Rousseau, *Emile,* trans. Barbara Foxley (New York: E. P. Dutton, 1963), p. 49; and *Social Contract,* trans. Maurice Cranston (New York: Penguin, 1968), pt. 2, sec. 12.
61. The discussion here and in the next section on the ways in which work is connected to social dignity is indebted to Judith N. Shklar, *American Citizenship: The Quest for Inclusion* (Cambridge, Mass.: Harvard University Press, 1991).
62. For a detailed analysis of the kind of comprehensive policies that would be necessary to implement these and similar conditions, see Ellwood, *Poor Support.*
63. Steven A. Holmes, "Out-of-Wedlock Births Up Since '83, Report Indicates," *New York Times,* July 20, 1994, p. 1. According to the Census Bureau, the figure for 1993 was 27 percent, but the proportion has probably grown significantly even since then.
64. See Irwin Garfinkel and Elizabeth Uhr, "A New Approach to Child Support," *Public Interest,* 75 (Spring 1984): 111–122.
65. Ellwood, *Poor Support,* p. 163.

66. Sweden has a successful system of child support along these lines, which guarantees children a level of support whether or not the government succeeds in collecting from absentee parents. See Alfred Kahn and Sheila B. Kamerman, *Income Transfers for Families with Children: An Eight-Country Study* (Philadelphia: Temple University Press, 1983).

67. See Ellwood, *Poor Support*, pp. 114–116.

68. Kathryn Edin and Christopher Jencks, "Reforming Welfare," in *Rethinking Social Policy: Race, Poverty, and the Underclass,* ed. Christopher Jencks (Cambridge, Mass.: Harvard University Press, 1992), pp. 205–208. The authors point out: "The essence of the 'welfare trap' is not that welfare warps women's personalities or makes them pathologically dependent, though that may occasionally happen. The essence of the trap is that, although welfare pays badly, low-wage jobs pay even worse" (p. 225).

69. A combination of significant increases in child support, child care allowances, minimum wage, and earned income tax credit which provided $16,000 for a single-parent family of three would pose no risk of discouraging parents from working. In the present system (depending on where they live), parents on welfare receive an amount ranging from barely less to slightly more disposable income than they would receive if they worked full-time at a job that pays $10,000 a year. This is less than two thirds of what is taken to be the poverty threshold for a mother and two children—$16,000. See the analysis in Edin and Jencks, "Reforming Welfare," pp. 223–226.

70. Although the state did not make major efforts to create jobs, the system did impose strict requirements on welfare recipients that encouraged them to seek and hold jobs that were available. According to one analysis, these requirements contributed significantly to the reduction in the number of citizens on welfare in the state. See Lawrence M. Mead, "The New Paternalism in Action: Welfare Reform in Wisconsin," Wisconsin Policy Research Institute, Milwaukee, January 1995, pp. 4–17.

71. For how and why job creation might work for two-parent families, one-parent families, and residents of the inner-city ghetto, see Ellwood, *Poor Support*, pp. 121–124, 178–183, 222–223. For a further defense of a policy of guaranteed employment, see Arneson, "Is Work Special?"

72. Some analysts propose a less drastic way: "The only reasonably sure way to protect dependent children from poverty is to see to it that their families receive more money. And the only way to provide more money without reducing parents' incentives to become self-supporting is to link increased payments to increased support for work effort and self-improvement." Theodore R. Marmor, Jerry L. Mashaw, and Philip L. Harvey, *America's Misunderstood Welfare State* (New York: Basic Books, 1990), p. 125.

73. Lally Weymouth, "Building Self-Sufficiency," *Washington Post*, March 27, 1992, p. A21.

74. The fair value of political liberty requires a far more comprehensive program of reforms than we can discuss here. For example, securing for everyone the effective opportunity to deliberate depends on educating all children to be capable of exercising their rights and responsibilities as equal citizens. Education shares with

fair workfare the aim of securing the fair value of political liberty. For a discussion of other reforms necessary to realize the fair value of political liberty, see John Rawls, *A Theory of Justice* (Cambridge, Mass.: Harvard University Press, 1971), pp. 225–227.

75. Shklar, *American Citizenship*, p. 99.
76. Ibid. Shklar cites T. H. Marshall's defense of welfare rights in *The Right to Welfare and Other Essays* (New York: Free Press, 1981), pp. 11, 83–103.
77. Shklar, *American Citizenship*, p. 64.
78. For a cogent statement of the rationale for such changes, as well as some specific proposals, see Susan Moller Okin, *Justice, Gender, and the Family* (New York: Basic Books, 1989), pp. 170–186.
79. Shklar describes and criticizes these beliefs in *American Citizenship*, pp. 96, 98.
80. Sidney Verba and Norman Nie, *Participation in America* (Chicago: University of Chicago Press, 1987), pp. 129–133, 334–341; and M. Margaret Conway, *Political Participation in the United States*, 2d ed. (Washington, D.C.: Congressional Quarterly Press, 1991), pp. 21–27.
81. "Welfare Mothers Fight Back," *The Progressive*, 57 (December 1993): 961.
82. Galloway, "Politics of Welfare Reform," p. 1A.
83. John Stuart Mill, *Considerations on Representative Government*, in *Collected Works of John Stuart Mill*, ed. John M. Robson, vol. 19 (Toronto: University of Toronto Press, 1977), chap. 3, p. 68.
84. A more pessimistic view is presented by Claus Offe, who argues that, because the structural conditions in modern societies encourage just the opposite of public-regarding deliberation, democracies are not likely to provide adequate social welfare in the future. See Claus Offe, "Democracy against the Welfare State?," in Moon, *Responsibility, Rights, and Welfare*, pp. 189–228.

9. The Ambiguity of Fair Opportunity

1. See note 2 in Chapter 1, citing Robert K. Fullinwider, "Affirmative Action at AT&T," in *Ethics and Politics*, ed. Amy Gutmann and Dennis Thompson, 2d ed. (Chicago: Nelson-Hall, 1990), pp. 213, 217.
2. Having an adequate job, however, is in our terms a basic opportunity good. We do not discuss this important aspect of work—and the complications that arise under conditions of less than full employment—because, for the purposes of a deliberative perspective, it raises many of the same general issues that we discussed in the case of health care. Jobs differ from health care in two respects that are relevant to a deliberative perspective. First, it is not reasonable for citizens to demand more health care than they need to live a long, healthy life. By contrast, it is not unreasonable for citizens to want a better job than they "need." People value employment for the challenges, satisfactions, status, and remuneration that it may offer, not only for the security it provides for a decent life. Second, jobs are generally not distributed on the basis of need because jobs are valuable not only or even primarily for what they can contribute to the well-being of those who hold them. Society takes an interest in jobs because they contribute to producing socially valuable goods and services, and to enhancing political citizenship.

On the latter, see the discussion of "Earning as Empowerment" in chapter 8 at n. 75 ff.

3. This understanding of the contrast between the liberal and egalitarian interpretations of opportunity, which appears often in the writings of critics of preferential hiring, is found in Charles Frankel, "The New Egalitarianism and the Old," *Commentary*, 56 (September 1973): 54–61; Irving Kristol, "About Equality," *Commentary*, 54 (November 1972): 41–47; Robert Nisbet, "The Pursuit of Equality," *Public Interest*, 35 (Spring 1974): 103–120; and Daniel Bell, "On Meritocracy and Equality," *Public Interest*, 29 (Fall 1972): 29–68.

4. Fullinwider, "Affirmative Action," pp. 214, 217.

5. Information about this case used in this chapter comes mainly from Fullinwider, "Affirmative Action," pp. 211–218.

6. *EEOC v. AT&T*, 365 F. Supp. 1105 (1973) at 1108, cited in Fullinwider, "Affirmative Action," p. 211.

7. Thomas Nagel, whose egalitarianism is developed from the standpoint of impartiality rather than reciprocity, also appears to regard this demand as carrying equality too far, but for somewhat different reasons. See Thomas Nagel, *Equality and Partiality* (Oxford: Oxford University Press, 1991), esp. pp. 63–74.

8. Iris Marion Young, *Justice and the Politics of Difference* (Princeton: Princeton University Press, 1990), pp. 192–225.

9. This seems to be the main implication that Young (ibid.) wants to draw from the fact that the criteria are not objective or impartial.

10. See, e.g., this argument from a theorist who emphasizes rights: Judith Jarvis Thomson, "Preferential Hiring," in *Equality and Preferential Treatment*, ed. Marshall Cohen et al., (Princeton: Princeton University Press, 1977), pp. 19–39. Compare the argument of Michael Walzer, who emphasizes the social meaning of practices, but comes to the same conclusion affirming the difference between a right to a job and a right to equal consideration, in *Spheres of Justice: A Defense of Pluralism and Equality* (New York: Basic Books, 1983), pp. 135–139.

11. Walzer, *Spheres of Justice*, p. 145.

12. For a critic of preferential hiring who claims that the distinction collapses, see Alan H. Goldman, "Affirmative Action," in Cohen et al., *Equality and Preferential Treatment*, pp. 192–209.

13. In the case of AT&T, it is unlikely that the company would have instituted quotas if the Model Plan had not required them. The hiring freeze that the plan required caused a great deal of "disgruntlement" and some protest among employees. See Fullinwider, "Affirmative Action," p. 216. An affirmative action plan without preferential hiring would probably have caused less dissatisfaction, and would therefore have been more resistant to pressures to turn goals into quotas.

14. Goldman, "Affirmative Action," pp. 192–209. See also Nathan Glazer, "Racial Quotas," in *Racial Preference and Racial Justice: The New Affirmative Action Controversy*, ed. Russell Nieli (Washington, D.C.: Ethics and Public Policy Center, 1991), pp. 6–19; and Thomas Sowell, *Civil Rights: Rhetoric or Reality?* (New York: William Morrow, 1984).

15. Goldman, "Affirmative Action," p. 198.

16. See Joan Scott, "Deconstructing Equality-Versus-Difference: Or the Uses of Post-structural Theory for Feminism," *Feminist Studies,* 14 (Spring 1988): 33–50.

17. Shelby Steele, *The Content of Our Character: A New Vision of Race in America* (New York: Harper, 1991), p. 124. See also Glenn C. Loury, "Why Should We Care about Group Inequality?," *Social Philosophy and Policy,* 5 (1987): 253–263.

18. For a more extensive discussion of distributive justice in education, see Amy Gutmann, *Democratic Education* (Princeton: Princeton University Press, 1987), pp. 127–170 and 194–222.

19. Fullinwider, "Affirmative Action," p. 214.

20. See Alfred W. Blumrosen, *Modern Law: The Law Transmission System and Equal Employment Opportunity* (Madison: University of Wisconsin Press, 1993), esp. p. 210; and *Affirmative Action to Open the Doors of Job Opportunity: A Policy of Fairness and Compassion That Has Worked,* report of the Citizens' Commission on Civil Rights, Center for National Policy Review, Catholic University, Washington, D.C. (June 1984), pp. 60–61. The AT&T case was not atypical. Fifteen months after the agreement with AT&T, the EEOC together with the Justice and Labor departments entered into a "Steel Industry Settlement" with nine major steel companies and the United Steelworkers of America that was similar to the AT&T plan, providing not only compensation for past discrimination but also hiring "goals" for women and minorities.

21. Fullinwider, "Affirmative Action," p. 217.

22. For an analysis and survey of the major arguments about affirmative action and preferential hiring, see Michel Rosenfeld, *Affirmative Action and Justice* (New Haven: Yale University Press, 1991).

23. Ronald Dworkin, "Bakke's Case: Are Quotas Unfair?," in *A Matter of Principle* (Cambridge, Mass.: Harvard University Press, 1985), p. 299.

24. Ibid.

25. See Jacqueline Jordan Irvine, *Black Students and School Failure* (New York: Greenwood Press, 1990), pp. 40–42; and Kofi Lomotey, *African-American Principals: School Leadership and Success* (New York: Greenwood Press, 1989).

26. *Regents of University of California v. Bakke,* 438 U.S. 265 (1978).

27. For a careful analysis of the conditions under which "reaction qualifications" may be morally legitimate factors in hiring decisions, see Alan Wertheimer, "Jobs, Qualifications, and Preferences," *Ethics,* 94 (October 1983): 99–112.

28. Ronald Dworkin, "Reverse Discrimination," in *Taking Rights Seriously* (Cambridge, Mass.: Harvard University Press, 1977), p. 234. Here Dworkin is reconstructing a utilitarian argument, and may himself prefer to use what he calls an "ideal" argument, though he does not develop such an argument in this case.

29. Thomson, "Preferential Hiring," pp. 19–48.

30. Testimony no. 7 to the House Special Subcommittee on Education (of the Committee on Education and Labor), September 23, 1974.

31. Ibid.; emphasis added.

32. See, e.g., Dale L. Hiestand, *Discrimination in Employment: An Appraisal of the Research* (Ann Arbor: University of Michigan and National Manpower Task Force, 1970); Anthony H. Pascal, ed., *Racial Discrimination in Economic Life*

(Lexington, Mass.: Lexington Books, 1972); and Catherine R. Stimpson, ed., *Discrimination against Women: Congressional Hearings on Equal Rights in Education and Employment* (New York: Bowler Books, 1973).

33. See Thomas Hobbes, *De Corpore,* in vol. 4 of *The English Works of Thomas Hobbes,* ed. William Molesworth (London: J. Bohn 1839), p. 53.

34. Lyndon B. Johnson, "Commencement Address at Howard University," June 4, 1965, in *Public Papers of the Presidents, 1965,* bk. 2 (Washington, D.C.: G.P.O., 1966), pp. 635–639.

35. For the best statement and analysis of such an argument, see George Sher, "Justifying Reverse Discrimination in Employment," in Cohen et al., *Equality and Preferential Treatment,* pp. 49–60.

36. Thomson, "Preferential Hiring," p. 38.

37. Loury, "Why Should We care about Group Inequality?," p. 263.

38. Ibid., pp. 268–269.

39. The argument here is a reconstruction of arguments put forward by several different writers, most notably Owen Fiss, "Groups and the Equal Protection Clause," in Cohen et al., *Equality and Preferential Treatment,* pp. 84–154; and Young, *Justice and the Politics of Difference,* pp. 156–191.

40. Fiss, "Groups and the Equal Protection Clause," p. 148

41. Ibid., p. 150.

42. Ibid., p. 163.

43. Walzer, *Spheres of Justice,* p. 154. For an extensive argument favoring reparations, see Boris J. Bittker, *The Case for Black Reparations* (New York: Random House 1973).

44. Walzer, *Spheres of Justice,* p. 154.

45. From the dissent of Associate Justice Antonin Scalia in the case of *Johnson v. Transport Agency, Santa Clara County,* 480 U.S. 616 (1987), at 677.

46. *Regents of University of California v. Bakke,* 438 U.S. 265 (1978), at 407.

47. See, for example, Richard Wasserstrom, "One Way to Understand and Defend Programs of Preferential Treatment," in *The Moral Foundations of Civil Rights,* ed. Robert K. Fullinwider and Claudia Mills (Totowa, N.J.: Rowman and Littlefield, 1986), p. 46. Except for its denial that anyone is wronged or treated unfairly by preferential treatment, Wasserstrom's case for preferential treatment converges with the one that we construct, and invokes the kinds of considerations on which critics and advocates of preferential treatment should be able to agree (pp. 46–55). By not admitting the unfairness of passing over better-qualified persons, however, Wasserstrom implies that there is nothing morally preferable about a society in which preferential treatment is unnecessary except that it is no longer a "system of racial disadvantage and oppression" (p. 48). Compare Dworkin's discussion and critical revisions of the utilitarian case for preferential hiring in "Reverse Discrimination," pp. 227–239.

48. See Herbert R. Northrup and John A. Larson, *The Impact of the AT&T-EEO Consent Decree* (Philadelphia: University of Pennsylvania, Industrial Research Unit, 1981), p. 24.

Index

Abortion, 3, 5, 16, 20, 60; and government, 12, 61, 159; federal subsidies for, 11, 15, 47, 82–83, 88–90, 108, 363n1b; and self-interest, 20, 21; and incompatibility of values, 24–25; and justice, 35; and violence, 44; legalization of, 61–62, 74–75, 84, 88, 107, 129, 130–131, 138, 139, 374n3, 375n21, 381n37, 384n1; debate over, 74–77, 79, 82–90, 357, 361, 376n35; and civic integrity, 81–82; and taxes, 89–90; and public policymaking, 107, 138–141, 163, 346, 351. *See also* Rights: abortion

Abramson, Jeffrey, 385n17

Abramson, Jill, 382nn47,50

Accommodation. *See* Mutual respect

Accountability, 8, 12, 52; principle of, 15, 199, 348, 349, 351; and publicity, 97, 104, 107, 115, 117, 118, 121, 123, 125; scope of, 128–164, 351; and representative democracy, 130–132; deliberative, 150–153, 175, 227, 228; obstacles to, 173–178; conditions of, 197, 201, 229, 352, 355, 356; and mutual dependence, 293

Ackerman, Bruce, 365n11, 371n68, 373n74

Adams, Robert M., 383n64

Adatto, Kiku, 391n29

Adoption, 231, 236, 243

Affirmative action, 5, 313–314, 315, 323, 342, 363n2b, 408n13; and fairness, 12,

307, 332, 341. *See also* Discrimination; Preferential hiring

AHCCCS. *See* Arizona Health Care Cost Containment System

Aid to Families with Dependent Children (AFDC), 82, 275, 282, 286, 287, 288, 404nn31,39

Akron v. Akron Center for Reproductive Health, Inc., 378n50

Allende, Salvador, 118, 383n59

Allison, Graham, 383n59

American Association of Physicians and Surgeons, Inc., v. Clinton, 383n56

American Association of University Professors, 330

American Smelting and Refining Company (Asarco; Tacoma, Washington), 167–181, 184–188 passim, 193–194, 196, 197, 351, 352, 354

American Telephone and Telegraph Company (AT&T): preferential hiring at, 11, 14, 307, 315, 325–326, 329–330, 333, 334, 339, 342, 346, 357; and publicity, 15, 16, 109, 311, 315–317, 318, 319, 350; Model Affirmative Action Plan of, 309, 314, 322–324, 327, 331–332, 340, 343–344, 363n2, 408n13

Anderson, Elizabeth, 248, 392n42, 398nn35,36, 399nn37,39,41, 400n48

Aponte, Robert, 404n35

Applbaum, Arthur Isak, 369n44